# Classic Writings on Instructional Technology

## VOLUME 2

**Donald P. Ely**
Syracuse University

**Tjeerd Plomp**
University of Twente

2001
Libraries Unlimited, Inc.
Englewood, Colorado

LIBRARIES UNLIMITED, INC.
P.O. Box 6633
Englewood, CO 80155-6633
1-800-237-6124
www.lu.com


**Library of Congress Cataloging-in-Publication Data**

Library of Congress has catalogued previous volume.

Classic writings on instructional technology / Donald P. Ely, Tjeerd
    Plomp [editors].
        xix, 257 p. 17x25 cm. -- (Instructional technology series)
        Includes bibliographical references and index.
        ISBN 1-56308-230-6
        1. Educational technology. 2. Instructional systems--Design.
    3. Teaching--Aids and devices. 4. Audio-visual education. I. Ely,
    Donald P. II. Plomp, Tjeerd. III. Series.
    LB1028.3.C617        1996
    370.3'078--dc20                                                    96-3668
                                                                          CIP


Volume 2: ISBN 1-56308-854-1

# Contents

## Part 1
## Definition and Conceptual Background

## Part 2
## Design and Development Functions

## Part 3
# Delivery Options

## Part 4
# The Profession

# Contents for Volume 1

## Part 4
# The Profession

### Professions in the Audio-Visual Field

**Professionalizing the Audio-Visual Field**
   *James D. Finn*

   *Bibliography*

   *Index*

# Introduction

Two of life's questions are relevant to one's professional life as well: "Where have I been?" and "Where am I going?" This book emphasizes the former while taking the position that the future depends largely upon what has been said in the past. The National Archives in Washington, D.C., displays an engraved stone at the entrance: "What is past is prologue." The essence of that statement provides the background for this publication.

## Purpose

This book continues the purposes of Volume 1: to provide a convenient collection of seminal papers that are considered to be foundations for the field of instructional technology and to document some of the field's history through documents that are perceived to be major contributors to the conceptual growth of the field. The introduction to Volume 1 underscored the importance of this literature in understanding current developments.

This book attempts to provide a partial conceptual history of the primary works that often are sidestepped for more recent interpretations of the older gems. When historians do history, they go to the original sources, not secondary interpretations and digests.

Each of the articles in this Volume is more concerned with the "why" rather than the "how" of the field. Each work marks the introduction of important and timeless ideas that have withstood the test of time. Some reviewers of the first Volume indicated that there are more up-to-date articles than the ones that were included. Granted, but they do not fall within the scope of "classic writings." For the most part, the current publications draw upon ideas and rationales that were first published in earlier times and continue to be cited in contemporary writings.

## Audience

This book is intended for "foundations" or "trends and issues" courses in graduate educational technology programs. It is also a reference resource for professors and advanced graduate students who are seeking original articles that may be difficult to find. Individuals who are new to the field and are trying to determine its philosophical and conceptual base should benefit from these articles, which provide a substantive grounding for the principles and procedures that are required in applied settings. For any professional it is important not only to know "how," but also "why." Such is the nature of this publication.

# Relationship of Volumes 1 and 2

The original plan for Volume 1 included about a dozen articles that were eventually eliminated because of space limitations. Those that were published (see the Table of Contents for Volume 1 preceding this introduction) included four articles from the 1940s and 1950s, seven from the 1960s and six from the 1970s. The publisher supports a second Volume where later classics of the 1970s, 1980s, and early 1990s—and one resurrected from the 1960s, have been included. Many of the articles omitted in Volume 1 are now in Volume 2. We remain committed to the definition of "classic" that framed the selection for Volume 1: ". . . those books and articles that have withstood the test of time and are still read and quoted."

# The Selection Process

Unused nominations for Volume 1 were reactivated and others were sought from leaders in the Professors of Instructional Development and Technology (PIDT) group that meets annually. The editors also added their favorites. With a list of more than fifty nominees, frequency of citation in the Social Science Citation Index was used as one screen. Frequency of mention in current books that cover the scope of instructional technology offered still another measure. Included in the review were the *Handbook of Research on Educational Communications and Technology,* edited by Jonassen, *Instructional Development Paradigms* by Dills and Romiszowski, Gagné's *Foundations of Educational Technology*, and Anglin's 2nd edition of *Instructional Technology: Past, Present and Future.* The list of titles was again submitted to a PIDT "jury." Final selections were difficult because there were wide discrepancies among the titles chosen and many qualified articles had to be eliminated because of space limitation.

It is not possible to be completely unbiased about the articles selected. The editors had to take some liberty in the selection process by applying personal criteria, especially to articles that were written by European authors. European authors are not frequently recognized by North American professionals. It is likely that the list of articles selected would be quite different if determined by other editors.

Everyone has "favorites" depending upon personal experiences with the literature. Perhaps there will be a Volume 3 that will pick up those highly ranked items that were not included in Volume 2. It is possible, too, that the World Wide Web might provide a new source of classics.

# Organization of This Volume

The editors decided to use the same organization as Volume 1, which is roughly congruent with the domains in *Instructional Technology: The Definition and Domains of the Field* by Seels and Richey. The overview of "The Field and Its Definition" and "The Profession" offer unifying elements along with the separate sections.

1. Definition and Conceptual Background

    The Field and Its Definition

    Theory and Rationale

2.  Design and Development Functions

    Design and Development

    Evaluation

3.  Delivery Options

    Media and Technology

    Methods and Techniques

4.  The Profession

# Changes

One change that seemed necessary was to introduce each section with a brief essay about the articles in it. This addition provided opportunities to list other articles that were not included with a brief explanation about their contributions to the conceptual development of that particular element of the field. It also permitted the addition of books that have been influential. The nature of these two volumes with "classic articles" means that they are not amenable to the inclusion of books. However, three readings in this book have been reproduced from book chapters.

The mini-essays should provide some additional background about the articles themselves as well as about related publications; they should also help to provide a context for the articles that follow.

## Part 1

# Definition and Conceptual Background

**Robert Heinich (1984):**
*The Proper Study of Instructional Technology*

## The Field and Its Definitions

Robert Heinich is the only author to be represented in both Volumes 1 and 2 of *Classic Writing on Instructional Technology*. In Volume 1, his article "Is There a Field of Educational Communications and Technology?" is located in the same section of the book as the present article. Over the years, Heinich has been active in defining the field and his appearance again in this Volume confirms the importance of these contributions.

Robert Heinich has been a provocative writer and ardent advocate for under-standing the "true" nature of the field. Many of his early ideas were formed while a doctoral student at the University of Southern California under the tutelege of James D. Finn. His dissertation, renamed "Technology and the Management of Instruction," was published as a monograph by the Association for Educational Communications and Technology (AECT) in 1970 and stands today as one of the defining statements of the field. This publication was the impetus, in the 1980s, for a request to update and elaborate the original ideas and concepts of the 1970 monograph; it was a unanimous choice of the professionals who recommended articles for this volume.

In this article, Heinich provides a historical context of the field's growth and development as a backdrop for his contention that "technology is the base" of the field. He reiterates the importance of Galbraith's definition of technology as ". . . the systematic application of scientific and other organized knowledge to practical tasks" (Galbraith, 1967). He goes on to discuss the characteristics and principles that extend the definition to educational technology: 1) replicability; 2) reliability; 3) algorithmic decision making; 4) communication and control; and 5) the effect of scale.

In an attempt to relate technology to the education professions, Heinich reviews the relationship of teacher unions to the acceptance of technology in schools and also to the early education reform movement of the 1960s and 1970s. He views teacher unions as a potential barrier to the acceptance and use of technology in the schools.

The concluding part of the article reviews progress (and the lack of it) in matters of research in the field. He calls for a shift of emphasis from education to technology as an appropriate next step for the field.

# Theory and Rationale

### J. S. Brown, A. Collins, and P. Duguid (1989): *Situated Cognition and the Culture of Learning*

### D. H. Jonassen (1991): *Objectivism Versus Constructivism: Do We Need a New Philosophical Paradigm?*

The field of instructional technology borrows much of its theory and rationale from other fields and disciplines: communication, management, technology, perception, sociology, and instructional and learning psychology. In recent years, as the practitioners in the field have focussed on learning; the psychology of instruction and the psychology of learning have dominated the deliberations of designers. One of the latest entries into the theory and rationale realm is "constructivism." The interest in constructivistic approaches to learning is largely in response to the earlier and prominent use of behavioral approaches to teaching and learning. With continuing challenges to "behavioral objectives" something had to replace or modify the generic concept of "learning outcomes."

Richard Clark (1994) joined the voices of Thomas Duffy and David Jonassen (1991) in praise of the cognitive sciences as a more useful rationale upon which to build support for instructional design. The term *constructivism* emerged as a descriptor for this growing movement.

Constructivism grew in popularity among instructional designers and developers in the early 1990s. One of the most frequently quoted articles in this area is "Situated Cognition and the Culture of Learning" by Brown, Collins, and Duguid (1989). The research and development efforts of the Cognition and Technology Group at Vanderbilt (CTGV, 1997), especially with their "Jasper" Project, encompassed many of the concepts in the new wave of learning outcomes. "Generative learning" is another term associated with this trend in the field. "Objectivism" entered the debate as a counterpoint to constructivism (Jonassen, 1991).

Both the Brown, Collins, and Duguid and the Jonassen articles in this section introduce some of the basic concepts in this arena. Brown, Collins, and Duguid (1989) draw upon cognitive factors that are "situated," and state that learning in such contexts is an amalgamation of "activity, context, and culture in which it is developed and used."

They point out that "conventional schooling too often ignores the influence of the school culture on what is learned in schools" and call for cognitive apprenticeships. The examples given in this article are from the field of mathematics but should be generalizable to other subjects.

Jonassen (1991) refers to the article of Brown, Collins, and Duguid as an application of constructivism. In his article, he defines "objectivism" as "knowing and learning . . . processes for representing and mirroring reality." For Jonassen, "constructivism . . . is a process of actively interpreting and constructing individual knowledge representations." He contrasts the two extremes and concludes that no commitment to one approach or the other should be made before the instructional design procedure begins. The decision rests on the context in which the learning is to occur.

In his concern for context, Jonassen refers to Brown, Collins, and Duguid's call for real-world environments that create contexts that are more relevant for the learner than traditional instructional settings. In such contexts, teaching from scripts or predetermined instructional procedures, the learner is expected to solve learning problems rather than to generate a standard response. The assumptions of objectivism and constructivism listed in Table 1.1 of Jonassen's article provide a useful catalog of comparisons between the two approaches.

Give some credit to Jonassen for not succumbing to the unyielding advocacy position that often characterizes new approaches to old problems and procedures. He repeatedly says that constructivism is not a panacea but, rather, another process that should be within the arsenal of instructional design. Duffy and Jonassen (1991, 1994) extend the basic concepts and applications of constructivism in the realm of instructional design.

# References

Clark, R. E. 1994. *How the cognitive sciences are changing our profession.* In H. Stolovitch and E. Keeps, eds., *Handbook of human performance technology.* New York: Macmillan.

Cognition and Technology Group at Vanderbilt (CTGV). 1997. *The Jasper project.* Hillsdale, N.J.: Lawrence Erlbaum.

Duffy, T. M., and D. H. Jonassen. 1991. Constructivism: New implications for instructional technology? *Educational Technology* 31:5. 2–7.

Duffy, T. M., and D. H. Jonassen, eds. 1992. *Constructivism and the technology of instruction: A Conversation.* Hillsdale, N.J.: Lawrence Erlbaum.

# The Proper Study of Instructional Technology

## Robert Heinich

*This is the 10th ERIC/ECTJ Annual Review Paper, preparation of which was supported by the ERIC (Educational Resources Information Center) Clearinghouse on Information Resources, Syracuse University. The material in this article was prepared pursuant to a contract with the National Institute of Education, U.S. Department of Education. Contractors undertaking such projects under government sponsorship are encouraged to express their judgment in professional and technical matters with freedom. Points of view or opinions do not necessarily represent the official view or opinion of the NIE.—Ed.*

This article originated in a request to update my monograph *Technology and the Management of Instruction* (Heinich, 1970). Since its publication, I have explored and extended the basic premises of the monograph in a series of fugitive and quasi-fugitive papers. I welcomed the opportunity to pull together the main ideas of those papers and present them under a unifying conceptual framework. Prior reading of the monograph will be helpful but it is not essential.

*Warning:* This article is not intended to be read by anyone other than an instructional technologist. Do not yield to the temptation to show this to your dean, administrator, or superior. Under penalty of stripping you of your behavioral objectives, do not, above all, show this to faculty!

From: Heinich, R. M. (1984). The proper study of instructional technology. *Educational Communication and Technology Journal* 32(3):67–87. Reprinted with permission of Association for Educational Communications and Technology.

To be radical is to grasp the root. The root of instructional technology is technology itself. Instructional technology as a field of study is better considered as a subset of technology in general rather than as a subset of Education (or, in the orientation of some members of the field, Psychology). Because technologies of instruction[1] have developed to the point of being able to range from helping an instructor improve a lesson to serving as the modus operandi of an entire institution (such as the Open University), the field of instructional technology, and therefore its study, has grown beyond the restrictive boundaries of Education as exemplified in schools and departments of education in colleges and universities.

The majority of academic departments of instructional technology emerged from media (occasionally educational psychology) departments or programs in Schools of Education.[2] As implied above, the reason was the historical use of media as tools to improve teacher performance; this relationship not only set organizational and institutional patterns but also shaped the directions of scholarly activity. The consequences were and are limitations on the development of theory, research, and practice.

Concomitantly, media service units operating within school systems, colleges, and universities find themselves in institutional settings that assign total curricular and instructional authority to individual faculty. As these service groups struggle to evolve into instructional technology units, they eventually face a decision-making structure that neither encourages nor facilitates the full application of the technology at their command; this makes using the products of their efforts subject to the vagaries of temporary casts of characters. In formal education, the assignment of instructional authority to faculty is taken for granted. Rarely does a counterpart authority exist to institutionalize technologically-based instruction. The consequences are the same limitations on the development of theory, research, and practice.[3]

## *Limitations*

Because training teachers is the main business of Schools of Education, preparing teachers to use media effectively and preparing service personnel to help teachers select media are assumed by the Schools and the programs to be the main functions and the primary intellectual interests of media programs. As a result, the energies of faculties are directed toward service courses rather than toward building the knowledge base of instructional technology. The basic assumption of teacher education is that final instructional decisions, whether based on careful planning or on spontaneity, are made at the moment of interaction between teacher and students. Consequently, media faculty find themselves accepting the priority of their administrative home: improving the performance of teachers in classrooms by providing stimulus materials and showing teachers how to use them. My complaint is that, although improving teacher performance is a good thing, accepting that function as a primary basis for theory-building, research, and practice imposes severe limitations on the intellectual growth and professional development of instructional technology. Before I elaborate on this point, I want to state the foundation of instructional technology.

In contrast to the underlying assumption of teacher education, the basic premise of instructional technology is that all instructional contingencies can be managed through space and time (i.e., they can be incorporated into the interaction between student and material and/or device). Our inability to do so in any given situation is viewed as a temporary deficiency in our knowledge base. Primary emphasis is given to the development of more powerful technologies of instruction along with the development of organizational structures that facilitate their use; secondary emphasis is given to improvement of teacher performance. (As we shall see later, this order of priority raises the question of the competence level required of the individual in direct contact with learners.) As a *strategy,* as an *approach to solving problems,* this basic premise of instructional technology expands theory, research, and development, redirects our efforts to different client systems, and leads to lines of inquiry in direct opposition to the assumptions of teacher education. The following are offered in illustration.

In traditional education, curriculum and instruction are regarded as related but separable processes: Instruction is the responsibility of individual faculty assigned to courses. In other words, curriculum is planned independently of its adoption. When instructors are responsible for both curriculum and instruction, they regard each as separate activities. Providing stimulus materials for this paradigm is what was expected of us.[4] The cause-and-effect relationship in specific instructional situations, therefore, was not under our control. But as our technologies of instruction became more sophisticated, more reliable, and more powerful, we realized that curriculum and instruction can be (and in certain cases must be) developed at the same time. For example, if a course is to be designed as programmed instruction, or CAI, or video, etc., instruction is designed into the delivery system. Cause-and-effect relationships can be identified, studied, and managed.[5] Research and development based on a theoretical construct that requires manipulation of all variables, including instructors, can lead us to an instructional science and technology capable of radically altering the institution of education.[6]

However, our colleagues in Education, and other faculty, are reluctant to accept instructional technology as an alternative method of structuring education; they are also less than eager to view us in any other than the service role of provider or designer of stimulus materials. They do not want the craft nature of instruction disturbed by technology. I would like to draw on an example from general technology and a parallel from education to illustrate this crucial point:

---

Suppose a sales representative from a machine tool maker demonstrates a new tool to cut threads to the manager of a plant that manufactures machine screws. The new tool permits a faster cut, doesn't wear out as quickly, and is easier to mount in the lathe. The foreman wastes no time in showing the new tool to the lathe operators, who are delighted to try it out. Here is an innovation that obviously has a high probability of being accepted by the workforce.

The following year, the sales representative demonstrates to the manager of the plant a new lathe that *automatically* fashions machine screws. Fewer operators are needed to produce the same volume of screws. The plant manager immediately recognizes an innovation that will have an impact drastically different from that of the tool the plant adopted the previous year. Here now is a device that will appeal to the owner of the plant because it will make the company more cost-effective. The consumer benefits also because the unit price of machine screws will drop. In the long run, the workforce benefits from the expanded job markets that result. But in the short run, the manager knows that the lathe operators will not look kindly on a machine that will do their jobs.[7]

---

(This should go without saying, but I am not suggesting by this analogy that learners can be treated like machine screws. The point is that perspective and insight can be gained by studying how similar problems have been resolved in other areas of technology.)

By contrast, consider the place of the textbook in the instructional scheme of things. The textbook is worth examining because it has been around for so long and has become so much a part of the system that we tend not to think of it as a product of technology. The textbook endures to a great extent because of the symbiotic relationship that has developed over a long time between it and the teacher. Publishers have found that the symbiotic relationship is disturbed when the book assumes too much of the instructional burden. A text is essentially a course of study (a curriculum) between hard covers. It requires the teacher to translate it into instruction. If the text translates itself into instruction, as in a programmed book, the symbiotic relationship is disturbed and the text is rejected. The more "pedagogical aids" (in publishers' parlance) provided with the text the better, but there is an important difference between pedagogical aids and self-instruction: The former underscores the need for the teacher. The point is that text adopters are telling publishers that the text should be supportive, not threatening. For the same reason, producers find it easier to sell individual film titles than a course on film (or video). Producers of CAI will find a readier market for individual lessons than for complete courses.

In general, the development of instructional technology has disturbed the symbiotic relationship between instructional materials and teachers. I see why, and I can readily understand teachers' reactions: They reject the implied change in the power structure. Correlatively, curriculum personnel and teachers resist instructional technologists when we move toward the union of curriculum and instruction in designing mediated instruction.

We as a field have failed to learn important lessons from our experiences in introducing new technologies of instruction. Reflection on those experiences and on the two examples given above should give us more insight into the reasons we need to look elsewhere for intellectual kinship. Consider the following:

## Misunderstanding of Client Systems

If the manager of the plant had tried to convince the lathe operators to adopt the automatic screw machine, we know what the answer would have been. Yet this is precisely what we have done and continue to do in the institutions we serve. We have tended to treat all technological innovations the same way in reference to client systems: Introduction of television systems is seen as little different from the introduction of an overhead projector. We have failed to understand that the overhead projector (and other devices) does not disturb power relationships (it is a "better tool"), but that a television system can disturb power relationships. Faculty, like lathe operators, prefer the power relationships the way they are and maintain them by reducing all technologies to the status of "tools." Doing so keeps everything in place.

Analysis and recognition of the differential effects of technology on power relationships can lead us away from butting our heads against a stone wall and toward an understanding of why the system reacts the way it does and what will change the performances of the characters involved.

It follows that the same holds true for our research efforts. We act as though faculty are the clients of our research when, in reality, inquiry into most of the systemic aspects of instructional technology is most pertinent to clients other than faculty: administrators, school boards, boards of trustees, legislators, and so forth. It is up to us to demonstrate to those clients the policy issues implicit in technology. Even in such traditional areas of research as message design, we frequently assume that faculty are our clients rather than the producers of materials they really are: Faculty are not normally in a position to incorporate research findings into the *design* of materials.

## Instructional Development into Faculty Development

Instructional development departments in higher education frequently find themselves pushed more and more into faculty development; this results in less and less effort expended on instructional development. Faculty development and instructional development are not the same. Faculty development is concerned with improving the performance of individual instructors, with little regard for instructional development as we define it. Sometimes the fond hope is that faculty can be trained to perform instructional development. The problem is that the institution rewards the performance of the individual, not of the instructional system.

The original concept of instructional development as being able to account for *all* variables, including instructors, has eroded under institutional pressure; the system does not permit this general accountability to occur. Again, inquiry into the infrastructure that supports the basic assumption of instructional authority in the present system would help us understand the reason and show us how the rules of the game should be changed.

I conclude this section with the observation that the more successful the instructional development department and the more capable its personnel, the more it will be pushed into faculty development: The instructional development department thus becomes a victim of its own success. This observation is not meant to denigrate these and other activities that serve the purposes of the institution and reward those who perform them. The point is that instructional technologists need to recognize when they are performing functions that do not further their conceptual framework and that delude them into misconceptions of what they are about.

## From Leadership to Consultation

The erosion of the instructional development concept has its consequences in the gradual shift from leadership to consultation. After all, it's hard to remain a revolutionary when your cause is rejected but you prevail! Many still espouse the cause, but the lure of profit from the current system softens the protest. It's sort of like being a Norman Thomas socialist (for those of you who remember)—and the system rather enjoys its "safe" rebels!

Seriously, we must understand what is happening to us when our role changes as the system modifies our intellectual concepts. To prevent any misunderstanding, I am neither belittling the acquisition of consulting skills nor criticizing people for doing their jobs as best they can. It is important that we learn to work well with clients. But the consulting skills needed in anticipation of leading a design team are different from those needed to advise about "better tools." The latter implies acceptance of the status quo.

## Acceptance of Institutional Relationships

Perhaps the most serious consequence of our academic origins is our acceptance of the institutional relationships and governing structure of formal education. This applies to a good extent to training programs because they tend to look to education for models. By accepting the underlying assumptions of traditional educational practice, we automatically accept the infrastructure of the institutions that have evolved in support of those assumptions. We grew up academically supporting faculty and are uncomfortable when shaking off that encumbering intellectual heritage. We project the same attitudes into our service roles and back off from the logical consequences of our technology.

A number of reasons for the discomfort come to mind:

1. *A disturbing sense of disloyalty to our "upbringing" in Education and to our colleagues among the faculty.* Typical of this state of mind are the frequent reassurances we utter about not replacing teachers with technology; our unease over our presumption that *we could* replace much of what goes on in education; the legacy of our training in Education that instruction is best when created ad hoc or when "the teachable moment" is at hand (one of the hoariest myths of Education); and so forth.

   Even some of our most advanced prophets in instructional technology suffered from this syndrome. For example, James D. Finn, who along with Charles F. Hoban did the most to lead us into a brave new world of technology, balked at the changes in client systems and personnel behavior implied by the consequences of his work. He could deal with it in the abstract, as he did in "Technology and the Instructional Process" (Finn, 1960), but not at the personal level. He received his training during the height of the progressive education movement and could not bring himself to break away by challenging its precepts from the point of view of technology. Ironically, his John Dewey Society lecture, "A Walk on the Altered Side," is his finest attempt to drag Education into the world of technology (Finn, 1962).

   To a considerable degree, those parts of the field that came up through programmed instruction and television escaped this syndrome—at least concerning academic orientation. Unhampered by educationists, the programmed instruction enthusiasts quickly saw the revolutionary nature of what they wrought. The realities of institutional restraints brought them crashing back to earth. Unfortunately, the television people got caught up in the delivery system and thought that all one needed was a dynamic personality and a camera. Such organizations as the Agency for Instructional Television and the Children's Television Workshop have been correcting that mistake. Those entering the field from the computer area are repeating the television mistake: They don't realize that programmed instruction, not the machine itself, is their intellectual fountainhead.

2. *Cognitive dissonance caused by the discrepancy between what we can do and what the "establishment" permits us to do.* This is related to my previous statement about being a revolutionary whose cause is rejected; or if you can't lick 'em, join 'em. Cognitive dissonance is reduced (even eliminated) by convincing oneself that change can come about only by personal persuasion, better research evidence, and improved courseware: comforting but false.

3. *The necessity to change from a nurturing to a commanding role (and from a support to a design role).* This is a particularly important problem that may solve itself in the long run but causes difficulties in the short run. It is a problem that plagues any profession or trade in fundamental transition. One aspect of the problem is a personality dimension: If people have

chosen a profession because it is primarily supportive or nurturing, can they take charge when changes in the profession demand it? Obviously some can, but the question is addressed to the average professional. Is the denial of instructional technology's potential by individual professionals an implicit refusal to accept an unanticipated level of responsibility? For example, can a media specialist in a school become an instructional technologist? Can a person who is trained to expect someone else to make curricular decisions and another someone else to make instructional decisions move into a truly collaborative design role as an instructional technologist? Another aspect is the question of different talents as well as of different personality. Is the talent for curricular and instructional design qualitatively different from the talent required to perform traditional service functions? Do we need to tap another labor pool, or is a drastic change in training enough? (And where do those training programs come from?) The same is true of media service roles in higher education. Kerr's (1977) study of the perceptions of media personnel in the schools underscores the need for more work in this area.

Educationists, almost as a professional posture, assume that the education professions should emerge from the basic teaching pool and, further, that all education professionals should first be trained as teachers. I would challenge this position by returning to the lathe example. The talent *that designed* the automatic lathe is fundamentally different—by initial selection and by training—from the talent that *operated* the lathe. Was it necessary for the *designers* of automatic lathes to be *operators* of lathes before exercising their design skills?

The legacy of a nurturing role also haunts the professional association with the longest history in the field—the Association for Educational Communications and Technology (AECT). Because AECT originated as a department of the National Education Association and remained so for almost half a century, it looked to the parent association to deal with major policy issues and generally accepted the paternalism implied. AECT has not as yet succeeded in developing a strong, independent, and commanding voice of its own.

4. *The difficulty of analyzing our own profession.* First let me hasten to state that blame for this item cannot be laid at the door of Education but is, rather, inherent in our academic jobs. Allow me to illustrate with an anecdote: A few years ago, I was working with an economist on cost effectiveness of technologically-based instructional systems. As it became apparent that, under certain circumstances, cost effectiveness could be improved by reducing the labor intensiveness of instruction, he suddenly exclaimed, "Bob, do you realize we're talking about our jobs?" Our own vested interests as faculty can interfere with our scholarly inquiry into the impact of technology on education institutions. We need to discipline ourselves to separate our jobs from our intellectual study.

We need also to deal with our own cognitive dissonance that arises from the discrepancy between what we profess about the design of instruction and how we ourselves instruct. There is a collective respose and an individual response to this dilemma. The collective response shows that our performance is under the same pressures and forces that shape the performance of our colleagues in other schools and departments. In other words, if the rules of the game shape the performance of the players, we are playing by the same rules. The individual response has to do with our capabilities as instructors.

## Different Solutions to Educational Problems

We tend to seek solutions to education problems through technology, to Education through teaching personnel. The two are often in direct conflict. At present, the United States is lamenting the sad state of instruction in the schools. The National Commission on Excellence in Education reminds us that the gains of the education reforms of the 1950s and 1960s have been dissipated and the support systems that evolved during that period have been allowed to fall apart. The nation is where it was twenty-five years ago: in desperate need of high-quality education, particularly in science and math. Education's response is to train more teachers, retrain teachers now in service, and pay them more.

What is our response? What have we learned from the experience of the 1950s and 1960s? For our purpose here, the two lessons we should have learned are these:

- More teachers will not improve science and math instruction.

- The reliance then placed on technologies of instruction to carry the burden of reform was appropriate and is even more so today because of our vastly improved capabilities in the design and delivery of instruction.[8]

The large-scale experiment in Wisconsin using the Harvey White filmed course in physics (Wittich, Pella, & Wedemeyer, 1960), the successful use of filmed courses by the Rocky Mountain Area Project for Small High Schools (Anderson, 1969), the experience of the Physical Science Study Committee and the rationale behind it (Marsh, 1964), the Individually Prescribed Instruction Program and other technologically based programs should reinforce us in the belief that comprehensive use of technology can result in better instruction in schools more quickly than can be achieved solely by training teachers. But in these days of falling enrollments in Schools of Education, how far would we get by advocating an approach to the crisis in the schools that does not hold out much hope for increasing credit-hour production and for filling summer session classes once again?

I must stress that I haven't been setting up a good-guys-versus-bad-guys conflict. There is nothing inherently "bad" about them and "good" about us. Winston Churchill has been credited with the observation, "First we shape our buildings and then our buildings shape us." Education institutions evolved from basic assumptions about how instruction should be managed. Those institutions now reinforce the assumptions that created them by shaping the behaviors of the faculties and administrators who work in them. Our assumptions about the management of instruction (if you agree with me) are fundamentally different. We need to understand that. Survival depends on establishing our own intellectual identity. Contrary to what many of us currently believe, capitulation makes us vulnerable because then we can be easily co-opted; we must make a distinction between our administrative "home" and our intellectual foundations.

By establishing our own identity, we stand a much better chance of demonstrating that the future of Education can be enhanced if we broaden its mission to include all approaches to designing, delivering, and managing instruction. For example, curriculum faculty tend to restrict themselves to curriculum-building within one institutional framework: the schools. Our recent moves into the human resources development arena can lead curriculum faculty into an institution-free concept of curriculum-building. In this way, we can help other departments increase their survival abilities.

Concerning our service functions, establishing our own intellectual identity would put us in a much stronger position to demonstrate the cost effectiveness of our approach to curricular and instructional tasks. As technology becomes more comprehensive, more sophisticated, more pervasive, its consideration and use move to higher and higher levels of decision making: Selecting instructional materials to supplement a lesson affects only one instructor; using telecommunications and information technology to create an autonomous institution involves the legislature and a governing board. Are we intellectually ready to address both levels and all others in between?

# The Hope of the 1960s

Do you have a feeling of déjà vu about the current situation in education? If so, then you were around during the latter part of the 1950s and the decade of the 1960s. Public criticism and Soviet scientific success combined to put pressure on the schools to improve instructional effectiveness and academic standards. We in instructional technology knew we had the methods and techniques needed to do the job. The 1950s saw the teaching of entire courses by television and then by film. The emergence of the programmed instruction movement gave us great confidence in our ability to design effective and replicable instruction—and isn't that what America needed even more than a good five-cent cigar? Extensive national curriculum projects were mounted; these resulted in courses with appropriate academic rigor that were backed up by well-developed packages of materials. We discovered systems theory, and instructional development emerged as a process and a method to set in motion a systems approach to instruction.

Business and industry caught the fever. Mergers of electronics and publishing firms became commonplace; they saw the real need for comprehensive, complex packages of instruction. Much money was invested. Many good products were developed, but few were bought and fewer were used. Hardware manufacturers also saw a vast market for their equipment. Although federal money made purchasing equipment easier, much of it wound up on shelves in closets: technological tools whose use was vitiated by an absence of a commitment to technology as process.

A funny thing happened on our way to the systems approach and instructional development: We stumbled over the rigidity of educational governance and the craft structure of education institutions. We completely misread the institutional framework of which we are a part. A. Rupert Hall, a historian of technology, once commented that "Scientific knowledge is of little material value if the object of technological proficiency is the manufacture of objects of luxury; hence, in backward contemporary societies, the arbitrary installation of a few modern industrial plants, without modification of the basic economy, has little more result than to allow the rich to adopt Cadillacs and television in place of more barbarous means of ostentation" (Hall 1963). This is precisely what happened in education—except the part about "barbarous means of ostentation"! We must study our institutions from the viewpoint of general technology to understand how the "basic economy" can be changed to make our processes and products central rather than "objects of luxury."

# Technology Is the Base

## *Definition and Characteristics of Technology*

By asserting an intellectual position independent of Education and education institutions, we can examine what we are about in terms of theory, research, and practice from a different perspective. But what perspective? As I stated in the lead paragraph, I propose that instructional technology be regarded as a subset of technology in general. A definition of technology, then, would be helpful.

Agreeing on a definition of technology that can be applied to all stages of history may be impossible. Early technology evolved primarily through accident and trial and error. Although the fortuitous discovery is still important, contemporary technology is mainly the result of a constantly expanding knowledge base. A definition that fits early technology does not apply to advanced technology, and vice versa. Unfortunately for our use, the word was coined during a time that used it to describe what artisans do. For a long time, therefore, dictionaries defined technology as "the systematic treatment of an art." New dictionaries and recent revisions of older ones are using definitions that better fit contemporary technology. *Webster's New Collegiate Dictionary* defines technology as "the totality of the means employed to provide objects necessary for human sustenance and comfort" and "a technical method of achieving a practical purpose."

Nor is it useful to define technology too broadly. Perhaps in reaction to the conventional view of technology as machines, it has become fashionable in certain circles to represent just about anything that uses organized thought as technology. In responding to one such definition, Peter Drucker dryly remarked that, according to the speaker, a fox who has learned to cross a highway without getting killed has acquired technology.

Neither technique nor method, in itself, is technology. A teaching technique is not technology. Neither is my method of organizing a manuscript. I have read prestigious reports that represented a seating chart as technology in the classroom; this trivializes technology. (For example, see Goodlad, 1983, p. 469.)

In 1967, I used Galbraith's definition: "Technology means the systematic application of scientific and other organized knowledge to practical tasks" (Galbraith, 1967). It is still useful. Daniel Bell, the eminent sociologist, defines technology as "the instrumental ordering of human experience within a logic of efficient means, and the direction of nature to use its power for material gain" (Bell, 1973). These two definitions fit our field particularly well.

Valuable as they are, definitions are still abstract. To better understand how instructional technology benefits by considering it a subset of technology, we need to look at characteristics and principles of technology that extend into our field. Consider the following:

1. *Replicability.* Certainly the most obvious characteristic of technology is doing things in a reproducible manner. This characteristic changes the goal of technology from serving the few to enriching the lives of everyone. The technological (not scientific) developments and inventions that led to the Industrial Revolution shifted control of technology from the artisan to the skilled tool designer and maker, thereby forever changing the primary purpose of technology from the production of luxury items to mass production of items of necessity. Some historians of technology claim that technology began with the Industrial Revolution. Before that, all production was craft-based.

A hallmark of technology, which makes it into a producer of plenty, is that reproduction is much cheaper than invention and development; the general economy is geared to make that possible. The economy of education does not facilitate the kind of distribution that can amortize the costs of invention and development over large enough units to realize the benefits of large-scale production. The economy of education is based on the reinvention of instruction each year. Each instructional act is viewed as the work of an artisan.

2. *Reliability.* As Hoban (1962) put it, "In forty years, this concept of newer media in education has grown from one of a device for a lesson presentation to one of a complete system of remotely controlled instruction covering an entire course." I have addressed this point earlier, but some of you may be thinking that the reliability of our technology is still not very high. Perhaps so, but remember, it doesn't take much to be more reliable than what's currently in the classroom. The other point we must remember is that the potential for improving a technology is far greater than that of improving a craft, and the benefits of an improved technology can be realized more quickly than those of an improved craft.

3. *Algorithmic decision making.* As Bell (1973) put it:

---

Technology is dearly more than the physical manipulation of nature. There is an "intellectual technology" as well. An algorithm is a "decision ride," a judgment of one or another alternative course to be taken, under varying conditions, to solve a problem. In this sense we have technology whenever we can substitute algorithms for human judgment. (p. 52)

---

He goes on to state that new intellectual technology, although on a "continuum with classical technology," transposes it to a higher qualitative level. Algorithmic decision making in the design of instruction, based on our improved knowledge of human learning, raises our technology to a new qualitative level. Any process that lends itself to algorithmic treatment can be replicated reliably.

Bell concludes his discussion of algorithms with this grand statement:

---

Beyond this is a larger dream, the formalization of a theory of choice through stochastic, probabilistic, and deterministic methods . . . If the computer is the "tool," then decision theory is its master. Just as Pascal sought to throw dice with God, or the physiocrats to draw a perfect grid to array all economic exchanges among men, so the decision theorists, and the new intellectual technology, seek their own *tableau entier*—the compass of rationality itself. (pp. 52–53)

---

Isn't this the dream implied by the Hoban quote and implied by the assumption that I earlier asserted as underlying instructional technology?

4. *Communication and control.* There is little need to elaborate on this point—it is the one with which we are most familiar. Marshall McLuhan and his global village, Edmund Carpenter, and a host of others have made us aware that we are all within "earshot" of each other. What we have not grasped in education is that our notion of narrow institutional authority is completely dissonant with our ability to deliver instruction wherever the students are and in whatever social groups they choose to form. We can learn from general technology how social institutions can be reshaped by changes in communication systems.

5. *The effect of scale.* Implied in the first four items is the effect of changes in scale caused by an ever-improving technology. As a number of people have pointed out, a sufficient quantitative change causes a qualitative change—a change in scale can mean a change in institutional form. Using a television camera as an image magnifier is a vastly different concept of scale than using television systems to create an institution. The printing press created a totally different scale in the distribution of knowledge, thereby changing the social fabric of western Europe. Finn (1960) once commented that instructional technology has developed to the point where it is now possible not only to replace the teacher but also the entire school system, a logical extension of the Hoban quote—increasing the scale increases the range of control. When the linear extension of a technological form reaches its limits, an increase in scale can only occur when the form itself is abandoned. For example, when the limits of piston-driven aircraft engines were reached, the aviation industry shifted to the jet engine. When the limits of an institution to accommodate technological developments are reached, either the institution changes under the pressure to increase scale, or the technology is artificially restrained to fit the institution. As I will point out later, our situation in education begs the question: Have we reached the limits of our institutional frameworks to facilitate the scale of our present and potential instructional technology? The above are not intended to be exhaustive, just illustrative of the kinship between our field and technology.

The beginnings of exploring their relationship have been made. Finn and Hoban in the same year, 1956, separately but not independently, drew parallels between certain problems in instruction and the systems approach to organizational efforts in industry and the military—Hoban in his keynote address to the second Lake Okoboji conference and Finn in a series of editorials in a long-defunct journal called *Teaching Tools.*

Finn later borrowed a principle of thermodynamics, negative entropy, to explain a phenomenon he observed in using technology in education. He maintained that injecting technology into an instructional system has the same organizing effect as introducing additional energy into a thermodynamic system (Finn, 1959). One of the most frequent observations made by television instructors in the 1950s had to do with how much more tightly organized the television lesson was compared to the same lesson taught in class. Any of us in this field, regardless of the medium in which we work, can easily find examples of how the introduction of technology has caused a higher level of organization.

The concept of negative entropy lends itself to experimental verification, but, unfortunately, our fixation on learning gains as a dependent variable obscures opportunities to explore *system* effects of technology. Cabeceiras (1972) did take note of Finn's interpretation of negative entropy in a study on the effect of using an overhead projector on the verbal behavior of teachers. However, he mentioned it only in the conclusion of his article; it was not part of the theoretical framework that generated his hypotheses. Many of the studies in programmed instruction reported the achievement of specified behaviors in less time when the material was programmed. However, I know of none that attempted to attribute the effect to the programing itself—nor were the findings related to negative entropy. The Nebraska studies of film in social studies reported that with film, a year of U.S. history could be taught in a much shorter time. An example of negative entropy? A secondary analysis of studies in various media where time or any other manifestation of negative entropy was a factor could verify the construct. We may even find that learning gains are more accurately attributable to negative entropy than to the medium used.

A study of technology would turn up other principles, laws, and postulates that have some counterpart in instructional technology. Pursuing them can give us important insights into the system aspects of instructional technology.

# Technology and Institutional Relationships

A goodly part of our intellectual difficulty is the limited way in which we think of technology in the context of institutional and societal relationships. I have mentioned that as technology becomes more sophisticated and more pervasive in effect, consideration of its use must be raised to higher and higher levels of decision making. Review the machine screw example I used earlier. The decision to replace the entire lathe is of a completely different order than replacing the cutting tool. The quote from Hoban that I used in discussing *Reliability* can be paraphrased as follows:

In forty years, this concept of newer media in education has grown from the concern of an instructor in choosing a device for a lesson presentation to the concern of a state legislature in considering the establishment of a university based on instructional technology.

This is the societal reality of the change in scale noted by Hoban. But, for reasons cited earlier, we have difficulties grasping the full implications of this type of policy shift. My contention is that we can find better guidance in how to deal successfully with these issues in the history of technology than we can from our historic roots in Education.

# From Craft to Technology

Many of the issues we now face have been dealt with previously—often quite previously—in other sectors of society. For example, one of the main, if not the main, conceptual issues we face is the change in instruction from a craft to a technological culture. There are many facets to this issue. I will touch on several for purposes of illustration. How do institutions respond when threatened by technology? If they survive, why do they survive and in what changed form? The medieval guilds dominated the production of goods in Europe. Today's teaching profession has certain characteristics of the craft guilds. As the merchant guilds gradually took over the production of goods they had traditionally only marketed, conflicts between the two types of guilds became frequent and often violent. The craft guilds eventually lost out not only because of the gradual development of manufacturing but also because of improved transportation and communication. What lessons might we learn by knowing more about this early encounter between craft and budding technology?

In our own time, the labor-management-technology relationship can best be understood by reviewing the history of craft unionism during the first half of the twentieth century. Some of you may be uncomfortable with this; but regardless of the stand individual teachers take, there is little question that the organized teaching profession is far closer to unionism than it is to professionalism. The main questions are these: At what stage of unionism are they, and by studying the labor movement in general, what future developments might we expect? What should our relationship be to both management and labor?

We have very little research on how the growth of teacher militancy and unionism can affect our freedom to apply the full range of our technological capabilities to large-scale instructional problems. Yet, the research we do have indicates that we should be paying closer attention to these matters. Dawson's (1971) study of attitudes of members of the education profession toward media, and Schaefer's (1974) study of the implications of negotiated contracts on instructional technology are good but old. Schaefer's, in particular, needs to be updated because it documented a movement in its early stages.

The evidence we have seems to indicate that organized teacher activity parallels the craft union movement in industry. The ways in which the labor movement tried to protect its members from the encroachment of technology are very similar to how teacher groups seek to maintain the labor-intensive character of instruction. How and under what circumstances certain craft unions have accommodated (and are accommodating) technological change could help us analyze our own problems with the clash between the craft and technology of instruction.

Studying the specialization of labor and its evolution in the history of technology could give us important insights into how the craft-to-technology issue might manifest itself in the organization of instructional systems. Specialization of labor can be fully exploited only in a technologically-based system. By studying the nature of work as technology changed crafts and industries, we can obtain a more objective viewpoint of how instructional relationships might become more specialized and how instructional responsibilities could be assigned to those specialties. In presentations on this topic, I often use three film clips to demonstrate how technology changes the nature of work.[9] One of the clips contrasts the cutting out of an aircraft stabilizer by a craft method—using a template to scribe the outline of the stabilizer and to manually guide the cutting blade—to the same job performed by a machine controlled by a magnetic tape. The crew of workers cutting out the stabilizer is subtly contrasted with the technical knowledge of the designers of the machine and programmers of the control tape.

The second clip shows the hand crafting of glass objects contrasted with the manufacture of glass products. The important questions raised by the film clip are these: Under what circumstances of societal need do we call upon the labor-intensive, emotionally satisfying hand crafting of glass, and when should we rely on the efficiency of the manufacturing process? Certainly both are necessary. If technology had not entered the glass-making business, most of us would still be drinking out of gourds. The marketplace makes the decision in industry. But what are the mechanisms in a subculture in which the marketplace does not make the decisions? How do we reap the benefits of the specialization of labor in instruction?

The third clip documents the development of the Pap test. A scanning device analyzes cells from a smear and sends the information to a computer. Normal cells are ignored by the computer, but suspect ones are called to the attention of cytotechnicians for careful examination. It would be impossible for cytotechnicians to handle the volume of smears without the computer. Here for our study is another model of how labor can be deployed more effectively. All three film clips are examples of how the nature of work is changed when technological processes are applied to complex tasks.

It should be clear by now that instructional technology is aligned much more closely with management than it is with labor, despite what our sympathies may be at any given time. Those of us employed in higher education are more likely to romanticize our relationship with the teaching profession, partly because we are not normally on the firing line of militancy and partly because most of us are instructional technologists as well as teachers. But make no mistake about it, when we moved as a field from "a device to support a lesson" to the design of instructional systems, we also moved from the side of labor to that of management. I am not suggesting any open hostility to the teaching profession—far from it; what I am saying is that the very nature of our capabilities makes us an instrument of management. Suppose, as an extreme example, that teachers in a school system or institution plan to go on strike. Under pressure from public and governing boards, the chief administrator calls you into his or her office and asks you to draw up and prepare to execute a plan to use technology to keep instruction going. Choose your response: "Yes, Sir or Madam," or "I'd rather work somewhere else."

Those instructional technologists working in business and industry are far more likely to know where loyalty lies. Training is more easily identified with management goals. Regardless of whether management supports effective or ineffective instruction (and management often does both), we are hired to carry out management's decisions. As more and more instructional technologists take positions in nonformal education settings, the weight of their experiences will influence the labor-management perspective of the programs from which they graduated.

The reorientation of instructional technology from its craft origins to its technology present and future is critical to the continued well-being of the field. Depending on a craft orientation makes instructional technology dispensable—like luxury goods in a time of retrenchment. Technology builds systems that collapse if the technological support—men, machines, methods—is removed (e.g., the importance of the telephone to the conduct of business or the importance of the school bus to the consolidation of schools). Except in such rare instances as the British Open University, we are not even close to that kind of dependency.

# Technology and the Education Professions

One of the aspects of technology least understood by the education professions is the way in which technology changes institutional and professional relationships. Even that part of the academic community whose job it is to study the impact of technology on society generally takes an "it-can't-happen-here" attitude toward the subject of its study and its own profession. Although it is a function of higher education to analyze the problems of society, the difficulty here is that the problem of society to be analyzed happens to be one's own professional function. Many people have pointed out that it is almost impossible for someone to analyze critically an activity in which he or she is presently engaged. Perhaps the best and most objective research on the education professions can be done only by those without an occupational vested interest.

To get a better feel for how technology might affect the education professions, it might help to look at selected examples of how technology has changed other professions; that is, to see how technology affects professions uniquely rather than look for isomorphic models. Technology does not change all professions in the same way. The extent to which technology can subsume certain kinds of professional tasks and how the profession (or craft) responds determine how technology changes a profession.

Of the various professions connected to the health sciences, perhaps pharmacy has been affected the most by industrial (rather than professional) technology. The traditional professional skills of the pharmacist in compounding drugs has been incorporated into the manufacturing process by the drug industry. Rapid advancements in pharmacology made the manufacture of drugs imperative; pharmacists couldn't possibly keep up with the chemistry. Thus the role of the pharmacist changed from pill roller to pill dispenser, the result being a crisis in the training of pharmacists. Some schools of pharmacy want to shift the emphasis of their curriculum to that of how to run a small business. In other words, they are willing to acknowledge that the drug industry has made it unnecessary to teach the prospective pharmacist the intricacies of chemistry. Other schools of pharmacy want to create a higher role for certain pharmacists as an intermediary between physician and patient, particularly in states where prescriptions must be written in generic terms. In at least one state, California, hospitals are required to retain a registered pharmacist as an advisor to patients on medication.

It should be mentioned that the faculties of schools of pharmacy are neither prepared nor interested in teaching their students how to run a small business; they are prepared to teach chemistry, and want to teach chemistry, necessary or not. This reminds me of the account by Morison (1966) of the change by necessity from sail to steam power in naval vessels during the American Civil War. The admirals had resisted the introduction of steam before the war, but they were forced to accept it because of the tactical advantages it gave them. However, after the war, the admirals went back to rejecting steam because commanding a sailing vessel projected the image of what a naval officer *should* be—and it was certainly not standing on a bridge against a backdrop of black smoke! What is the proper image of the professor?

The main parallel to the education professions of the pharmacy example is the incorporation of professional expertise into a technological process. A little over two decades ago, when the academic disciplines first initiated large-scale curriculum revision projects, one of the main arguments advanced for doing so was that teachers in the public schools did not have the opportunity to maintain expertise in their respective disciplines. For example, the Physical Science Study Committee (PSSC) pointed out that many developments in physics had not found their way into the classrooms of the public schools. The PSSC thought it necessary to reestablish the link between the members of the discipline and the students in high school. The new developments in physics, of course, would be incorporated into the PSSC materials. When Jerome Bruner initiated the curriculum innovation that became known as Man—A Course of Study, he not only mentioned the difficulties of public school teachers in keeping abreast of developments in academic areas but he also stressed that teachers did not know how to develop problem-solving materials for children. In other words, he believed that methodological as well as substantive developments should be incorporated into the materials developed by the project. The Individually-Prescribed Instruction (IPI) program developed at the University of Pittsburgh is another example of how the instructional expertise of the professional has been built into the materials. The professional role of the teacher has been limited to determining whether each student is ready to go on to the next unit. Obviously, that function could have also been built into the materials, but politically it was necessary for the IPI program to maintain a professional role for the teachers in those classrooms. The parallel to pharmacy is made even more striking by the use of the word "prescribed" in the title of the program.

The physician and the dentist have managed to remain on top of technological developments in their professions. Physicians (and dentists to a lesser degree) have been able to delegate lower-skill, lower-return tasks to specially created technical specialties, thereby reserving high-skill, high-return tasks for themselves. Much of the technology of medicine is designed to increase the flow of patients through the doctor's office, even at the price of passing on those costs to the patients. The use of cheap, disposable materials (such as disposable hypodermic needles) and elaborate machinery (body X-ray machinery, for example) fits this pattern. The important point is that physicians have realized that increasing the number of patients handled raises income. They have also realized that their long-range interests lie in differentiation of staff.

Although dentists have moved in the same general direction as physicians, they appear to rest on a plateau. However, in at least one area, dental technology places the dentist in danger of losing control of a lucrative professional task. Until recently, all states stipulated that only a dentist can actually place a denture in the mouth of a patient. The manufacturers of dentures claim that those regulations are now obsolete. They maintain that the technology of both manufacturing and dentures has advanced to the point where the professional care of the dentist is not necessary; technicians can handle the entire process from the initial impression to the placement of the denture in the patient's mouth. Oregon became the first state to allow someone other than a dentist to fit and place dentures.

Both physicians and dentists long ago abandoned the notion that the individual in most frequent contact with a patient is in the best position to know what that patient needs. In Education, we continue to cling to that myth. We are reluctant to move to an organizational structure that permits subprofessionals to have the most frequent contact with students and reserves professional contact for specific instructionally oriented purposes.

Until recently, law was a profession about as unaffected by technology as education. As with education, it is difficult to see how the work of a lawyer might be affected by the introduction of technology. However, as mentioned at the beginning of this section, technology influences professions in different ways. Technology is about to change the profession of law, not by altering what a lawyer does when representing a client but by changing the way in which the accumulated wisdom of the profession is made available, and to whom. Both the identification of pertinent provisions of the law and the precedents relied on for interpretation of the law are basically problems of information codification, storage, and retrieval. As we all know, those problems are amenable to computer technology. In the past, companies that specialized in gathering and selling information in the form of monthly or annual compilations in print form sold their products primarily to law firms and law libraries. Processing this information in relation to a specific case was still the job of the lawyer. Computer processing of information, however, makes it possible to change that. To the chagrin of lawyers, some of these legal information companies are now making their services available to anyone willing to pay their fee. The most immediate clients for such services are small companies and businesses that cannot afford expensive legal services in connection with minor legal problems. It is certainly not too difficult to see that certain classes of legal problems, regardless of the size of the company, could be handled by a legal information processing firm. It is easy to foresee a time when individuals with such problems as divorce, real estate sales, leases, adoption procedures, etc., could take advantage of legal services provided at the end of a computer terminal. How the American Bar Association reacts to these developments will be interesting.

A final example examines a case where, because of technological developments, the power relationship between two occupations has reversed. The newspaper and magazine business has for a long time been dictated to by the International Typographical Union (ITU). This Union has traditionally looked at the American Newspaper Guild (made up of reporters, editors, etc.) as a strange mixture of union and professional association. The American Newspaper Guild has never exercised the same kind of control as the ITU. However, computer-controlled typesetting has made it possible for reporters to compose and set final copy without manual typesetting. Suddenly, the members of the newspaper guild are in a position to cooperate in the elimination of many typographical union jobs.

These are but a few examples of how technology has changed professions and, of course, the institutions of which those professions are a part. Although we cannot make a literal translation from these examples to the education professions, certainly we can learn lessons from each.

The education professional most directly affected by instructional technology is the teacher; however, many other education professions are affected directly and indirectly.

Instructional technology can take over much of what teachers traditionally do. The extent of the takeover is a function of subject, grade level, nature of the students (for example, normal, handicapped), etc. There is no question that the ratio of professional and paraprofessional personnel to students can be changed drastically. For example, the ratio of professional to paraprofessional in Banneker School (Gary, Indiana) during the performance contract changed significantly. Douglas Ellson of Indiana University has developed programmed reading for inner-city children in which all the instruction is incorporated into the program, adult supervision being limited to motivation and the tender loving care that children need constantly; Ellson has successfully used mothers from the neighborhood to perform that function. In this particular situation, the paraprofessional is the only one in direct, constant contact with the student.

In the 1950s, when Alexander Stoddard, and Lloyd Trump were developing a model of school organization often referred to as the Trump Plan, reliance was placed on the differentiation of staff, with an emphasis on paraprofessionals taking over much of the routine work of the classroom teacher. As an expression of the impact of technology on the profession, this model most closely resembles that of the physician and dentist. Lower-skill tasks are delegated to someone else, reserving the higher-skill tasks to professional attention. Stoddard and Trump were wise in realizing that the organizational pattern of the school would have to be changed along with professional roles; otherwise, just the very structure of organization would continue to force teachers to perform much as they had before. This is very clearly revealed in the study conducted by Eaton H. Conant (1973) in the Portland (Oregon) public schools. The Conant study was probably the most extensive work productivity analysis of the classroom ever undertaken. It should be required reading. We need more studies of that kind.

Administrators as well as teachers will be affected by the shift to technology. During the Banneker performance contract, Behavioral Research Laboratories found it necessary to hire a second principal to supervise the instructional program, leaving the officially appointed principal to continue doing what principals do. The principal's image of himself was not that of an implementer of curricular and instructional change nor was it that of disturber of the personnel status quo (Wilson, 1973).

The purpose of this section is not to predict what the education professions will become in the future but to point out that the study of how professions and trades in other areas are affected by technology can help us plan for a much more variegated profession than we have at present.

# Research and Development

In 1990, I participated in a Delphi study on trends in instructional technology. One of the statements asked about the future importance of research "to conduct studies to establish the validity of instructional technology." When the results of the first round came back, I was not surprised to find my response to that item at complete variance with the responses of the other participants. I rated the item as of no importance, but the others thought it very important. My reply did not mean that I think research is unimportant but, rather, that the *stated purpose* of research is unimportant. The implied wishful thought in the item is that success would crown our efforts if only we could "prove" unequivocally the effectiveness of technologically-based instruction.[*]

First, we already have more research than we need for that purpose; second, the primary purpose of research in any applied field is to improve, not prove, the technology; third, at this stage of our development, research on the specific instruments of instruction is far less important than research on the systems for which they are intended. The first I will ignore; I want to address the second and third.

A technology is not accepted or rejected on the basis of comparative performance in its beginning stages. If this were so, railroads would not have been built because the early locomotive lost a race to a horse, and the automobile would never have survived the derisive taunt, "Get a horse!" Had education researchers had been around at the time of Gutenberg, they would have immediately conducted research to determine whether people would learn from the printed page as well as or better than from hand-lettered manuscripts. When they found no significant difference, they would have urged the abandonment of the newfangled device, thereby completely missing the significance of movable type.[10] A technology survives because of faith, continuing internal improvement, an institutional structure that encourages and facilitates continued development, and an environment that permits a new technology to seek the best avenues for its contribution. For example, as of now, technologically-based instruction is finding its most ready acceptance in distance education and in underdeveloped countries where highly structured low-cost learning systems are making instruction cost-effective, as in Project Impact in the Philippines (Wooten, Jansen, & Warren, 1982). Study of the history of technological innovations would throw considerable light on the survival features of inventions.

By the way, the obverse of the above is that educators do not need research to adopt an innovation that they favor or to continue what they now do. We are all familiar with the challenge, "What evidence do you have that (any medium) really teaches?" Pick up the other end of the stick. Suppose we stood in every classroom doorway in the country and asked the instructors about to enter, "What evidence do you have that what you are about to do the next 50 minutes will be effective—or that it is the best way to present the material?" The difference is that they don't have to answer because they possess something far more important than research: They possess authority. The moral is that lack of research evidence can be used to stalemate an innovation, but it is of no importance when people want to do what they have the authority to do.

---

[*] By now you, too, should be asking, "If you build a better mousetrap, is it the mice who rush to buy it?"

I stated that technology needs to improve constantly to survive. Usually, this type of improvement is development rather than research: how to design CAI courseware, how to develop more effective instructional television, how to develop reliable low-cost learning systems, etc. At this time, it is more important to develop and refine techniques and methods of instructional design than to pursue, for example, the "attributes" of media in experimental settings. Basic or conclusion-oriented research is important, but we are woefully behind on applied or decision-oriented research, and our ultimate survival lies there. However, my fear is that researchers who are disenchanted with research on and with media will move in the direction of performing conclusion-oriented research in constructs in psychology rather than move into decision-oriented development in the design of instructional systems. This is the implication of a recent review of research by Clark (1983). It is difficult not to conclude that researchers committed to experimental methods and laboratory settings find it more difficult to change methods and settings than they do the field of inquiry. I would much prefer that our capable researchers get involved in developmental problems of instructional systems. Applied fields don't hesitate to use methods and materials that work even though explanations as to why they work aren't available. Medicine, for example, has many remedies and techniques that are effective but for which there are no explanations. Similarly, our researchers should not be hesitant about exploring complex systems problems even though the exact nature of individual elements are not known.

At the 1983 meeting of the Society for the History of Technology, one of the presenters discussed this issue in relation to chemical engineering. His point was that chemical engineers are not chemists but managers of chemical processes. They need to know as much (or more) physics and math as they do chemistry. By definition, any applied field is concerned with means and ends as opposed to a "pure" field of inquiry, which is concerned with cause-and-effect relationships. This is also a classic distinction between theory and practice: Theory is concerned with cause and effect, practice with means and ends. This is not to say that there are no theoretical constructs in an applied field but that the means-ends relationship is paramount. This also means that an applied field can have an existence independent of the theoretical concerns of contributing disciplines. For example, the shift from Newtonian to Einsteinian physics had virtually no effect on mechanical engineering, even though physics is the main contributing discipline. We need to remember this when we attempt to make literal translations from contributing disciplines (e.g., learning psychology) to the applied field of instructional technology.

Hoban (1965) once commented that "the central problem of education is not learning but the management of learning, and that the teaching-learning relationship is subsumed under the management of learning" (p. 124). Instruction is the management of learning, and instructional management, like engineering, is a class of its own made up of a complex organization of men, machines, and processes. A large-scale instructional problem may not be best analyzed in terms of individual personalogical variables or isolated media attributes but by a consideration of demographics of students, organizational relationships, the sociology of the instructional environment, delivery systems, etc. The laboratory approach of many of our researchers frequently is not compatible with instructional management realities. For example, elegant algorithmic decision charts idealizing the selection of media are meaningless when real-life decisions are based on completely different factors: accessibility of materials, level of supervision required, display requirements, delivery system capability, etc. We spend too much time telling practitioners what they *should* be doing and not enough in finding out which conditions shape their decisions. Pursuing the latter would take us out into the field for more "naturalistic" inquiry. The current interest in naturalistic methods came out of the evaluation movement—a decision-oriented, situation-specific line of inquiry. Through the use of naturalistic inquiry, I am sure that we will discover important factors, such as the earlier discussion of negative entropy, that have been ignored too long in instructional management. Latham (1974), Taylor (1981), and Kerr (1977) have asked the type of questions that can lead to important system-related findings. Siegel and Corkland (1964) proposed a conceptual framework for investigating the "instructional gestalt," as they termed it, that bears reexamination, particularly because of their inclusion of the teacher as a variable. Their framework allows for a combination of quantitative and naturalistic methods.

Our obsession with learning gains as *the* dependent variable, and our acceptance of teacher appraisals of treatments have obscured important aspects of what I refer to as the sociology of instruction—more critical in instructional management than in comparative learning gains. For example, the Wisconsin experiment in the use of the Harvey White physics course on film was undertaken to show what we already knew: Films can teach as well as classroom teachers. The *important* findings of the study, reported in an almost off-hand manner, should have told us much about the effects of teacher hostility to the filmed course (Scott, 1960). The major conclusion of the study should have dealt with how to design an instructional environment that would be conducive to the use of mediated courses. Unfortunately, the NSD finding on learning gains relegated the study to the ho-hum category. Qualitative methods used as an integral part of the experiment could have forced the important issues to the forefront. Such methods would even lead to different interpretations of learning gains. The Scott report and the Anaheim ITV studies led me to postulate the John Henry effect: One of the causes of NSD results is that the teachers of the *control* groups perform at maximum rather than typical levels (Heinich, 1970).

We must remember that research techniques designed to establish cause-and-effect relationships may not be suitable for means-ends problems. Research designs and statistical techniques most appropriate for conclusion-oriented research may impose artificial and unrealistic constraints on decision-oriented (situation-specific) questions. The inappropriateness of using techniques based on normative testing in criterion-referenced situations is one example that has gained recognition. Even more critical is that conclusion-oriented research designs elegantly *isolate* treatment effects, when what is often sought in decision-oriented research is a methodology that shows how treatments can *reinforce* each other. The techniques of operations research in engineering and business administration are more "simpatico" with decision-oriented problems in instructional systems.

We have emulated science in our research for too long. There are many reasons for this, a few implied earlier, but surely the higher status accorded science over technology in higher education and the public's virtual adoration of SCIENCE are important factors. History of science departments abound in higher education, but history of technology departments are much scarcer. "Science" in a department title is prestigious, if misleading. A friend agreed with me that his department was far more concerned with technology than with science, but his department is called "Computer Science." Where is the science in "Library Science" or "Information Science"? "Techniques" would be a better label at the rudimentary level; at the more complex level, "technology" is far more appropriate. (Then there's "Political Science"—but I wouldn't want it as a "technology" either!) The space shuttle completes a mission, and it's a great "scientific" achievement. Technology was more responsible than science. Anyone connected with the space program is a scientist, even the engineers! Our field has had fair success with getting "technology" in department titles but very little success in getting acknowledgment of the technological nature of our major research questions and problems.

We need to reexamine our posture toward the science-technology relationship. We, along with many others, tend to believe that basic research lays the groundwork for invention in a fairly direct way. Because of this general belief, the Department of Defense (DoD) invested about 10 billion dollars from 1945 to 1966 in scientific research with about 25 percent going to undirected, basic research. Growing doubt about the relationship between research and invention led the DoD to mount Project Hindsight, an eight-year study of the key contributions to the development of the weapons systems then the backbone of U.S. defense. The thirteen teams of scientists and engineers isolated some 700 developments. They concluded that 91 percent were technological and 9 percent were classifiable as science. Of the second category, only two events, or three-tenths of 1 percent, were the results of undirected, basic research. Needless to say, the scientific community reacted with shock. In an attempt to redress Project Hindsight, a subsequent study, TRACES, cited five recent innovations as dependent on scientific research (Layton, 1971). As Layton points out, "The question, therefore, is not whether science has influenced technology but rather the precise nature of the interaction" (p. 564). We would do well to ponder the relationship between science and technology, and between research and development, in our own field. As a backdrop for such a study I suggest another article by Layton (1974), "Technology as Knowledge."

# Where Do We Go from Here?

I hope that by now I have established sufficient cause to consider shifting the intellectual base of instructional technology from education to technology. By doing so, we can more freely explore the consequences of the techniques, methods, instruments, and processes inherent in our continuously developing field. The opportunities for unfettered scholarly inquiry become far more extensive. As Hoban (1965) pointed out, "The term *educational media* does not, in itself, suggest the ramifications for research, educational policy, and operating procedures which are inherent in the term *technology of education*" (p. 124). But as I mentioned, dependence on Education on the part of many of our academic programs and on the institutions within which our service units function can inhibit intellectual freedom. If the basic position of this article is to be furthered, I would expect those programs not dependent on undergraduate or graduate certification of education professionals to take the lead. It helps greatly if the academic program is not too intimately linked to a service unit within the same institution. Within those programs, leadership will have to come from individuals who perform scholarly inquiry for its own sake, who do not have one eye (or both) constantly on the alert for the next consulting opportunity—too many of our people are intellectually "bought" by consulting arrangements.

There was much more scholarly activity along the lines of this article during the 1960s than there is now. Skinner (and his followers), Finn, and Hoban made us aware that our technologies of instruction could lead to a redesign of the system. Indiana, Michigan State, Syracuse, and the University of Southern California were particularly productive in generating conferences, papers, and dissertations that explored the potential of the "systems approach." Florida State's excellent program was born as a direct result of the ferment of that period; with good intellectual leadership, it quickly established itself as a leading program. The impetus of the scholarly thrust of the 1960s must be recaptured, and not necessarily by the same institutions. I must make the observation that much of the leadership that does exist is directed to ventures in developing countries. It's time to bring it home.

Although iconoclastic scholarly activity may best be done in the kind of programs I have specified, certainly all programs can move in the direction of pertinent research and development. Surely they can start moving away from experimental to field-based studies that can add so much to the development of informed practice. A climate of acceptance for dissertations based on naturalistic methods should be generated. I hasten to add that I am not implying less rigorous study. In my view, a naturalistic study must be more disciplined, more perceptive, if less mathematical, than an experimental study. Those in our academic programs who claim administration as their specialty must carry their interest into the realm of policy and governance and begin to study education institutions not as givens but as complex organizations whose governing rules are amenable to inquiry and eventual change. The results of these studies should find their way into the important journals not only of the field but also of education and training. Convention programs should provide forums for work in progress as well as for completed studies.

It should be clear that we are in dire need of scholars. One of the inevitable characteristics of professional schools is that they turn out too many practitioners and not enough scholars. By scholar I mean someone who is prepared to examine his or her own field according to its basic premises, its status, and its place in the general scheme of things—a reflective, thinking individual. We need skilled practitioners, but we also need scholars to study and guide what the practitioners do. We are fortunate indeed when we find someone who is both practitioner and scholar.

In about 1980, I was sitting in a bar in the Los Angeles airport with a friend who I had roomed with as an undergraduate. We had not seen each other for about fifteen years. As we talked about our respective fields—he is on the English faculty of one of the University of California campuses—I commented that there are many capable people in my field, but few scholars. He was gracious enough to turn my comment around by saying that in his field there were many scholars but few capable people. When we meet again, I hope I can tell him that the balance in my field has shifted.

# Notes

1. I am using the definition of "technology of instruction" as it appears in the Association for Educational Communications and Technology (1977) Glossary (p. 177): The specific process used to design a specific type of reliable and validated instructional product/instructional systems component (e.g., the process used to develop programmed instructional materials is a technology of instruction).

2. The reader needs to keep in mind that I am discussing academic programs that prepare professionals for the field, not individuals who are practicing in the field. We can think of individuals who emerged from a variety of backgrounds, primarily psychology, but if they are part of an academic program that prepares instructional technologists, that program is highly likely to be in a School of Education. The programs at the Rochester Institute of Technology, the New York Institute of Technology, and the Twente University of Technology (See ECTJ, 1983, 31, 239–245) are exceptions worth watching. All are relatively new and based in technology, not in Education. Are they aberrations or a trend?

3. Suppose a programmed text (or a CAI course) enables students to reach the same (or better) level of performance as a traditional course. There is no office in the university that can say, "Any student who goes through the programmed text and passes the exam automatically receives credit for that course and the credit counts toward the degree." Isn't that what happens when a faculty member is assigned a course? The ramifications of institutionalization are complex. I hope to deal with them in the near future.

4. It should not be surprising then that this field began in exhortation and advocacy. These are dead ends. If this is all one has, what does one do when advocacy is either no longer necessary or hits a plateau? Without content, one is left with teaching little more than technique and mechanics, and with service programs with little more than service functions.

5. I have expressed this principle as a law: Technology makes instruction visible (Heinich 1970). Its corollary: Research on teacher behavior is unreliable—replication is uncertain.

6. A slender volume by Dewey (1929) was extremely helpful in reinforcing my ideas on this subject. I urge all of you to seek it out. The following excerpts are from pages 8–15. Note that I would often use "technology" where Dewey uses "science."

---

The important thing is to discover those traits in virtue of which various fields are called scientific. When we raise the question in this way, we are led to put emphasis upon methods of dealing with subject-matter rather than to look for uniform objective traits in subject-matter. From this point of view, science signifies, I take it, the existence of systematic methods of inquiry, which, when they are brought to bear on a range of facts, enable us to understand them better and to control them more intelligently, less haphazardly and with less routine.

There is an intellectual technique by which discovery and organization of material go on cumulatively, and by means of which one inquirer can repeat the researches of another, confirm or discredit them, and add still more to the capital stock of knowledge. Moreover, the methods when they are used tend to perfect themselves, to suggest new problems, new investigations, which refine old procedures and create new and better ones.

The question as to the sources of a science of education is, then, to be taken in this sense. What are the ways by means of which the function of education in all its branches and phases—selection of material for the curriculum, methods of instruction and discipline, organization and administration of schools—can be conducted with systematic increase of intelligent control and understanding? What are the materials upon which we may—and should—draw in order that educational activities may become in a less degree products of routine, tradition, accident and transitory accidental influences? From what sources shall we draw so that there shall be steady and cumulative growth of intelligent, communicable insight and power of direction?

This digression seems to be justified not merely because those who object to the idea of a science put personality and its unique gifts in opposition to science, but also because those who recommend science sometimes urge that uniformity of procedure will be its consequence, So it seems worthwhile to dwell on the fact that in the subjects best developed from the scientific point of new, the opposite is the case. Command of scientific methods and systematized subject-matter liberates individuals; it enables them to see new problems, devise new procedures, and, in general, makes for diversification rather than for set uniformity. But at the same time these diversifications have a cumulative effect in an advance shared by all workers in the field.

Engineering is, in actual practice, an art. But it is an art that progressively incorporates more and more of science into itself, more of mathematics, physics and chemistry. It is the kind of art it is precisely because of a content of scientific subject-matter which guides it as a practical operation. There is room for the original and daring projects of exceptional individuals. But their distinction lies not in the fact that they turn their backs upon science, but in the fact that they make new integrations of scientific material and turn it to new and previously unfamiliar and unforeseen uses. When, in education, the psychologist or observer and experimentalist in any field reduces his findings to a rule which is to be uniformly

> adopted, then, only, is there a result which is objectionable and destructive of the free play of education as an art.
>
> But this happens not because of scientific method but because of departure from it. It is not the capable engineer who treats scientific findings as imposing upon him a certain course which is to be rigidly adhered to: it is the third- or fourth-rate man who adopts this course. Even more, it is the unskilled day laborer who follows it. For even if the practice adopted is one that follows from science and could not have been discovered or employed except for science, when it is converted into a uniform rule of procedure it becomes an empirical rule-of-thumb procedure—just as a person may use a table of logarithms mechanically without knowing anything about mathematics.

At the risk of putting words in Dewey's mouth, I believe he is urging a transition from a craft to a technology.

7. This example originally appeared in Heinich, 1983a.

8. This argument originally appeared in Heinich, 1983b.

9. The film clips on the aircraft stabilizer and the Pap test are from the Edward R. Murrow See It Now program "Automation" that appeared on CBS in June 1957. The film is still available. The clip on the glass industry is from the film "Glass" by Bert Haanstra.

10. In case you think this farfetched, an abstract of a funded research project came to my attention in about 1990 that is as absurd. The study in question sought to determine whether students would learn from microfiche as well as they learn from the printed page. Surprise—no significant difference! The future of microfiche hardly hangs on the outcome of such research.

# References

Anderson, F. A. 1969. The responsibilities of state education agencies for education. In E. L. Morphet and D. L. Jesser, eds., *Planning for effective utilization of technology in education.* New York: Citation Press.

Bell, D. Technology, nature and society. 1973. In *Technology and the frontier of knowledge.* Garden City, N.Y.: Doubleday.

Cabeceiras, J. 1972. Observed differences in teacher verbal behavior when using and not using the overhead projector. *AV Communication Review* 20:271–280.

Clark, R. E. 1983. Reconsidering research on learning from media. *Review of Educational Research* 53:445–459.

Conant, E. H. 1973. *Teacher and paraprofessional work productivity.* Lexington, Mass.: D. C. Heath.

Dawson, P. 1971. Teacher militancy and instructional media. *AV Communication Review.* 19:184–197.

Dewey, J. 1929. *The sources of a science of education.* New York: Horace Liveright.

Finn, J. D. 1959. Directions for theory in audiovisual communications. In J. V. Edling, ed., *The new media in education.* Sacramento, Calif.: Sacramento State College.

———. 1962. A walk on the altered side. *Phi Delta Kappan* 44 (October):29–34. Reprinted in R. McBeath, ed., *Extending education through technology.* Washington, D.C.: Association for Educational Communications and Technology, 1972.

Galbraith, J. K. 1967. *The new industrial state.* Boston: Houghton Mifflin.

Goodlad, J. I. 1983. A study of schooling: Some findings and hypotheses. *Phi Delta Kappan* 64 (March):465–470.

Hall, A. R. 1963. The changing technical act. In C. F. Stover, ed., *The technological order.* Detroit: Wayne State University Press.

Heinich, R. 1970. *Technology and the management of instruction.* Washington, D.C.: Association for Educational Communications and Technology.

―――. 1983. Instructional technology and decisionmaking. *Educational Considerations* 10 (Spring): 25–26.(a)

―――. 1983. Legal aspects of alternative staffing patterns and educational technology. *Synthesis* (Newsletter of the Southwest Educational Development Laboratory, Austin, Texas) 6 (May 31):1–6.(b)

Heinich, R., and K. Ebert. 1976. *Legal Barriers to educational technology and instructional productivity* (NIE Grant No. NfG-G-74-0036). Washington, D.C.: National Institute of Education.

Hoban, C. F. 1962. *Research in new media in education.* Paper presented to the American Association of Colleges for Teacher Education, Washington, D.C.

―――. 1965. From theory to policy decisions. *AV Communication Review* 13:121–139.

Kerr, S. T. Are there instructional developers in the schools? *AV Communication Review* 197, no. 25: 243–267.

Latham, C. 1974. Measuring teacher responses to instructional materials. Exceptional Child Center, Utah State University.

Layton, E. 1971. Mirror-image twins: The communitie of science and technology in 19th century America. *Technology and Culture* 12:562–580.

―――. 1974. Technology as knowledge. *Technology and Culture* 15:31–41.

Marsh, P. E. 1964. Wellsprings of strategy: Considerations affecting innovations by the PSSC. In M. B. Miles, ed. *Innovations in education.* New York: Columbia University, Teachers College.

Morison, E. E. 1966. *Men, machines and modern times.* Cambridge, Mass.: M.I.T. Press.

Schaefer, W. J. 1974. *A study of negotiated contracts and their actual and perceived effects on school district media programs.* Unpublished doctoral dissertation, Indiana University.

Scott, D. T. 1960. Teaching high school physics, through the use of films. *AV Communication Review* 8:220–221.

Siegel, L., and L. Corkland. 1964. Instructional gestalt: A conceptual framework and design for educational research. *AV Communication Review* 12:16–45.

Taylor, W. D. 1981. Teachers and materials: The selection process. In *Secondary school video: A facilitator's guide.* Bloomington, Ind.: Agency for Instructional Television.

Wilson, J., and A. Banneker. 1973. *A case study of educational change.* Homewood, Ill.: ETC Publications. Based on *Some effects of performance contracting on the school organization: A case study of educational change.* Unpublished doctoral dissertation, Indiana University, 1973.

Wittich, W. A., M. O. Pelia, and C. A. Wedemeyer. 1960. The Wisconsin physics film evaluation project. *AV Communication Review* 8:156–157.

Wooten, J., W. Jansen, and M. K. Warren. 1983. *Project impact: A low-cost alternative for universal primary education in the Philippines.* Washington, D.C.: Agency for International Development.

# Author

*ROBERT HEINICH is professor, Instructional Systems Technology, School of Education, Indiana University, Bloomington, IN 47405.*

# 2

# Situated Cognition and the Culture of Learning

## John Seely Brown, Allan Collins, and Paul Duguid

*Many teaching practices implicitly assume that conceptual knowledge can be abstracted from the situations in which it is learned and used. This article argues that this assumption inevitably limits the effectiveness of such practices. Drawing on recent research into cognition as it is manifest in everyday activity, the authors argue that knowledge is situated, being in part a product of the activity, context, and culture in which it is developed and used. They discuss how this view of knowledge affects our understanding of learning, and they note that conventional schooling too often ignores the influence of school culture on what is learned in school. As an alternative to conventional practices, they propose cognitive apprenticeship (Collins, Brown, and Newman, in press), which honors the situated nature of knowledge. They examine two examples of mathematics instructions that exhibit certain key features of this approach to teaching.*

The breach between learning and use, which is captured by the folk categories "know what" and "know how," may well be a product of the structure and practices of our education system. Many methods of didactic education assume a separation between knowing and doing, treating knowledge as an integral, self-sufficient substance, theoretically independent of the situations in which it is learned and used. The primary concern of schools often seems to be the transfer of this substance, which comprises abstract, decontextualized formal concepts. The activity and context in which learning takes place are thus regarded as merely ancillary to learning—pedagogically useful, of course, but fundamentally distinct, and even neutral, with respect to what is learned.

Recent investigations of learning, however, challenge this separating of what is learned from how it is learned and used.[1] The activity in which knowledge is developed and deployed, scholars now argue, is not separable from or ancillary to learning and cognition. Nor is it neutral. Rather, it is an integral part of what is learned. Situations might be said to co-produce knowledge through activity. Learning and cognition, it is now possible to argue, are fundamentally situated.

In this paper, we try to explain in a deliberately speculative way, the reasons activity and situations are integral to cognition and learning, and how different ideas of what is appropriate learning activity produce very different results. We suggest that, by ignoring the situated nature of cognition, education defeats its own goal of providing useable, robust knowledge. And conversely, we argue that approaches such as *cognitive apprenticeship* (Collins, Brown, and Newman, in press) that embed learning in activity and make deliberate use of the social and physical context are more in line with the understanding of learning and cognition that is emerging from research.

# Situated Knowledge and Learning

Miller and Gildea's (1987) work on vocabulary teaching has shown how the assumption that knowing and doing can be separated leads to a teaching method that ignores the way situations structure cognition. Their work has described how children are taught words from dictionary definitions and from a few exemplary sentences, and they have compared this method with the way vocabulary is normally learned outside school.

People generally learn words in the context of ordinary communication; this process is startlingly fast and successful. Miller and Gildea note that by listening, talking, and reading, the average seventeen-year-old has learned vocabulary at a rate of 5,000 words per year (13 per day) for over sixteen years. By contrast, learning words from abstract definitions and sentences taken out of the context of normal use, the way vocabulary has often been taught, is slow and generally unsuccessful. There is barely enough classroom time to teach more than 100 to 200 words per year. Moreover, much of what is taught turns out to be almost useless in practice. The authors give the following examples of students' uses of vocabulary that has been acquired this way:

> *Me and my parents correlate, because without them I wouldn't be here.*
>
> *I was meticulous about falling off the cliff.*
>
> *Mrs. Morrow stimulated the soup.*[2]

Given the method, such mistakes seem unavoidable. Teaching from dictionaries assumes that definitions and exemplary sentences are self-contained pieces of knowledge. But words and sentences are not islands, entire unto themselves. Language use would involve an unremitting confrontation with ambiguity, polysemy, nuance, metaphor, and so forth were these not resolved with the extralinguistic help that the context of an utterance provides (Nunberg, 1978).

Prominent among the intricacies of language that depend on extralinguistic help are *indexical* words—words such as *I, here, now, next, tomorrow, afterwards, this.* Indexical terms are those that "index," or more plainly point to a part of the situation in which communication is being conducted.[3] They are not merely context-sensitive; they are completely context-dependent. Such words as *I* or *now,* for instance, can be interpreted only in the context of their use. Surprisingly, all words can be seen as at least partially indexical (Barwise & Perry, 1983).

Experienced readers implicitly understand that words are situated; they ask for the rest of the sentence or for the context before committing themselves to an interpretation of a word. And when they consult dictionaries, they have in mind situated examples of usage. The situation as well as the dictionary supports the interpretation. But the students who produced the sentences listed above had no support from a normal communicative situation. In tasks such as theirs, dictionary definitions are assumed to be self-sufficient. The extralinguistic props that would structure, constrain, and ultimately allow interpretation in normal communication are ignored.

Learning from dictionaries, like any method that tries to teach abstract concepts independently of authentic situations, overlooks the way understanding is developed through continued, situated use. This development, which involves complex social negotiations, does not crystallize into a categorical definition. Because it is dependent on situations and negotiations, the meaning of a word cannot, in principle, be captured by a definition, even when the definition is supported by a couple of exemplary sentences.

All knowledge is, we believe, like language: Its constituent parts index the world and so are inextricably a product of the activity and situations in which they are produced. A concept, for example, will continuously evolve with each new occasion of use, because new situations, negotiations, and activities inevitably recast it in a new, more densely textured form. And so a concept, as with the meaning of a word, is always under construction. This would also appear to be true of apparently well-defined, abstract technical concepts. Even these are not wholly definable and defy categorical description; part of their meaning is always inherited from the context of use.

## Learning and Tools

To explore the idea that concepts are situated as well as progressively developed through activity, we should abandon any notion that they are abstract, self-contained entities. Instead, it may be more useful to consider conceptual knowledge as, in some ways, similar to a set of tools.[4] Tools share several significant features with knowledge: They can be fully understood only through use, and using them entails changing the user's view of the world and adopting the belief system of the culture in which they are used.

First, if knowledge is thought of as tools, we can illustrate Whitehead's (1929) distinction between the mere acquisition of inert concepts and the development of useful, robust knowledge. It is quite possible to acquire a tool but to be unable to use it. Similarly, it is common for students to acquire algorithms, routines, and decontextualized definitions that they cannot use and that, therefore, lie inert. Unfortunately, this problem is not always apparent. Old-fashioned pocket knives, for example, come with a device for removing stones from horses' hooves. People owning pocket knives that have this device may know its use and be able to talk wisely about horses, hooves, and stones. But they may never betray—or even recognize—that they would not begin to know how to use this implement on a horse. Similarly, students can often manipulate algorithms, routines, and definitions they have acquired with apparent competence and yet not reveal, to their teachers or themselves, that they would have no idea what to do should they come upon the domain equivalent to that of a limping horse.

People who use tools rather than just acquire them, by contrast, build an increasingly rich implicit understanding of the world in which they use the tools and of the tools themselves. The understanding, both of the world and of the tool, continuously changes as a result of their interaction. Learning and acting are, interestingly, indistinct, learning being a continuous, lifelong process resulting from acting in situations.

Learning how to use a tool involves far more than can be accounted for in any set of explicit rules. The occasions and conditions for use arise directly from the activities of each community that uses the tool, framed by the way members of that community see the world. The community and its viewpoint, quite as much as the tool itself, determine how a tool is used. Thus, carpenters and cabinet makers use chisels differently. Because tools and the way they are used reflect the particular accumulated insights of communities, it is not possible to use a tool appropriately without understanding the community or culture in which it is used.

Conceptual tools similarly reflect the cumulative wisdom of the culture in which they are used and the insights and experience of individuals; their meaning is not invariant but a product of negotiation within the community. Again, appropriate use is not simply a function of the abstract concept alone. It is a function of the culture and the activities in which the concept has been developed. Just as carpenters and cabinet makers use chisels differently, so physicists and engineers use mathematical formulae differently. Activity, concept, and culture are interdependent. No one can be completely understood without the other two. Learning must involve all three. Teaching methods often try to impart abstracted concepts as fixed, well-defined, independent entities that can be explored in prototypical examples and textbook exercises. But such exemplification cannot provide the important insights into either the culture or the authentic activities of members of that culture that learners need.

To talk about academic disciplines, professions, or even manual trades as communities or cultures will perhaps seem strange. Yet communities of practitioners are connected by more than their ostensible tasks: They are bound by intricate, socially constructed webs of belief, which are essential to understanding what they do (Geertz, 1983). The activities of many communities are unfathomable, unless they are viewed from within the culture. The culture and the use of a tool interact to determine the way practitioners see the world; and the way the world appears to them determines the culture's understanding of the world and of the tools. Unfortunately, students are too often asked to use the tools of a discipline without being able to adopt its culture. To learn to use tools as practitioners use them, a student, like an apprentice, must enter that community and its culture. Thus, in a significant way, learning is, we believe, a process of enculturation.

## *Learning and Enculturation*

Enculturating may, at first, appear to have little to do with learning; but it is what people do when they learn to speak, read, and write, or when they become school children, office workers, researchers, and so on. From a very early age and throughout their lives, people, consciously or unconsciously, adopt the behavior and belief systems of new social groups. Given the chance to observe and practice *in situ* the members of a culture and their behavior, people pick up relevant jargon, imitate behavior, and gradually begin to act in accordance with its norms. These cultural practices are often recondite and complex. Nonetheless, given the opportunity to observe and practice them, people adopt them with great success. Students, for instance, can quickly gain an implicit sense of what is suitable diction, what makes a relevant question, what is legitimate or illegitimate behavior in a particular activity. The ease and success with which people do this (as opposed to the intricacy of describing what it entails) not only belie the immense importance of the process but obscure learning as a product of the ambient culture rather than of explicit teaching.

Too often the practices of contemporary schooling deny students the chance to engage the relevant domain culture because that culture is not in evidence. Although students are shown the tools of many academic cultures in the course of a school career, the pervasive cultures that they observe, in which they participate, and which some enter quite effectively are the cultures of school life itself. These cultures can be unintentionally antithetical to useful domain learning. The ways schools use dictionaries, or math formulae, or historical analysis are very different from the ways practitioners use them (Schoenfeld, in press). Thus, students may pass exams (a distinctive part of school cultures) but still not be able to use a domain's conceptual tools in authentic practice.

This is not to suggest that all students of math or history should become professional mathematicians or historians but to claim that for students to learn these subjects (and not just to learn about them), they need much more than abstract concepts and self-contained examples. They need to be exposed to the use of a domain's conceptual tools in authentic activity—to teachers acting as practitioners and using these tools in wrestling with problems of the world. Such activity can tease out the way a mathematician or historian looks at the world and solves emergent problems. The process may appear informal, but it is nonetheless full-blooded, authentic activity that can be deeply informative—in a way that textbook examples and declarative explanations are not.

# Authentic Activity

Our case so far rests on an undefined distinction between authentic and school activity. If we take learning to be a process of enculturation, it is possible to clarify this distinction and to explain why much schoolwork is inauthentic and thus not fully productive of useful learning.

The activities of a domain are framed by its culture. Their meaning and purpose are socially constructed through negotiations among present and past members. Activities thus cohere in a way that is, in theory, if not always in practice, accessible to members who move within the social framework. These coherent, meaningful, and purposeful activities are *authentic,* according to the definition of the term we use here. Authentic activities then, are most simply defined as the ordinary practices of the culture.

This is not to say that authentic activity can only be pursued by experts. Apprentice tailors (Lave, 1988a), for instance, begin their training by ironing finished garments (which tacitly teaches them a lot about cutting and sewing). Ironing is simple, valuable, and absolutely authentic. Students of Palincsar and Brown's (1984) reciprocal teaching of reading may read elementary texts, but they develop authentic strategies that are recognized by all readers. The students in Miller and Gildea's study, by contrast, were given a strategy that is a poor extrapolation of experienced readers' situated use of dictionaries.

School activity too often tends to be hybrid, implicitly framed by one culture, but explicitly attributed to another. Classroom activity very much takes place within the culture of schools, although it is attributed to the culture of readers, writers, mathematicians, historians, economists, geographers, and so forth. Many of the activities students undertake are simply not the activities of practitioners and would not make sense or be endorsed by the cultures to which they are attributed. This hybrid activity, furthermore, limits students' access to the important structuring and supporting cues that arise from the context. What students do tends to be ersatz activity.

Archetypal school activity is very different from what we have in mind when we talk of authentic activity, because it is very different from what authentic practitioners do. When authentic activities are transferred to the classroom, their context is inevitably transmuted; they become classroom tasks and part of the school culture. Classroom procedures, as a result, are then applied to what have become classroom tasks. The system of learning and using (and, of course, testing) thereafter remains hermetically sealed within the self-confirming culture of the school. Consequently, contrary to the aim of schooling, success within this culture often has little bearing on performance elsewhere.

Math word problems, for instance, are generally encoded in a syntax and diction that is common only to other math problems. Thus, the word problems of a textbook of 1478 are instantly recognizable today (Lave, 1988c). But word problems are as foreign to authentic math practice as Miller and Gildea's example of dictionary learning is to the practices of readers and writers. By participating in such ersatz activities, students are likely to misconceive entirely what it is that practitioners actually do. As a result, students can easily be introduced to a formalistic, intimidating view of math that encourages a culture of math phobia rather than one of authentic math activity.

In the creation of classroom tasks, the apparently peripheral features of authentic tasks—such as the extralinguistic supports involved in the interpretation of communication—are often dismissed as "noise" from which salient features can be abstracted for the purpose of teaching. But the context of activity is an extraordinarily complex network from which practitioners draw essential support. The source of such support is often only tacitly recognized by practitioners, or even by teachers or designers of simulations. Classroom tasks, therefore, can completely fail to provide the contextual features that allow authentic activity. At the same time, students may come to rely, in important but little noticed ways, on features of the classroom context, in which the task is now embedded, that are wholly absent from and alien to authentic activity. Thus, much of what is learned in school, if it was learned through such activity, may apply only to the ersatz activity.

## Activities of Students, Practitioners, and Just Plain Folks

The idea that most school activity exists in a culture of its own is central to understanding many of the difficulties of learning in school. Jean Lave's ethnographic studies of learning and everyday activity (1988b) reveal how different schooling is from the activities and culture that give meaning and purpose to what students learn elsewhere. Lave focuses on the behavior of JPFs (just plain folks) and records that the ways they learn are quite distinct from what students are asked to do.

Three categories primarily concern us here: JPFs, students, and practitioners. Put most simply, when JPFs aspire to learn a particular set of practices, they have two apparent options. First, they can enculturate through apprenticeship. Becoming an apprentice doesn't involve a qualitative change from what JPFs normally do. People enculturate into different communities all the time. The apprentices' behavior and the JPFs' behavior can thus be thought of as pretty much the same.[5]

The second, and now more conventional option is to enter a school as a student. Schools, however, do seem to demand a qualitative change in behavior. What the student is expected to do and what a JPF does are significantly different. The student enters the school culture while ostensibly being taught something else. And the general strategies for intuitive reasoning, for resolving issues, and for negotiating meaning that people develop through everyday activity are superseded by the precise, well-defined problems, formal definitions, and symbol manipulation of much school activity.

We try to represent this discontinuity in Table 2.1, which compares the salient features of JPF, practitioner, and putative student behavior.

*Table 2.1.* JPF, Practitioner, and Student Activity

|  | JFPs | Students | Practitioners |
|---|---|---|---|
| reasoning with: | causal stories | laws | causal models |
| acting on: | situations | symbols | conceptual situations |
| resolving: | emergent problems and dilemmas | well-defined problems | ill-defined problems |
| producing: | negotiable meaning & socially constructed understanding | fixed meaning & immutable concepts | negotiable meaning & socially constructed understanding |

This table is mainly intended to make apparent that, in our terms, there is a great similarity between JPFs' and practitioners' activity. Both have their activities situated in the cultures in which they work, within which they negotiate meanings and construct understanding. The issues and problems they face arise out of, are defined by, and are resolved within the constraints of the activity they are pursuing.

Lave's work (1988b) provides a good example of a JPF engaged in authentic activity using the context in which an issue emerged to help find a resolution. The example comes from a study of a Weight Watchers class, whose participants were preparing their carefully regulated meals under instruction.

---

*In this case they were to fix a serving of cottage cheese, supposing the amount laid out for the meal was three-quarters of the two-thirds cup the program allowed. The problem solver in this example began the task muttering that he had taken a calculus course in college. . . . Then after a pause, he suddenly announced that he had "got it!" From then on he appeared certain he was correct, even before carrying out the procedure. He filled a measuring cup two-thirds full of cottage cheese, dumped it out on the cutting board, patted it into a circle, marked a cross on it, scooped away one quadrant, and served the rest.*

*Thus, "take three-quarters of two-thirds of a cup of cottage cheese" was not just the problem statement but also the solution to the problem and the procedure for solving it. The setting was part of the calculating process and the solution was simply the problem statement, enacted with the setting. At no time did the Weight Watcher check his procedure against a paper and pencil algorithm, which would have produced 3/4 cup x 2/3 cup = 1/2 cup. Instead, the coincidence of the problem, setting, and enactment was the means by which checking took place. (p. 165)*

---

The dieter's solution path was expedient and drew on the sort of inventiveness that characterizes the activity of both JPFs and practitioners. It reflected the nature of the activity, the resources available, and the sort of resolution required in a way that problem solving relies on that abstracted knowledge cannot.

This inventive resolution depended on the dieter's seeing the problem in the particular context, which itself was embedded in ongoing activity. And this again is characteristic of both JPFs and experts. The dieter's position gave him privileged access to the solution path he chose. (This probably accounts for the certainty he expressed before beginning his calculation.) He was thus able to see the problem and its resolution in terms of the measuring cup, cutting board, and knife. Activity-tool-culture (cooking-kitchen utensils-dieting) moved in step throughout this procedure because of the way the problem was seen and the task performed. The entire micro-routine simply became one more step on the road to a meal.[6] Knowing and doing were interlocked and inseparable.

This sort of problem solving is carried out in conjunction with the environment and is quite distinct from the processing solely inside heads that many teaching practices implicitly endorse. By off-loading part of the cognitive task onto the environment, the dieter automatically used his environment to help solve the problem. His actions were not in any way exceptional; they resemble many ordinary working practices. Scribner (1984) records, for instance, how complex calculations can be performed by practitioners who use their environment directly. In the case she studied, dairy loaders used the configuration of crates they were filling and emptying almost like an elaborate abacus. Nor are such problem-solving strategies limited to the physical or social environment: This sort of reliance on situations can be seen in the work of physicists, who see "through" formulae by envisioning a physical situation, which then provides support for inferences and approximations (deKleer & Brown, 1984). Hutchins' (in press) study of intricate collaborative naval navigation records the way people distribute the burden across the environment as well as the group. The resulting cognitive activity can then be explained only in relation to its context. Hutchins observes that

---

[W]hen the context of cognition is ignored it is impossible to see the contribution of structure in the environment, in artifacts, and in other people to the organization of mental processes. Instead of taking problems out of the context of their creation and providing them with an extraneous framework, JPFs seem particularly adept at solving them within the framework of the context that produced them. This allows JPFs to share the burdens of both defining and solving the problem with the task environment as they respond in 1 real time.

---

The adequacy of the solution they reach becomes apparent in relation to the role it must play in allowing activity to continue. The problem, the solution, and the cognition involved in getting between the two cannot be isolated from the context in which they are embedded.

Even though students are expected to behave differently, they inevitably do behave like the JPFs they are and solve most of their problems in their own situated way. Schoenfeld (in press) describes mathematics students using well-known but unacknowledged strategies, such as the position of a problem in a particular section of the book (e.g., the first questions at the end of chapters are always simple ones, and the last usually demand concepts from earlier chapters), or the occurrence of a particular word in the problem (e.g., "left" signals a subtraction problem), to find solutions quickly and efficiently. Such ploys indicate how thoroughly learners really are situated, and how they always lean on whatever context is available for help. Within the practices of schooling, these strategies can obviously be very effective. But the school situation is specialized. Viewed from outside, where problems do not come in textbooks, a dependency on such school-based cues makes the learning fragile.

Furthermore, although schooling seeks to encourage problem solving, it disregards most of the inventive heuristics that students bring to the classroom; it thus implicitly devalues not just individual heuristics, which may be fragile, but the entire process of inventive problem solving. Lave (198c) describes how some students find it necessary to disguise effective strategies so that teachers believe the problems have been solved in the approved way.

## *Structuring Activity*

Authentic activity, as we have argued, is important for learners because it is the only way they gain access to the standpoint that enables practitioners to act meaningfully and purposefully. Authentic activity shapes or hones their tools; how and why remain to be explained. Activity also provides experience, which is plainly important for subsequent action. Here, we try to explain some of the products of activity as idiosyncratic "indexicalized" representations.

Representations arising out of activity cannot easily (or perhaps at all) be replaced by descriptions. Plans, as Suchman argues (1987), are distinct from situated actions. Most people will agree that a picture of a complex machine in a manual is distinctly different from how the machine actually looks. (In an intriguing way you need the machine to understand the manual, as much as the manual to understand the machine.) The perceptions resulting from actions are a central feature in learning as well as in activity. How a person perceives activity may be determined by tools and their appropriated use. What they perceive, however, contributes to how they behave and learn. Different activities produce different indexicalized representations, not equivalent, universal ones; thus, the activity that led to those representations plays a central role in learning.

Representations are, we suggest, indexicalized rather in the way that language is. That is to say, they are dependent on context. In face-to-face conversations, people can interpret indexical expressions (containing such words as *I, you, here, now, that,* etc.), because they have access to the indexed features of the situation, although people rarely notice the significance of the surroundings to their understanding. The importance of the surroundings becomes apparent, however, when they try to hold similar conversations at a distance. Then indexical expressions become problematic until ways are found to secure their interpretation by situating their reference (see, for instance, Rubin 1980, on the difference between speech and writing).

Perhaps the best way to discover the importance and efficiency of indexical terms and their embedding context is to imagine discourse without them. Authors of a collaborative work such as this one will recognize the problem if they have ever discussed the paper over the phone. "What you say here" is not a very useful remark. *Here* in this setting needs an elaborate description (such as "page 3, second full paragraph, fifth sentence," beginning . . . ) and can often lead to conversations at cross purposes. The problem gets more difficult in conference calls, when *you* becomes as ambiguous as *here* is unclear. The contents of a shared environment make a central contribution to conversation.

When the immediacy of indexical terms is replaced by descriptions, the nature of discourse changes and understanding becomes much more problematic. Indexical terms are virtually transparent. They draw little or no attention to themselves. They do not necessarily add significantly to the difficulty of understanding a proposition in which they occur, but simply point to the subject under discussion, which then provides essential structure for the discourse. Descriptions, by comparison, are at best translucent and at worst opaque, intruding emphatically between speakers and their subjects. The audience has first to focus on the descriptions and try to interpret them and find what they might refer to. Only then can the proposition in which they are embedded be understood. (However elaborate, a description does not merely replace the indexical word.) The more elaborate the description is in an attempt to be unambiguous, the more opaque it is in danger of becoming. And in some circumstances, the indexical term simply cannot be replaced (Perry, 1979).

Knowledge, we suggest, similarly indexes the situation in which it arises and is used: The embedding circumstances efficiently provide essential parts of its structure and meaning. So knowledge, which comes coded by and connected to the activity and environment in which it is developed, is spread across its component parts, some of which are in the mind and some in the world, much as the final picture on a jigsaw is spread across its component pieces.

As Hutchins (in press), Pea (1988), and others point out, the structure of cognition is widely distributed across the social and physical environment. And we suggest that the environment, therefore, makes important contributions to the indexical representations people form in activity. These representations, in turn, contribute to future activity. Indexical representations developed through engagement in a task may greatly increase the efficiency with which subsequent tasks can be done, providing part of the environment that structures the representations remains invariant; this is evident in the ability to perform tasks that cannot be described or remembered in the absence of the situation. Recurring features of the environment may thus afford recurrent sequences of actions. Memory and subsequent actions, as knots in handkerchiefs and other *aides memoires* reveal, are not context-independent processes. Routines (Agre, 1985) may well be a product of this sort of indexicalization. Thus, authentic activity becomes a central component of learning.

Indexicality indicates that knowledge, and not just learning, is situated, one of the key points of the concept. A corollary of this is that learning methods that are embedded in authentic situations are not merely useful; they are essential.

# Learning Through Cognitive Apprenticeship

We have been working toward a conception of human learning and reasoning that, we feel, it is important for school practices to honor. Though there are many innovative teachers, schools, and programs that act otherwise, prevalent school practices assume, more often than not, that knowledge is individual and self-structured, that schools are neutral with respect to what is learned, that concepts are abstract, relatively fixed, and unaffected by the activity through which they are acquired and used, and that JPF behavior should be discouraged.

Cognitive apprenticeship (Collins, Brown, & Newman, in press), whose mechanisms we have, to some extent, been trying to elucidate, embraces methods that stand in contradistinction to these practices. Cognitive apprenticeship methods try to enculturate students into authentic practices through activity and social interaction in a way similar to that evident—and evidently successful—in craft apprenticeship. In this section, we examine briefly two examples of mathematics teaching in an attempt to illustrate how some of the characteristics of learning that we have discussed can be honored in the classroom. We use examples from mathematics in part because that is where some of the most innovative work in teaching can be found; but we firmly believe that this sort of teaching is possible not just in mathematics.

## *Schoenfeld's Teaching of Problem Solving*

Schoenfeld's teaching of problem solving (1985, in press) deliberately attempts to generate mathematical practice and to show college students how to think about the world mathematically, how to see the world through the mathematician's eyes, and how to use the mathematician's tools. Schoenfeld's approach goes well beyond simply giving students problem-solving strategies; much more important, it provides students with the opportunity to enter the culture of mathematical practice.

Schoenfeld's students bring problems to class that he and they investigate mathematically. His students can witness and participate in spontaneous mathematical thinking and see mathematics as a sense-making pursuit. This approach is distinctive because, before graduate school, few students have the opportunity to watch their teachers engaged in mathematical practice, yet the students are expected to understand the nature of that practice.

In one case (Schoenfeld, in press), he and his class faced the problem of the magic square (see Figure 2.1). Though the problem is relatively straightforward, the collaborative work involved in solving it and, which is important, in analyzing the solution helped reveal to the class the way mathematicians look at problems. The class worked collectively through a number of strategies, which, on reflection, they recognized as

Courtesy of the Carnegie Library of Pittsburgh

**The tentmakers and the apprentice.**

Can you place the digits 1, 2, 3, 4, 5, 6, 7, 8, 9 in the box below, so that the sum of the digits along each row, each column, and each diagonal is the same? The completed box is called a *magic square*.

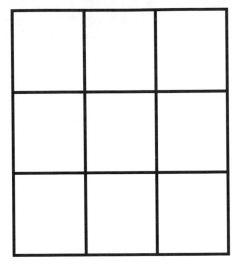

***Fig. 2.1.*** **The magic square problem.**

more general and more powerful mathematical ideas. In discussing whether 9 can go in the center of the square, they developed the ideas of "focusing on key points that give leverage," and "exploiting extreme cases." Although Schoenfeld may appear to be teaching strategy rather than subject matter, he was, more fundamentally, building with his class a mathematical belief system around his own and the class's intuitive responses to the problem.

As an indication that Schoenfeld's class was working in the culture of mathematics, not in the culture of schooling, he did not have the students stop at what, in culture of school practice, would mark the end: an answer.

---

*Are we done? In most mathematics classes the answer is "yes." Early in the semester, my students all say, "yes," expecting me to go on to another problem. My answer, however, is a resounding "no." In most classes, so-called "problems" are exercises; you are done when you've shown that you've mastered the relevant technique by getting the answer. (Schoenfeld, in press)*

---

His class's goal, by contrast, was to understand the mathematical nature of magic square, and it was in part by doing this that the belief system was exemplified. The class explored other possible magic squares and discovered general principles (e.g., an algebraic form for describing the squares). It also led to further generalizable mathematical strategies, less commonly seen in classroom practice, such as working forward from an initial solution; using systematic generating procedures; finding more than one way to solve a problem. Schoenfeld is consistently careful to emphasize that all such strategies are illustrated in action, developed by the class, and not declared by the teacher. In Schoenfeld's classes, the belief system is instilled in the only way it can be, through practice in which the students participate.

## *Lampert's Teaching of Multiplication*

Lampert (1986) also involves her students in mathematical exploration, which she tries to make continuous with their everyday knowledge. She has devised methods for teaching mathematics to fourth-grade students that lead, through activity and social construction in the culture, from students' implicit understanding of the world beyond the classroom to the sort of robust learning that direct teaching of algorithms usually fails to achieve.

She starts teaching multiplication, for example, in the context of coin problems, because in the community of fourth-grade students, there is usually a strong, implicit, shared understanding of coins. Next, the students create stories for multiplication problems, drawing on their implicit knowledge to delineate various examples of multiplication. Then, in the context of the coin problems and stories the community has created, Lampert helps them toward the abstract algorithm that everyone learns for multidigit multiplication. Thus, the method presents the algorithm as one more useful strategy to help her students resolve community problems.

The first phase of teaching starts with simple coin problems, such as "using only nickels and pennies, make 82 cents." With such problems, Lampert helps her students explore their implicit knowledge. Then, in the second phase, the students create stories for multiplication problems (see Figure 2.2). They perform a series of decompositions and discover that there is no one, magically "right" decomposition decreed by authority, just more and less useful decompositions whose *use* is judged in the context of the problem to be solved and the interests of the problem solvers. The third phase of instruction gradually introduces students to the standard algorithm, now that such an algorithm has a meaning and a purpose in their community. The students' procedure parallels the story problems they had created. Eventually, they find ways to shorten the process, and they usually arrive at the standard algorithm, justifying their findings with the stories they created earlier.

Through this method, students develop a composite understanding of four different kinds of mathematical knowledge: a) *intuitive knowledge,* the kind of shortcuts people invent when doing multiplication problems in authentic settings; b) *computational knowledge,* the basic algorithms that are usually taught; c) *concrete knowledge,* the kind of concrete models of the algorithm associated with the stories the students created; and d) *principled knowledge,* the principles such as associativity and commutativity that underlie the algorithmic manipulations of numbers. Lampert tries to inculcate an inseparable understanding of these kinds of knowledge and the connections between them, and thus to bridge the huge gap that emerges from much conventional teaching between conceptual knowledge and problem solving activity—between, as we characterized them at the beginning, knowing and doing.

This approach fosters procedures that are characteristic of cognitive apprenticeship:

- *By beginning with a task embedded in a familiar activity, it shows the students the legitimacy of their implicit knowledge and its availability as scaffolding in apparently unfamiliar tasks.*

- *By pointing to different decompositions, it stresses that heuristics are not absolute, but assessed with respect to a particular task—and that even algorithms can be assessed in this way.*

- *By allowing students to generate their own solution paths, it helps make them conscious, creative members of the culture of problem-solving mathematicians. And, in enculturating through this activity, they acquire some of the culture's tools—a shared vocabulary and the means to discuss, reflect upon, evaluate, and validate community procedures in a collaborative process.*

Schoenfeld's approach differs principally in its strong emphasis on exposing students to the authentic ways of thinking of a culture and its conceptual viewpoint as much as to its subject matter.

Figure 2.3 shows how, in the terms of cognitive apprenticeship, we can represent the progress of the students from embedded activity to general principles of the culture. In this sequence, apprenticeship and coaching in a domain begin by providing modeling *in situ* and scaffolding for students to get started in an authentic activity. As the students gain more self-confidence and control, they move into a more autonomous phase of collaborative learning in which they begin to participate consciously in the culture. The social network within the culture helps them develop its language and belief systems and promotes the process of enculturation. Collaboration also leads to articulation of strategies, which can then be discussed and reflected upon; this, in turn, fosters generalizing, which is grounded in the students' situated understanding. From here, students can use their fledgling conceptual knowledge in activity and see that activity in a new light, which in turn leads to the further development of conceptual knowledge.

In language learning, for instance, the original frail understanding of a word is developed and extended through subsequent use and social negotiation, though each use is obviously situated. Miller and Gildea (1978) describe two stages of this process. The first, in which people learn the word and assign it a semantic category (e.g., the word "olive" is first assigned to the general category of color words), is quickly done. The second, in which distinctions within this semantic category (e.g., between olive and other colors) are explored as the word occurs again and again, is a far more gradual process, which "may never be completely finished" (p. 95). This second phase of word learning corresponds to the development through activity of all conceptual knowledge. The threadbare concepts that initially develop out of activity are gradually given texture as they are deployed in different situations.

# Apprenticeship and Cognition

The development of concepts out of and through continuing authentic activity is the approach of cognitive apprenticeship—a term closely allied to our image of knowledge as a tool. Cognitive apprenticeship supports learning in a domain by enabling students to acquire, develop, and use cognitive tools in authentic domain activity. Similarly, craft apprenticeship enables apprentices to acquire and develop the tools and skills of their craft through authentic work at, and membership in, their trade. Through this process, apprentices enter the culture of practice. So the term *apprenticeship* helps to emphasize the centrality of activity in learning and knowledge and highlights the inherently context-dependent, situated, and enculturating nature of learning. And *apprenticeship* also suggests the paradigm of situated modeling, coaching, and fading (Collins, Brown, & Newman, in press) whereby teachers or coaches promote learning, first by making explicit their tacit knowledge or by modeling their strategies for students in authentic activity. Teachers and colleagues then support their students' attempts at doing the task. And finally, they empower their students to continue independently. The progressive process of learning and enculturation perhaps argues that *Increasingly Complex Micro-worlds* (see Burton, Brown, & Fischer, 1984) can be replaced by increasing complex enculturating environments.

T: Can anyone give me a story that could go with this multiplication... 12 x 4?

S1: There were 12 jars, and each had 4 butterflies in it.

T: And if I did this multiplication and found the answer, what would I know about those jars and butterflies?

S1: You'd know you had that many butterflies altogether.

T: Okay, here are the jars. [*Draws a picture to represent the jars of butterflies—see diagram.*] The stars in them will stand for butterflies. Now, it will be easier for us to count how many butterflies there are altogether, if we think of the jars in groups. And as usual, the mathematician's favorite number for thinking about groups is?

S2: 10

T: Each of these 10 jars has 4 butterflies in it. [*Draws a loop around 10 jars.*]...

T: Suppose I erase my circle and go back to looking at the 12 jars again altogether. Is there any other way I could group them to make it easier for us to count all the butterflies?

S6: You could do 6 and 6.

T: Now, how many do I have in this group?

S7: 24

T: How did you figure that out?

S7: 8 and 8 and 8. [*He puts the 6 jars together into 3 pairs, intuitively finding a grouping that made the figuring easier for him.*]

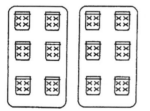

T: That's 3 x 8. It's also 6 x 4. Now, how many are in this group?

S6: 24. It's the same. They both have 6 jars.

T: And now how many are there altogether?

S8: 24 and 24 is 48.

T: Do we get the same number of butterflies as before? Why?

S8: Yeah, because we have the same number of jars and they still have 4 butterflies in each.

Note: From Lampert, 1986.

*Fig. 2.2.* **Story problems for teaching multiplication.**

*Cognitive* emphasizes that apprenticeship techniques actually reach well beyond the physical skills usually associated with apprenticeship to the kinds of cognitive skills more normally associated with conventional schooling. This extension is not as incompatible with traditional apprenticeship as it may at first seem. If our argument for the inseparability of knowing and doing is correct, the physical skills usually associated with apprenticeship embody important cognitive skills. Certainly many professions with generally acknowledged cognitive content, such as law, medicine, architecture, and business, have nonetheless traditionally been learned through apprenticeship.

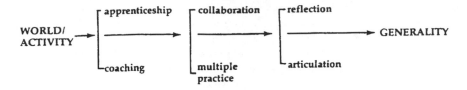

*Fig. 2.3.* **Students' progress from embedded activity in generality.**

Moreover, advanced graduate students in the humanities, the social sciences, and the physical sciences acquire their extremely refined research skills through the apprenticeships they serve with senior researchers. It is then that they, like all apprentices, must recognize and resolve the ill-defined problems that issue out of authentic activity, in contrast to the well-defined exercises that are typically given to them in textbooks and on exams throughout their earlier schooling. In short, at this stage, students no longer behave as students but as practitioners, and develop their conceptual understanding through social interaction and collaboration in the culture of the domain, not of the school.

In essence, cognitive apprenticeship attempts to promote learning within the nexus of activity, tool, and culture that we have described. Learning, both outside and inside school, advances through collaborative social interaction and the social construction of knowledge. Resnick has pointed out (1988) that throughout most of their lives people learn and work collaboratively, not individually, as they are asked to do in many schools. Lampert's and Schoenfeld's work, Scardamalia, Bereiter, and Steinbach's teaching of writing (1984), and Palincsar and Brown's (1984) work with reciprocal teaching of reading all employ some form of social interaction, social construction of knowledge, and collaboration.

Within a culture, ideas are exchanged and modified and belief systems developed and appropriated through conversation and narratives; these must be promoted, not inhibited. Though they are often anathema to traditional schooling, they are an essential component of social interaction and, thus, of learning. They provide access to much of the distributed knowledge and elaborate support of the social matrix (Orr, 1987). Learning environments, then, must allow narratives to circulate and "war stories" to be added to the collective wisdom of the community.

The role of narratives and conversations is perhaps more complex than might first appear. An intriguing role in learning is played by "legitimate peripheral participation," where people who are not taking part directly in a particular activity learn a great deal from their legitimate position on the periphery (Lave & Wenger, in preparation). It is a mistake to think that important discourse in learning is always direct and declarative; indeed, peripheral participation is particularly important for people entering the culture because, to gain a sense of how expertise is manifest in conversation and other activities, they need to observe how practitioners at various levels behave and talk.

# Cognitive Apprenticeship and Collaborative Learning

If, as we propose, learning is a process of enculturating that is supported in part through social interaction and the circulation of narrative, groups of practitioners are particularly important, for it is only within groups that social interaction and conversation can take place. Salient features of group learning include the following:

- *Collective problem solving. Groups are not just a convenient way to accumulate the individual knowledge of their members. They give rise synergistically to insights and solutions that would not come about without them (Schoenfeld, in preparation).*

- *Displaying multiple roles. Successful execution of most individual tasks requires that students understand the many roles needed for carrying out any cognitive task. Teaching one person to play all the roles entailed by authentic activity and to reflect productively upon his or her performance is one of the monumental tasks of education. The group, however, permits different roles to be displayed and engenders reflective narratives and discussions about the aptness of those roles.*

- *Confronting ineffective strategies and misconceptions. We know from an extensive literature (diSessa, 1982, 1983, 1986; McCloskey, Caramazza, & Green, 1986; White, 1983) that students have many misconceptions about qualitative phenomena in physics. Teachers rarely have the opportunity to hear enough of what students think, to recognise when the information that is offered back by students is only a surface retelling for school purposes (the handing back of an uncomprehended tool, as we described it at the beginning) that may mask deep misconceptions about the physical world and problem-solving strategies. Groups however, can be efficient in drawing out, confronting, and discussing misconceptions and ineffective strategies.*

- *Providing collaborative work skills. Students who are taught individually rather than collaboratively can fail to develop skills needed for collaborative work. In the collaboration conditions of the workplace, knowing how to learn and work collaboratively is increasingly important. If people are going to learn and work in conjunction with others, they must be given the situated opportunity to develop those skills.*

In looking at Schoenfeld's and Lampert's teaching, in noting what we believe are important features of their methods, and in stressing social interaction and collaborative learning, we are trying to show how teaching through a form of apprenticeship can accommodate the new view of knowledge and learning we have been outlining. The increasing role of the teacher as a master to apprentices, and the teachers' use of authentic domain activity as a major part of teaching, will, perhaps, once and for all, dismiss George Bernard Shaw's scurrilous criticism of teachers, "He who can, does. He who cannot, teaches." His comment may then be replaced with Alexander Pope's hopeful "Let such teach others who themselves excell."

# Conclusion—Toward an Epistemology of Situated Cognition

Much research investigating situated features of cognition remains to be done. It is, however, already possible to begin serious reappraisal of the assumptions about learning that underlie current classroom practice (see, for example Resnick, 1988; Shanker, 1988).

Determining what should be made explicit in teaching and what should be left implicit is one of the particularly difficult challenges for research (which exceptional teachers may solve independently). A common strategy in trying to overcome difficult pedagogic problems is to make as much as possible explicit; thus, we have ended up with wholly inappropriate methods of teaching. Whatever the domain, explication often lifts implicit and possibly even nonconceptual constraints (Cussins, 1988) out of the embedding world and tries to make them explicit or conceptual. These now take a place in our ontology and become something more to learn about rather than simply something useful in learning. But indexical representations gain their efficiency by leaving much of the context underrepresented or implicit. Future work into situated cognition, from which educational practices will benefit, must, among other things, try to frame a convincing account of the relationship between explicit knowledge and implicit understanding.

We have described here only a fragment of an agenda for a fully developed theory of situated cognition. There remains major theoretical work to shift the traditional focus of education. For centuries, the epistemology that has guided educational practice has concentrated primarily on conceptual representation and has made its relation to objects in the world problematic by assuming that, cognitively, representation is prior to all else. A theory of situated cognition suggests that activity and perception are importantly and epistemologically prior—at a nonconceptual level—to conceptualization and that it is on them that more attention needs to be focused. An epistemology that begins with activity and perception, which are first and foremost embedded in the world, may simply bypass the classical problem of reference—of mediating conceptual representations.

In conclusion, the unheralded importance of activity and enculturation to learning suggests that much common educational practice is the victim of an inadequate epistemology. A new epistemology might hold the key to a dramatic improvement in learning and a completely new perspective on education.

# Notes

1. All work in this area is, to a greater or lesser degree, built upon the research of activity theorists such as Vygotsky, Leontiev, and others. For examples of recent work, see, for instance, Rogoff and Lave 1984; Scribner, 1984; Hutchins, in press; Engestrom 1987; Lave and Wenger, in preparation; and in particular Lave 1977, 1988a, 1988b, 1988c, in preparation. Anyone familiar with Jean Lave's work on learning, apprenticeship, and everyday cognition will realize at once that we are deeply indebted to her groundbreaking work.

2. The dictionary definitions that the students used in writing these sentences are as follows: *Correlate*—be related one to the other; *meticulous—very careful; stimulate*—stir up. They were given these definitions with little or no contextual help, so it would be unfair to regard the students as foolish for using the words as they did.

3. In the linguistics literature, the term *deixis* is often used instead of *indexicality*. See, for example, J. Fillmore, Santa Cruz Lectures.

4. This image is, of course, not original. For the way it is developed here, we are particularly indebted to Richard Burton, who explored it during a symposium on education organized by the Secretary of Education of Kentucky and to D. N. Perkins' book *Knowledge as Design* (1986).

5. The JPF must, of course, have access to a culture and become what Lave and Wenger (in preparation) call a "legitimate peripheral participant." And, of course, an apprentice usually has to do a great deal of work. We are not trying to suggest that anything magical occurs in the process of enculturation. (Medical interns testify to how hard it can be.) But the process, we stress, is not qualitatively different from what people do all the time in adopting the behavior and belief systems of their peers.

6. To get some sense of how foreign this is to school tasks, it might be useful to imagine the impropriety of a student's being given this problem and asked, "Does the dieter have a measuring cup, cutting board, and knife at hand?" Though word problems are meant to ground theory in activity, the things that structure activity are denied to the problem solvers. Textbooks ask students to solve supposedly "real-life" questions about people who do very unreal things, such as driving at constant speeds in straight lines or filling leaking troughs with leaking buckets. Students are usually not allowed to indulge in real-life speculation. Their everyday inventiveness is constrained by prescribing and proscribing ways in which the solution must be found. The ubiquitous Mr. Smith might, after all, wisely repair the hole in his bucket or fill the trough with a hose. Sitting down and calculating how many journeys it will take with a leaking bucket is probably the very last thing he would do. (See also Lave, 1988c.)

Editor's Note: *In an effort to encourage informed discussion and debate on the themes of this article, the new ER will publish a set of commentaries in the May 1989 issue.*

*Acknowledgement: Many of the ideas in this paper emerged from group discussions at the Institute for Research on Learning. We are especially grateful to James Greeno, Jean Lave, Susan Newman, Roy Pea, and John Rheinfrank, who read earlier drafts and commented on them with great care. We are also grateful to Richard Burton, William Clancey, and Alan Schoenfeld for helpful and insightful contributions. More generally, we would like to acknowledge the influence of Brian Cantzvell Smith's pioneering research into a theory of computation and semantics built on notions of situatedness, embeddedness, and embodiedness; of Susan Stucky's important new idealization of mind in terms of "radical" efficiency rather than of rationality; and also of the work on indexicality of Philip Agre and David Chapman.*

*This research was supported in part by the Personnel and Training Research Programs, Psychological Sciences Division, Office of Naval Research, under Contract NO. N00014-C-85-0026. Contract Authority Identification Number, NR 667-540.*

*An extended version of this article will appear as IRL report No. 88-0008 (available from the Institute for Research on Learning) and as BBN Research Report 6886 (available from Bolt Beranek & Newman Inc.).*

# References

Agre, P. 1985. *Routines*. MIT Al Memo.

Barwise, K. J., and J. Perry. 1983. *Situations and attitudes*. Cambridge, Mass.: MIT Press.

Burton, R., J. S. Brown, and G. Fischer. 1984. Skiing as a model of instruction. In B. Rogoff and J. Lave, eds., *Everyday cognition: Its development in social context* (pp. 139–150). Cambridge, Mass.: Harvard University Press.

Collins, A., J. S. Brown, and S. E. Newman. In press. Cognitive apprenticeship: Teaching the craft of reading, writing and mathematics. In L.B. Resnick, ed., *Knowing, learning, and instruction: Essays in honor of Robert Glaser*. Hillsdale: N.J.: Lawrence Erlbaum.

Cussins, A. 1988. *The connectionist construction of concepts*. (SSL Research Report). Palo Alto, Calif.: Xerox Palo Alto Research Center.

deKleer, J., and J. S. Brown. 1984. A qualitative physics based on confluences. *Artificial Intelligence Journal* 24:1–3.

diSessa, A. 1982. Unlearning Aristotelian physics: A study of knowledge-based learning. *Cognitive Science* 6:37–75.

———. 1983. Phenomenology and the evolution of intuition. In D. Gentner and A. Stevens, eds., *Mental models* (pp. 15–33). Hillsdale, N.J.: Lawrence Erlbaum.

———. 1986. Knowledge in pieces. In G. Forman and A. Pufall, eds., *Constructivism in the computer age*. Hillsdale, N.J.: Lawrence Erlbaum.

Engestrom, Y. 1987. *Learning by expanding*. Helsinki: Orienta-Konsulit Oy.

Fillmore, J. 1974. *Santa Cruz lectures on deixis*. Bloomington, Ind.: Indiana University Linguistics Club.

Geertz, C. 1983. *Local knowledge*. New York: Basic Books.

Hutchins, E. In press. Learning to navigate. In S. Chalkin and J. Lave, eds., *Situated Learning*. New York: Cambridge University Press.

Lampert, M. 1986. Knowing, doing, and teaching multiplication. *Cognition and Instruction* 3:305–342.

Lave, J. 1977. Tailor-made experiments and evaluating the intellectual consequences of apprenticeship training. *The Quarterly Newsletter of the Institute for Comparative Human Development* 1:1–3.

———. 1988a. *The culture of acquisition and the practice of understanding*. (IRL report 88-00087). Palo Alto, Calif.: Institute for Research on Learning.

———. 1988b. *Cognition in practice*. Boston: Cambridge.

———. 1988c. *Word problems: A microcosm of theories of learning*. Paper presented at AERA annual conference, New Orleans, La.

————. In preparation. *Tailored learning: Education and everyday practice among craftsmen in West Africa.*

Lave, J., and E. Wenger. In preparation. *Situated learning: Legitimate peripheral participation.*

McCloskey, M., A. Caramazza, and B. Green. 1980. Curvilinear motion in the absence of external forces: Naïve beliefs about the motion of objects. *Science* 210:1139–1141.

Miller, G. A., and P. M. Gildea. 1987. How children learn words. *Scientific American* 257, no. 3:94–99.

Nunberg, G. 1978. *The pragmatics of reference.* Bloomington, Ind.: Indiana University Linguistics Club.

Orr, J. 1987. *Talking about machines.* (SSL Report). Palo Alto, Calif.: Xerox Palo Alto Research Center.

Palincsar, A. S. 1986. Metacognitive strategy instruction. *Exceptional Children* 53:118–124.

Palincsar, A. S., and A. L. Brown. 1984. Reciprocal teaching of comprehension-fostering and monitoring activities. *Cognition and Instruction* 1:117–175.

Pea, R. D. 1988. *Distributed intelligence in learning and reasoning processes.* Paper presented at the meeting of the Cognitive Science Society, Montreal.

Perkins, D. N. 1986. *Knowledge as design.* Hillsdale, N.J.: Lawrence Erlbaum.

Perry, J. 1979. The problem of the essentia indexical. *Nous* 13:3–21.

Resnick, L. 1988. Learning in school and out. *Educational Researcher* 16, no. 9:13–20.

Rogoff, B., and Lave, J., eds. 1984. *Everyday cognition: Its development in social context.* Cambridge, Mass.: Harvard University Press.

Rubin, A. 1980. A theoretical taxonomy or the differences between oral and written language. In R. J. Spiro, B. C. Bruce, and W. Brewer, eds., *Theoretical issues in reading comprehension* (pp. 411–438). Hillsdale, N.J.: Lawrence Erlbaum.

Scardamalia, M., C. Bereiter, and R. Steinbach. 1984. Teachability of reflective processes in written composition. *Cognitive Science* 8:173–190.

Schoenfeld, A. H. 1985. *Mathematical problem solving.* Orlando, Fla.: Academic Press.

————. In press. On mathematics as sense-making: An informal attack on the unfortunate divorce of formal and informal mathematics. In D. N. Perkins, J. Segal, and J. Voss, eds., *Informal reasoning and education.* Hillsdale, N.J.: Lawrence Erlbaum.

Scribner, S. 1984. Studying working intelligence. In B. Rogoff and J. Lave, eds., *Everyday cognition: Its development in social context* (pp. 9–40). Cambridge, Mass.: Harvard University Press.

Shanker, A. 1988. Exploring the missing connection. *New York Times*, E7.

Suchman, L. 1987. *Plans and situated actions.* New York: Cambridge University Press.

White, B. 1983. Sources of difficulty in understanding Newtonian dynamics. *Cognitive Science* 7:41–65.

Whitehead, A. N. 1929. *The aims of education.* Cambridge, Mass.: Cambridge University Press.

# Author

*JOHN SEELY BROWN and PAUL DUGUID are at the Institute for Research on Learning, 2550 Hanover Street, Palo Alto, CA 94304.*

*ALLAN COLLINS is at BNN Inc, 10 Moulton Street, Cambridge, MA 02238.*

# 3

# Objectivism Versus Constructivism:

## Do We Need a New Philosophical Paradigm?

### David H. Jonassen

*Many scholars in the instructional systems field have addressed the paradigm shift in the field of learning psychology and its implications for instructional systems technology (IST). This article analyzes the philosophical assumptions underlying IST and its behavioral and cognitive foundations, each of which is primarily objectivistic, which means that knowing and learning are processes for representing and mirroring reality. The philosophical assumptions of objectivism are then contrasted with constructivism, which holds that knowing is a process of actively interpreting and constructing individual knowledge representations. The implications of constructivism for IST provide a context for asking the reader to consider to what extent our field should consider this philosophical paradigm shift.*

Learning theory has undergone a major revolution during the past few decades. Beginning in the late 1950s with psychologists such as Chomsky, Simon, and Miller, learning psychology underwent a scientific revolution or paradigm shift (Kuhn, 1962) in which theories and models of learning from the cognitive sciences are now more commonly used to explain learning processes than the behavioral explanations they supplanted, especially those that require higher-order thinking (Gardner, 1985).

From: Jonassen, D. H. (1991) Objectivism vs. constructivisim: Do we need a new paradigm? *Educational Technology Research & Development* 39(3):5–14. Reprinted with permission of Association for Educational Communication and Technology.

For most of the first half of the twentieth century, behavioral laws provided the most prominent conceptions of learning. Learning, according to behaviorism, is a change in the behavioral dispositions of an organism. Learning behaviors, according to behaviorists, can be shaped by selective reinforcement. Because learning is equated with behavioral outcomes, behavioral laws excluded the role of mental operations. Behaviorists such as Skinner were unwilling to acknowledge the existence of the mind or the act of knowing because these are not observable. Because the existence of the mind[**] could not be proven from the observation of behavior, and because behaviorists were concerned primarily with discovering the laws of human behavior, the mind was an unnecessary construct in the learning process. Behaviorists "believe that the construct of mind does more harm than good; that it makes more sense to talk about neurological structures or about overt behaviors than about ideas, concepts or rules" (Gardner, 1985, p. 39); and that discussing these entities is misleading and incoherent. The exclusion of the mind from the learning process by behavioral laws was a primary theoretical cause of the paradigm shift in learning psychology.

Learning, according to cognitive psychology, is concerned not so much with behavioral responses, but rather with what learners know and how they acquire it. The cognitive revolution first enlisted the neo-behaviorists, who posited a role for the mind but relegated it to "black-box" status because they could not comprehend or understand it. The revolution concluded by not only acknowledging the mind, but also by studying its functions and processes. Cognitive activity is embodied in mental states that enable humans to construct mental representations and manipulate them through the use of symbols (Fodor, 1981). The mind is the agent of learning, and so it is both appropriate and necessary to study it from a mentalistic perspective, according to cognitive theorists. Unlike the behaviorists, who were only concerned with what learners do, cognitive psychologists are interested in what learners know and how they come to acquire it.

# Influences of the Cognitive Revolution on IST

Instructional systems technology evolved with a behaviorist foundation, therefore its theory base was naturally influenced by many of the behaviorists' assumptions. Fundamental IST processes, such as task analysis, behavioral objectives, criterion-referenced evaluation and mathemagenic strategies all reflect a behavioristic tradition. For instance, the first true technology of instruction—programmed instruction—was essentially an application of operant conditioning wherein the learner's behavior was shaped by the reinforcement of desired learning behaviors. Behavioristic assumptions therefore delimited the types of questions generated by research and theory development in the IST field.

During the 1990s, IST consciously rejected many (though certainly not all) of its behavioristic assumptions and accommodated a new set of psychological assumptions about learning from the cognitive sciences. Winn (1975), a leader in this transition, invoked an "open systems model of the learner," a more organismic view of the learner as one who interacts with the environment and acquires knowledge, skills, and competence

[**]The term *mind* is used often in this paper to refer to the covert, mental operations that give rise to consciousness and cognition. The term is not meant to posit a separate Cartesian entity, but rather the ability to think.

from it. But the roots of behaviorism extend deeply into IST practice. Acceptance of the mentalistic perspective from the cognitive sciences has been inconsistent. Therefore, Winn (1989) is still promoting the use of cognitive instructional strategies, less reductionistic forms of analysis, and a more holistic approach to conceiving learner interactions in a field that still focuses on learning behaviors.

The urging of cognitive models and processes of instructional design has echoed through our journals and conferences for over a decade (Champagne, Klopfer, & Gunstone, 1982; DiVesta & Rieber, 1987; Jonassen, 1985a; Wildman & Burton, 1981). Why have these calls had so little effect on IST theory and practice? Does cognitive psychology not provide a more valid model of learning than behaviorism? This article argues that perhaps cognitive psychology has not provided enough of a paradigm shift; that behavioral and many cognitive instructional design processes are based on a restrictive set of philosophical assumptions that do not adequately conceptualize the mental states of the learner; and that perhaps a new philosophical paradigm shift is needed in IST.

## *Limitations of the Cognitive Theory of Learning*

### The Role of the Mind in Learning

Perhaps IST has not accommodated or even adequately conceptualized the mind in its theories of learning because the psychological revolution did not include a commensurate philosophical revolution in the field to adequately accommodate the mind. Cognitive theory conceives of mental processes, but it does not make the philosophical assumptions necessary to extricate itself from the constraints of Cartesian dualism. Descartes believed that the mind stands apart and operates independently of the body, which is a different sort of entity (Gardner, 1985). He posited great powers to the mind, but was unable to say what the mind really does. Is the mind the sole source or agent of learning, or is learning the result of neurochemical reactions that occur in the body? Does the mind therefore exist within the body? Descartes believed both.

Many cognitive scientists believe that the mind is a material entity that controls the actions of the knower. Others believe that the mind and the consciousness it enables are not material but spiritual, and hence not bound by physical entities. Cognitive theorists are also caught in the theoretical trap of dualism; the agents of learning are therefore not clear to them because they, like Descartes, are unable to apply consistent epistemic criteria to study the existence of the mind.

Most current cognitive psychologists begin with the assumption that the role of mental activities is to represent the real world. Information-processing theorists, for instance, use cognitive task analysis to represent the mental operations that must be performed to accomplish the task, assuming that a most appropriate sequence of mental activities exists; these activities are externally manipulated by the teacher or the instruction. Cognitive learning models isolate mental operations in order to discover the most efficient mapping of external reality onto learners. Even Piaget, whose epistemological theory is alleged to be one of the most constructivistic, assumed that mental constructions were representations of the real world to which the learner had to "accommodate" (Bruner, 1986). The inconsistency of Piaget's position was that, like Descartes and many cognitive theorists, he posited epistemic characteristics to the mind but did not employ epistemic criteria for describing or evaluating the role of mental activities in learning.

The mind, according to Piaget and most cognitive psychologists, can only be thought of as a reference tool to the real world.

Contemporary cognitive theorists are asking whether the mind is merely a tool for reproducing the real world, or whether it produces its own unique conception of events or objects that is based on individual conceptions of reality. This new group of cognitive theorists is driving the revolution that is the subject of this article (Bruner, 1986, 1990; Churchland, 1984; Goodman, 1984). The new cognitive revolution escapes the trap of dualism and conceives the proper study of man through a more interpretive approach to cognition concerned with "meaning-making" (Bruner, 1990).

## Is There an Objective Reality?

Another limitation of current cognitive theories is the philosophical position about the mind (defined in the next section as *objectivism*) that regards thinking as effective only if it adequately describes some "objective reality." Bruner (1986, p. 95) asks, "Is a science of thinking not a science until it meets the criteria of objectifiability?" Is the mind merely a reflexive agent for re-presenting a societally accepted reality? Our Western cultural belief system accepts the existence of a real world. For instance, the journal that you are reading now is real. It is simple to describe its physical attributes: black ink on white paper. However, what each reader believes this article to be, and, more important, what each reader believes it to mean, may not be so easily referenced to any objective reality, at least none that appears obvious. If our learning theory assumes that we construct meaning for objects and events by interpreting our perceptions of them according to our past experiences, beliefs, and biases, then each of us mentally represents our own personal reality. Each reality is somewhat different, because each person's experiences and resulting apperceptions are different. These differences in interpretation are proof, *ipso facto,* of the individual constructed nature of reality.

## *Consequent Effects on IST*

To restate the hypothesis of this article, a potential explanation for the lack of a paradigm shift in IST is that both behavioral and cognitive conceptions of instruction seek to analyze, decompose, and simplify tasks to make instruction—and by inference, learning—easier and more efficient. The process of reducing the complexity of learning tasks, whether cognitively or behaviorally based, may well be misrepresenting the thinking or mental processing required by the task. Such decomposition also misrepresents the nature of the content, which is often fraught with irregularity and complexity (Spiro, Coulson, Feltovich, & Anderson, 1988). In attempting to simplify the learning to improve instructional efficiency and effectiveness, IST may be short-circuiting relevant mental processing. Designers' attempts to simplify learning risk supplanting the complexity that is inherent in the learning process or the task to be learned.

The implicit goal of many instructional strategies espoused by instructional designers appears to be to supplant thinking rather than to engage or enhance it (Salomon, 1979). The explicit goal of IST is more efficient "knowledge transmission." Designers use their objective tools (e.g., task analysis) to determine an objective reality, which they then try to map onto learners through embedding instructional strategies that control learning behavior. But knowledge transmission tacitly assumes that 1) we all agree on what reality is, and 2) we all use essentially the same process for understanding it. A number of cognitive researchers, whose positions are described later in this article, question these assumptions and present alternative conceptions of learning that are based on different philosophical assumptions; their assumptions are based upon constructivism. In the next section, these constructivistic assumptions are contrasted with the assumptions of current behavioral, cognitive, and IST beliefs, which are based on objectivism.

# Comparing Philosophical Paradigms

In this section, alternative conceptions of how we perceive objects and conceive reality are compared. These theories of thinking and learning are *objectivism* and *constructivism.*

One purpose of this article is to describe the philosophical assumptions of these theories. This article argues that behavioral psychology, most of cognitive psychology, and IST are firmly rooted in objectivism. The implications of a philosophical paradigm shift to constructivism for IST are considered later. Ultimately, the reader must judge the meaningfulness of each theory in generating his or her own view of reality, learning, and instruction.

This article proceeds by describing the differences in these alternative positions for a theory of understanding and learning. To contrast their assumptions, the two theories are generally described as polar extremes on a continuum from externally mediated reality (objectivism) to internally mediated reality (constructivism). Most theorists, however, take positions that fall somewhere in the middle of the continuum.

To explain any philosophy, its metaphysics and epistemology must be described; these are the foundations of any philosophy. Metaphysics (more specifically, a branch known as *ontology*) describes the nature of reality, that is, the assumptions we hold about the physical world. Epistemology is the study of the nature of knowledge and thought. How we come to know and what we know are integrally related and essential to any philosophy of understanding. Objectivism and constructivism are contrasted on the basis of metaphysical and epistemological criteria.

Table 3.1 lists assumptions that both objectivism and constructivism make about reality, the mind, thought, meaning, and symbols. These convey the metaphysical and the epistemological assumptions of the poles of the continuum described above.

## *Objectivism*

Objectivism has its roots in *realism* and *essentialism* (Lakoff, 1987). Realism, needless to say, believes in the existence of the real world, external to humans and independent of human experience. This belief relies on the existence of reliable knowledge about the world, knowledge that we, as humans, strive to gain. What is epistemically important to this position is that it assumes that we all gain the same understanding. Essentialism holds that, among the properties that make up this stable knowledge, the existence of essential properties makes an entity a particular thing. Lakoff claims that objectivism is a special case of essentialism.

***Table 3.1.*** **Assumptions Inherent in Objectivism and Constructivism**

|  | *Objectivism* | *Constructivism* |
|---|---|---|
| *Reality* (real world) | External to the knower | Determined by the knower |
|  |  | Dependent upon human mental activity |
|  | Stucture determined by entitites, properties, and relations | Product of mind |
|  |  | Symbolic procedures construct reality |
|  | Structure can be modeled | Structure relies on experiences/ interpretations |
| *Mind* | Processor of symbols | Builder of symbols |
|  | Mirror of nature | Perceiver/interpreter of nature |
|  | Abstract machine for manipulating symbols | Conceptual system for constructing reality |
| *Thought* | Disembodied: independent of human experience | Embodied: grows out of bodily reality |
|  | Governed by external reality | Grounded in perception/construction |
|  | Reflects external reality | Grows out of physical and social experience |
|  | Manipulates abstract symbols | Imaginative: enables abstract thought |
|  | Represents (mirrors) reality | More than representation (mirrors) of reality |
|  | Atomistic: decomposable into "building blocks" | Gestalt properties |
|  | Algorithmic | Relies on ecological structure of conceptual system |
|  | Classification | Building cognitive models |
| *Meaning* | Corresponds to entities and categories in the world | Does not rely on correspondence to world |
|  | Independent of the understanding of any organism | Dependent upon undersanding |
|  | External to the understander | Determined by understander |
| *Symbols* | Represent reality | Tools for constructing reality |
|  | Internal representations of external reality ("building blocks") | Representations of internal reality |

The important metaphysical position that objectivism makes (see Table 3.1) is that the world is real, that it is structured, and that its structure can be modeled for the learner. The epistemology of objectivism holds that the purpose of the mind is to "mirror" that reality and its structure. It does so by thought processes that manipulate abstract symbols (primarily language) that represent that reality; those thought processes are analyzable and decomposable. The meaning that the thought processes produce is external to the understander and is determined by the structure of the real world. Learning consists of grasping the referents of words; that is, the kinds of entities or concepts that the words denote in reality (Rand, 1966). Objectivism assumes that learning is the process of mapping those entities or concepts onto learners.

Objectivism—the more common scientific conception of reality—holds that we as learners assimilate an objective reality. The role of education is to help students learn about the real world; students are not encouraged to make their own interpretations of what they perceive; the teacher or the instruction interprets events for them. Learners are told about the world and are expected to replicate its content and structure in their thinking.

## *Constructivism*

Constructivism claims that reality is more in the mind of the knower, that the knower constructs a reality, or at least interprets it, based upon his or her apperceptions. The emphasis in objectivism is on the *object* of our knowing, whereas constructivism is concerned with how we *construct* knowledge. How one constructs knowledge is a function of previous experiences, of mental structures, and of beliefs that one uses to interpret objects and events. Constructivism does not preclude the existence of an external reality; it merely claims that each of us constructs our own reality through interpreting perceptual experiences of the external world.

This view of constructivism is not an example of *solipsism,* which claims that the mind can only know its own interpretations, that reality is individualistic. We are able to comprehend a variety of interpretations and use those in arriving at our own interpretation; for instance, some of us interpret the wars in Vietnam, Granada, and Iraq as the obligation of a democratic state to defend the rights of nations oppressed by the evils of communism or dictatorships; others believe these wars represent the avaricious protection of the rights of multinational corporations to perpetuate a decadent lifestyle. How correct is either view?

The assumptions of constructivism are fundamentally different from those of objectivism. Radical constructivists (Goodman, 1984; von Glasersfeld, 1984; Watzlawick, 1984) believe that there is no real world, no objective reality that is independent of human mental activity. In Goodman's view, our personal world is created by the mind, therefore no one world is any more real than any other. There is no single reality or any objective entity that can be described in any objective way; rather, the real world is a product of the mind that constructs that world. A less radical form of constructivism holds that the mind is instrumental and essential in interpreting events, objects, and perspectives on the real world, and that those interpretations comprise a knowledge base that is personal and individualistic. The mind filters input from the world in making those interpretations.

Bruner (1986) claims that constructivism began with Kant, who, in his *Critique of Pure Reason,* argued for *a priori* knowledge that precedes all reasoning. It is what we know, and we map it onto *a posteriori* knowledge, which is what we perceive from our interactions with the environment. But what we know as individuals is what the mind produces. Kant believed in the external, physical world (noumena), but we know it only through our sensations (phenomena)—how the world appears to us.

Constructivism, founded on Kantian beliefs, claims that reality is constructed by the knower based upon mental activity. Humans are perceivers and interpreters who construct their own reality through engaging in those mental activities: "Cogito, ergo sum" (I think, therefore I am—Descartes). Therefore, the existence of the individual is predicated on his or her own constructions.

According to constructivists, thinking is grounded in the perception of physical and social experiences, which can only be comprehended by the mind. The mind produces mental models that explain to the knower what he or she has perceived. Rather than being driven by external structures, these mental models are *a priori,* according to Kant.

The important epistemological assumption of constructivism holds that meaning is a function of how the individual creates meaning from his or her experiences. We all conceive of the external reality somewhat differently, based on our unique set of experiences with the world and our beliefs about them.

# Applications of Constructivism

Many educators and cognitive psychologists are working to develop more constructivistic environments and instructional prescriptions (Duffy & Jonassen, in press). Perhaps the most important of these prescriptions is the provision of instruction in relevant contexts (Jonassen, 1991a). *Situated cognition* (Brown, Collins, & Duguid, 1988; Resnick, 1987) argues that learning occurs most effectively in context, and that context becomes an important part of the knowledge base associated with that learning. Rather than decontextualizing learning in isolated school environments, we should create real-world environments that employ the context in which the learning is relevant. A related approach requires learners to serve a *cognitive apprenticeship* (Collins, 1990; Collins, Brown, & Newman, 1987). Just as a craftsman would not teach an apprentice using prepared scripts, instructional environments and teachers should focus on realistic approaches to solving real-world problems rather than use predetermined instructional sequences. The instructor is a coach and analyzer of the strategies used to solve these problems.

Another important strategy is the presentation of multiple perspectives to learners. *Cognitive flexibility theory* is a conceptual model for instruction that facilitates the advanced acquisition of knowledge in ill-structured knowledge domains. Flexibility theory (Spiro et al., 1988) avoids oversimplifying instruction by stressing conceptual interrelatedness, providing multiple representations or perspectives on the content because there is no single schema (no objective reality), and emphasizing case-based instruction that provides multiple perspectives or themes inherent in the cases.

The approaches represented by these authors are clearly cognitive and also make constructivistic assumptions, yet there is an objectivistic grounding to them. Constructivism is not the panacea for all of the instructional problems in education and training, no more than other theories and technologies are. Yet all are designed to make learning a more realistic and meaningful process.

# Implications of Constructivism for IST: Do We Need Another Revolution?

IST is not ignorant of cognitive learning theory; many of its innovations, such as elaboration theory and information processing analysis, are based on cognitive theories. Yet IST begins, as do these cognitive theories, with an objectivistic world view, secure in the belief that the purpose of instruction is that of transfer agent, transferring objective information to learners. Perhaps the greatest epistemological concern about this assumption is that students learn without interpretation or reconstruction what is transferred to them. Constructivism claims that learners can only interpret information in the context of their own experiences, and that what they interpret will, to some extent, be individualistic. As designers, we may intend to map a particular reality onto learners, but ultimately they interpret our messages in the context of their own experiences and knowledge, and construct meaning relative to their own needs, backgrounds, and interests. Rather than attempting to map the structure of an external reality onto learners, constructivists recommend that we help them to construct their own meaningful and conceptually functional representations of the external world.

If IST were to accommodate some of these constructivistic assumptions, these are some of the changes in practice that could result:

- *Instructional goals and objectives would be negotiated, not imposed.* Instructional designers cannot impose a prescribed reality on learners because each learner will interpret that reality somewhat differently. Therefore, the outcomes of learning will vary somewhat, and objectives, if they are useful at all, would be a negotiating tool for guiding learners during the learning process and for self-evaluation of learning outcomes. This prescription is especially problematic for training design, which is typically based on the solution of specific, perceived problems. Most training is, almost by definition, convergent and objectivistic, because it supports explicit performance goals.

- *Task and content analysis would focus lesson identifying and prescribing a single, best sequence for learning.* Task analysis would concentrate more on considering appropriate interpretations and providing the intellectual tools that are necessary for helping learners to construct knowledge. These tools, and the environments containing them, should not only accommodate but also promote multiple interpretations of reality.

- *The goal of IST would be less concerned with prescribing mathemagenic instructional strategies necessary to lead learners to specific learning behaviors.* Rather than presenting instructional treatments, designers would provide generative, mental construction "tool kits" embedded in relevant learning environments that facilitate knowledge construction by learners. This generative-mathemagenic distinction (Jonassen, 1985b) refers more to the control of mental processing than to levels of processing. Constructivists believe that learning is internally controlled and mediated by the learner. Objectivists believe that learning is externally mediated by the instructional strategies that predetermine the required mental activities that give rise to acquiring the elements of an external reality.

- *Evaluation of learning would become less criterion-referenced.* If you believe, as radical constructivists do, that no objective reality is uniformly interpretable by all learners, then assessing the acquisition of such a reality is not possible. A less radical view suggests that learners will interpret perspectives differently, therefore evaluation processes should accommodate a wider variety of response options. Evaluation of learning, according to constructivists, should become more goal-free (Jonassen, 1991b; Scriven, 1983); evaluation would become less of a reinforcement or control tool and more of a self-analysis tool.

# Conclusion

Much of cognitive psychology and most of IST currently are grounded in objectivism. Objectivists believe that the goal of instruction is to map an external reality onto learners. Perhaps the most common conception of instruction based upon objectivist thinking is the "transmission of knowledge," a knowledge that is prescribed by subject matter analysis. Objectivists accomplish this task analysis, whether it is behavioral or cognitive task analysis, by determining what reality should be learned and how it should be acquired.

Constructivists warn that the "knowledge" transmitted may not be the knowledge constructed by the learner. They maintain that, rather than prescribe learning outcomes, instruction should focus on providing tools and environments for helping learners interpret the multiple perspectives of the world in creating their own world view. In answer to Bruner's question about whether a science of thinking must be objectifiable, constructivists contend that it is unnecessary, but objectivists believe that, to be transmitted and assessed, learning and thinking can and must be objectified.

If we as a field choose to adopt a more constructivistic view of instruction, we assume the need for a philosophical revolution of some dimension in our field to support the psychological revolution that has been underway for over a decade. Constructivists claim that we need a *philosophy of understanding* to support our *psychology of understanding*. This philosophy of understanding is "constructivism," claims Goodman (1984), and it comprises a philosophy of science and a philosophy of art, as well as a philosophy of cognition.

Objectivism and constructivism represent alternative conceptions of learning and thinking, much like the artist-scientist, two-worlds dialectic (Snow, 1960). The IST world is largely scientific and objectivistic. Goodman (1984) claims that constructivism is an increasingly popular philosophy that may be applied to cognitive science and, by inference, to IST.

The intention and conclusion of this article is *not* that we reject all of our objectivistic assumptions in favor of the constructivistic assumptions. Objectivists would argue against that recommendation from the pragmatic perspective that any nonobjectivist or nonrealist position is inoperable, that constructivism is antecedent to academic chaos. IST should not necessarily adopt a radical constructivistic view that thought is completely individualistic, that all of us cannot interpret the world in a similar manner. Such a position is solipsistic and *would* surely lead to intellectual chaos and the inability to communicate. Besides, the socially negotiated meaning that underlies "common knowledge" is part of the constructivist belief.

Yet constructivism holds important lessons for how to interpret the results of learning and for how to design environments to support learning. Those environments must engage learners in negotiating meaning and in socially constructing reality. Educators have always been the agents of control, so that societal reinforcement (social learning theory remains firmly rooted in behaviorism) is predicated on assimilating enough of its objective reality. If we, as educators or designers, relinquish that control, learners must assume it. The objectivistic research on learner control suggests that because learners are often unable or unwilling to assume greater personal responsibility for learning, learning should be externally mediated by instructional interventions. Constructivists argue that the type of control that is invested in learners in such studies precludes "meaning making."

Because learning obviously entails constructivistic and objectivistic activities, the most realistic model of learning lies somewhere on the continuum between these positions. Instructional design is a prescriptive theory based upon descriptive theories of learning (Reigeluth, 1983). Instructional design and the learning theories that support it are largely objectivistic. The implications of many descriptive learning theories are obvious for a prescriptive theory of instruction and its related practice; however, constructivistic theories of learning remain largely descriptive. The implications of constructivism probably are not well enough established to support a prescriptive theory of instruction, yet some of the implications are becoming more obvious (Duffy & Jonassen, in press).

It is reasonable for IST to consider the implications of constructivism for instructional systems. Foremost, researchers and designers should question our long-standing but delusive presumption that we can always control what individuals learn. At best, teachers and designers constrain learning, but to maximize individual learning, we may have to yield some control and instead prepare learners to regulate their own learning by providing supportive rather than intervening learning environments.

A final caveat: When integrating constructivism into the instructional design process, the nature of the learning and the context in which it will occur should be considered before committing to one theory or the other. For instance, the outcomes of air traffic controller training probably should not be individualistic or primarily constructed, yet designers must recognize that controllers' perceptions of their roles and functions will differ somewhat. The intent of this article is not to suggest that designers adopt constructivism as they have so many other potential panaceas, but that they reflect upon and articulate their conceptions of knowing and learning and adapt their methodology accordingly. When asked to commit to either the objectivistic or constructivistic camp, the designer will be best served by replying that it depends upon the context.

# Author's Note

*Thanks to Roberts Braden, Peggy Cole, Scott Grabinger, Marty Tessmer, and Brent Wilson, as well as the ETR&D editorial consultants, who reviewed this manuscript, for helping me to reconstruct these ideas based upon their interpretations of earlier drafts. This article was completed while the author was a visiting professor on the Instructional Technology faculty at the University of Twente, Netherlands. Thanks to their chair, Professor Sanne Dijkstra.*

# References

Brown, J. S., A. Collins, and P. Duguid. 1988. Situated cognition and the culture of learning. *Educational Researcher* 18, no.1:32–42.

Bruner, J. 1986. *Actual minds, possible worlds.* Cambridge, Mass.: Harvard University Press.

———. 1990. *Acts of meaning.* Cambridge, Mass.: Harvard University Press.

Champagne, A. B., L. E. Klopfer, and R. F. Gunstone. 1982. Cognitive research and the design of science instruction. *Educational Psychologist* 17:31–51.

Churchland, P. 1984. *Matter and consciousness: A contemporary introduction to the philosophy of mind.* Cambridge, Mass.: MIT Press.

Collins, A. 1990. Cognitive apprenticeship and instructional technology. In L. Idol and B. E. Jones, eds., *Educational values and cognitive instruction: Implications for reform.* Hillsdale, N.J.: Lawrence Erlbaum.

Collins, A., J. S. Brown, and S. E. Newman. 1987. Cognitive apprenticeship: Teaching the craft of reading, writing, and mathematics. In L. Resnick, ed., *Learning, knowing, and instruction: Essays in honor of Robert Glaser* (pp. 453–494). Hillsdale, N.J.: Lawrence Erlbaum.

DiVesta, F. J., and L. P. Reiber. 1987. Characteristics of cognitive engineering: The next generation of instructional systems. *Educational Communications and Technology Journal* 35:213–230.

Duffy, T., and D. H. Jonassen. In press. *Instructional principles for constructivist learning environments.* Hillsdale, N.J.: Lawrence Erlbaum.

Fodor, J. 1981. *Representations: Philosophical essays on the foundations of cognitive science.* Cambridge, Mass.: MIT Press.

Gardner, H. 1985. *The mind's new science: A history of the cognitive revolution.* New York: Basic Books.

Goodman, N. 1984. Of *mind and other matters.* Cambridge, Mass.: Harvard University Press.

Jonassen, D. H. 1985a. Learning strategies: A new educational technology. *Programmed Learning and Educational Technology* 22:26–34.

———. 1985b. Mathemagenic vs. generative control of text processing. In D. H. Jonassen, ed., *The technology of text,* vol. 2. Englewood Cliffs, N.J.: Educational Technology Publications.

———. 1991a. Context is everything. *Educational Technology* 31, no. 6:33–34.

———. 1991b. Evaluating constructivistic learning. *Educational technology* 31, no. 9: 28–33.

Kuhn, T. 1962. *The structure of scientific revolutions.* Chicago: University of Chicago Press.

Lakoff, G. 1987. *Women, fire, and dangerous things: What categories reveal about the mind.* Chicago: University of Chicago Press.

Rand, A. 1966. *Introduction to objectivist epistemology.* New York: New American Library.

Reigeluth, C. M. 1983. Introduction. In C. M. Reigeluth, ed., *Instructional-design theories and models: The current state of the art.* Hillsdale, N.J.: Lawrence Erlbaum.

Resnick, L. 1987. Learning in school and out. *Educational Researcher* 16, no. 2:13–20.

Salomon, G. 1979. *The interaction of media, cognition and learning.* San Francisco: Jossey-Bass.

Scriven, M. 1983. *Evaluation models: Viewpoints on educational and human services evaluation.* Boston: Kluwer-Nijhoff.

Snow, C. P. 1960. *The two cultures and the scientific revolution.* New York: New American Library.

Spiro, R. J., R. L. Coulson, P. J. Feltavich, and D. K. Anderson. 1988. *Cognitive flexibility theory: Advanced knowledge acquisition in ill-structured domains* (Technical Report No. 441). Champaign, Ill.: University of Illinois, Center for the Study of Reading.

von Glasersfeld, E. 198). Radical constructivism. In P. Watzlawick, ed., *The invented reality.* Cambridge, Mass.: Harvard University Press.

Watzlawick, P. 1984. *The invented reality.* Cambridge, Mass.: Harvard University Press.

Wildman, T., and J. Burton. 1981. Integrating learning theory with instructional design, *Journal of Instructional Development* 4, no. 3:5–14.

Winn, W. 1975. An open system model of learning. *AV Communication Review* 23:5–33.

———. 1989. Some implications of cognitive theory for instructional design. *Instructional Science* 19:53–69.

## Part 2

# Design and Development Functions

### Walter Dick and Lou Carey (1978):
### *The Systematic Design of Instruction:*
### *Origins of Systematically Designed Instruction*

### Charles M. Reigeluth (1979):
### *In Search of a Better Way to*
### *Organize Instruction: The Elaboration Theory*

### Michael J. Hannafin (1992):
### *Emerging Technologies, ISD,*
### *and Learning Environments: Critical Perspectives*

## Design and Development

Design is one of the major domains described in *Instructional Technology: The Definition and Domains of the Field* (Seels and Richey, 1994). This sector of the multiple domains diagram includes instructional systems design (ISD), message design, instructional strategies, and learner characteristics. These elements account for a major portion of the theories and applications to teaching and learning within the field of instructional technology.

The systems concept captured the imagination of early pioneers of the field who were seeking unique aspects of instruction that distinguish instructional technology from traditional principles of teaching and learning. The 1965 article, "On the Design of Educational Systems," by C. West Churchman (in Volume 1 of *Classic Writings*) was one of the precursors to systems thinking. About the same time, the National Special Media Institutes (Michigan State University, Syracuse University, Teaching Research of the Oregon State System of Higher Education, and the University of Southern California) created the Instructional Development Institute (IDI) using a systematic approach in its design and in its content. This five-day Institute was eventually disseminated to over 20,000 public school personnel during the 1970s.

In 1978, Walter Dick and Lee Carey of Florida State University authored *The Systematic Design of Instruction*. This textbook, now in its sixth edition, has become a standard in the field. The model that was used in the first edition has been altered only slightly in the latest edition. The first chapter of the 1978 edition is included here because it introduced the systematic design concept for both the academics and the practitioners.

**67**

It is generic in that there are several dozen other models, some developed before and some after, that incorporate the basic concepts of the Dick and Carey model. It has withstood the test of time and is probably one of the most recognized models of its kind.

To obtain an overview of the many models that are systematic (currently, "systemic") in nature, the *Survey of Instructional Development Models,* third edition (Gustafson and Branch, 1997) describes models in three taxonomic categories: 1) classroom-oriented models, that is, those models that individual teachers use in designing local instruction; 2) product development models used primarily in the design of specific instructional resources; and 3) system-oriented models that are usually involved in large-scale instructional developments such as school or university curricula and major training programs in business and industry. The Dick and Carey model, along with many other models, provide concepts and procedures that are basic foundations of the field.

Other theorists and instructional developers have gone beyond the foundation models to emphasize specific aspects that enhance the basic models, or to focus on specific contexts or categories of problems. For example, Reigeluth's elaboration theory, described in his article, "In Search of a Better Way to Organize Instruction: The Elaboration Theory," focuses on the organization of instruction rather than on all the elements of the design process. He uses an analogy of the "zoom" lens, which takes in a wide-angle view of the entire instructional environment and later zooms in on specific levels or steps in the process. After appropriate treatments at each level, the designer zooms out and concentrates on the next level until the desired level of application is reached for all the elements of the process.

Reigeluth has expanded elaboration theory in articles on task analysis and design (Reigeluth and Rodgers, 1980) and in his book, *Instructional Design Theories and Models: An Overview of Their Current Status* (Reigeluth, 1983).

With the emergence of computers as integral parts of many contemporary delivery systems, the writings of Michael Hannafin have been especially useful. One of his first major efforts was a textbook, *The Design, Development and Evaluation of Instructional Software* (Hannafin and Peck, 1988). A later publication, "Emerging Technologies, ISD, and Learning Environments: Critical Perspectives" is included in this volume because it synthesizes both the applications of computer-based instruction since the 1960s and the developments in research and theory. This article underscores the importance of systemic development of instruction with the computer as one of the integral components. It redefines the learner-computer interface and provides a rationale for new computer-mediated learning environments. It builds on instructional systems design (ISD) concepts and provides transition rationales for years to come.

# References

Churchman, C. W. 1965. On the design of educational systems. *Audiovisual Instruction* 10, no. 5:361–365.

Gustafson, K. L., and R. M. Branch, eds. 1997. *Survey of instructional development models, third edition.* Syracuse, N.Y.: ERIC Clearinghouse on Information and Technology.

Hannafin, M. J., and K. L. Peck. 1988. *The design, development and evaluation of instructional software.* New York: Macmillan.

Reigeluth, C. M ., ed. 1983. *Instructional design theories and models: Overview of their current status.* Hillsdale, N.J.: Lawrence Erlbaum.

Reigeluth, C. M., and C. A. Rodgers. 1980. The elaboration theory of instruction: Prescriptions for task analysis and design. *NSPI Journal* 19, no. 1:16–26.

Seels, B. B., and R. C. Richey. 1994. *Instructional technology: The definition and domains of the field.* Washington, D.C.: Association for Educational Communications and Technology.

# Evaluation

## Gene E. Hall, Susan F. Loucks, William L. Rutherford, and Beulah W. Newlove (1975): *Levels of Use of the Innovation: A Framework for Analyzing Innovation Adoption*

## Lee L. Cronbach (1963): *Course Improvement Through Evaluation*

Evaluation has always been a part of instructional design and development; recently, it has become more pervasive. Traditionally, evaluation has been something that was most frequently done after instruction. Currently it is integral to the process from beginning to end; for example, the emphasis on "needs assessment" or "front-end analysis" is considered to be essential (Kaufman 1977). (Kaufman's "Needs Assessment: Internal and External" is included in *Classic Writings,* Volume 1.) This step in the ISD process has been refined by Rossett (1987) and is now considered to be one of the essential evaluative components of the process.

When new ideas, procedures, instructional systems, and/or curricula are introduced through the ISD process, they are often thought of as innovations within the contexts where they will be put into practice. Innovations in the instructional process usually are implemented after they have gone through diffusion and adoption stages (Rogers, 1994). The implementation stage is often clouded with ambiguity because professionals who are involved have no systematic approach with which to determine the extent of implementation. Hall, Loucks, Rutherford and Newlove (1975) recognized the need for evaluating the extent to which an innovation has been adopted. Their article spells out the "Level of Use" (LoU) concept that clearly assists in the evaluation process.

LoU is a matrix that defines eight levels of use in seven distinct categories: knowledge, acquiring information, sharing, assessing, planning, status reporting, and performing. Each level is preceded by a "decision point" that leads to the next level. The descriptions clearly describe the behaviors that are expected at each level for each category. Further research on the LoU matrix is reported in Hall and Loucks (1977).

Whenever evaluation of instruction is mentioned, the terms, *formative evaluation* and *summative evaluation* are often used, terms and concepts usually attributed to Michael Scriven. They are described, along with his concept of "goal-free" evaluation in his "Methodology of Evaluation" paper (1967). In that paper, Scriven admits a "special obligation" to Lee Cronbach's 1963 paper, reprinted here. A 1991 paper by Scriven, "Beyond Formative and Summative Evaluation," again confirms his debt to Cronbach's paper. It seems appropriate, therefore, to include the genesis of the concept from Cronbach directly in this volume.

Scriven does not see formative and summative evaluation as two types of evaluation; he does interpret these concepts in terms of the roles they play in the evaluation process. In the formative role, the purpose of evaluation is to improve a course or program; the summative role is reserved primarily for determining the worth of a program. Cronbach outlines the principles of formative evaluation—a tool used more frequently than summative evaluation in the ISD process. His closing statement says it all:

Evaluation is a fundamental part of curriculum development, not an appendage. Its job is to collect facts the course developer can and will use to do a better job, and facts from which a deeper understanding of the educational process will emerge. (p. 683)

The two papers that represent evaluation in this volume just scratch the surface of the many roles that evaluation plays in the process of teaching and learning. The instructional designer should be knowledgeable and competent in applying these and other evaluation concepts to the ISD process.

# References

Hall, G., and S. Loucks. 1977. A developmental model for determining whether the treatment is actually implemented. *American Educational Research Journal* 14, no. 3:263–276.

Kaufman, R. 1977. Needs assessment: Internal and external. *Journal of Instructional Development* 1, no.1:5–8.

Rogers, E. M. 1995. *Diffusion of innovations,* 4th edition. New York: Free Press.

Rossett, A. 1987. *Training needs assessment.* Englewood Cliffs, N.J.: Educational Technology Publications.

Scriven, M. 1967. The methodology of evaluation. In *Perspectives of curriculum evaluation.* Chicago: Rand McNally, 39–83.

———. 1991. Beyond formative and summative evaluation. In M. W. McLaughlin and D. C. Phillips, eds. *Evaluation and education: at quarter century,* pp. 19–64. 90th Yearbook of the National Society for the Study of Education, part II. Chicago: University of Chicago Press.

# 4

# The Systematic Design of Instruction:

## Origins of Systematically Designed Instruction

### Walter Dick and Lou Carey

We educators are sometimes the last persons to recognize the magnitude of changes that are taking place in our own profession. Perhaps it is because we are so close to the trees that we cannot see the forest. If we consider for a moment what has happened in public education during the past decade, however, we can see that there has been a tremendous broadening of the content included in the academic curriculum as new subject matter is added. Career education and environmental education have emerged as separate instructional areas or have been integrated into existing courses. In addition, advanced placement courses have been added for talented high-school students, and colleges and universities are granting advanced placement in their own programs to these students. There has also been a steady increase in the amount and type of in-service training provided for persons already on the job.

Vocational/technical schools have been growing at increasing rates and are providing instructional opportunities which have been unavailable to many students in the past. In addition, schools have added more work-study programs which have permitted students to stay in school and complete their formal programs whole working at part-time employment.

More dramatic types of changes have occurred in the establishment of both public and private alternative schools. These schools attempt to use radically different procedures to reach the specially talented, or the less capable student.

There have been other types of changes in the last decade such as the consolidation of rural schools in order to maximize the use of resources and the employment of business management techniques in schools to get the most from the available resources. Likewise, teachers in more and more school districts are becoming organized as unions begin to play a role in public education.

During this time, students have become freer in their expression of their feelings about what is right and what is wrong in the culture and in the schools. It appears they have established a different type of relationship with their peers and with school personnel. Young people have defused for themselves what they will consider success and nonsuccess in their culture. No longer will they accept the traditional value that everyone must go to college to succeed. They, too, are looking for alternatives.

Nowhere is there more evidence of an effort to try to serve the needs of students than in the trend toward systematically designed instruction in education. In the past, teachers have been taught that they should attend to the needs of each and every individual student. But, teachers were employed in classrooms where their only alternative was to treat the students as a group and proceed in a lockstep manner to try to provide the best instruction for the total group. In essence they were not provided with the methodology required to attend to individual student needs. Systematically designed instruction provides teachers with statements of exact skills to be learned. These statements can be used to determine each student's instructional needs in order to tailor instruction to each student as much as possible.

# Major Approaches to Instruction

If asked, each reader could probably provide a definition of individualized instruction and believe it was fairly accurate and reflective of the current thinking of most educators about individualization. If these definitions were shared, however, one might find almost as many definitions of individualized instruction as there are persons using the term. Current definitions vary from those that say students will proceed at their own rate through a prescribed set of materials to reach a predetermined set of objectives, to definitions that say students will be free to select their own means of achieving their own objectives. These two types of definitions reflect in part the two traditions which have contributed the most to the growth of systematically designed instruction. These two approaches may be characterized as the *humanistic approach* and the behavioral science or *systems approach* to instruction.

Educators who consider themselves in the humanistic camp have a genuine interest in the total development of individual children. They recognize the importance of individual differences and believe that the essence of an outstanding education is to show genuine care and concern for students as they attempt to define those areas of learning which are important and relevant to them. There is a strong focus on the personal growth and development of the individual student. This emphasis on individual personal development and human relationships is an attempt to counteract the increasing alienation which students encounter in their society and perhaps in their own homes. The rapid growth of the book sales in personal development and in the establishment of various personal development groups reflects society's interest in these same problems.

It is probably no overstatement to say that most teachers view themselves as humanists. Surveys indicate that many select the teaching profession because of their interest in helping students. Teachers are almost always concerned about the feelings, attitudes, beliefs, and values of students, that is, about those things which make an individual distinctly human. Many teacher-training programs can also be viewed as humanistic, since they focus upon the importance of the interactive relationship between the teacher and the student and emphasize such aspects of the educational process as flexibility and adaptability, methods of learning, self-actualization, discovery methods, and promotion of each student's individuality. In essence, humanistically oriented teachers believe that there is no best way to manage a classroom or to organize a learning experience. They believe there is no single formula for good teaching, but rather a number of approaches, one or more being appropriate for the needs of a particular student.

Some teachers prefer a behavioral approach to teaching. These individuals tend to view the teacher as one responsible for instruction in cultural heritage, social responsibilities, and specific subject matter. They believe that these matters can not be left to the individual interests of students alone. This type of teacher emphasizes a carefully prepared lesson plan, logically organized material, and specific educational objectives and tends to emphasize "getting the correct answer." In essence, these teachers prefer a systematic approach which utilizes research knowledge on the conditions of learning required for students to achieve clearly defined outcomes. Much of the knowledge already gained through research is now used in the development of instructional materials, but little has been incorporated into teacher-training programs.

The systematic approach to instruction had its initial impact on the development of programmed instruction. This medium of instruction emphasizes the importance of a precise definition of what it is that the student will learn and the importance of careful structuring of instructional materials. Programmed instruction requires the active participation of students in instruction to facilitate achievement of given objectives. Many of the teaching principles of programmed instruction are applied today in the systematic design of instructional materials, although programmed instruction per se is not in great use.

Both of these instructional approaches—the humanistic and the behavioral—emphasize the significance of individual differences and the necessity for providing appropriate instruction to the student. More and more teachers, especially at the elementary school level, have begun to individualize their instruction in the classroom. They have either designed their own systems and modified materials for their students, or they have adopted one of the national individualized instruction systems such as Individually Prescribed Instruction (IPI), Plan for Learning According to Needs (PLAN), or Individually Guided Education (IGE). These national programs provide schools with descriptions of procedures as well as materials and teacher-training aids to implement individualized instruction. As a result of these efforts, there has been more and more interest shown in the development of new and effective instructional techniques for individualized instruction.

It should be noted that while in academic circles representatives of humanism and behaviorism debate the merits of their approaches, there is little evidence of this conflict when one views individualized instruction in use in classrooms. Recent studies by Fox and DeVault (1974) indicate that the best examples of individualized instruction are those that blend the best of both the humanistic and the systems approaches to instruction. Though this book will stress the behavioral science approach to designing, developing, and evaluating instruction, the authors are in full accord with Fox and DeVault's position that the humanistic and systems approaches must be integrated in the classroom to provide the best atmosphere for effective student learning.

# The Role of the Teacher

If the trend in education is toward a genuine integration of humanism and behaviorism, then how will this affect the role of the teacher? It is our thesis that the primary role of the teacher is that of designer of instruction, with accompanying roles of implementor and evaluator of instruction. This is a critical statement to consider. If education is to meet the needs of individual students through provision of appropriate knowledge and training in important skills, there must be increased dependence upon well-designed, effective instruction. Teacher-dependent, group-paced instruction can no longer serve as the primary model for the teacher. Conversely, teachers have been, are, and will continue to be designers of at least some of their own instructional materials. Some of the best teachers have been doing this intuitively for years. However, it will become more important for teachers to have technical skills that will enable them to design and implement instruction in the classroom. In addition, they must be prepared to make wise decisions about the selection of materials developed elsewhere. Knowledge of instructional design techniques will greatly enhance each teacher's ability to select such materials wisely. Certainly, not all instruction will (or should) be based totally on the use of instructional materials. Interactive classroom instruction will continue, and such instruction should be planned and designed with the same precision as that used in designing instructional materials.

The integration of the humanistic and behaviorist approaches means a change in the teacher's role. There is a reduced need for the teacher to disseminate information. Obviously, the teacher must be concerned with the act of teaching. The expanded role includes monitoring the progress of students using individualized materials, tutoring and counseling students, conducting small-group discussions, assisting with special projects, and, when necessary, presenting major topics to an entire class. The teacher must also act as evaluator— not only of student success in the learning process but also of the instructional process itself. Did the instruction work? For which students, and to what extent? What components of the instruction failed? What aspects could be improved? Teachers should answer these questions systematically and use their answers to redesign the instruction for future use.

Although the skills of implementation and evaluation of instruction are crucial to the teacher, an equally critical skill is that of instructional design. Principles that have been successfully applied by professional instructional designers can prove equally valuable to the instructor. One can apply them to the design of instruction or to the selection or modification of existing materials. One can also use them in the design of a strategy that incorporates a collection of varying instructional modes, including interactive instruction and group activities in the classroom. This text is designed primarily to teach the skills associated with instructional design and evaluation processes, with considerable emphasis also given to the application of these skills to the selection of instructional materials, the development of lesson strategies, and the implementation of instruction in the classroom.

The authors recognize that, although in the real world, teachers are unable to design materials for all their own instruction, it is important that teachers obtain the required skills to design materials because of the applicability of such skills to other parts of the instructional process. Because of this emphasis on instructional design skills, for the remainder of this text the teacher will be referred to interchangeably as the instructor or the instructional designer. These references are not made to professionals who have a full-time responsibility for designing instructional materials, but rather to the teacher who has the ongoing responsibility for teaching specific content to a specific group of learners. Having considered this evolving role of the instructor, we now examine the nature of the instructional materials used in individualized instructional programs. The paragraphs that follow describe these materials.

# Characteristics of Instructional Materials

The types of instructional materials which are typically used in systematically designed instruction have come to be referred to as modules. Just as there is no universally accepted definition of individualized instruction, similarly there is no general definition of a module. An analogy may help in this explanation. Consider the technique known in the building industry as *modular construction.* Various components of a building are built and assembled in a factory and shipped to the construction site. These components, or modules, are then assembled in a particular configuration that results in the construction of a new budding. Workers are still required to drive the nails and place the screws and bolts which hold the entire structure together. They also pour the foundation and add the finishing touches that make it a sound and secure building.

One may consider modular instruction in much the same way. A module is a self-contained or self-instructional unit of instruction that has an integrated theme, provides students with information needed to acquire specified knowledge and skills, and serves as one component of a total curriculum.

Most instructors would agree with the definition given above. However, they would differ on a number of the specific characteristics of modules. For example, the length of time required for students to study a module may vary from one to fifteen hours. Even less time may be required for very young children. Some designers will insist that a module of instruction should include at least two alternative conceptual presentations of the instructional materials and preferably two or more modes of presentation to accommodate individual differences. Other designers would not agree that all these alternatives are necessary.

In addition, some instructors would argue that a module should be strictly self-contained. That is, a student should be able to achieve all the objectives which are stated in the module without interacting with the teacher or other individuals. Other instructors will specifically include in the design of the module the participation of peers, teachers, and outsiders in order to involve the student in a variety of interactive activities.

Many instructors even differ on whether students should be informed of the major objectives for a module. Some insist that students should receive precise statements of the objectives for a module, while others argue that objectives may be reworded at a level more appropriate for the student, or that objectives may be omitted all together.

Regardless of the issues listed above, most modules require the students to interact actively with the instructional materials rather than simply allowing the students to read the materials passively. The students are asked to perform various types of learning tasks and receive feedback on that performance. There is some type of testing strategy that tells the students if they achieved mastery of the content and what they should do if they did not.

Based upon the description in prior paragraphs, how would you recognize a module if you saw one? In its most simple form, a module might be a typewritten statement to students that says what it is they are about to learn and how they will be tested. It would provide printed or typed instructional materials as well as some practice test items. A self-test which might be used prior to taking a terminal test could also be included.

The most complex module might contain all of the items listed above, but might also incorporate a number of alternative sets of materials from which the student could choose the most appropriate one for him or herself. Alternative media forms such as audiotapes or filmstrips could also be included. In addition, the student might go to a laboratory to conduct an experiment or go outside the school to gather information.

Regardless of the complexity of a module, it should be validated; that is, it should be demonstrated that students learn from it—that they can perform the skills as described in the objectives for the module. Methods have been developed which are used to obtain information from students as a module is being developed to improve its quality. After the module has been completed, data are collected which are used to demonstrate the extent to which the module is effective in bringing about anticipated changes in student behavior.

This empirical approach to the development of instruction most distinctly differentiates the systems approach from prior approaches to designing instruction. In the next section, the general systems approach to designing instruction will be presented. The importance of empirical evaluations and revisions of instruction will become more apparent in later chapters.

# A Systems Approach Model
# for Instructional Design

Given the need to develop instructional materials, what is the best method to accomplish the task? One seemingly reasonable approach is to use an existing module as a model. There are several problems associated with this approach. Any given module is designed to teach a particular type of learning to a particular type of student. What is needed is a more generalized model—one which will describe the procedures for developing a module regardless of the type of learner or the type of learning which is to occur.

One general model for designing instructional materials is referred to as *the systems approach model*. We emphasize, however, that there is no single systems-approach model for designing instruction. There are a number of models which bear the label "systems approach," and all of them share most of the same basic components. The systems approach model, which will be presented in this book, includes the major components that are included in other models, but this model is perhaps less complex than some.

The systems approach models are an outgrowth of over twenty years of research into the learning process. Each component of the model is based upon theoretical or research outcomes which demonstrate the effectiveness of that component. The model brings together in one coherent whole many of the concepts that you may have already encountered in a variety of educational situations. For example, you undoubtedly have heard of behavioral objectives and may have already developed some yourself. Such terms as *criterion-referenced testing* and *formative evaluation* may also be familiar. The model will show how these terms, and the processes associated with them, are interrelated and how these procedures can be used to produce instructional materials that work.

The model, as it is presented here, is based upon both research and a considerable amount of practical experience in its application. We suggest that the novice instructional designer use the model principally in the sequence and manner that we present it in this chapter. Hundreds of students who have done so have produced effective instructional materials. On the other hand, we acknowledge that in particular circumstances and with increased experience with a model, you may change the model in order to meet those particular circumstances. Also, we expect that more research and experience will help to amplify the procedures associated with each component of the model.

In the section that follows, we will present the general systems approach model (and you can read it) in much the same way as a cookbook recipe—you do this and then that and you have a pie. When you begin to use a recipe in your own kitchen, however, it takes on greater meaning, just as the model will when you begin to involve your own interests with the topic you have selected: you develop your own instructional resources, you select your own set of learners, and so on. Your perspective on the model will probably change greatly. In essence, your use of your own kitchen, your own ingredients, and your own personal touch will result in a unique product.

This discussion is a roundabout way of saying that there are two levels at which this book may be used by the reader. The first is at an academic, cognitive level at which you learn new terminology, concepts, and how they may be integrated as an approach to designing instructional materials. The second level is at a productive or developmental level, and it sharply differs from the first. It involves the production of your own module at the same time that you study these units. This combination of the conceptual and productive study of a systems approach model seems to provide a depth of perspective on these techniques which is nearly impossible to obtain by studying only the cognitive information.

The model which will be described in detail in succeeding chapters is graphically presented in Figure 4.1. The model includes eight interconnected boxes and a major line that shows feedback from the last box to the earlier boxes. The boxes refer to sets of procedures and techniques which are employed by the instructional designer to design, produce, evaluate, and revise an instructional module. The steps will be briefly described in sequence. Each will be described in much greater detail in later chapters.

## *Components of the Systems Approach Model*

### Identifying an Instructional Goal

The first step in the model is to determine what it is that you want students to be able to do when they have completed your instruction. The definition of the instructional goal may be derived from a statement of goals, from a needs assessment with regard to a particular curriculum, or from practical experience with learning difficulties of students in the classroom.

### Conducting an Instructional Analysis

After you identify the instructional goal, you will analyze it in order to identify the subordinate skills that a student must learn in order to achieve that goal. This process may result in the identification of concepts, rules, and information which a student needs, or the identification of steps in a procedural sequence which must be followed to perform a particular process.

### Identifying Entry Behaviors and Characteristics

In addition to identifying the substance of the content which must be included in the instruction, it will be necessary to identify the specific skills that students must have prior to beginning instruction. You need to determine not only the specific knowledge and skills students must have in order to be ready to use the module, but also the general characteristics of the learners which may be important to the design of the instruction. These characteristics might include special interests, maturation level, attention span, and so on.

### Writing Performance Objectives

Based on the instructional analysis and the statement of entry behaviors and characteristics, you will write specific statements of what it is the students will be able to do when they complete your module. These statements, which are derived from the skills identified in the instructional analysis, will identify the skills students will learn, the conditions under which they must perform these skills, and the criteria for successful performance.

### Developing Criterion-Referenced Tests

Based on the objectives you have written, you then develop assessment instruments which are parallel to and measure the student's ability to achieve what you described in the objectives. Major emphasis is placed on relating the kind of behavior described in the objective's to that which is required in the assessment instruments.

## Developing an Instructional Strategy

Given information from the five preceding steps, you will now begin to identify the strategy which you will use in the instructional module to reach the terminal objective. The strategy will include sections on preinstructional activities, presentation of information, practice and feedback, testing, and follow-through activities. The strategy will be based upon current outcomes of learning research, current knowledge of the learning process, content to be taught, and the characteristics of the students who will use the materials. These same features can be used to select materials and to develop a strategy for interactive classroom instruction.

## Developing and Selecting Instruction

In this step you will utilize your instructional strategy to produce the instructional module. The module will include a student manual, instructional materials, tests, and a teacher's guide. Whether you develop original materials for the module will depend upon the type of learning to be taught, the availability of existing relevant materials, and developmental resources available to you. Criteria for selecting from among existing materials will be provided.

## Designing and Conducting the Formative Evaluation

Following the completion of a draft of the module, a series of evaluations are conducted to determine how effectively the module works and to collect data which may be used to identify how to improve the module. The three types of formative evaluation are referred to as one-on-one evaluation, small-group evaluation, and field evaluation. Each type of evaluation provides the designer with a different type of information which can be used to improve the instructional module. Similar techniques can be applied to the formative evaluation of selected materials or a strategy for classroom instruction.

## Revising Instruction

The final step (and the first step in a repeat cycle) is revising the instruction. Data are summarized from various formative evaluations and interpreted in such a way as to attempt to identify difficulties experienced by learners in achieving the objectives of the module, and to relate these difficulties to specific deficiencies in the module. The line in Figure 4.1 labeled "Revising Instruction" indicates that the data from a formative evaluation is not simply used to revise the module itself, but is used to help reexamine the validity of the instructional analysis and the assumptions about the entry behaviors of students. It is necessary to reexamine statements of performance objectives and test items in the light of collected data. The instructional strategy is reviewed and finally all this is incorporated into revisions of the module to make it a more effective instructional tool.

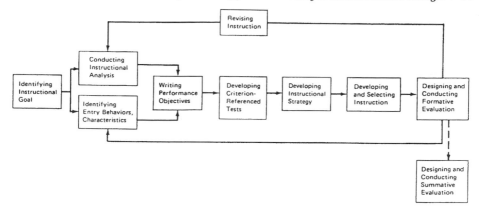

***Fig. 4.1.*** **Systems Approach Model for Designing Instruction.**

## Conducting Summative Evaluation

The dotted line in Figure 4.1 indicates that although summative evaluation is the culminating evaluation of the effectiveness of instruction, it is not a part of the design process. It occurs only after the instruction has been formatively evaluated and sufficiently revised to meet the standards of the designer. Since the summative evaluation usually does not involve the designer of the instruction (but rather an independent evaluator), this component is not considered an integral component of the instructional design process, per se. However, there are direct implications from this step for the process of grading students, and this relationship is described in some depth in the text.

The nine basic steps represent the procedures which one employs when one uses the systems approach to designing instructional materials. The reason this set of procedures is referred to as a systems approach model is that it is made up of interacting components, each having its own input and output, which together produce predetermined products. A system also collects information which is fed back into the system so that the final product reaches the desired level of effectiveness.

The instructional design model described here is considered a systems approach model because there is a specific input, process, and output for each component. When instructional materials are being developed, data are collected and the module is reexamined in light of these data to make it as effective and efficient as possible.

Before concluding our discussion of the systems approach model, those things for which the model is not a solution should be made clear. As it stands, it is not a curriculum design model. In order to design a curriculum many more steps would be required prior to the identification of the instructional goals. Some of these techniques are known as goal identification analysis, needs assessment, and curriculum analysis. The model described here is intended to be used at that point when the instructor is able to identify a specific instructional goal. The model can and is being used in curriculum development projects after the instructional goals have been derived.

# References

Banathy, B. *Instructional systems.* Belmont, Calif.: Fearon Publishers, 1968.
    This small book for educators describes the nature of systems and how systems techniques can be applied to the design of instructional materials.

Fox, G. T., DeVault, M. V. Technology and humanism in the classroom: Frontiers of educational practice. *Educational Technology,* XIV (10), 7–13, 1974.
    This is an excellent discussion of the realities of the classroom and the importance of the blending of humanism and technology.

Kolesnik, W. B. *Humanism and/or behaviorism in education.* Boston: Allyn and Bacon, Inc., 1975.
    This book provides a very readable and enjoyable comparison between humanism and behaviorism, and points out the necessity for integrating these two approaches.

Talmage, H. (ed.). *Systems of individualizing instruction.* Berkeley, Calif.: McCutcheon Publishers, Inc., 1975.
    This book provides chapters on the theoretical bases for the individualization of instruction.

Weisgeber, R. A. *Developmental efforts in individualizing learning.* Itasca, Ill.: F. E. Peacock Publishers, Inc., 1971.
    This book contains descriptions of various materials and individualized instruction systems such as IPI, PLAN and IGE, as well as some locally developed programs.

*Note:* The journal, *Educational Technology,* carries many articles which are of interest to the instructional designer. Numerous applications of systematic design procedures are described. Empirical research and theory articles are also included.

# 5

# In Search of a Better Way to Organize Instruction:

## The Elaboration Theory

### Charles M. Reigeluth

The *elaboration theory* of instruction is an alternative to the standard way of organizing instruction based on a hierarchical task analysis. The hierarchical organization results in an instructional sequence that begins with highly fragmented, small pieces of the subject-matter content. Many educators have found its fragmentation to be demotivating. Many educational psychologists have found its parts-to-whole sequence to be inconsistent with much knowledge about how learning occurs most effectively—namely, schema theory and its predecessor, subsumption theory. And many instructional designers have found that "learning hierarchies" represent an incomplete basis upon which to make decisions about sequencing the instruction, primarily because learning hierarchies are only one aspect of the structure or subject-matter content. All this is not to deny that learning prerequisites exist nor to say that they are not important—they do exist and they are important. Rather this affirms that learning prerequisites are not a sufficient basis for organizing an entire course: Our knowledge must progress beyond the hierarchy. It is for these reasons that the elaboration theory is being developed.

From: Reigeluth, C. M. 1979. In search of a better way to organize instruction: The elaboration theory. *Journal of Instructional Development* 2(3):8–15. Reprinted with permission of Association for Educational Communications Technology.

# Context

Before describing the elaboration theory, I would like to place it within the context of instructional design in general. Instructional design theory can be thought of as being concerned with four major aspects of instruction (see Figure 5.1): 1) ways of organizing instruction, which include such concerns as sequencing and formatting the subject-matter content, 2) ways of delivering instruction, which is usually a matter of media selection, 3) ways of motivating students, which may be intrinsic or extrinsic, and 4) ways of managing the student's use of the other three aspects of instruction (Reigeluth & Merrill, 1979).

As Figure 5.1 indicates, it is helpful to think of ways for organizing instruction as being of two types, based on their scope. Micro strategies are ways of organizing instruction on a single topic, such as on a single concept or on a single principle. They include such strategy components as generalities (or definitions), instances (or examples), and practice. Macro strategies are ways of organizing those aspects of instruction that relate to more than one topic, such as sequencing the topics, showing interrelationships among the topics, and previewing or reviewing the topics. Task analysis is done primarily, if not exclusively, to develop this last type of strategy—specifically sequencing strategy.

The elaboration theory of instruction is a partial theory of instruction—it does not deal with all aspects of instruction. As is shown in Figure 5.1, it deals primarily with macro strategies for organizing instruction; but it also includes many motivational strategies, and the other aspects of instruction will be integrated with elaboration theory in the forseeable future. Merrill has done excellent work on micro strategies for organizing instruction (Merrill, Reigeluth, & Faust, 1979; Merrill, Richards, Schmidt, & Wood, 1977), and Keller (1979) and Dodge (1979) are making some excellent progress in the development of a motivational theory of instructional design.

## *The Elaboration Theory*

The elaboration theory of instruction states that if cognitive instruction is organized in a certain specified way, that instruction will result in higher levels of learning synthesis, retention, and affect. There is a limitation to this theory: The smaller the amount of inter-related subject-matter content, the less difference it will make. With a small enough number of topics, it doesn't make any difference how you sequence them, whether you show interrelationships among them, or whether you preview and review the topics (as long as there are no learning prerequisite relationships among them). The following is a description of that "certain specified way" of organizing instruction, which is called the elaboration model of instruction.

# The Elaboration Model

A good introduction to the nature of the elaboration model of instruction is an analogy with a zoom lens. Taking a look at a subject matter "through" the elaboration model is similar in many respects to looking at a picture through a zoom lens on a movie camera.

A person starts with a wide-angle view, which allows one to see the major parts of the picture and the major relationships among those parts (e.g., the composition or balance of the picture), but without any detail.

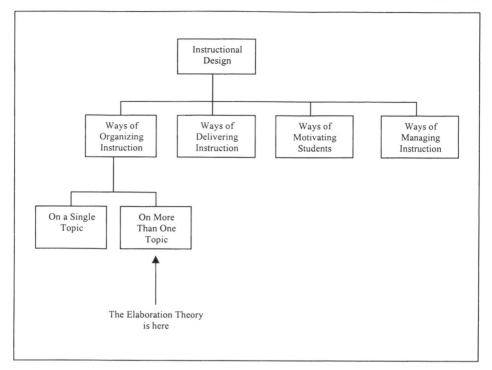

**Fig. 5.1.** The context of the elaboration theory in relation to other aspects of instructional design theory.

The person then zooms in on a part of the picture. Assume that, instead of being continuous, the zoom operates in steps, or in discrete levels. Zooming in at one level on a given part of the picture allows the person to see the major subparts. After having studied those subparts and their interrelationships, the person could then zoom back out to the wide-angle view to review the other parts of the whole picture and to review the context of this part within the whole picture.

The person continues this pattern of zooming in at one level to see the major subparts of a part and zooming back out for context and review, until the whole picture has been seen at the first level of detail. Then the person can follow the same zoom-in/zoom-out pattern for the second level of detail, the third level, and so on, until the desired level of detail is reached.

In a similar way, the elaboration model of instruction starts the student with an overview of the major parts of the subject matter, it elaborates on one of those parts to a certain level of detail (called the first level of elaboration), it reviews the overview and shows the context of that part within the overview (an expanded overview), it continues this pattern of elaboration/expanded overview for each part of the overview until all parts have been elaborated one level, and it follows the same pattern for further levels of elaboration. Of course, the zoom-lens analogy is just an analogy and therefore it has nonanalogous aspects. One such dissimilarity is that all the detail of the picture is actually present (although usually not noticed) in the wide-angle view, whereas the detail is not there at all in the overview of the subject matter.

Now, some people ask, "Don't you have to go through a lot of learning prerequisites to teach the overview?" The answer is a definite "no." In fact, few unmastered learning prerequisites (if any) exist at the level of the overview. As a learner works to deeper levels of detail, increasingly complex prerequisites will need to be introduced. If, however, they are introduced only at the level of detail at which they are necessary, there will be only a few prerequisites at each level; and learners will want to learn those prerequisites because they will see their importance for learning at the level of detail that now interests them.

The general-to-detailed organization prescribed by the elaboration model helps to ensure that learners are always aware of the context and importance of the topics that are being taught. It allows learners to learn at the level of detail that is most appropriate and meaningful to them at any given state in the development of their knowledge; and the learner never has to struggle through a series of learning prerequisites that are on too deep a level of detail to be interesting or meaningful at the initial stages of instruction.

Unfortunately, the zoom-lens approach has not been used much in instruction, in spite of its fundamental simplicity and intuitive rationale. Many textbooks begin with the "lens" zoomed in to the level of detail deemed appropriate for the intended student population, and they proceed—with the "lens" locked on that level of detail—to pan across the entire subject matter. This method has had unfortunate consequences for synthesis, retention, and motivation. Many instructional developers begin with the lens zoomed all the way in and proceed in a highly fragmented manner to pan across a small part and zoom out a bit on that part, pan across another small part and zoom out a bit on it, and so on until the whole scene has been covered and, to some limited degree, integrated. This has also had unfortunate consequences for synthesis, retention, and motivation. And some educators have intuitively groped for an elaboration-type approach with no guidelines on how to do it; this has been a good deal less effective than is possible for maximizing synthesis, retention, and motivation.

The major reason for the zoom-lens approach in instruction is not used is probably that the hierarchical approach was well-articulated and was a natural outgrowth of a strong behavioral orientation in educational psychology. This in effect put "blinders" on most of the few people who were working on instructional design strategies and methodology.

To summarize, the elaboration model of instruction starts by presenting knowledge at a general or simplified level—in the form of a special kind of overview. Then it proceeds to add detail or complexity in "layers" across the entire breadth of the content of the course (or curriculum), one layer at a time, until the desired level of detail or complexity is reached. It is important to emphasize, though, that the elaboration model prescribes a special kind of overview, and it prescribes a special way in which the elaboration is to occur. The following is as close as we can come (without sacrificing clarity) to a nontechnical introduction to these special aspects of the elaboration model.

## The Epitome

We do not like to use the word "overview" because its meaning is vague—it means different things to different people. Also, we believe that a certain specific kind of overview is superior to other kinds. Among other things, our overview must epitomize the subject matter that is to be taught, instead of summarizing it. Hence, we have named it the *epitome*. An epitome has two "critical characteristics" that distinguish it from other types of overviews: It epitomizes the subject matter of the course (or curriculum) rather than summarizing it; and it has a single "orientation"—which means that it emphasizes a single type of content.

With respect to epitomizing the subject matter of the course (or curriculum), an epitome is formed by "boiling down" the course content to its essence. It does not preview all the course content; rather it presents a few fundamental topics that convey the essence of the entire content. Those topics are chosen or derived in such a way that all the remaining course content provides more detail or more complex knowledge about the epitome. Although an epitome is very general, it is not purely abstract. Because "general" and "abstract are often confused, this distinction will be discussed in greater detail later.

With respect to having an orientation, the epitome emphasizes any one of three types of content: concepts, procedures, or principles. A concept is a set of objects, events, or ideas that share certain characteristics. Knowing a concept entails being able to identify, recognize, classify, or describe what something is. A procedure is a set of actions that are intended to achieve an end; it is often referred to as a skill, a technique, or a method. Knowing a procedure entails knowing how to do something. A principle is a change relationship—it indicates the relationship between a change in one thing and a change in something else; it describes causes or effects by identifying what will happen as a result of a given change (the effect) or why something happens (the cause). These three emphases are referred to respectively as a conceptual orientation, a procedural orientation, and a theoretical orientation. The orientation is selected on the basis of the general goals or purpose of the course (or curriculum). All three types of content may appear in the epitome, but one type receives primary emphasis; and the epitome is formed by epitomizing the orientation type of content and then introducing whatever of the other two types of content are highly relevant. More will be said about this below.

I mentioned above that an epitome is general but is not purely abstract. The terms *general* and *abstract* are often confused. It is helpful to think of three continua: 1) general to detailed; 2) simple to complex; and 3) abstract to concrete. These three continua are illustrated in Figure 5.2. The first two are similar to each other, but the third is different.

The general-to-detailed continuum refers primarily to a continuum formed by subdividing things (concepts or procedures) or by lumping things (concepts or subprocedures) together. "General" has breadth (things lumped together), but "detailed" is usually narrow (subdivisions). In Figure 5.2(a), "polar bear" is a more detailed concept than "animal." The simple-to-complex continuum refers primarily to a continuum formed by adding or removing things (principles or procedures). "Simple" has few things, but "complex" has many things. In Figure 5.2(b), the procedure for subtracting multi-digit numbers is more complex than the procedure for subtracting single-digit numbers. Additional complexity can be added by introducing subprocedures for "borrowing" when the top number is smaller than the bottom number. The abstract-to-concrete continuum refers to tangibility—and there are two major types of tangibility. First, generalities are abstract, and instances are usually concrete—the definition of a tree is abstract, but a specific tree (an object) is concrete; this is the most important abstract-to-concrete continuum for instructional theory. Second, some concepts are considered abstract because their instances are not tangible. "Intelligence" is a good example of an abstract concept. This second abstract-to-concrete continuum is largely irrelevant for our purposes.

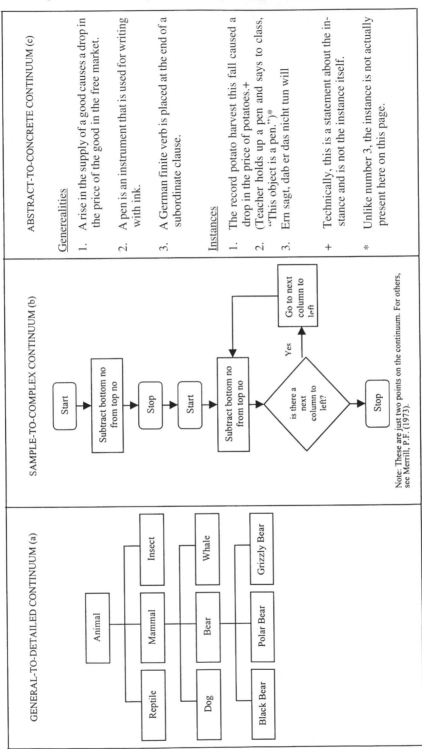

*Fig. 5.2.* **Illustrations of three continua that are often confused.**

On the basis of these distinctions, an epitome is always either very general or very simple—it must be, to epitomize the instructional content. But it should never be purely abstract. According to *Merrill's Component Display Theory* (Merrill, Reigeluth, & Faust, 1979), it should contain the following for each topic it presents: a generality (e.g., the definition of a concept), some instances of that generality (e.g., examples of the concept), and some practice for the student in applying the generality to new instances. As a rough guide, an epitome usually contains about six (plus or minus three) topics—that is, about six generalities, along with some instances and practice items for each. These topics may be any combination of concepts, procedures, and/or principles. Figures 5.3 and 5.4 illustrate the nature of each of the three kinds of epitomes: conceptual, theoretical, and procedural.

---

**Theoretical Epitome**

1. The law (principle) of supply and demand.
   a. The principle of what causes changes to occur in the quantity demanded and the quantity supplied (price changes).
   b. The principle of why prices change in a free market economy.
2. The principle of why changes occur in supply schedules or demand schedules.
3. The concepts of supply, supply schedule, and demand curve.
4. The concepts of demand, demand schedule, and demand curve.
5. The concept of changes in quantity supplied or demanded.
6. The concept of changes in supply schedules or demand schedules.
7. The concept of equilibrium price.

Practically all principles of economics can be viewed as elaborations on the law of supply and demand, including those that relate to monopoly, regulation, price fixing and planned economies.

**Conceptual Epitome**

1. Definition of economics.
2. Definition of subdivisions of economics:
   a. Definition of macro economics
   b. Definition of micro economics
   c. Definition of comparative economics
   d. Definition of international economics
   e. Definition of labor economics
   f. Definition of managerial economics.

Practically all concepts in economics can be viewed as elaborations on these concepts (i.e. as further subdivisions -either parts or kinds- of these concepts).

---

*Fig. 5.3.* **The instructional contents for a theoretical epitome and for a conceptual epitome for an introductory course in economics.**

1.  There are four major stages in the multidimensional analysis and interpretation of creative literature:
    a.  Identifying elements of the dramatic framework—character and plot.
    b.  Combining the elements into composites appropriate for analysis of their literal meaning—analysis of character and plot.
    c.  Figuratively interpreting the elements—symbolism through character, mood, tone.
    d.  Making a judgment of worth—personal relevance, universality.

(This procedure is simplified by introducing only *two* elements for the analyses in a and b, *three* in c, and *two* in d. It is further simplified by introducing only those procedures and concepts necessary for the analysis and interpretation of a *short poem*. Complexity is added later by increasing the number of elements used in each stage of analysis of interpretation and by introducing procedures and concepts needed for analyzing and interpreting more complicated types of creative literature.)

2.  Concepts necessary for performing the procedure in 1.
    a.  Character
    b.  Plot
    c.  Symbolism
    d.  Mood
    e.  Tone
    f.  Universality

**Fig. 5.4.** The instructional content for a procedural epitome for an introductory course in literature. (I appreciate the help of Faith Stein in the preparation of this figure.)

## A Level-1 Elaboration

A level-1 elaboration is a part of the instruction that provides some more detailed or complex knowledge on an aspect of the epitome. It should not include all of the more detailed or complex knowledge on that aspect. Rather, a level-1 elaboration should itself be an epitome of all of the more detailed or complex knowledge on that aspect, just as zooming in one level provides a slightly more detailed wide-angle view of one part of the picture. There is usually a level-1 elaboration for each aspect of the epitome, but an aspect is not the same thing as a topic. It is possible that a level-1 elaboration may elaborate to some extent on all the topics in the epitome, or perhaps even on a relationship among those topics.

The depth to which a level-1 elaboration should elaborate on an aspect of the epitome is somewhat variable (i.e., the discrete levels on the zoom lens are variable, not always constant and equal in the amount of detail added). The most important factor for deciding on the depth of a given level-1 elaboration is student learning load. It is important that the student learning load be neither too large nor too small, for either will impede the instruction's efficiency, effectiveness (especially for retention), and appeal. The number of topics that represent the optimal learning load will vary with students' ability, the complexity of topics, and student's familiarity with the topics. The breadth of a level-1 elaboration will usually be fairly difficult to adjust; hence, optimizing the student learning load in a given elaboration can often be done mainly by varying the depth of that elaboration.

Figure 5.5 illustrates the nature of a level-1 elaboration on the theoretical epitome in Figure 5.3, and Figure 5.6 illustrates the nature of a level-1 elaboration on the procedural epitome in Figure 5.4.

---

1. Principle of increasing marginal costs as an explanation for the shape of the supply curve.
2. Principle of profit maximization for individual firms.
3. Procedure of marginal analysis to arrive at profit maximization.
4. Concepts of fixed and variable costs.
5. Concepts of total average, and marginal costs.
6. Concepts of break-even point and shut-down point.

---

*Fig. 5.5.* The instructional content for a level-1 elaboration on the theoretical epitome in Figure 5.3. This level-1 elaboration elaborates on the supply aspect of the law of supply and demand by presenting more complex principles that relate to supply.

---

1. How to identify other elements of the dramatic framework -setting, perspective, and language.
2. How to combine the elements into composites appropriate for analysis of their literal meaning -(1) analysis of character, plot, and setting, (2) analysis of perspective, character, and plot, and (3) analysis of language.
3. Concepts of setting, perspective, and language.
4. Concepts of types and patterns of imagery (in language).
5. Procedure for analyzing imagery.
6. Concept of prosody.
7. Procedure for analyzing prosody.

---

*Fig. 5.6.* The instructional content for a level-1 elaboration on the procedural epitome in Figure 5.4. This level-1 elaboration just on stages a and b—which must be elaborated at the same time because of their interrelatedness. It elaborates on these two stages by adding elements that need to be identified (in stage a of Figure 5.4) and analyzed in combination (in stage b of Figure 5.4). (I appreciate the help of Faith Stein in the preparation of this figure.)

## Other Elaborations

A level-2 elaboration is identical to a level-1 elaboration with the exception that it elaborates on an aspect of a level-1 elaboration rather than on an aspect of the epitome. In a similar manner, a level-3 elaboration provides more detail or complexity on an aspect of a level-2 elaboration, and so on for elaborations at deeper levels of detail/complexity. In all cases, an elaboration at one level of detail/complexity should be an epitome for all the lower level elaborations that elaborate on it.

According to this kind of organization, elaborations that are on the same level are different from each other with respect to their instructional content (i.e., their topics are different from each other); but elaborations that are on different levels are similar to each other with respect to their instructional content (i.e., their topics are similar), because each level has the same content as the previous levels, only at a level of greater detail/complexity; this provides an important systematic review mechanism—more will be said about this shortly.

## Expanded Epitome

After each elaboration, the instruction presents a summarizer and an expanded epitome, equivalent to the zoom-out-for-context-and-review activity in the zoom-lens analogy. The summarizer is comprised of a concise generality for each topic presented in the elaboration. The expanded epitome does two things: It synthesizes the topics presented within the elaboration (internal synthesis), and it shows the relationship of those topics (and relationships) to the rest of the topics (and relationships) that have been taught (external synthesis).

## Summary of the Elaboration Model

In summary, the elaboration model is as follows (see Figure 5.7). First, the epitome is presented to the student. Then a level-1 elaboration is presented to provide more detail on an aspect of the orientation content in the epitome (the aspect that is most important or contributes most to an understanding of the entire orientation structure). Next a summarizer and an expanded epitome are presented. Another level-1 elaboration and its summarizer and expanded epitome are presented. This pattern of level-1 elaboration followed by its summarizer and expanded epitome continues until all aspects of the orientation content that were presented in the epitome have been elaborated one level. Then a level-2 elaboration is presented to provide more detail on an aspect of the orientation content that was presented in one of the level-1 elaborations. As always, this elaboration is followed by a summarizer and an expanded epitome. This pattern continues until all the aspects of the orientation content presented in all the level-1 elaborations have been elaborated one level (unless the objectives of the course or the nature of the subject matter exempt a level-1 elaboration from being further elaborated). Additional levels of elaboration are provided in the same manner—an elaboration followed by a summarizer and an expanded epitome—until the level of detail/complexity specified by the objectives is attained in all aspects of the orientation content of the course.

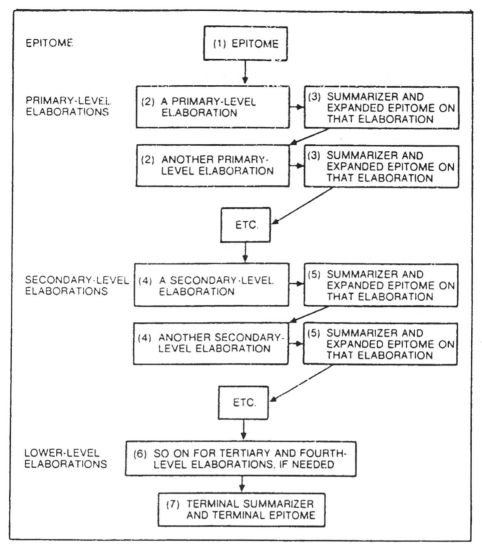

*Fig. 5.7.* **A diagramatic representation of the elaboration model of instruction.**

It should be noted that systematic review takes place in three ways: First, each level of elaboration covers content similar to that in the previous level (only with some additional detail and related topics). Learning this more detailed version of the same content stimulates or incorporates review of that earlier part of the course content. Second, the summarizer at the end of each elaboration reviews the content that was just presented in that elaboration; it does this by providing a concise generality for each topic. And third, the expanded epitome at the end of each elaboration constantly reviews the major content that was presented in earlier elaborations.

# Using the Elaboration Model

We have developed a fairly detailed set of procedures for designing instruction according to the elaboration model (Reigeluth, Merrill, Wilson & Spiller, 1978). A major part of those procedures is the analysis of the instructional content as to four types of subject-matter structures. A subject-matter structure shows a single kind of relationship that exists within a subject matter. Figure 5.2(a) shows part of a subject matter structure. The four types of subject-matter structures are conceptual, procedural, theoretical, and learning structures. (Learning structures show learning prerequisite relations within the subject matter.) It is beyond the scope of this paper to describe and illustrate each of these four types of structures. The interested reader is referred to Reigeluth, Merrill, and Bunderson 1978.

There are six major steps for designing instruction according to the elaboration model (see Figure 5.8). First, one must select an orientation—either conceptual, procedural, or theoretical—on the basis of the goals or purpose of the instruction. Second, one must develop an orientation structure for that orientation. The orientation structure depicts the orientation content (either concepts, procedures, or principles) in the most detailed/complex version that the student needs to learn; this is a form of content analysis or task description. Next, the orientation structure is analyzed in a systematic manner to determine which aspect(s) of the orientation content will be presented in the epitome and which aspects will be presented in each level of elaboration. In this way, the "skeleton" of the instruction is developed on the basis of epitomizing and elaborating on a single type of content.

The fourth major step is to embellish the "skeleton" by adding the other two types of content at the lowest appropriate levels of detail. This is usually done by "nesting" the remaining subject matter structures within different parts of the skeleton. Learning prerequisites are one of the considerations that enter in at this point.

When all the instructional content has been allocated to the different levels of elaboration, it is important to establish the scope and depth of each individual elaboration that will comprise each level. The scope is usually predetermined by the orientation topic and its necessary supporting topics. The depth is then determined on the basis of achieving an optimal student learning load, as described above.

Sixth, and finally, some of the internal structure of each elaboration within each level can be planned. The sequence of topics within an elaboration is decided on the basis of contribution to an understanding of the entire orientation structure (but of course within the constraints of learning prerequisites); the locations of synthesizers and summarizers are also determined.

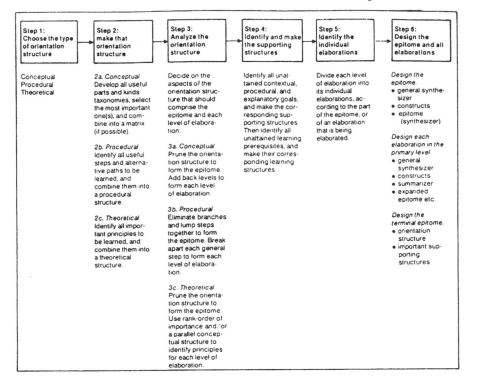

| Step 1:<br>Choose the type of orientation structure | Step 2:<br>make that orientation structure | Step 3:<br>Analyze the orientation structure | Step 4:<br>Identify and make the supporting structures | Step 5:<br>Identify the individual elaborations | Step 6:<br>Design the epitome and all elaborations |
|---|---|---|---|---|---|
| Conceptual<br>Procedural<br>Theoretical | *2a. Conceptual*<br>Develop all useful parts and kinds taxonomies, select the most important one(s), and combine into a matrix (if possible).<br><br>*2b. Procedural*<br>Identify all useful steps and alternative paths to be learned, and combine them into a procedural structure.<br><br>*2c. Theoretical*<br>Identify all important principles to be learned, and combine them into a theoretical structure. | Decide on the aspects of the orientation structure that should comprise the epitome and each level of elaboration.<br><br>*3a. Conceptual*<br>Prune the orientation structure to form the epitome. Add back levels to form each level of elaboration.<br><br>*3b. Procedural*<br>Eliminate branches and lump steps together to form the epitome. Break apart each general step to form each level of elaboration.<br><br>*3c. Theoretical*<br>Prune the orientation structure to form the epitome. Use rank-order of importance and/or a parallel conceptual structure to identify principles for each level of elaboration. | Identify all unattained contextual, procedural, and explanatory goals, and make the corresponding supporting structures. Then identify all unattained learning prerequisites, and make their corresponding learning structures. | Divide each level of elaboration into its individual elaborations, according to the part of the epitome, or of an elaboration, that is being elaborated. | *Design the epitome.*<br>• general synthesizer<br>• constructs<br>• epitome (synthesizer)<br><br>*Design each elaboration in the primary level*<br>• general synthesizer<br>• constructs<br>• summarizer<br>• expanded epitome etc.<br><br>*Design the terminal epitome.*<br>• orientation structure<br>• important supporting structures |

***Fig. 5.8.*** **The six-step design procedure for structuring the instruction in any course entailing cognitive subject matter.**

This concludes the "macro" design process, at which point the "micro" design process begins—decisions about how to organize the instruction on a single topic. We have spelled out these procedures for designing instruction in much greater detail elsewhere (Reigeluth, Merrill, Wilson, & Spiller, 1978).

## The Need for Research

The model and procedures as described above have undergone limited field testing and virtually no research. It may turn out that having a complete expanded epitome after every single elaboration is inefficient and unnecessary (especially after lower-level elaborations). It may also turn out that it is unnecessary for a student to study all level-1 elaborations before proceeding to a level-2 elaboration, a situation that would have important implications for learner-controlled selection and sequencing of topics. Indeed, a student could now truly follow his or her interests in approaching a subject matter; this would be particularly valuable in adult and continuing education contexts.

It is also likely that a large, full-scale field test of the design procedures will reveal more effective and efficient ways to design instruction according to the model.

The elaboration model as developed to date is a tentative move in a much-needed direction. It does not yet have the maturity and validation of the currently used approaches to instructional design, but the need for alternatives should be clear. There is great potential for the elaboration model to meet that need.

## Author's Note

*Several people helped the author in the development of the elaboration model: David Merrill, Brent G. Wilson, Reginald T. Spiller, and Robert F. Norton of Courseware, Incorporated. The development of this model was made possible by funding from Brigham Young University and from the Navy Personnel Research and Development Center (NPRDC) in San Diego. Work for NPRDC was done as a project of Courseware, Incorporated.*

## References

Dodge, B. 1979. Designing curiosity into instructional materials: A theory-based approach. In J. M. Keller, chairperson, in paper presented at symposium, Motivation and Instructional Design. A symposium presented at the annual convention of the Association for Educational Communications and Technology, New Orleans. (The symposium papers are available through ERIC.)

Keller, J. 1979. Motivation and instructional design: A theoretical perspective. In J. M. Keller, chairperson, symposium, Motivation and Instructional Design. A symposium presented at the annual convention of the Association for Educational Communications and Technology, New Orleans. (The symposium papers are available through ERIC.)

Merrill, M. D., C. M. Reigeluth, and G. W. Faust. 1970. The instructional quality profile: A curriculum evaluation and design tool. In H. F. O'Neil, Jr., ed., *Procedures for instructional systems development.* New York: Academic Press.

Merrill, M. D., R. A. Richards, R. V. Schmidt, and N. D. Wood. 1977. *The instructional strategy diagnostic profile training manual.* San Diego: Courseware.

Reigeluth, C. M., and M. D. Merrill. 1979. Classes of instructional variables. *Educational Technology* (March):5–24.

Reigeluth, C. M., M. D. Merrill, and C. V. Bunderson. 1978. The structure of subject-matter content and its instructional design implications. *Instructional Science* 7:107–126.

Reigeluth, C. M., M. D. Merrill, B. G. Wilson, and R. T. Spiller. July 1978. *Final report on the structural strategy diagnostic profile project.* A final report submitted to the Navy Personnel Research and Development Center, San Diego, California.

# 6

# Emerging Technologies, ISD, and Learning Environments:

## Critical Perspectives

### Michael J. Hannafin

*During the past three decades, interest in computer-based instruction (CBI) has grown dramatically. Enhanced power, increased availability of peripheral devices, and developments in hypermedia have created extraordinary capabilities. At the same time, there have been significant, though largely unexploited, advances in research, theory, and practice. Collectively, these advances offer the potential to redefine learner-computer interaction. A rationale for, and description of, computer-mediated learning environments— multifaceted, integrated systems that promote learning through student-centered activities—are presented in this article.*

During the past twenty to thirty years, the field of instructional systems design (ISD) has prospered in many ways. The number of graduate training programs has grown dramatically. Program graduates have readily obtained employment in the fast-growing training field, with projections of continued growth into the twenty-first century. Indeed, with its outcome-driven, performance orientation, the ISD field has been a unique success story.

From: Hannafin, M. J. 1992. Emerging technologies, ISD, and learning environments: Critical perspectives. *Educational Technology Research & Development* 40(1):49–63. Reprinted with permission of Association for Educational Communications and Technology.

Despite well-documented growth, the field has failed to evolve in many ways. Developments in cognitive psychology, for example, have implications beyond our predominating externally centered designs (West, Farmer, & Wolff, 1991). Advances in computers and related hardware technologies have far outstripped prevailing design methodologies. The field remains insulated from developments of considerable consequence for improving learning, and isolated collectively from intellectual communities where significant work in next-generation learning systems has occurred.

The purposes of this article are to examine the role of ISD in rapidly changing delivery systems and to explore the relevance of developments in learning environments and emerging technologies for the ISD field.

# ISD Evolution and the Technology Revolution

Despite the proliferation of models and perspectives in systems approaches (see, for example, reviews by Andrews & Goodson, 1980; Gustafson, 1991; and Schiffman, 1991), few substantive changes have been observed in ISD processes and procedures during the past three decades. The differences between models are often related more to level of detail, terminology, and emphasis than to clearly differentiated foundations, assumptions, and learning paradigms. The basic systems approaches to instructional design and development have been applied similarly across traditional instructional media.

ISD methods and models have also been applied successfully to computer-based instruction (CBI). Recently, however, new generations of hybrid computer-based instructional systems, called emerging technologies, have expanded the designer's tool kit dramatically (Hannafin & Rieber, 1989a; 1989b). The phrase "emerging technologies" emphasizes creating or extending functions and attributes across developing technologies, as opposed to attributing differences to specific media such as interactive video, computer-based instruction, compact disk-interactive (CD-1), electronic databases (including textual, visual, and aural), and alternative input and output devices. In effect, emerging technologies represent, to varying degrees, the technological capacity to present, manipulate, control, or otherwise manage educational activities.

Although most educators concede that emerging technologies can revolutionize our historic notions of teaching and learning, some are convinced that the application of ISD methods alone will not support such a transformation (Carroll, 1990). Our methods and models are primarily externally directed and content-driven (Johnsen & Taylor, 1991); they emphasize the attainment of highly prescribed objective outcomes and the organization of to-be-learned *lesson content,* not the largely unique and individual organization of *knowledge.* Alternative perspectives may be needed to optimize the value of emerging technologies.

Thus far, the ISD field has not significantly influenced the quest for alternatives; indeed, in many cases, we have deterred such efforts. We have re-hosted traditional ISD via computer technology, but have not reassessed the basic foundations or assumptions of our models. The core components of our models—objectives, learning hierarchies and sequences, emphasis on convergent instructional activities—become the cornerstones of our craft. To question them is regarded as heresy.

One significant consequence has been the insulation from fields where ISD's theoretical orientation is not embraced. The innovative activities of individuals, groups, and entire fields outside the ISD conunnity are often viewed with disdain or antagonism. Much of the seminal work in artificial intelligence and expert systems has gone unnoticed (see Lawler & Yazdani, 1987). With a few notable exceptions (see, for example, Jonassen, 1986, 1988, 1991; Kinzie & Berdel, 1990; Streibel, 1988), technological developments in hypermedia have failed to alter instructional strategies appreciably. Constructivist models of teaching and acquiring knowledge (Perkins, 1991), widespread throughout the sciences, have been challenged as impractical (Merrill, Li, & Jones, 1990c). Cooperative teaching and learning work—even in projects explicitly focusing on computer adaptations (Johnson & Johnson, 1986)—have scarcely influenced typical CBI design. ISD's insulation from the broader world of teaching, learning, and technology has contributed to its isolation from mainstream educational trends, theory, and research.

# The Evolution of Computer-Based Learning Environments

The concept of integrated supporting activities centered around topical themes is neither new nor revolutionary. Since the early work of John Dewey (1933), idealized visions of learning environments have evolved. Students should develop interests in problems or theme areas, acquire varying degrees of formal knowledge, explore first-hand how relationships between current and other concepts might be established, pursue advanced applications of the concepts under study, and generate new learning goals and priorities; yet rarely have these visions been realized. In virtually all cases, the logistics of adopting integrated learning systems have proved daunting.

Emerging technologies, and their implications for the design of learning environments, offer considerable promise. Learning environments are comprehensive integrated systems that promote engagement through student-centered activities, including guided presentations, manipulations, and explorations among interrelated learning themes (Hannafin & Gall, 1990). Several essential elements are reflected in this definition: Integration implies that the environment is constructed to support the student in accessing existing conceptual linkages or in building new ones; activities are provided that support the individual's efforts to mediate his or her learning; guidance supports the learner's decision making within the learning environment; and themes help to organize contexts, often in the form of a problem to be solved or an orienting goal, that bind the features and activities of the environment.

Learning environments supply interactive, complementary activities that help student-centered learning. Students are guided (rather than directed) in the availability and use of appropriate activities, each of which is linked conceptually around unifying learning themes. Individually, each component permits students to pursue understanding within established parameters. Students might, for example, select a manipulation tool, request tutoring on a topic, or request elaborations of key terms. Collectively, however, the components provide a rich set of resources that progressively broaden, rather than converge upon, learning themes.

## *Roots and Influences*

Learning environments are neither singular in their attributes nor distinctly classifiable in a conventional sense. Instead, they refer to a class of systems that integrate, to varying degrees, tools, resources, and pedagogical features that deepen comprehension. Several developments have influenced their evolution: 1) problems with traditional notions of learning; 2) shifts in psychological paradigms; 3) emphasis on student-centered learning; 4) unprecedented technological developments; 5) developments outside the ISD field; and 6) efforts within the ISD field.

## Limitations of Traditional Learning Outcomes

Several authorities have cited shortcomings in traditional views of learning. For example, Salomon and Perkins (1989) noted that traditional methods support primarily "low road" transfer, that is, transfer that is largely regulated by the limiting focus and nature of the instructional stimuli. Bransford, Franks, Vye, & Sherwood (1989) detailed problems of "inert knowledge"—knowledge that has been acquired and demonstrated in a conventional sense but that has little value to the learner in interpreting, modifying, or otherwise influencing performance. Such knowledge may take the form of momentary learning, where knowledge is consciously retained until circumstances mediating the retention (e.g., a test) are completed. Inert knowledge exists as "islands of information," which, although independently retrievable, provide little mutual or interactive value.

Spiro's work in cognitive flexibility (see, for example, Spiro, Coulson, Feltovich, & Coulson, 1988; Spiro, Feltovich, Jacobson, & Coulson, 1991; Spiro & Jengh, 1990), conducted extensively with medical students, emphasized the problems of ill-structured knowledge, that is, domains where precise meaning or utility cannot be provided. Whereas the simplest of elements in a complex domain can almost always be taught, advanced knowledge invariably requires insights and knowledge that cannot be taught algorithmically; limitations exist in the ability to comprehend fully new or complex domains. As a result, topics are often taught and learned in simplistic, incomplete ways. Subsequently, learners apply simplistic understanding to more complex aspects of the domain. Teaching strategies need to promote flexibility to enable students to organize and invoke knowledge in varied ways under conditions neither fully known nor understood during encoding, as well as to foster "high road" (mindful abstractions) transfer.

Other examples of problems associated with traditional teaching methods have been reported. Andrea di Sessa (1982) demonstrated that even advanced students suffer from naive misconceptions of fundamental Aristotelian science concepts. Perkins and Simmons (1988) provided an extensive analysis of common misunderstandings in science, mathematics, and computer programming. Much of the problem, according to the authors, can be traced to dogmatic teaching methods that promote regimental—and incomplete—understanding. Indeed, there is compelling evidence that negative transfer and durability are consequences associated with incorrect initial learning (see also Hannafin, 1988; McDermott, 1984).

Flexible teaching methods may militate against many problems associated with naive learning. Constructivists, for instance, view errors as largely transitional and functional if supporting educational methods are provided. They allow the student to evolve beliefs that can be modified, updated, and otherwise reconstructed as additional knowledge and experience is attained. Knowledge and beliefs about knowledge, even when erroneous, help the student generate hypotheses about the relationships among objects, information, and events. Mistaken ideas help to establish tentative, dynamic beliefs that are subsequently used to interpret new, apparently contradictory evidence. In effect, the student learns not solely what is correct in an objective sense, but the insight that accompanies progressive refinements in understanding. In this context, errors are seen as supporting, not hampering, meaningful learning. (See Yackel, Cobb, Wood, Wheatley, & Merkel, 1990, for a more detailed account of the role of errors from constructivist perspectives.)

Successful teaching encompasses a broad range of activities that are organized loosely around broad, orienting educational goals. Apart from providing instructional "events" (Gagné, Briggs, & Wager, 1988), good teachers pose questions requiring comparisons and informed speculation. Further, they require student self-assessments and stimulate ways to assist in integrating knowledge (Shuell, 1988). In effect, they supply methods that invoke greater introspection and reflection by the student during learning. Good teachers acquire expertise that rarely limits their functions as knowledge disseminators. Instead, they focus on activities that cause students to process information in unique ways that deepen understanding. Effective teaching rarely embodies simple telling and is rarely limited to the transmission of formal knowledge (Berliner, 1990).

Ironically, although countless definitions have been offered for ISD, few have been presented for instruction; one can comfortably infer, however, that instruction is an organized set of methods, materials, and assessments designed to promote competence in defined outcomes (cf. Dick, 1991). Instruction is directive in nature; instructional designers typically structure both the content and the methods used to convey lesson content. Lesson content is given priorities and organized into instructional sequences; activities are developed to support intended learning; and learners proceed through prescribed activities and sequences. Even in cases where learner control is provided, it typically provides externally dictated access to embedded instructional strategies (such as help, glossaries, quantity or complexity of examples or questions) and segments (such as menu selection affecting lesson segment order and continuation-termination decision points). The learner may or may not decide which (and sometimes when) available options will be used.

Although instruction, as operationalized in ISD, may be effective for defined outcomes, it may be comparatively ineffective for broader learning goals. In many cases, learning goals and activities are substantially less explicit, identifiable, and singular, while being substantially more complex, individual, and internally centered, than as addressed via instructional design methods (Kember & Murphy, 1990). For many educators, traditional instructional procedures are too rigid to be adapted and require too many assumptions about the nature of external control in knowledge acquisition.

## *Shifts in Paradigms*

Successful learning requires more than literal encoding of defined aspects of formal instruction. It requires that knowledge be assimilated, perceptions of value, meaning, and importance be derived, existing knowledge be evaluated concurrently with new knowledge, and knowledge be reconstructed accordingly (Hannafin & Rieber, 1989a). These are principally internal, learner-directed processes that can be supported, but not explicitly regulated, externally.

ISD methods, and instructional design products, are largely convergent and reductionistic in nature: They are perceived as focusing on the part rather than the whole. They emphasize the systematic organization of to-be-learned lesson information and the design of activities that support the acquisition of discretely defined knowledge and skills. This process invariably requires the student to learn according to the sequence and structure of progressively ordered, externally imposed instructional activities. In many cases, especially where the external structuring of knowledge and learning of clearly specified content and procedures are required, such methods are effective and valuable.

In other cases, neither external structuring nor strict outcome-based accountability is emphasized. In some fields, learning emphasizes process over product; relevant domains are situated within contexts in which they derive meaning (Bereiter, 1990; Brown, Collins, & Duguid, 1989). In science, for example, authorities have argued that the demise of scientific reasoning among today's youth can be traced to the treatment of science as discrete knowledge that is presented to children. Students are taught facts, rules, and "truths" of scientific disciplines, but they acquire few insights. In many cases, scientists value the processes of scientific reasoning and inquiry (called "sciencing") far greater than formal scientific knowledge (DeVito & Krockover, 1980a; 1980b). For ISD, this requires more than an identification of the formal knowledge and skills of a complex domain; it requires an understanding of the evolution of understanding, the importance of acquiring insight, and awareness of mechanisms that induce student engagement.

Shifts emphasizing the individual's role in mediating learning, and in the corresponding design implications, have played an important role in the evolution of learning environments. Significant work in cognitive psychology, for example, has yielded teaching and instructing guidelines that represent a significant shift in the locus of activity. External agents (teachers, instructional materials) are viewed increasingly as activators for learning rather than as mediators of knowledge.

Developments in situated cognition (Brown, Collins, & Duguid, 1989) and related work in anchored instruction (Cognition and Technology Group at Vanderbilt, 1990) are also significant. Such perspectives view cognition and the circumstances supporting learning as inseparable. Rather than decontextualizing learning by isolating and making explicit "required" elements, it may be fundamentally more productive to embed desired elements within "authentic" activities wherein the knowledge and skills naturally reside. Consistent with, while also extending, cognitive views, learning is more inherently meaningful when relevant contexts are available and appropriately structured.

In Bereiter's (1991) treatment of connectionism, a construct studied widely both in cognitive science and among artificial intelligence researchers, distinctions are drawn between cognition as a rule-based versus a connection-based activity. Popular notions of cognition presume that thinking is a process guided by complex sets of rules which, if fully understood, enable cognitive processes to be mapped more or less algorithmically. Connectivists reason that the relationships among connected elements adapt dynamically as varied circumstances affect different member elements in different ways. Learners need not be trained in all procedures likely to be useful, but must evolve strategies for how to manipulate connected elements to adapt to varied circumstances. In effect, knowledge resides in the connections themselves—their richness, strength, and complexity—not in the individual collection of data elements. Such a perspective requires that learning be stimulated not by mastery of formal knowledge, but by activities that progressively refine and qualify relationships between connected elements.

Constructivists have also influenced the evolution. Paris and Byrnes (1989) described several principles undergirding constructivist approaches. Constructivists perceive that the individual, as an active organism, possesses intrinsic motivation to seek information; these motivations should be exploited, not neutralized, during learning. Next, understanding is thought to transcend the information given. Learners continuously interpret events and form opinions and tentative conclusions based upon their interpretations. Constructivists believe that mental representations change with development. Constructivists also note that progressive refinements in understanding occur; learning is a continuous rather than a discrete process. Constructivists further believe that developmental constraints on learning exist. This has been characterized as the "zone of proximal development," a cognitive readiness that is essential to profit from given activities (Vygotsky, 1978). Finally, constructivists note that reflection and reconstruction need to be promoted over activities that emphasize assimilation alone.

Recent interest in contextualizing learning experiences has been widespread. This has taken the form of anchoring instruction within powerful real-life problems or of situating cognition in relevant contexts (Cognition and Technology Group, 1990). Such paradigms rely heavily on the power of a supporting context to embed a variety of potentially complex problems. In such projects, the selection and design of the supporting context effectively drives the strength of the anchored learning, and vice versa.

# Student-Centered Learning

Interest in student-centered learning has grown dramatically during the past decade. Student-centered learning systems essentially define the student as the principal arbiter in making judgments as to what, when, and how learning will occur. Typically, students not only select and sequence educational activities, but identify, create, cultivate, pursue, and satisfy their individual learning needs (Hooper & Hannafin, 1991). Student-centered learning systems tacitly presume that students possess the metacognitive skills needed to make effective judgments, or that they can be induced to make appropriate choices through advice, hints, or guided reflection.

The implications for design are that emphasis is typically focused on supporting student-initiated lesson navigation, providing an organizing theme or context for lesson activities, and embedding aids and support in the form of help, elaboration, and other resources that can be selected by the student to improve understanding. Successful student-centered learning systems require that a sufficient array of resources be available to enable students to assess and address knowledge and skill needs as they evolve. The role of instruction in such environments is to provide substantive support for student-initiated knowledge or skill development, not necessarily to provide the principal vehicle for knowledge transmission. In certain cases, students might successfully learn important knowledge and skills and derive in-depth understandings, yet receive no formal instruction.

Student-centered learning systems have taken many forms. For example, several researchers and theorists, largely apart from the ISD field, have espoused the virtues of student-centered microworlds (e.g., Levin & Waugh, 1987). Microworlds are incubators for knowledge, that is, systems that provide environments where learning is nurtured rather than knowledge taught (Papert, 1980). Papert's conceptual framework, influenced more by developmental than pedagogical theory, emphasizes the "model of children as builders of their own intellectual structures" (p. 7). Although macro-environments for intellectual development (LOGO in particular) have been challenged within the ISD field, enthusiasm for student- versus instruction-centered learning is considerable and widespread (e.g., Duffy & Jonassen, 1991; Hannafin & Rieber, 1989b; Kember & Murphy, 1990; Perkins, 1991).

Nevertheless, student-centered learning environments do encompass their own set of complex problems. The capacity of many students to mediate their learning in accountability-based educational settings has not been demonstrated; indeed, many students are too ill-equipped to make effective choices during a lesson (Steinberg, 1989). In effect, because much of what mediates effective student choice is related to prior knowledge, student-centered environments may prove inefficient or ineffective (Merrill, Li, & Jones, 1990c). In addition, because of typical student-centered environments are nondirective, students may focus their attention on relatively unimportant lesson features or content. Students' individual needs to seek knowledge and pursue their own evolving interests may be satisfied, but fundamental knowledge and skills may not be learned (Dick, 1991). Few challenge the goal of supporting the unique intellectual development of learners, but the pedagogical implications remain debatable.

# Rapid Technological Advances

Unprecedented technological refinements have been reported in high-density optical storage, miniaturization, input and output, and connectivity among technological devices; this expanded tool kit has enabled designers to vary presentation stimuli in ways heretofore impossible. Objects can be presented in forms that closely represent their objective properties, supporting the design of extraordinarily realistic simulations. Considerations of human factors, both in the structure of activities and in the nature of human-computer transactions, are now addressable. For example, the application of real-time, input-output design principles in aviation allow simulation of the sensory aspects of both a pilot's actions (e.g., mistakes causing engine stall) and reactions (e.g., G-force increases during acceleration).

The management capabilities of the computer, especially in data manipulation, have also improved dramatically. The ability to build and rapidly access large and complex databases, in forms ranging from expert knowledge representations, to encyclopedic resources, to image libraries, to personal knowledge representations, greatly expands the volume of information that can be immediately addressed. By overcoming the many logistical limitations inherent in traditional instructional units or modules, computer-supported learning environments have become increasingly viable.

The developments of overarching significance for learning environments, however, are in hypermedia. Hypermedia refers to computer-mediated access to elements contained in varied media (Marchionini, 1988). The designer's tool kit can be extended substantially by linking a variety of knowledge resources found across a range of media. However, the key dimension in hypermedia is not simply the ability to link media, but the ability to manage how linkages occur. At the designer's discretion, linkages can range from completely unmanaged, allowing the student to access any information from any of the available resources at any time based on individual beliefs, to tightly managed, contingent on precisely prescribed relationships that constrain access and based on beliefs external to the student. Hypermedia not only permit the construction of exceptionally elaborate conventional instructional designs but also enable sophisticated alternative learning environments that stand in sharp contrast to conventional practice.

Hardware technology has far surpassed the sophistication of our associated design technology (Hannafin, 1989). Often we have simply "harnessed" technology, assimilating new technologies to accommodate our traditional notions of instructional design. In other instances, there exists no obvious organized system for making judgments about technology use. New design notions must evolve if we are to optimize the capability of emerging technologies for learning.

## External Research and Development

Outside the ISD field, several trends have emerged. Innovative prototypes and full-scale operational learning systems have flourished. A decided emphasis has been placed on creating qualitatively different learning experiences rather than re-hosting older ones. Learning systems are widely viewed as a means rather than an end, especially in educational settings (cf. Salomon, Perkins, & Globerson, 1991). The overriding goals of such systems are to promote application and manipulation of knowledge, not simply to acquire the knowledge itself.

Significant advances have also been reported in allied fields. Although artificial intelligence (AI) is still in its infancy, significant work has been reported on its implications for the design of learning environments (see Brown, 1989, and Lawler & Yazdani, 1987). Efforts to support expert AI-based diagnoses, subject matter analyses, teaching tactics, and teaching strategies have also been reported (Ohlsson, 1987). Attempts to better understand the nature of how experts reason have been widespread.

Duchastel (1990) described various types of cognitive tools, each of which supports functions distinct from those typically considered in the ISD field. Tools, in this context, refer to features that augment an individual's ability to learn or act. Power tools "augment cognition of a structural nature" (p. 4; see also empowering environments per J. S. Brown, 1985). They support comprehension by helping to overcome misconceptions while guiding the formation of mental models. Students used diSessa and White's (1982) "dynaturtle" to manipulate operationally several Aristotelian physics concepts, for which misconceptions were common. (See also Rieber's article in this issue.) Assimilatory tools, on the other hand, help individuals to integrate information within existing schemata. They help the individual to make sense of the theoretically limitless ranges of data and information available in various forms, sources, and media. Such tools permit on-demand access to relevant resources, such as in many hypertext systems, when the individual's need to know has been established.

Concern over the limited perspectives of the instructional design field has also been expressed. John Carroll (1990) concluded that ISD, by overemphasizing the role of formal instruction versus concrete experience, has failed to provide meaningful educational experiences via the computer. The preoccupation with objective specification is, in large measure, an artifact of the ISD field's own history, not necessarily a response to the priorities of the varied fields where learning is valued. Experience, inquiry manipulation, prediction, and a host of other learning processes are widely viewed as being at least as essential to successful learning as the attendant formal knowledge. Instructional perspectives alone may limit our views of the design of more inclusive computer-based learning environments.

Not surprisingly, the activity boom outside the ISD field has suffered as well as prospered. Despite tremendous growth in activity, there appears to be no overriding framework guiding system design and no theoretical foundation undergirding most efforts (Spiro & Jehng, 1990). Projects rarely reflect strong grounding in contemporary psychological or pedagogical research and theory. The efforts have been fragmented; the processes are often intuitive and untested. Few attempts have been made to study such systems empirically, and consensus has yet to be reached as to their design. Our field has a significant opportunity to make design methods for systems of diverse conceptual roots operational.

## ISD Contributions

Merrill, Li, and Jones (1990a) detailed several shortcomings of traditional ISD that have become increasingly apparent with emerging instructional technologies. Problems cited were excessive fragmentation, the closed nature of ISD processes, and the tendency to promote passive rather than active learning. Although Merrill, Li, and Jones (1990b) retain a commitment to instruction-centered paradigms, they underscore many of the problems inherent in traditional ISD practice.

At the same time, increased attention has focused on reconceptualizing some basic elements of instructional design. Gagné and Merrill (1990), for instance, acknowledged a "need for treating human performance at a somewhat higher level of abstraction than is usual in most instructional design models" (p. 24). Successful performance, they suggest, is more typically the application of complex sets of knowledge and skills, not the acquisition of the knowledge and skills in isolation. They described a need to identify learning goals that, in effect, require concurrent integration of multiple objectives.

Other recent developments related to alternative approaches have been reported. In response to Merrill's second-generation instructional design model, Kember and Murphy (1990) described a host of alternative directions for instructional designs rooted in constructivism. During the 1991 annual meetings of the Association of Educational

Communications and Technology and American Educational Research Association, several sessions emphasizing alternative approaches were conducted. Recently, *Educational Technology* published a special issue related to constructivism, instructionism, and educational technology in which several authorities presented alternative empirical or theoretical approaches (see, for example, Duffy & Jonassen, 1991; Cognition and Technology Group, 1991; Perkins, 1991; Spiro et al., 1991). This renewed attention reflects a growing recognition of, and interest in, alternative perspectives in learning system design.

Although new and potentially revolutionary possibilities exist, many problems remain. As a field, we must acquire a better sense of our fit with contemporary developments. We need to broaden our notions of design to better understand emerging technologies and the views of others; but we must also seek to influence future developments in thoughtful and productive ways. We need extended design methodologies, the likes of which are only beginning to emerge.

Perhaps the time has come to critically reexamine the foundations, assumptions, and procedures of our craft. Instructional design reflects expert views on the structure of content and strategies designed to *teach* content, not necessarily the manner in which knowledge could or should be *learned.* Instruction may be algorithmic, but learning is not; an instructional design provides one way—not necessarily the only way or the best way—to promote learning.

# Learning Environments:
# Classifications and Examples

Learning environments share a variety of dimensions: scope, activities (user and educational), and content integration methods; these are shown in Figure 6.1. Each dimension exists as a continuum, and learning environments possess attributes along each continuum. The remainder of this article focuses on learning environments and the ways in which they exemplify one or more of the shared dimensions.

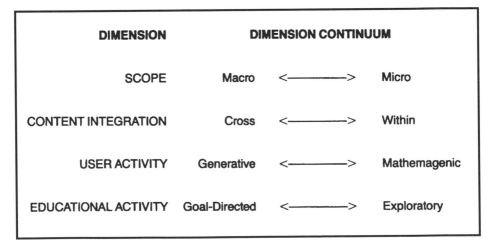

*Fig. 6.1.* Dimensions of learning environment.

# Scope

Scope refers to the inclusiveness of the environment, both with respect to content coverage and to the extent that educational features are available to the learner.

## Macro-Level Environments

Macro-level learning environments emphasize comprehensive treatment among interrelated information, concepts, and activities. They attempt to provide vehicles for broadening the context for the lesson while enabling students to pursue interests or needs beyond the parameters typically provided in isolated lessons.

*ScienceVision* (formerly *Science Quest*) provides a rich set of complementary activities in a hypermedia environment (Litchfield, 1990). Students are provided a wide range of tools and resources from which to explore the various features of the environment; these range from simple glossaries to video encyclopedias to advice from experts to manipulation components, and so on. In addition, a significant array of both on- and off-line resources (e.g., log books) and activities (e.g., project options) are provided. The system incorporates concepts from several fields and varied methods of student-centered learning. (See also Tobin and Dawson's article in this issue.)

## Micro-Level Environments

Micro-environments focus on a relatively discrete domain and permit detailed examinations and explorations between interrelated skills and concepts. Although micro-environments are not integrated explicitly with a larger range of concepts, they often represent a synthesis of several skills and concepts.

Streibel and colleagues developed MENDEL, a learning environment that provides learning resources rather than instruction in the solving of prescribed genetics problems (Streibel, Stewart, Koedinger, Collins, & Jungck, 1987). Students initially construct tentative hypotheses regarding individual genetics experiments; the computer subsequently generates data consistent with expert notions of predicted outcomes. However, MENDEL neither instructs students in "correct" procedures nor solves the problem for them (even though an expert system is available to do so). Instead, the system provides expert advice to students on how to evaluate their own predictions and hypotheses and how to reassess their assumptions to test progressively more refined hypotheses.

# User Activity

Learning environments also vary as a function of learner activity. For example, many learning environments provide complex methods for accessing existing information; others emphasize the creation of environments that support the representation of knowledge.

## Generative Environments

Generative environments rely on the individual (or group of individuals) to create, elaborate, or otherwise represent knowledge. Typically, they supply either a context within which students produce actions designed to clarify, manipulate, or otherwise explore the environment, or a framework within which student representations of meaning can be generated. In the first case, the situation essentially guides individual cognition; in the second, the elements of the representation system guide students' actions.

The Cognition and Technology Group at Vanderbilt University (1990, 1991) has anchored mathematics instruction in relevant real-life contexts. Within these contexts, students are not so much taught as provided circumstances within which critical mathematics problem-solving skills are naturally embedded. Rather than being taught the reasoning skills in a directive manner, students investigate alternatives and determine information requirements. Students generate plans, identify knowledge requirements, test their plans, and revise them as needed to solve the problem.

Scardamalia and her colleagues created *Computer-Supported International Learning Environment* (CSILE), a prototype designed to support students in the purposeful, intentional processing of lesson information (Scardamalia, Bereiter, McLean, Swallow, & Woodruff, 1989). Using CSILE, groups of students generate knowledge bases, including student notes, related text, drawings, graphs, tabular data, and so forth. The system represents alternate ways that individuals organize and understand concepts and provides various heuristics and guidelines that assist students in the construction of a shared knowledge base. Rather than presupposing explicit external structure to the knowledge base, CSILE provides support for individuals or groups to organize and construct knowledge in unique ways.

## Mathemagenic Environments

Among the most common applications of hypermedia learning environments are those that support access to various representations of content. To vary the manner in which information is organized as well as the method in which it is provided in many systems, students might be permitted to access existing glossaries, video clips, encyclopedic information, tutorial instruction, and other representations of to-be-learned content. The content is structured externally and is often available in multiple ways to permit the student to learn according to externally generated notions of meaning.

At Brown University, Yankelovich and colleagues applied advanced hypertext methods in the design of an environment called *Dicken's Web* (Yankelovich, Haan, Meyrowitz, & Drucker, 1988). Conceptual ties (links) to related literary concepts (nodes) were established to connect related textual materials, permitting students to move rapidly among networks of concepts. The environment allows students to construct their own sets of relationships within the network; this allows the system to learn and subsequently invoke individual representations of the lesson content. The system is designed to support connections beyond a particular author or topic by providing cross-topic linkages and pathways.

## *Educational Activity*

The nature of the educational activity—the emphasis on goal-directed, intentional learning versus student-directed exploration—is another dimension that differentiates learning environments.

# Goal-Directed Environments

Goal-directed environments emphasize intended competence, facility, or comprehension. The activities are designed to support a defined set of learning outcomes. Students may be provided considerable flexibility in employing the features of the environment, but all features are structured to promote fluency in prescribed areas.

Harless (1986) reported the design of a sophisticated hypermedia environment designed to simulate intake and follow-up treatment plans required of emergency room physicians. Although a variety of alternative videodisc scenarios could be presented—and many variations could evolve, depending on the physicians' responses and the evolving health of the patients—the goals were consistently prescribed. Physicians-in-training identified symptoms, selected needed procedures and tests, determined whether to admit a patient, prescribed and followed up on treatment plans, and so on. The environment provided ongoing and summative feedback to the participant as to patient status as well as the success and cost of treatment.

# Exploratory Environments

Exploratory environments emphasize processes more than outcomes, at least insofar as intended learning is concerned. Often, students are encouraged to alter, explore, or otherwise manipulate the parameters of the environment in examining possible outcomes; the emphasis is on learning as a constructive, individually mediated process rather than as an accountability-based process based upon external notions of importance and relevance.

*Geometric Supposer* (Schwartz & Yerulshamy, 1987), for instance, focuses on a comparatively narrow range of mathematics topics but provides an unusually powerful array of tools that promote deeper processing and understanding. There are no explicit performance expectations; instead, support is provided for student-centered exploration and manipulation. Students receive tools that enable them to explore, predict, and manipulate geometric phenomena to create highly visual and interactive experiences with geometry.

# *Content Integration*

Although content integration is a trademark of all learning environments, the manner in which integration occurs can vary widely. In many cases, the environment promotes integration among closely allied knowledge or concepts; in others, the environment emphasizes content integration beyond the range normally associated with a given topic or subject.

# Cross-Content Integration

Cross-content integration attempts to minimize the explicit or implicit boundaries of subject matter by featuring information, concepts, and skills in varied contexts. Multiplication skills, for example, might be integrated with social studies (e.g., one candidate receiving three times more votes than another); with language (e.g., one word having three times more letters than another); with science (e.g., one weight being three times heavier than another); and so on. Skills and knowledge are not isolated and taught out of context; they are introduced and developed within a variety of meaningful contexts.

Again, *ScienceVision* integrates content across various fields. Several related areas (e.g., citizenship, mathematics, career education) are represented within a relevant context. For example, information regarding a range of careers related to the environment is nested within an ecology unit; the information is provided through descriptive information as well as through interviews with various professionals in the field. Additionally, a number of mathematical concepts are presented in context, as are various mapping methods and activities. Students, again within the context of a real-life problem, also explore the rights and responsibilities of individuals to protect and maintain environmental standards. Although the main theme is related to science, the content is heavily contextualized and integrated with other related fields.

## Within-Content Integration

Content integration can also be focussed within given domains. For example, in learning the meaning of the term *freedom,* students might receive a variety of situations and examples from history that exemplify concepts related to freedom. The context may shift from the flight of the Pilgrims to the early Revolutionary War to the repression of slaves to current-day examples of civil rights violations. All instances enrich the understanding of freedom within the context of history; all presumably enrich students' understanding of freedom within historical contexts.

Spiro et al. (1988; 1991) reported the development of hypertext systems designed to broaden the ways in which advanced, often ill-structured, knowledge can be acquired. One system, *Cardioworld Explorer,* focuses on the complexities involved in understanding complex, conditional aspects of the cardiovascular system. Another system, *Exploring Thematic Structure in Citizen Kane,* merges original film and portions of text to promote advanced understanding of a film in which segments can be reexamined for meaning from multiple perspectives. In this system, conditionally relevant knowledge—knowledge that assumes different meaning under different circumstances—is explored from multiple perspectives to promote cognitive flexibility.

Varied and powerful learning environments have been developed to reflect a diversity of pedagogical processes that differ vastly among the systems themselves as well as from typical ISD methods; these samples represent only a fraction of the available applications. Increasingly, open-ended systems such as those mentioned are redefining "state-of-the-art."

# Emerging Technologies, ISD, and the Future of Learning Environments

How, or will, the ISD field influence future developments in computer-mediated learning environments? Collectively, we cling to our historic views about teaching, learning, and instructing. Perhaps we have been blinded by our own success; indeed, significant innovations have been advanced, yet we are not yet partners in such developments.

What can the ISD field learn from developments in emerging technologies? Learning environments offer alternatives—potentially powerful and effective alternatives—to many traditional instructional goals. The goal of instruction, like the goal of learning environments, is to support learning; however, the foundations, assumptions, and methods of instruction are distinct. Instruction seeks to build competence according to external conventions; learning environments seek to induce it through internal mediation. Individuals can, and in some cases must, assume a greater role in regulating, and not merely participating in, lesson activities.

Alternative approaches are often complementary to current practice, but they can also be at odds with it. It is not difficult for ISD professionals to envision environments where knowledge is passed on through traditional instructional methodologies while tools and resources are provided to enrich and elaborate, i.e., as supplemental or enrichment activities for instruction. However, this is not the only way nor is it the method of choice in many fields. We must learn to understand and respect alternative approaches if we expect to influence their evolution.

ISD can also make significant contributions to emerging technology. We have extracted enviable precision in the processes used to plan, adopt, and validate educational solutions. Few fields offer logical design and development procedures of comparable power or sophistication. We have also evolved robust psychological and pedagogical foundations from which to generate empirically referenced design guidelines and heuristics. We have assisted learners during complex lesson navigation, refined human factors considerations, improved the design of complementary messages, developed protocols for screen design, and so on. In many cases, these are precisely the areas where learning environment design needs are most acute.

The problems and limitations of learning environments must also be addressed. Although evidence of application to widely varied lesson content has been demonstrated, some learning tasks are certainly more amenable than others to the features and components of the learning environment. Further, not all important activities must be delivered via computer. High-technology solutions need not be employed where they are unnecessary; indeed, there is much to be learned about the pragmatic aspects of learning environments.

This article is not intended to diminish either the importance or the successes of the ISD field. ISD procedures have proven efficient, effective, and valuable across a wide array of problems and settings. The question is not whether instruction has a place in the computer-based learning environments of the future, for it most certainly does. The critical question may be, "Is that enough?"

Will the ISD field assume a significant role in conceptualizing more inclusive computer-based learning environments in the future? Is instruction as historically operationalized sufficient to accomplish the more inclusive goals of successful learning? Are the models employed to develop instruction robust enough to accommodate learning goals that are qualitatively different from those traditionally addressed? If so, how do we apply them? If not, upon what are our designs based? These are significant questions. They require significant answers.

# References

Andrews, D., and L. Goodson. 1980. A comparative analysis of models of instructional design. *Journal of Instructional Development* 3:2–16.

Bereiter, C. 1990. Aspects of educational learning theory. *Review of Educational Research* 60:603–624.

———. 1991. Implications of connectionism for thinking about rules. *Educational Researcher* 20, no. 3:2–9.

Berliner, D. November 1990. *Expertise in pedagogy: Implications for reform.* Paper presented at the Dean's Seminar Series, Florida State University, Tallahassee, Florida.

Bransford, J., J. Franks, N. Vye, and R. Sherwood. 1989. New approaches to instruction: Because wisdom can't be told. In S. Vosniadou and A. Ortony, eds., *Similarity and analogical reasoning.* New York: Cambridge University Press.

Brown, J. S. 1985. Process versus product: A perspective on tools for communal and informal electronic learning. *Journal of Educational Computing Research* 1:179–201.

———. 1989. Toward a new epistemology for learning. In C. Frasson and J. Gauthiar, eds., *Intelligent tutoring systems at the crossroad of AI and education.* Norwood, N.J.: Ablex.

Brown, J. S., A. Collins, and P. Duguid. 1989. Situated cognition and the culture of learning. *Educational Researcher* 18, no. 1:32–41.

Carroll, J. 1990. *The Nurnberg Funnel: Designing minimalist instruction for practical computer skill.* Cambridge, Mass.: MIT Press.

Cognition and Technology Group at Vanderbilt. 1990. Anchored instruction and its relationship to situated cognition. *Educational Researcher* 19, no. 6:2–10.

———. 1991. Technology and the design of generative learning environments. *Educational Technology* 31, no. 5:34–40.

DeVito, A., and G. Krockover. 1980a. *Creative sciencing: A practical approach.* 2d ed. Boston: Little, Brown.

———. 1980b. *Creative sciencing: Ideas and activities for teachers and children.* 2d ed. Boston: Little, Brown.

Dewey, J. 1933. *How we think.* Boston: Heath.

Dick, W. 1991. An instructional designers view of constructivism. *Educational Technology* 31, no. 5:41–44.

diSessa, A. 1982. Unlearning Aristotelian physics: A study of knowledge-based learning. *Cognitive Science* 6:37–75.

diSessa, A., and B. White. 1982. Learning physics from a dynaturtle. *Byte* 7:324.

Duchastel, P. 1990. Assimilatory tools for informal learning: Prospects for ICAI. *Instructional Science* 19:3–9.

Duffy, T., and D. Jonassen. 1991. Constructivism: New implications for instructional technology? *Educational Technology* 31, no. 5:7–12.

Gagné, R., and M. D. Merrill. 1990. Integrative goals for instructional design. *Educational Technology Research and Development* 38:23–30.

Gagné, R., L. Briggs, and W. Wager. 1988. *Principles of instructional design.* 3d ed. New York: Holt, Rinehart, & Winston.

Gustafson, K. 1991. *Survey of ID models.* 2d ed. Syracuse, N.Y.: ERIC Clearinghouse of Information Resources.

Hannafin, M. J. 1988. The effects of instructional explicitness of learning error persistence. *Contemporary Educational Psychology* 13:126–132.

———. 1989. Interaction strategies and emerging instructional technologies: Psychological perspectives. *Canadian Journal of Educational Communication* 18:167–179.

Hannafin, M. J., and J. Gall. October, 1990. *Emerging instructional technologies and learning environments: From instruction- to learner-centered models.* Paper presented at the annual meeting of the Association for the Development of ComputerBased Instructional Systems, San Diego, California.

Hannafin, M. J., and L. P. Rieber. 1989a. Psychological foundations of instructional design for emerging computer-based instructional technologies: Part 1. *Educational Technology Research and Development* 37:91–101.

———. 1989b. Psychological foundations of instructional design for emerging computer-based instructional technologies: Part II. *Educational Technology Research and Development* 37:102–114.

Harless, W. 1986. An interactive videodisc drama: The case of Frank Hall. *Journal of Computer-Based Instruction* 13:113–116.

Hooper, S., and M. J. Hannafin. 1991. Psychological perspectives on emerging instructional technologies: A critical analysis. *Educational Psychologist* 26:69–95.

Johnsen, J., and W. Taylor. 1991. Instructional technology and unforeseen value conflicts: Toward a critique. In G. Anglin, ed., *Instructional technology: Past, present, and future.* Englewood, Colo.: Libraries Unlimited.

Johnson, D., and R. Johnson. 1986. Computer-assisted cooperative learning. *Educational Technology* 26:12–18.

Jonassen, D. 1986. Hypertext principles for courseware design. *Educational Psychologist* 21:269–292.

———. 1988. Designing structured hypertext and structuring access to hypertext. *Educational Technology* 28, no. 11:13–16.

———. 1991. Hypertext as instructional design. *Educational Technology Research and Development* 39:83–92.

Kember, D., and D. Murphy. 1990. Alternative new directions for instructional design. *Educational Technology* 30, no. 8:42–47.

Kinzie, M., and R. Berdel. 1990. Design and use of hypermedia systems. *Educational Technology Research and Development* 38:61–M.

Lawler, R., and M. Yazdani, eds. 1987. *Artificial intelligence and education.* Vol. 1. Norwood, N.J.: Ablex.

Levin, J., and M. Waugh. 1987. Educational simulation tools, games, and microworlds: Compuer-based environments for learning. *International Journal of Educational Research* 12, no. 1:71–79.

Litchfield, B. 1990. Science Quest: A multimedia inquiry based videodisc science curriculum. *Instruction Delivery System* 4, no. 3:12–17.

Marchionini, G. 1988. Hypermedia and learning: Freedom and chaos. *Educational Technology* 28, no. 1:8–12.

McDermott, L. 1984. Research on conceptual understanding in mechanics. *Physics Today* 37:24–32.

Merrill, M. D., Z. Li, and M. Jones. 1990a. Limitations of first generation instructional design. *Educational Technology* 30, no 1:7–11.

———. 1990b. The second generation instructional design research program. *Educational Technology* 30, no. 3:26–31.

———. 1990c. ID2 and constructivist theory. *Educational Technology* 30, no. 12:52–55.

Ohlsson, S. 1987. Some principles of intelligent tutoring. In R. Lawler and M. Yazdani, eds. *Artificial intelligence education,* vol. 1. Norwood, N.J.: Ablex.

Papert, S. 1980. *Mindstorms.* New York: Basic Books.

Paris, S., and J. Byrnes. 1989. The constructivist approach to self-regulation and learning in the classroom. In Zimmerman and Schunk, eds. *Self-regulated learning and academic theory, research, and practice* (pp. 169–199). New York: Springer-Verlag.

Perkins, D. 1991. Technology meets constructivism: Do they make a marriage? *Educational Technology* 31, no. 5:18–23.

Perkins, D., and R. Simmons. 1988. Patterns of misunderstanding: An integrative model for science, math, and programming. *Review of Educational Research* 58:303–326.

Salomon, G., and D. Perkins. 1989. Rocky roads to transfer: Rethinking mechanisms of a neglected phenomenon. *Educational Psychologist* 24:111–142.

Salomon, G., D. Perkins, and T. Globerson. 1991. Partners in cognition: Extending human intelligence with intelligent technologies. *Educational Researcher* 29, no. 3:2–9.

Scardamalia, M., C. Bereiter, R. McLean, J. Swallow, and E. Woodruff. 1989. Computer-supported intentional learning environments. *Journal of Educational Computing Research* 5:51–68.

Schiffman, S. 1991. Instructional systems design: Five views from the field. In G. Angfin, ed., *Instructional technology: Past, present, and future.* Englewood, Colo.: Libraries Unlimited.

Schuell, T. 1988. The role of the student in learning from instruction. *Contemporary Educational Psychology* 13:276–295.

Schwartz, J., and M. Yerulshamy. 1987. The "Geometric Supposer": Using microcomputers to restore invention to the learning of mathematics. In D. Perkins, J. Lochead, and J. Bishop, eds., *Thinking: Proceedings of the international conference* (pp. 525–536). Hillsdale, N.J.: Lawrence Erlbaum.

Spiro, R., and J. Jengh. 1990. Cognitive flexibility, random access instruction, and hypertext: Theory and technology for non-linear and multidimensional traversal of complex subject matter. In D. Nix and R. Spiro, eds., *Cognition, education, and multimedia: Exploring ideas in high technology* (pp. 163–205). Hillsdale, N.J.: Lawrence Erlbaum.

Spiro, R., R. Coulson, P. Feltovich, and D. Anderson. 1988. Cognitive flexibility theory: Advanced knowledge acquisition in W-structured domains. In *Tenth Annual Conference of the Cognitive Science Society* (pp. 375–383). Hillsdale, N.J.: Lawrence Erlbaum.

Spiro, R. J., P. L. Feltoavich, M. J. Jacobson, and R. L. Coulson. 1991. Cognitive flexibility, constructivism, and hypertext: Random access instruction for advanced knowledge acquisition in W-structured domains. *Educational Technology* 31, no. 5:24–33.

Steinberg, E. 1989. Cognition and learner control: A literature review, 1977–1988. *Journal of Computer-Based Instruction* 16:117–121.

Streibel, M. 1988. Instructional plans and situated learning: The challenge of Suchman's theory of situated action for instructional designers and instructional systems. *Journal of Visual Literacy* 9, no. 2:8–34.

Streibel, M., J. Stewart, K. Koedinger, A. Collins, and J. Jungck. 1987. MENDEL: An intelligent computer tutoring system for genetics problem solving, conjecturing, and understanding. *Machine-Mediated Learning* 2, nos. 1&2:129–159.

Vygotsky, L. 1978. *Mind in society: The development of higher psychological processes.* Cambridge, Mass.: Harvard University Press.

West, C., J. Farmer, and P. Wolff. 1991. *Instructional design: Implications from cognitive science.* Englewood Cliffs, N.J.: Prentice Hall.

Yackel, E., P. Cobb, T. Wood, G. Wheatley, and G. Merkel. 1990. The importance of social interactions in children's construction of mathematical knowledge. In T. Cooney, ed., *1990 Yearbook of the National Council of Teachers of Mathematics.* Reston, Va.: NCTM.

Yankelovich, N., B. Haan, N. Meyrowitz, and S. Drucker. 1988. Intermedia: The concept and the construction of a seamless information environment. *Computer* 21, no. 1:81– .

# 7

# Levels of Use of the Innovation:

## A Framework for Analyzing Innovation Adoption

### Gene E. Hall, Susan F. Loucks,
### William L. Rutherford, and Beulah W. Newlove[*]

Change and the tendency to embrace or to resist it seem always to have been a part of the human condition. Change leads to consternation and indignation for some, shock for others, and hope for a few. Because of this inherent potential for trauma, defining concepts and developing measurement procedures for assessing what is actually accomplished by change is difficult and challenging work. All too frequently, the affective dimension of change draws a veil that obscures the work the innovation users are doing. In this paper, we describe a hypothesized dimension of innovation adoption that we have defined and are measuring, and that attempts to assess the work the individual innovation user does in using an innovation (1, 2). The dimension seems to have power for practitioners, researchers, and theoreticians alike—particularly in education, where innovation adoption is so widespread and the public interest in change is so intense.

We have found, based on our experiences in the field as practitioners and adoption agents as well as on our past research efforts, that "change," or innovation adoption, is not accomplished just because a decision maker has announced it. Instead, the various members of a user system, such as teachers and professors, demonstrate a wide variation in the type and degree of their use of an innovation. One of the reasons for this variation is that innovation adoption is a process rather than a decision-point, which is commonly overlooked; it is a process that each innovation user experiences individually. A basic assumption of our present research is that this variation in use by each individual innovation user must be behaviorally described and systematically accounted for if innovations are to be used with maximum effectiveness.

*Reprinted with permission. Copyright by the American Association of Colleges for Teacher Education. Hall, G., Loucks, S., et al., "Levels of use of the innovation: A framework for analysing innovation adoption." *Journal of Teacher Education* 23(1), (January/February, 1975): pp. 52–56.

We recognize that such other variables as organizational climate, intervention strategies, and characteristics of decision makers should be considered. However, we and others have found that, the character of the outside variables notwithstanding, what actually happens in the individual application of an innovation is open to tremendous variation.

# Levels of Innovation Use

So that we can account for the individual variation in use of an innovation, we have attempted to articulate the *Levels of Use of the Innovation,* a concept described in the *Concerns-Based Adoption Model* (CBAM) (3). The model proposes eight discrete levels an individual may demonstrate in using an innovation; these levels range from ignorance of the innovation to an active, sophisticated, and highly effective use of it and, further, to active searching for a superseding innovation. It is further hypothesized that growth in using an innovation (movement toward higher levels) by most individuals is developmental. Normally, individuals do not use an innovation for the first or even the second time as effectively and efficiently as they do after four or five cycles.

The Levels of Use (LoU) dimension describes the various behaviors of the innovation user through various stages—from spending most efforts in *orienting,* to *managing,* and finally to *integrating* use of the innovation. Before use, the individual becomes familiar with and increasingly knowledgeable about the innovation. First use is typically disjointed, management problems being quite common. With continued use, management becomes routine, and the user (teacher or professor) is able to direct more effort toward increased effectiveness for the clients (learners) and integrate what he or she is doing with what others are doing. Obviously, these advanced levels of use are not attained merely by using the innovation through several cycles. Experience is essential but not sufficient to ensure that a given individual will develop high-quality use of an innovation.

The LoU dimension is targeted toward describing behaviors of innovation users and does not at all focus on attitudinal, motivational, or other affective aspects of the user. The dimension does not attempt to explain causality. Instead, the LoU dimension is an attempt to define operationally various states of innovation user behavior; that is, what the user is *doing.* The reason the innovation user does certain things (the why) is a reasonable question only after how the user behaves can be systematically described and measured.

# The LoU Chart

To organize the various behaviors characteristic of each level in a manageable way, a framework of indices and decision points has been developed. Operationally defining the concept of LoU in this way greatly increases the probability that the phenomenon of use can be understood and measured validly and reliably. This framework, the "LoU Chart," is presented in its fully defined form as Figure 7.1. We have found this full articulation to be very helpful for work in the field as well as vital for research because it provides many indices and data points that can be tapped to determine precisely where an innovation user is.

In studying the LoU Chart, note that in addition to defining the eight Levels of Use, each level is further defined according to seven subparts, or *categories.* These categories represent the key functions that users carry out when they are using an innovation. At each level, the category descriptions represent the typical behaviors that users at that level are engaged in; however, an individual may not be on the same level in all seven categories, as is illustrated in the following description. When such variations occur, they become further clues for interpretation by the adoption agent and the researcher.

## LEVELS OF USE

| SCALE POINT DEFINITIONS OF THE LEVELS OF USE OF THE INNOVATION | *CATEGORIES* | | |
|---|---|---|---|
| | KNOWLEDGE | ACQUIRING INFORMATION | SHARING |
| Levels of Use are distinct states that represent observably different types of behavior and patterns of innovation use as established by individuals and groups. These levels characterize a user's development in acquiring new skills and varying use of the innovation. Each level encompasses a range of behaviors, but is limited by a set of identifiable Decision Points. For descriptive purposes, each level is defined by seven categories. | That which the user knows about characteristics of the innovation, how to use it, and consequence of its use. This is cognitive knowledge related to using the innovation, not feelings or attitudes. | Solicits information about the innovation in a variety of ways, including questioning resource persons, corresponding with resource agencies, reviewing printed materials, and making visits. | Discusses the innovation with others. Shares plans, ideas, resources, outcomes, and problems related to use of the innovation. |
| **LEVEL 0** NON-USE: State in which the user has little or no knowledge of the innovation, no involvement with the innovation and is doing nothing toward becoming involved. | Knows nothing about this or similar innovations or has only very limited general knowledge of efforts to develop innovations in the area. | Takes little or no action to solicit information beyond reviewing descriptive information about this or similar innovations when it happens to come to personal attention. | Is not communicating with others about the innovation beyond possibly acknowledging that the innovation exists. |
| **DECISION POINT A** | *Takes action to learn more detailed information about the innovation.* | | |
| **LEVEL I** ORIENTATION: State in which the user has recently acquired or is acquiring information about the innovation and/or has recently explored or is exploring its value orientation and its demands upon user and user system. | Knows general information about the innovation such as origin, characteristics, and implementation requirements. | Seeks descriptive material about the innovation. Seeks opinions and knowledge of others through discussions, visits, or workshops. | Discusses the innovation in general terms and/or exchanges descriptive information, materials or ideas about the innovation and possible implications of its use. |
| **DECISION POINT B** | *Makes a decision to use the innovation by establishing a time to begin.* | | |
| **LEVEL II** PREPARATION: State in which the user is preparing for first use of the innovation. | Knows logistical requirements, necessary resources and timing to initial use of the innovation, and details of initial experiences for clients. | Seeks information and resources specifically related to preparation for use of the innovation in own setting. | Discusses resources needed for initial use of the innovation. Joins others in pre-use training and in planning for resources, logistics, schedules, etc. In preparation for first use. |

*Fig. 7.1.* **The LoU Chart.**

| DECISION POINT C | Changes, if any, and uses are dominated by user needs. | | |
|---|---|---|---|
| **LEVEL III**<br>MECHANICAL USE: State in which the user focuses most effort on the short-term day-to-day use of the innovation with little time for reflection. Changes in use are made more to meet user needs than client needs. The user is primarily engaged in a step-wise attempt to master the tasks required to use the innovation, often resulting in disjoined and superficial use. | Knows on a day-to-day basis the requirements for using the innovation. Is more knowledgeable on short-term activities and effects than long-range activities and effects of use of the innovation. | Solicits management information about such things as logistics, scheduling techniques, and ideas for reducing amount of time and work required of user. | Discusses management and logistical issues related to use of the innovation. Resources and materials are shared for purposes of reducing management, flow and logistical problems related to use of the innovation. |
| **DECISION POINT D-1** | A routine pattern of use is established. | | |
| **LEVEL IV A**<br>ROUTINE: Use of the innovation is stabilized. Few if any changes are being made in ongoing use. Little preparation or thought is being given to improving innovation use of its consequences. | Knows both short- and long-term requirements for use and how to use the innovation with minimum effort or stress. | Makes no special efforts to seek information as a part of ongoing use of the innovation. | Describes current use of the innovation with little or no references to ways of changing use. |
| **DECISION POINT D-2** | Changes use of the innovation based on formal or informal evaluation in order to increase client outcomes. | | |
| **LEVEL IV B;**<br>REFINEMENT: State in which the user varies the use of the innovation to increase the impact on clients within immediate sphere of influence. Variations are based on knowledge of both short- and long-term consequences for clients. | Knows cognitive and affective effects of the innovation on clients and ways for increasing impact on clients. | Solicits information and materials that focus specifically on changing use of the innovation to affect client outcomes. | Discusses own methods of modifying use of the innovation to change client outcomes. |
| **DECISION POINT E** | Initiates changes in use of innovation based on input of an coordination with what colleagues are doing. | | |
| **LEVEL V**<br>INTEGRATION: State in which the user is combining own efforts to use the innovation with related activities of colleagues to achieve a collective impact on clients within their common sphere of influence. | Knows how to coordinate own use of the innovation with colleagues to provide a collective impact on clients. | Solicits information and opinions for the purpose of collaborating with others in use of the innovation. | Discusses efforts to increase client impact through collaboration with others on personal use of the innovation. |

***Fig. 7.1.*** **The LoU Chart (continued).**

| DECISION POINT F | *Begins exploring alternatives to or major modifications of the innovation presently in use.* | | |
|---|---|---|---|
| **LEVEL VI**<br>RENEWAL: State in which the user reevaluates the quality of use of the innovation, seeks major modifications of or alternatives to present innovation to achieve increased impact on clients, examines new developments in the field, and explores new goals for self and the system. | Knows of alternatives that could be used to change or replace the present innovation that would improve the quality of outcomes of its use. | Seeks information and materials about other innovation as alternatives to the present innovation or for making major adaptations in the innovation. | Focuses discussions on identification of major alternatives or replacements for the current innovation. |

## *CATEGORIES*

| **ASSESSING**<br>Examines the potential or actual use of the innovation or some aspect of It. This can be a mental assessment or can involve actual collection and analysis of data. | **PLANNING**<br>Designs and outlines short- and/or long-range steps to be taken during process of innovation adoption, i.e., aligns resources, schedules, activities, meets with others to organize and/or coordinate use of the innovation. | **STATUS REPORTING**<br>Describes personal stand at the present time in relation to use of the innovation. | **PERFORMING**<br>Carries out the actions and activities entailed in operationalizing the innovation. |
|---|---|---|---|
| Takes no action to analyse the innovation, its characteristics, possible use, or consequences of use. | Schedules no time and specifies no steps for the study of use of the innovation. | Reports little or no personal involvement with the innovation. | Takes no discernible action toward learning about or using the innovation. The innovation and/or its accouterments are not present or in use. |
| Analyzes and compares materials, content, requirements for use, evaluation reports, potential outcomes, strengths and weaknesses for purpose of making a decision about use of the innovation. | Plans to gather necessary information and resources as needed to make a decision for or against use of the innovation. | Reports presently orienting self to what the innovation is and is not. | Explores the innovation and requirements for its use by talking to others about it, reviewing descriptive information and sample materials, attending orientation sessions, and observing others using it. |
| Analyzes detailed requirements and available resources for initial use of the innovation. | Identifies steps and procedures entailed in obtaining resources and organizing activities and events for initial use of the innovation. | Reports preparing self for initial use of the innovation. | Studies reference materials in depth, organizes resources and logistics, schedules and receives skill training in preparation for initial use. |

*Fig. 7.1.* **The LoU Chart (continued).**

| | | | |
|---|---|---|---|
| Determines own use of the innovation with respect to problems of logistics, management time, schedules resources, and general reactions of clients. | Plans for organizing and managing resources, activities, and events related primarily to immediate ongoing use of the innovation. Planned-for changes address managerial or logistical issues with a short-term perspective. | Reports that logistics, time, management, resource organization, etc. are the focus of most personal efforts to use the innovation. | Manages innovation with varying degrees of efficiency. Often lacks anticipation of immediate consequences. The flow of actions in the user and clients is often disjointed, uneven and uncertain. When changes are made, they are primarily in response to logistical and organizational problems. |
| Assesses use of the innovation in global terms without reference to making changes. Specific evaluation activities are limited to those that are administratively required with little attention paid to findings for the purpose of changing use. | Plans intermediate and long-range actions with little projected variation in how the innovation will be used. Planning focuses on routine use of resources, personnel, etc. | Reports that personal use of the innovation is going along satisfactorily with few if any problems. | Uses the innovation smoothly with minimal management problems: over time, there is little variation in pattern of use. |
| Assesses use of the innovation for the purpose of changing current practices to improve client outcomes. | Develops intermediate and long-range plans that anticipate possible and needed steps, resources, and events designed to enhance client outcomes. | Reports varying use of the innovation in order to change client outcomes. | Explores and experiments with alternative combinations of the innovation with existing practices to maximize client involvement and to optimize client outcomes. |
| Appraises collaborative use of the innovations in terms of client outcomes and strengths and weaknesses of the integrated effort. | Plans specific actions to coordinate own use of the innovation with others to achieve increased impact on clients. | Reports spending time and energy collaborating with others about integrating own use of the innovation. | Collaborates with others in use of the innovation as a means for expanding the innovation's impact on clients. Changes in use are made in coordination with others. |
| Analyzes advantages and disadvantages of major modifications or alternatives to the present innovation. | Plans activities that involve pursuit of alternatives to enhance or replace the innovation. | Reports considering major modifications of or alternatives to present use of the innovation. | Explores other innovations that could be used in combination with or in place of the present innovation in an attempt to develop more effective means of achieving client outcomes. |

*Fig. 7.1.* **The LoU Chart (continued).**

Although the concept of LoU represents a developmental growth continuum, key points distinguish each of the eight Levels of Use. These *Decision Points* are also described in the LoU Chart. By checking these points, it is possible to quickly assign an overall LoU to a given individual. The fuller complexity of what the user is doing can be assessed by probing further in each of the categories.

# Examining Levels of Use

An interesting approach to further examination of Levels of Use is to describe users as they progress from familiarization with to increased sophistication in using an innovation. As an illustration, consider a college professor and the use of instructional modules. In an initial observation, no trace of modules is observed in her instruction and she reports that she has never heard of them, is not actively looking for any information about them, and has no intention of using them. She is at LoU 0 with respect to every category. Often, however, individuals are found to know quite a bit about an innovation, giving them as high as Level II Knowledge, but still have no intention of using it. This stresses the importance of measuring Level of Use for each category independently and not assuming that all category scores will be the same. People with different "profiles" across the categories, although they have the same Level of Use for the majority of categories, may require wholly different interventions. In this example, someone with a high level of knowledge about an innovation would not require the same initial information as one with LoU Knowledge.

To continue with this example through one more Level of Use, a return visit six months later may find this professor orienting herself to instructional modules. Sample modules are stacked on her desk. She has a file of letters she has written for more information about modules, and she plans to attend a session on modules at an upcoming professional meeting. She can explain the characteristics of modules and the advantages and disadvantages of their use in her situation. Because she has begun to explore the possibilities for using modules, but has not yet made a decision, this individual is at overall LoU I. There is also enough information to put her at Level I for the Knowledge, Acquiring Information, Assessing, Planning, Status Reporting, and Performing categories. The return visit illustrates the developmental nature of Levels of Use.

Several other examples might be useful in understanding Levels of Use. An innovation user reports spending an inordinate amount of time getting materials together and that the best he can do is plan and prepare for student needs on a day-to-day basis. Much time is involved in correcting pre- and post-tests and crisis management of resources and facilities that he thought he had organized, but unforeseen problems continue to arise. The students seem to spend a lot of time waiting for the teacher or for materials needed to proceed. This is an obvious case of LoU III. Another user states that the materials and facilities needed to use the innovation are well organized and require little time. No changes are contemplated, and you observe none of the confusion or disjointedness of the Level III user. These are typical Level IV A behaviors, particularly concerning Knowledge, Planning, Status Reporting, and Performing.

Innovation users often never reach Level IV B. Many reasons for this can be postulated, but research shows that individuals who have used an innovation for many years often have never evaluated their use of it, and have never made significant changes. For the same reasons, many innovation users never proceed to Level V. At this level, with the intent to collectively increase student outcomes, the users begin to coordinate efforts with others who may be sharing the same students.

The rare LoU VI individuals are those who are searching above and beyond the present innovation for ways to increase student learning. This is an interesting Level of Use, because as soon as another innovation is explored, the user recycles to LoU I or II with respect to the new innovation. Thus, a full cycle is created.

# Discussion and Implications

The Concerns-Based Adoption Model and its LoU dimension are currently the subjects of intensive research. How many of our ideas will subsequently be demonstrated to be true will have to await the results of our studies and the tests of real-world practice. However, even now we have enough data to support the following implications of the LoU dimension:

1. First of all, if different LoU exist, and adopting an innovation is a developmental phenomenon that each user experiences individually, it must be acknowledged that some individuals will at times be at such less efficient levels as III or IV A. Once acknowledged, these levels need to be accepted as legitimate steps in growth toward sophisticated use. Strategies must then be developed that deal with a user's present LoU and facilitate growth. For example, support for innovation adoption needs to extend across several cycles of use rather than consist mainly of no support or an initial two-day "hit and run" workshop. It also seems likely that the same interventions will not be appropriate or relevant for all levels.

2. Our LoU research shows, and this relates to the above point, that after three cycles of use, from 30 to 40 percent of an innovation's users are stable at LoU IV A. If further dynamic increases in sophistication are desired, special interventions appear to be needed, probably during the third cycle.

3. The concept of LoU also applies to groups and entire institutions. Analysis of the underlying dynamics of a particular group or institutional LoU is a challenging multivariate area for study. Development of easily applied tools is vitally needed in this area for use by researchers and practitioners.

4. During our research, we have encountered problems in attempting to specify exactly what comprises a single innovation. One implication of this problem relates to such "innovation bundles" as individually guided education, or competency-based teacher education, in which several innovations are combined into "one" innovation. In our research, we find it necessary to assess a given user's LoU for each innovation within the "bundle." These specific LoU may or may not be the same for all of the component innovations. Managing and studying the adoption of these innovation bundles becomes much more difficult and complicated than it is for single innovations, such as changing from one textbook to another (which isn't always easy).

5. One of the key reasons, we think, that so many "evaluation" reports conclude with no significant differences between experimental innovative efforts and comparison efforts is attributable to LoU. In most evaluation studies, the summative (outcome) data are collected during the first cycle of use of the innovation when most of the users are probably at LoU III

and are not yet using the innovation effectively. Thus, it is unreasonable to anticipate significant achievement gains. We suspect that the effects of an innovation's use are different depending on the LoU of the user; this has some interesting implications for evaluation studies.

6. LoU represents one part of the complex process of innovation adoption. Another critical part is the affective dimension of innovation users; this dimension is included in the Concerns-Based Adoption Model as the concept of innovation user "concerns." In our present research, we are exploring the interrelationship of concerns with LoU and how these relate to other critical change variables.

We envision a time in the not-too-distant future when it will be possible to assess individuals within a school or college according to their Levels of Use and concerns about a particular innovation, and to select appropriate intervention strategies and tactics to ease their growth in using the innovation while minimizing the trauma of change.

# References

The work reported here has been conducted with the support of National Institute of Education contract OEC 6-10-108. The opinions expressed herein, however, are those of the authors and no endorsement by the National Institute of Education is implied.

The authors wish to make special acknowledgement of their coworkers on the Procedures for Adopting Educational Innovations Project who have also been involved in the development of the Levels of Use Chart.

Hall, G. E., R. C. Wallace, and W. E. Dossett. *A Developmental Conceptualization of the Adoption Process Within Educational institutions.* Austin: The Research and Development Center for Teacher Education, The University of Texas at Austin, 1973.

# 8

# Course Improvement Through Evaluation

## Lee J. Cronbach

The national interest in improving education has generated several highly important projects to improve curricula, particularly at the secondary-school level. In conferences of directors of "course content improvement" programs sponsored by the National Science Foundation, questions about evaluation are frequently raised.[1] Those who inquire about evaluation have various motives, ranging from sheer scientific curiosity about classroom events to a desire to assure a sponsor that money has been well spent. While the curriculum developers sincerely wish to use the skills of evaluation specialists, I am not certain that they have a clear picture of what evaluation can do and should try to do. And, on the other hand, I am becoming convinced that some techniques and habits of thought of the evaluation specialist are ill suited to current curriculum studies. To serve these studies, what philosophy and methods of evaluation are required? And, particularly, how must we depart from the familiar doctrines and rituals of the testing game?

## Programatic Decisions

To draw attention to its full range of functions, we may define "evaluation" broadly as the *collection and use of information to make decisions about an educational program.* The program may be a set of instructional materials distributed nationally, the instructional activities of a single school, or the educational experiences of a single pupil. Many types of decisions are to be made, and many varieties of information are useful. It becomes immediately apparent that evaluation is a diversified activity and that no one set of principles will suffice for all situations. But measurement specialists have so concentrated upon one process—the preparation of pencil-and-paper achievement tests for assigning scores to individual pupils—that the principles pertinent to that process have somehow become enshrined as the principles of evaluation. "Tests," we are told, "should fit the content of the curriculum." Also, "only those evaluation procedures should be used that yield reliable scores." These and other hallowed principles are not entirely appropriate to evaluation for course improvement. Before proceeding to support this contention, I wish

123

to distinguish among purposes of evaluation and to relate them to historical developments in testing and curriculum making.

We may separate three types of decisions for which evaluation is used:

1. Course improvement: deciding what instructional materials and methods are satisfactory and where change is needed.

2. Decisions about individuals: identifying the needs of the pupil for the sake of planning his instruction, judging pupil merit for purposes of selection and grouping, acquainting the pupil with his own progress and deficiencies.

3. Administrative regulation: judging how good the school system is, how good individual teachers are, etc.

Course improvement is set apart by its broad temporal and geographical reference; it involves the modification of recurrently used materials and methods. Developing a standard exercise to overcome a misunderstanding would be course improvement, but deciding, whether a certain pupil should work through that exercise would be an individual decision. Administrative regulation likewise is local in effect, whereas an improvement in a course is likely to be pertinent wherever the course is offered.

It was for the sake of course improvement that systematic evaluation was first introduced. When that famous muckraker Joseph Rice gave the same spelling test in a number of American schools, and so gave the first impetus to the educational testing movement, he was interested in evaluating a curriculum. Crusading against the extended spelling drills that then loomed large in the school schedule—"the spelling grind"—Rice collected evidence of their worthlessness so as to provoke curriculum revision. As the testing movement developed, however, it took on a different function.

# The Turning Tides

The greatest expansion of systematic achievement testing occurred in the 1920s. At that time, the content of any course was taken pretty much as established and beyond criticism save for small shifts of topical emphasis. At the administrator's direction, standard tests covering the curriculum were given to assess the efficiency of the teacher or the school system. Such administrative testing fell into disfavor when used injudiciously and heavyhandedly in the 1920s and 1930s. Administrators and accrediting agencies fell back upon descriptive features of the school program in judging adequacy. Instead of collecting direct evidence of educational impact, they judged schools in terms of size of budget, student-staff ratio, square feet of laboratory space, and the number of advanced credits accumulated by the teacher. This tide, it appears, is about to turn. On many university campuses, administrators wanting to know more about their product are installing "operations research offices." Testing directed toward quality control seems likely to increase in the lower schools as well, as is most forcefully indicated by the statewide testing recently ordered by the California legislature.

After 1930 or thereabouts, tests were given almost exclusively for judgments about individuals—to select students for advanced training, to assign marks within a class, and to diagnose individual competenses and deficiencies. For any such decisions, one wants precise and valid comparisons of one individual with other individuals or with a standard. Much of test theory and test technology has been concerned with making measurements precise. Important though precision is for most decisions about individuals, I shall argue that in evaluating courses we need not struggle to obtain precise scores for individuals.

While measurers have been well content with the devices used to make scores precise, they have been less complacent about validity. Prior to 1935, the pupil was examined mostly on factual knowledge and mastery of fundamental skills. Tyler's research and writings of that period developed awareness that higher mental processes are not evoked by simple factual tests, and that instruction that promotes factual knowledge may not promote—indeed, may interfere with—other more important educational outcomes. Tyler, Lindquist, and their students demonstrated that tests can be designed to measure such general educational outcomes as ability to comprehend scientific method. Whereas a student can prepare for a factual test only through a course of study that includes the facts tested, many different courses of study may promote the same general understandings and attitudes. In evaluating today's new curricula, it will clearly be important to appraise the student's general educational growth, which curriculum developers say is more important than mastery of the specific lessons presented. Note, for example, that the Biological Sciences Curriculum Study offers three courses with substantially different "subject matter" as alternative routes to much the same educational ends.

Although some instruments capable of measuring general outcomes were prepared during the 1930s, they were never very widely employed. The prevailing, philosophy of the curriculum, particularly among "progressives," called for developing a program to fit local requirements, capitalizing on the capacities and experiences of local pupils. The faith of the 1920s in a "standard" curriculum was replaced by a faith that the best learning experience would result from teacher-pupil planning in each classroom. Since each teacher or each class could choose different content and even different objectives, this philosophy left little place for standard testing.

# Tests as Training

Many evaluation specialists came to see test development as a strategy for training the teacher in service, so that the process of test making came to be valued more than the test—or the test data—that resulted. The following remarks by Bloom are representative of a whole school of thought.[2]

The criterion for determining the quality of a school and its educational functions would be the extent to which it achieves the objectives it has set for itself. . . . Our experiences suggest that unless the school has translated the objectives into specific and operational definitions, little is likely to be done about the objectives. They remain pious hopes and platitudes. . . . Participation of the teaching staff in selecting as well as constructing evaluation instruments has resulted in improved instruments on one hand and, on the other hand, it has resulted in clarifying the objectives of instruction and in making them real and meaningful to teachers. . . . When teachers have actively participated in defining objectives and in selecting or constructing evaluation instruments, they, return to the learning problems with great vigor and remarkable creativity. . . . Teachers who have become committed to a set of educational objectives which they thoroughly understand respond by developing a variety of learning experiences which are as diverse and as complex as the situation requires.

Thus, "evaluation" becomes a local and beneficial teacher-training activity. The benefit is attributed to thinking about what data to collect. Little is said about the actual use of test results; one has the impression that when test-making ends, the test itself is forgotten. Certainly there is little enthusiasm for refining tests so that they can be used in other schools, for to do so would be to rob those teachers of the benefits of working out their own objectives and instruments.

Bloom and Tyler describe both curriculum making and evaluation as integral parts of classroom instruction, which is necessarily decentralized. This outlook is far from that of "course improvement." The current national curriculum studies assume that curriculum making can be centralized. They prepare materials to be used in much the same way by teachers everywhere. It is assumed that having experts draft materials, and revising these after tryout, produces better instructional activities than the local teacher would be likely to devise. In this context, it seems wholly appropriate to have most tests prepared by a central staff and to have results returned to that staff to guide further course improvement.

When evaluation is carried out in the service of course improvement, the chief aim is to ascertain what effects the course has—that is, what changes it produces in pupils. This is not to inquire merely whether the course is effective or ineffective. Outcomes of instruction are multidimensional, and a satisfactory investigation will map out the effects of the course along these dimensions separately. To agglomerate many types of post-course performance into a single score is a mistake, because failure to achieve one objective is masked by success in another direction. Moreover, since a composite score embodies (and usually conceals) judgments about the importance of the various outcomes, only a report that treats the outcomes separately can be useful to educators who have different value hierarchies.

The greatest service evaluation can perform is to identify aspects of the course where revision is desirable. Those responsible for developing a course would like to present evidence that their course is effective. They are intrigued by the idea of having an "independent testing agency" render a judgment on their product. But to call in the evaluator only upon the completion of course development, to confirm what has been done, is to offer him a menial role and to make meager use of his services. To be influential in course improvement, evidence must become available midway in curriculum development, not in the home stretch, when the developer is naturally reluctant to tear open a supposedly finished body of materials and techniques. Evaluation, used to improve the course while it is still fluid, contributes more to improvement of education than evaluation used to appraise a product already placed on the market.

## Effects and Effectiveness

Insofar as possible, evaluation should be used to understand how the course produces its effects and what parameters influence its effectiveness. It is important to learn, for example, that the outcome of programmed instruction depends very much upon the attitude of the teacher; indeed, this may be more important than to learn that on the average such instruction produces slightly better or worse results than conventional instruction.

Hopefully, evaluation studies will go beyond reporting on this or that course and help us to understand educational learning. Such insight will, in the end, contribute to the development of all courses rather than just the course under test. In certain of the new curricula, there are data to suggest that aptitude measures correlate much less with end-of-course achievement than they do with achievement on early units (Ferris). This finding is not well confirmed, but it is highly significant if true. If it is true for the new curricula and only for them, it has one implication; if the same effect appears in traditional courses, it means something else. Either way, it provides food for thought for teachers, counselors, and theorists. Evaluation studies should generate knowledge about the nature of the abilities that constitute educational goals. Twenty years after the Eight-Year Study of the Progressive Education Association, its testing techniques are in good repute, but we still know very little about what these instruments measure. Consider "Application of Principles in Science." Is this in any sense a unitary ability? Or has the able student only mastered certain principles one by one? Is the ability demonstrated on a test of this sort more prognostic of any later achievement than is factual knowledge? Such questions ought to receive substantial attention, although to the makers of any one course they are of only peripheral interest.

The aim to compare one course with another should not dominate plans for evaluation. To be sure, decision makers have to choose between courses, and any evaluation report will be interpreted in part comparatively. But formally designed experiments, pitting one course against another, are rarely definitive enough to justify their cost. Differences between average test scores resulting from different courses are usually small relative to the wide differences among, and within classes taking the same course. At best, an experiment never does more than compare the present version of one course with the present version of another. A major effort to bring the losing contender nearer to perfection would be very likely to reverse the verdict of the experiment.

Any failure to equate the classes taking the competing courses will jeopardize the interpretation of an experiment—and such failures are almost inevitable. In testing a drug, we know that valid results cannot be obtained without a double-blind control in which the doses for half the subjects are inert placebos; the placebo and the drug look alike, so that neither doctor nor patient knows who is receiving medication. Without this control, the results are useless even when the state of the patient is checked by completely objective indices. In an educational experiment, it is difficult to keep pupils unaware that they are an experimental group. And it is quite impossible to neutralize the biases of the teacher as those of the doctor are neutralized in the double-blind design. It is thus never certain whether any observed advantage is attributable to the educational innovation as such, or to the greater energy that teachers and students put forth when a method is fresh and "experimental." Some have contended that any course, even the most excellent, loses much of its potency as soon as success enthrones it as "the traditional method."

# Weakness of Comparisons

Since group comparisons give equivocal results, I believe that a formal study should be designed primarily to determine the post-course performance of a well-described group with respect to many important objectives and side effects. Ours is a problem like that of the engineer examining a new automobile. He can set himself the task of defining its performance characteristics and its dependability. It would be merely distracting to put his question in the form, "Is this car better or worse than the competing brand?" Moreover, in an experiment where the treatments compared differ in a dozen respects, no understanding is gained from the fact that the experiment shows a numerical advantage in favor of the new course. No one knows which of the ingredients is responsible for the advantage. More analytic experiments are much more useful than field trials applying markedly dissimilar treatments to different groups. Small-scale, well-controlled studies can profitably be used to compare alternative versions of the same course; in such a study, the differences between treatments are few enough and well enough defined that the results have explanatory value.

The three purposes—course improvement, decisions about individuals, and administrative regulation—call for measurement procedures having, somewhat different qualities. When a test will be used to make an administrative judgment on the individual teacher, it is necessary to measure thoroughly and with conspicuous fairness; such testing if it is to cover more than one outcome, becomes extremely time consuming. In judging a course, however, one can make satisfactory interpretations from data collected on a sampling basis, with no pretence of measuring thoroughly the accomplishments of any one class. A similar point is to be made about testing, for decisions about individuals. A test of individuals must be conspicuously fair and extensive enough to provide a dependable score for each person. But if the performance will not influence the fate of the individual, we can ask him to perform tasks for which the course has not directly prepared him, and we can use techniques that would be prohibitively expensive if applied in a manner thorough enough to measure each person reliably.

Evaluation is too often visualized as the administration of a formal test, an hour or so in duration, at the close of a course. But there are many other methods for examining pupil performance, and pupil attainment is not the only basis for appraising a course.

It is quite appropriate to ask scholars whether the statements made in the course are consistent with the best contemporary knowledge. This is a sound and even a necessary procedure. One may go on to evaluate the pedagogy of the new course by soliciting opinions, but here there is considerable hazard. If the opinions are based on some preconception about teaching method, the findings will be controversial and very probably misleading. There are no theories of pedagogy so well established that one can say, without tryout, what will prove educative.

# Systematic Observation

One can accept the need for a pragmatic test of the curriculum and still employ opinions as a source of evidence. During the tryout stages of curriculum making, one relies heavily on the teachers' reports of pupil accomplishment—"Here they had trouble"; "This they found dull"; "Here they needed only half as many exercises as were provided," etc. This is behavior observation even though unsystematic, and it is of great value. The reason for shifting to systematic observation is that this is more impartial, more public, and sometimes more penetrating. While I bow to the historian or mathematician as a judge of the technical soundness of course content, I do not agree that the experienced history or mathematics teacher who tries out a course gives the best possible judgment on its effectiveness. Scholars have too often deluded themselves about their effectiveness as teachers— particularly, have they too often accepted parroting of words as evidence of insight—for their unaided judgment to be trusted. Systematic observation is costly, and introduces some delay between the moment of teaching and the feedback of results. Hence, systematic observation will never be the curriculum developer's sole source of evidence. Systematic data collection becomes profitable in the intermediate stages of curriculum development, after the more obvious bugs in early drafts have been dealt with.

The approaches to evaluation include process studies, proficiency measures, attitude measures, and follow-up studies. A process study is concerned with events taking place in the classroom, proficiency and attitude measures with chances observed in pupils, and follow-up studies with the later careers of those who participated in the course.

The follow-up study comes closest to observing ultimate educational contributions, but the completion of such a study is so far removed in time from the initial instruction that it is of minor value in improving the course or explaining its effects. The follow-up study differs strikingly from the other types of evaluation study in one respect. I have already expressed the view that evaluation should be primarily concerned with the effects of the course under study rather than with comparisons of courses. That is to say, I would emphasize departures of attained results from the ideal, differences in apparent effectiveness of different parts of the course, and differences from item to item; all these suggest places where the course could be strengthened. But this view cannot be applied to the follow-up study, which appraises effects of the course as a whole and which has very little meaning unless outcomes can be compared with some sort of base rate. Suppose we find that 65 percent of the boys graduating from an experimental curriculum enroll as scientific and technical majors in college. We cannot judge whether this is a high or low figure save by comparing it with the rate among boys who have not had the course. In a follow-up study, it is necessary to obtain data on a control group equated at least crudely to the experimental cases on the obvious demographic variables.

Despite the fact that such groups are hard to equate and that follow-up data do not tell much about how to improve the course, such studies should take place in research on the new curricula, whose national samples provide unusual opportunity for follow-up that can shed light on important questions. One obvious type of follow-up study traces the student's success in a college course founded upon the high-school course. One may examine the student's grades or ask him what topics in the college course he found himself poorly prepared for. It is hoped that some of the new science and mathematics courses will arouse greater interest than usual among girls; whether this hope is well founded can be checked by finding out what majors and what electives these ex-students pursue in college. Career choices likewise merit attention. Some proponents of the new curricula would like to see a greater flow of talent into basic science as distinct from technology, whereas others would regard this as potentially disastrous; but no one would regard facts about this flow as lacking significance.

# Measuring Meanings

Attitudes are prominent among the outcomes with which course developers are concerned. Attitudes are meanings or beliefs, not mere expressions of approval or disapproval. One's attitude toward science includes ideas about the matters on which a scientist can be an authority, about the benefits to be obtained from moon shots and studies of monkey mothers, and about depletion of natural resources. Equally important is the match between self-concept and concept of the field: What roles does science offer a person like me? Would I want to marry a scientist? And so on. Each learning activity also contributes to attitudes that reach far beyond any one subject, such as the pupil's sense of his own competence and desire to learn.

Attitudes can be measured in many ways; the choices revealed in follow-up studies, for example, are pertinent evidence. But measurement usually takes the form of direct or indirect questioning interviews, questionnaires, and the like are quite valuable when not trusted blindly. Certainly, we should take seriously any undesirable opinion expressed by a substantial proportion of the graduates of a course (e.g., the belief that the scientist speaks with peculiar authority on political and ethical questions, or the belief that mathematics is a finished subject rather than a field for current investigation).

Attitude questionnaires have been much criticized because they are subject to distortion, especially where the student hopes to gain by being less than frank. Particularly if the questions are asked in a context far removed from the experimental course, the returns are likely to be trustworthy. Thus, a general questionnaire administered through homerooms (or required English courses) may include questions about liking for various subjects and activities; these same questions administered by the mathematics teacher would give much less trustworthy data on attitude toward mathematics. While students may give reports more favorable than their true beliefs, this distortion is not likely to be greater one year than another, or greater among students who take an experimental course than among those who do not. In group averages, many distortions balance out. But questionnaires insufficiently valid for individual testing can be used in evaluating curricula, both because the student has little motive to distort and because the evaluator is comparing averages rather than individuals.

# Process and Proficiency

For measuring proficiency, techniques are likewise varied. Standardized tests are useful. But for course evaluation it makes sense to assign *different* questions to different students. Giving each student in a population of 500 the same test of 50 questions will provide far less information to the course developer than drawing, for each student 50 questions from a pool of, say, 700. The latter plan determines the mean success of about 75 representative students on every one of the 700 items; the former reports on only 50 items (Lord). Essay tests and open-ended questions, generally too expensive to use for routine evaluation, can profitably be employed to appraise certain abilities. One can go further and observe individuals or groups as they attack a research problem in the laboratory or work through some other complex problem. Since it is necessary to test only a representative sample of pupils, costs are not as serious a consideration as in routine testing. Additional aspects of proficiency testing will be considered below.

Process measures have especial value in showing how a course can be improved because they examine what happens during instruction. In the development of programmed instructional materials, for example, records are collected showing how many pupils miss each item presented; any piling up of errors implies a need for better explanation or a more gradual approach to a difficult topic. Immediately after showing a teaching film, one can interview students, perhaps asking them to describe a still photograph taken from the film. Misleading presentations, ideas given insufficient emphasis, and matters left unclear will be identified by such methods. Similar interviews can disclose what pupils take away from a laboratory activity or a discussion. A process study may turn attention to what the teacher does in the classroom. In those curricula that allow choice of topics, for example, it is worthwhile to find out which topics are chosen and how much time is allotted to each. A log of class activities (preferably recorded by a pupil rather than the teacher) will show which of the techniques suggested in a summer institute are actually adopted and which form "part of the new course" only in the developer's fantasies.

I have indicated that I consider item data to be more important than test scores. The total score may give confidence in a curriculum or give rise to discouragement, but it tells very little about how to produce further improvement. And, as Ferris has noted, such scores are quite likely to be mis- or overinterpreted. The score on a single item, or on a problem that demands several responses in succession, is more likely than the test score to suggest how to alter the presentation. When we accept item scores as useful, we need no longer think of evaluation as a one-shot, end-of-year operation. Proficiency can be measured at any moment, with particular interest attaching to those items most related to the recent lessons. Other items calling for general abilities can profitably be administered repeatedly during the course (perhaps to different random samples of pupils) so that we can begin to learn when and from what experiences change in these abilities comes.

In course evaluation, we need not be much concerned about making measuring instruments fit the curriculum. However startling this declaration may seem, and however contrary to the principles of evaluation for other purposes, this must be our position if we want to know what changes a course produces in the pupil.

An ideal evaluation would include measures of all the types of proficiency that might reasonably be desired in the area in question, not just the selected outcomes to which this curriculum directs substantial attention. If you wish only to know how well a curriculum is achieving its objectives, you fit the test to the curriculum; but if you wish to know how well the curriculum is serving the national interest, you measure all outcomes that might be worth striving for. One of the new mathematics courses may disavow any attempt to teach numerical trigonometry, and indeed, might discard nearly all computational work. It is still perfectly reasonable to ask how well graduates of the course can compute and can solve right triangles. Even if the course developers went so far as to contend that computational skill is no proper objective of secondary instruction, they will encounter educators and laymen who do not share their view. If it can be shown that students who come through the new course are fairly proficient in computation despite the lack of direct teaching, the doubters will be reassured. If not, the evidence makes clear how much is being sacrificed. Similarly, when the biologists offer alternative courses emphasizing microbiology and ecology, it is fair to ask how well the graduate of one course can understand issues treated in the other. Ideal evaluation in mathematics will collect evidence on all the abilities toward which a mathematics course might reasonably aim; likewise in biology, English, or any other subject.

Ferris states that the ACS Chemistry Test, however well constructed, is inadequate for evaluating the new CBA and CHEM programs because it does not cover their objectives. One can agree with this without regarding the ACS test as inappropriate to use with these courses. It is important that this test not stand *alone,* as the sole evaluation device. It will tell us something worth knowing namely, just how much "conventional" knowledge the new curriculum does or does not provide. The curriculum developers deliberately planned to sacrifice some of the conventional attainments and have nothing to fear from this measurement, competently interpreted (particularly if data are examined item by item).

# Security, Content, Terms

The demand that tests be closely matched to the aims of a course reflects awareness that examinations of the usual sort "determine what is taught." If questions are known in advance, students give more attention to learning their answers than to learning other aspects of the course. This is not necessarily detrimental. Wherever it is critically important to master certain content, the knowledge that it will be tested produces a desirable concentration of effort. On the other hand, learning the answer to a set question is by no means the same as acquiring understanding of whatever topic that question represents. There is, therefore, a possible advantage in using "secure" tests for course evaluation. Security is achieved only at a price: One must prepare new tests each year and consequently cannot make before-and-after comparisons with the same items. One would hope that the use of different items with different students, and the fact that there is less incentive to coach when no judgment is to be passed on the pupils and the teachers, would make security a less critical problem.

The distinction between factual tests and tests of higher mental processes, as elaborated for example in the *Taxonomy of Educational Objectives,* is of some value in planning tests, although classifying items as measures of knowledge, application, original problem solving, etc., is difficult and often impossible. Whether a given response represents rote recall or reasoning depends upon how the pupil has been taught, not solely upon the question asked. One may, for example, describe a biological environment and ask for predictions regarding the effect of a certain intervention. Students who have never dealt with ecological data will succeed or fail according to their general ability to reason about complex events; those who have studied ecological biology will be more likely to succeed, reasoning from specific principles; and those who have lived in such an ecology or read about it may answer successfully on the basis of memory. We rarely, therefore, will want to test whether a student "knows" or "does not know" certain material. Knowledge is a matter of degree. Two persons may be acquainted with the same facts or principles, but one will be more expert in his understanding, better able to cope with inconsistent data, irrelevant sources of confusion, and apparent exceptions to the principle. To measure intellectual competence is to measure depth, connectedness, and applicability of knowledge.

Too often, test questions are course-specific, stated in such a way that only the person who has been specifically taught to understand what is being asked for can answer the question. Such questions can usually be identified by their use of conventions. Some conventions are commonplace, and we can assume that all the pupils we test will know them. But a biology test that describes a metabolic process with the aid of the $\rightleftharpoons$ symbol presents difficulties for students who can think through the scientific question about equilibrium but are unfamiliar with the symbol. A trigonometry problem that requires use of a trigonometric table is unreasonable, unless we want to test familiarity with the conventional names of functions. The same problem in numerical trigonometry can be cast in a form clear to the average pupil *entering* high school; if necessary, the tables of functions can be presented along with a comprehensible explanation. So stated, the problem becomes course-independent. It is fair to ask whether graduates of the experimental course can solve such problems, not previously encountered, whereas it is pointless to ask whether they can answer questions whose language is strange to them. To be sure, knowledge of certain terminology is a significant objective of instruction, but for course evaluation, testing of terminology should very likely be separated from testing, of other understandings. To appraise understanding, of processes and relations, the fair question is one comprehensible to a pupil who has not taken the course. This is not to say that he should know the answer or the procedure to follow in attaining the answer, but he should understand what he is being asked. Such course independent questions can be used as standard instruments to investigate any instructional program.

Pupils who have not studied a topic will usually be less facile than those who have studied it. Graduates of my hypothetical mathematics course will take longer to solve trigonometry problems than will those who have studied trig. But speed and power should not be confused; in intellectual studies, power is almost always of greater importance. If the course equips the pupil to deal correctly, even though haltingly, with a topic not studied, we can expect him to develop facility later when that topic comes before him frequently.

# Two Types of Transfer

The chief objective in many of the new curricula seems to be to develop aptitude for mastering new materials in the field. A biology course cannot cover all valuable biological content, but it may reasonably aspire to equip the pupil to understand descriptions of unfamiliar organisms, to comprehend a new theory and the reasoning behind it, and to plan an experiment to test a new hypothesis. This is transfer of learning. It has been insufficiently recognized that there are two types of transfer. The two types shade into one another, being arranged on a continuum of immediacy of effect; we can label the more immediate pole *applicational transfer,* and speak of slower-acting effects as *gains in aptitude* (Ferguson, 1954).

Nearly all educational research on transfer has tested immediate performance on a partly new task. We teach pupils to solve equations in $x$, and include in the test equations stated in $a$ or $z$. We teach the principles of ecological balance by referring to forests, and as a transfer test, ask what effect pollution will have on the population of a lake. We describe an experiment not presented in the text, and ask the student to discuss possible interpretations and needed controls. Any of these tests can be administered in a short time. But the more significant type of transfer may be the increased ability to learn in a particular field. There is very likely a considerable difference between the ability to draw conclusions from a neatly finished experiment, and the ability to tease insight out of the disorderly and inconsistent observations that come with continuous laboratory work on a problem. The student who masters a good biology course may become better able to comprehend certain types of theory and data, so that he gains more from a subsequent year of study in ethnology; we do not measure this gain by testing his understanding of short passages in ethnology. There has rarely been an appraisal of ability to work through a problem situation or a complex body of knowledge over a period of days or months. Despite the practical difficulties that attend an attempt to measure the effect of a course on a person's subsequent learning, such "learning to learn" is so important that a serious effort should be made to detect such effects and to understand how they may be fostered.

The techniques of programmed instruction may be adapted to appraise learning ability. One may, for example, test the student's rate of mastery of a self-contained, programmed unit on the physics of heat or some other topic not studied. If the program is truly self-contained, every student can master it, but the one with greater scientific comprehension will hopefully make fewer errors and progress faster. The program can be prepared in several logically complete versions, ranging from one with very small "steps" to one with minimal internal redundancy, on the hypothesis that the better educated student could cope with the less redundant program. Moreover, he might prefer its greater elegance.

# Toward Deeper Understanding

Old habits of thought and long established techniques are poor guides to the evaluation required for course improvement. Traditionally, educational measurement has been chiefly concerned with producing fair and precise scores for comparing individuals. Educational experimentation has been concerned with comparing score averages of competing courses. But course evaluation calls for description of outcomes. This description should be made on the broadest possible scale, even at the sacrifice of superficial fairness and precision.

Course evaluation should ascertain what changes a course produces and should identify aspects of the course that need revision. The outcomes observed should include general outcomes ranging far beyond the content of the curriculum itself—attitudes, career choices, general understandings and intellectual powers, and aptitude for further learning in the field. Analysis of performance or single items or types of problems is more informative than analysis of composite scores. It is not necessary or desirable to give the same test to all pupils; rather, as many questions as possible should be given, each to a different, moderate sized sample of pupils. Costly techniques, such as interviews and essay tests, can profitably be applied to samples of pupils, whereas testing everyone would be out of the question.

Asking, the right questions about educational outcomes can do much to improve educational effectiveness. Even if the right data are collected, however, evaluation will have contributed too little if it only places a seal of approval on certain courses and casts others into disfavor. Evaluation is a fundamental part of curriculum development, not an appendage. Its job is to collect facts the course developer can and will use to do a better job, and facts from which a deeper understanding of the educational process will emerge.

# Notes

1. My comments on these questions, and on certain more significant questions that *should* have been raised, have been greatly clarified by the reactions of several of these directors and of my colleagues in evaluation to a draft of this paper. J. Thomas Hastings and Robert Heath have been especially helpful. What I voice, however, are my personal views, deliberately more provocative than "authoritative."—LJC

2. Elsewhere, Bloom's paper discusses evaluation for the new curricula. Attention may also be drawn to Tyler's highly pertinent paper.

# References

Bloom, B. S. Quality control in education. *Tomorrow's teaching*. Oklahoma City: Frontiers of Science Foundation, 1961, pp. 54–61.

Bloom, B. S. (Ed.). *Taxonomy of educational objectives*. New York: Longmans, Green, 1956.

Ferguson, G. A. On learning and human ability. *Canadian Journal of Pscyhology*, 1954, 8, 95–112.

Ferris, F. L. Jr. Testing in the new curriculums: Numerology, tyranny, or common sense? *School Review*, 1962, 70, 112–131.

Lord, F. M. Estimating norms by item-sampling. *Educational and Psychological Measurement*, 1962, 22, 259–268.

Tyler, R. W. The functions of measurement in improving instruction. In E. F. Lindquist (ed.) *Educational measurement*. Washington, D.C.: Amer. Council Educ., 1951. pp. 47–67.

## Part 3

# Delivery Options

**Richard E. Clark (1983):**
*Reconsidering Research on Learning from Media*

**Robert B. Kozma (1991):**
*Learning with Media*

**David Hawkridge (1990):**
*Who Needs Computers in Schools, and Why?*

**Malcolm L. Fleming (1987):**
*Displays and Communication*

## Media and Technology

Just after World War II, the field now known as educational, or instructional, technology emphasized audiovisual media as primary vehicles for improving instruction. Today, media continue to be a major part of design and development systems. Without delivery mechanisms, instructional technology would not exist.

At the same time, the danger of overemphasis on media and technology has been expressed by collegial critics such as Richard Clark. His review of literature here is an attempt to present a critical analysis of media studies using standard criteria for educational research. He sheds the all-too-typical advocacy approach that had been evident among practitioners and concludes "that there are no learning benefits to be gained from employing any specific medium to deliver instruction." This article has generated extensive debates within the profession. Clark continues to hold to his position in an often-discussed paper, "Media Will Never Influence Learning" (1994).

One of the major impacts of Clark's strong position is further reassessment of media's role in teaching and learning by instructional technologists. Robert Kozma wrote a quasi-rejoinder to Clark in his 1991 article in the Review of Educational Research, the same journal that published Clark's original article. It is an update of media research using a medium-by-medium approach. In his concluding section, he accuses Clark of creating an artificial analysis by separating media from methods of use. Kozma advocates the use of design principles as an appropriate context for analyzing media research. Use of these principles, according to Kozma, calls for a modification of Clark's position. Kozma is constructively critical of Clark's position and offers reasonable alternatives to it.

Kozma's article reviews some of the research on computer-based instruction, especially those studies that deal with mental representations and cognitive processes. The computer, in the settings where it is used, is not so much a medium but an amalgam of multimedia presentation using cognitive designs that are aimed at the improvement of learning.

The "debate" continued after the publication of these two articles. In crowded sessions at the annual AECT meeting in 1994 and in the pages of Educational Technology Research and Development (Clark, 1994a, 1994b; Kozma, 1994a, 1994b). Other articles (Reiser, Shrock, and Morrison) in the special issue of ETR&D (1994a) and in the follow-up issue (Tennyson, 1994b) continued to analyze each position and drew further questions regarding the influence of media on learning. The professional instructional technologist should be familiar with the arguments and ready to take a position.

A more fundamental question is raised by Hawkridge: "Who Needs Computers, and Why?" The article responds directly to the question by listing a series of rationales that cover the spectrum of computer uses in education. He contends that this question ought to be asked before adopting and setting priorities for the use of computers in schools and universities. The article is based on computer use in several developing countries of the world, but the principles are applicable anywhere.

The popular rationales for using computers in schools are: social, vocational, pedagogic, and catalytic—all of which are described in this article. Beyond the popular rationales are less obvious ones: information technology; industry rationale; the cost-effectiveness rationale; and the special-needs rationale. These less obvious but very real rationales are presented with a caustic twist. Hawkridge presents a balanced picture with both advantages and criticisms of each rationale. After his probing questions, he ends with a note of optimism about the future of computers in education.

Clark, Kozma, and Hawkridge talk about research findings. Fleming reports on research in detail. His article focuses on the learner and uses specific findings from the literature regarding media displays. Special emphasis is given to attention, perception, learning, concept formation, and other cognitive processes. His writing offers substantive principles about stimulation, order, strategy, and meaning that can be used by the designer of learning materials. This article is an overview of the same principles that originally appeared in a more comprehensive version (Fleming and Levie, 1978).

# References

Clark, R. E. 1994a. Media will never influence learning. *Educational Technology Research and Development* 42, no. 2:21–29.

———. 1994b. Media and method. *Educational Technology Research and Development* 42, no. 3:7–10.

Fleming, M., and W. H. Levie. 1978. *Instructional message design: principles from the behavioral sciences*. Englewood, N.J.: Educational Technology Publications.

Kozma, R. B. 1994a. Will media influence learning? Reframing the debate. *Educational Technology Research and Development* 42, no. 2:7–19.

———. 1994b. A reply: Media and methods. *Educational Technology Research and Development* 42, no. 3:11–14.

Morrison, G. 1994. The media effects question: "Unresolvable" or asking the right question? *Educational Technology Research and Development* 42, no 2:41–44.

Reiser, R. 1994. Clark's invitation to the dance: An instructional designers response. *Educational Technology Research and Development* 42, no. 2:45–48.

Shrock, S. 1994. The media influence debate: Read the fine print, but don't lose sight of the big picture. *Educational Technology Research and Development* 42, no. 2:49–53.

# Methods and Techniques

## John M. Keller (1987): *Development and Use of the ARCS Model of Motivational Design*

## Otto Peters (1983): *Distance Teaching and Industrial Production: A Comparative Interpretation in Outline*

Methods and techniques can also be called "instructional strategies." These are the procedures and protocols that are part of the design process; they differ from design and development functions in that they offer enhancements or alternatives to the basic designs. For example, the Keller article on motivation suggests specific actions that can be taken to improve teaching and learning. The Peters article suggests an alternative approach to teaching and learning that we call "distance education." Both of these articles are enhancements of the basic ISD process or alternative delivery systems.

Many other enhancements or alternatives would be candidates for this section. Feedback and problem solving are examples of cognitive enhancements. Simulations, games, hands-on activities, debates, and discovery learning are examples of methods or techniques that vary the process. Motivation was selected as an appropriate example here because it is so often neglected in the design process; distance education was selected because it takes an entirely different approach to teaching and learning.

Keller's ARCS model has become well known and widely used as an effective and practical approach to stimulate and involve individuals in the learning process. Keller asked that the original title be changed from "instructional design" to "motivational design." The elements of the model follow the ARCS mnemonic: Attention; Relevance; Confidence, and Satisfaction. Keller offers specific strategies for reaching each of these conditions in the design of instruction. His work is based on research studies that confirm the value of the ARCS construct (for example, Visser and Keller, 1990).

The current high interest in distance education is largely based on the panoply of delivery systems that emerged in the last three decades of the twentieth century. As more technological systems appeared that promised "anytime, anyplace" learning opportunities and provided opportunities for dialog between instructors and students, the revival of an earlier approach to studying at a distance, correspondence instruction, occurred and was updated. One of the first educators to envision the potential of the distance learning process in the present time was Otto Peters.

Otto Peters, a distance education pioneer in Germany, has written most of his professional contributions in German. The article here was revised and translated from a 1965 paper that introduced the concept of distance learning as "an industrial process." The publication of his chapter in "Theoretical Aspects of Correspondence Instruction" (Mackenzie and Christensen, 1971) confirmed that Peters was an early leader in this field. He credits Charles Wedemeyer (1981) from the University of Wisconsin with major contributions to the growth of distance education. Peters' fundamental ideas are so basic to the current interest in distance learning that his early paper is included in this volume.

Peters introduced the concept of production along the lines of an industrial process as the basic structure of distance education. He has called distance education the most industrialized form of teaching and learning. This mechanistic-sounding term has led to controversy among educators, who bristle at the thought of education as a production line. Yet Peters has remained firm in his defense of the concept that has led to use of the term, "fordism"—an obvious connection to the automobile production line introduced by Henry Ford in the 1920s. Peters' article presents his initial rationale for use of the concept. Readers should notice that he emphasizes the most industrialized form of teaching and learning and uses this interpretation as a description of distance education and not as an advocacy statement.

Peters continues to write and publish. His most recent book (1998) is a collection of his major papers in which he elaborates upon the industrial theme and other matters pertaining to the definition and conduct of distance education. Most of the works are translated from the original German.

# References

Peters, O. 1998. *Learning and teaching in distance education.* London: Kogan Page.

Visser, J., and J. M. Keller. 1990. The clinical use of motivational messages: An inquiry into the validity of the ARCS model of motivational design. *Instructional Science* 19, no. 6:467–500.

Wedemeyer, C. 1981. *Learning at the back door: Reflections on non-traditional learning in the lifespan.* Madison, Wis.: The University of Wisconsin Press.

# 9

# Reconsidering Research on Learning from Media

Richard E. Clark

*Recent meta-analyses and other studies of media's influence on learning are reviewed. Consistent evidence is found for the generalization that there are no learning benefits to be gained from employing any specific medium to deliver instruction. Research showing performance or timesaving gains from one or another medium are shown to be vulnerable to compelling rival hypotheses concerning the uncontrolled effects of instructional method and novelty. Problems with current media attribute and symbol system theories are described and suggestions made for more promising research directions.*

Studies of the influence of media on learning have been a fixed feature of educational research since Thorndike (1912) recommended pictures as a laborsaving device in instruction. Most of this research is buttressed by the hope that learning will be enhanced with the proper mix of medium, student, subject matter content, and learning task. A typical study compares the relative achievement of groups who have received similar subject matter from different media. This research has led to so-called "media selection" schemes or models (e.g., Reiser & Gagné, 1982). These models generally promise to incorporate existing research and practice into procedures for selecting the best medium or mix of media to deliver instruction. Most of these models base many of their prescriptions on presumed learning benefits from media (Jamison, Suppes, & Welles, 1974).

However, this article will argue that most current summaries and meta-analyses of media comparison studies clearly suggest that media do not influence learning under any conditions. Even in the few cases where dramatic changes in achievement or ability have followed the introduction of a medium, as was the case with television in El Salvador (Schramm, 1977), it was not the medium that caused the change but rather a curricular reform that accompanied the change. The best current evidence is that media are mere vehicles that deliver instruction but do not influence student achievement any more than the truck that delivers our groceries causes changes in our nutrition. Basically, the choice of vehicle might influence the cost or extent of distributing instruction, but only the content of the vehicle can influence achievement.

Although research often shows a slight learning advantage for newer media over more conventional instructional vehicles, this advantage will be shown to be vulnerable to compelling rival hypotheses. Among these rival explanations is evidence of artifact and confounding in existing studies, as well as biased editorial decisions that may favor research showing larger effect sizes for newer media. After summarizing evidence from current meta-analyses of media research, I will discuss the advantages and problems with current "media attribute" and "symbol system" theories and will conclude by suggesting tentative solutions to past problems and future directions for research involving media.

# Media Comparison Studies

In the 1960s, Lumsdaine (1963) and others (e.g., Mielke, 1968) argued that gross media comparison and selection studies might not pay off. They implied that media, when viewed as collections of mechanical instruments, such as television and computers, were sample delivery devices. Nevertheless, earlier reviewers also held the door open to learning effects from media by attributing much of the lack of significance in previous research to poor design and lack of adequate models or theory.

Lumsdaine (1963) dealt primarily with adequate studies that had used defensible methodology, and had found significant differences between treatments. With the benefit of hindsight, it is not surprising that most of the studies he selected for review employed media as simple vehicles for instructional methods, such as text organization, size of step in programming, cueing, repeated exposures, and prompting. These studies compared the effects of, for example, different step size in programmed instruction via television. Step size (and other methods), not television (or other media), was the focus of these studies; this is an example of what Salomon and Clark (1977) called research with media. In these studies, media are mere conveyances for the treatments being examined and are not the focus of the study, although the results are often mistakenly interpreted as suggesting benefits for various media. An example of instructional research with media would be a study that contrasted a logically organized audiotutorial lesson on photosynthesis with a randomly sequenced presentation of the same frames (cf. Clark & Snow, 1975; Salomon & Clark, 1977, for a review of similar studies). Perhaps as a result of this confusion, Lumsdaine (1963) reached few conclusions beyond the suggestion that media might reduce the cost of instruction when many students are served because "the cost of perfecting it can be prorated in terms of a denominator representing thousands of students" (p. 670).

A decade later, Glaser and Cooley (1973) and Levie and Dickie (1973) were cautious about media comparison studies, many of which apparently were still being conducted. Glaser and Cooley (1973) recommended using any acceptable medium as "a vehicle for making available to schools what psychologists have learned about learning" (p. 855). Levie and Dickie (1973) noted that most media comparison studies to that date had been fruitless and suggested that learning objectives can be attained through "instruction presented by any of a variety of different media" (p. 859). At that time, televised education was still a lively topic, and studies of computerized instruction were just beginning to appear.

During the past decade, television research seems to have diminished considerably, but computer-learning studies are now popular. This current research either belongs to the familiar but generally fruitless media comparison approach or focuses on the contents or methods being presented via different media (e.g., science teaching via computers). Generally, each new medium seems to attract its own set of advocates who make claims for improved learning and stimulate research questions that are similar to those asked about the previously popular medium. Most of the radio research approaches suggested in the 1950s (e.g., Hovland, Lumsdaine, & Sheffield, 1949) were similar to those employed by the television movement of the 1960s (e.g., Schramm, 1977) and to the more recent reports of the computer-assisted instruction studies of the 1970s and 1980s (e.g., Dixon & Judd, 1977). It seems that similar research questions have resulted in similar and ambiguous data. Media comparison studies, regardless of the media employed, tend to result in "no significant difference" conclusions (Mielke, 1968). These findings were incorrectly offered as evidence that different media were "equally effective" as conventional means in promoting learning. No significant difference results simply suggest that changes in the outcome scores (e.g., learning) did not result from any systematic differences in the treatments compared.

Occasionally, a study would find evidence for one or another medium. When this happens, Mielke (1968) has suggested that the active ingredient might be some uncontrolled aspect of the content or instructional strategy rather than the medium. When we investigate these positive studies, we find that the treatments are confounded; the evidence for this confounding may be found in the current meta-analyses of media comparison studies. The next section argues that the uncontrolled effects of novelty and instructional method account for the existing evidence for the effects of various media on learning gains.

# Reviews and Meta-Analyses of Media Research

One of the most interesting trends in the past decade has been a significant increase in the number of excellent reviews and meta-analyses of research comparing the learning advantage of various media. The results of these overviews of past comparison studies seem to be reasonably unambiguous and unanimous. Taken together, they provide strong evidence that media comparison studies that find causal connections between media and achievement are confounded.

## *Size of Effect of Media Treatments*

A recent series of meta-analyses of media comparison studies have been conducted by James Kulik and his colleagues at the University of Michigan (Cohen, Ebling, & Kulik, 1981; C. Kulik, Kulik, & Cohen, 1980; J. Kulik, Bangert, & Williams, 1983; J. Kulik, Kulik, & Cohen, 1979). These reviews employ the relatively new technology of meta-analysis (Glass, 1976), which provides more precise estimates of the effect size of various media treatments than were possible a few years ago. Previous reviews dealing primarily with "box score" sums of significant findings for media versus conventional instructional delivery were sometimes misleading. Effect-size estimates often were expressed in portions of standard score advantages for one or another type of treatment. This discussion will express effects in one of two ways: a) the number of standard deviations separating experimental and control groups, and b) as improvements in percentile scores on a final examination.

## Box Scores versus Effect Size

An illustration of the advantage of meta-analytical effect-size descriptions of past research over "box scores" is available in a recent review of Postlethwaite's audiotutorial instruction studies (J. Kulik, Kulik, & Cohen, 1979). The authors found 42 adequate studies, of which 29 favored audiotutorial instruction and only 13 favored conventional instruction. Of those 42, only 15 reported significant differences, but 11 of the 15 favored audiotutorial and only 4 favored conventional instruction. This type of box score analysis would strongly favor the learning benefits of the audiotutorial approach over more conventional means, whereas effect-size estimates of this data show only .2 standard deviations differences in the final exam scores of audiotutorial and conventional treatments. Kulik and his colleagues reported that this difference was equivalent to approximately 1.6 points on a 100-point final examination. This small effect is not instructionally significant and could easily be caused by confounding.

The most common sources of confounding in media research seem to be the uncontrolled effects of a) instructional method or content differences between treatments that are compared, and b) a novelty effect for newer media, which tends to disappear over time.

## Uncontrolled Method and Content Effects

In effect-size analyses, all adequate studies are surveyed. They involve a great variety of subject matter content, learning task types, and grade levels. The most common result of this type of survey is a small and positive effect for newer media over more conventional instructional delivery devices. When studies are subjected to meta-analysis, however, our first source of rival hypotheses, medium and method confusion, shows up.

The positive effect for media more or less disappears when the same instructor produces all treatments (C. Kulik, Kulik, & Cohen, 1980). Different teams of instructional designers or different teachers probably give different content and instructional methods to the treatments that are compared. If this is the case, we do not know whether to attribute the advantage to the medium or to the differences between content and method and the media being compared. If the effect for media tends to disappear when the same instructor or team designs contrasting treatments, however, we have reason to believe that the lack of difference is caused by greater control of nonmedium variables. It was Mielke (1968) who reminded us that, when examining the effects of different media, only the media being compared can be different; all other aspects of the treatments, including the subject matter content and method of instruction, must be identical.

# Meta-Analytic Evidence for Method and Content Confounding

In meta-analyses of college-level computerized versus conventional courses, an effect size of .51 results when different faculty teach the compared course (C. Kulik, Kulik, & Cohen, 1980). This effect reduces to .13 when one instructor plans and teaches both experimental and control courses. Presumably, the weak but positive finding for college use of computers over conventional media is a result of systematic but uncontrolled differences in content and/or method, contributed unintentionally by different teachers or designers.

## Time Savings with Computers

Another instance of this artifact may be found in studies that demonstrate considerable time savings generated by certain media. Comparisons of computer and conventional instruction often show 30 to 50 percent reductions in time to complete lessons for the computer groups (C. Kulik, Kulik, & Cohen, 1980; Kulik, Bangert, & Williams, 1983). A plausible rival hypothesis here is the possible effects of the greater effort invested in newer media programs than in conventional presentations of the same material. Comparing this increased effort invested in computer instruction to that afforded conventional instruction might be likened to sponsoring a race between a precision-engineered racer and the family car. The difference in effort presumably involves more instructional design and development, which results in more effective instructional methods for the students in computer treatments. Presumably, the students in other treatments would fare as well if given the advantage of this additional design effort, which produces more effective presentations requiring less time to complete.

## Exchanging Method for Media in Instructional Research

There is evidence in these meta-analyses that the method of instruction leads more directly and powerfully to learning. Glaser (1976) defines instructional methods as "the conditions which can be implemented to foster the acquisition of competence" (p. 1). Variables such as instructional methods appear to foster learning, not media. For example, instructional programs such as the Keller (1968) personalized system of instruction (PSI) and programmed instruction (PI) contain methods that seek to add structure, shorter steps, reduced verbal loads, and self-pacing to lessons. Each, however, is typically associated with a different medium. The PSI (Keller plan) approach is usually presented by text, and PI is often the preferred approach of those who design computer-assisted instruction. When studies of PI via text and via computer-assisted instruction are compared for their effect size, they are similar. Both seem to show about a .2 standard deviation final examination advantage over conventional instruction (C. Kulik, Kulik, & Cohen, 1980). A compelling hypothesis to explain this similarity might be that most computerized instruction is merely the presentation of PI or PSI via a computer.

When computer and PI effects are compared with the use of visuals in televised or audiotutorial laboratories, the PI and computer studies show about a 30 percent larger effect size. The largest effect size, however, is reserved for the PSI approach. The description of this instructional program tends to focus on its essential methods rather than on a medium. Perhaps as a result, it typically results in a .5 standard deviation effect size when compared with conventional, computer, PI, or visual instruction (C. Kulik, Kulik, & Cohen, 1980). This would indicate that when we begin to separate method from medium we may begin to explain more significant amounts of learning variance.

# Uncontrolled Novelty Effects with Newer Media

A second, though probably less important source of confounding, is the increased effort and attention research subjects tend to give to media that are novel to them. The increased attention paid by students sometimes results in increased effort or persistence, which yields achievement gains. If they are caused by a novelty effect, these gains tend to diminish as students become more familiar with the new medium. This was the case in reviews of computer-assisted instruction at the secondary school level (grades 6 to 12) (Kulik, Bangert, & Williams, 1983). An average effect size of .32 (e.g., a rise in exam scores from the 50th to the 63rd percentile) for computer courses tended to dissipate significantly in longer duration studies. In studies lasting four weeks or less, computer effects were .56 standard deviations. This reduced to .3 in studies lasting from five to eight weeks and further reduced to the familiar .2 effect after eight weeks of data collection. Cohen (1977) describes an effect size of .2 as "weak," and notes that it accounts for less than 1 percent of the variance in a comparison. Cohen, Ebling, and Kulik (1981) report a similar phenomenon in their review of visual-based instruction (e.g., film, television, pictures). Although the reduction in effect size for longer duration studies approached significance (about .065 alpha), there were a number of comparisons of methods mixed with different visual media, which makes interpretation difficult.

In their review of computer use in college, C. Kulik, Kulik, and Cohen (1980) did not find any evidence for this novelty effect. In their comparison of studies lasting one or two hours with those that held weekly sessions for an entire semester, the effect sizes were roughly the same. Computers present less novel experiences for college subjects than for secondary school students.

# Editorial Decisions and Distortion of Effect Estimates

There is also some evidence for the hypothesis that journal editors typically select research that finds stronger effects for newer media. Kulik, Bangert, and Williams (1983) reported .21 and .3 effect sizes for unpublished and dissertation studies respectively. Published studies averaged effect sizes of .47 standard deviations, which is considerably larger. J. Kulik, Kulik, and Cohen (1979) found similar evidence in an analysis of audiotutorial instruction studies. Published studies showed a 3.8 percent final examination advantage for audiotutorial methods over conventional instruction (.31 standard deviations), but this reduced to a .6 percent advantage for the same method in unpublished studies.

## *A Research Caution*

Based on this consistent evidence, it seems reasonable to advise strongly against future media comparison research. Five decades of research suggest that there are no learning benefits to be gained from employing different media in instruction, regardless of their obviously attractive features or advertised superiority. All existing surveys of this research indicate that confounding has contributed to the studies attributing learning benefits to one medium over another and that the great majority of these comparison studies clearly indicate no significant differences.

This situation is analogous to the problems encountered in research on teaching. In that area, the teacher was constantly confused with teaching. Improvements in research findings result when specific teaching behaviors compete to influence learning rather than different types of teachers (Rosenshine, 1971). Where learning benefits are at issue, therefore, it is the method, aptitude, and task variables of instruction that should be investigated. Studies comparing the relative achievement advantages of one medium over another will inevitably confound medium with method of instruction.

# Recent Directions: Media Attribute Research Examined

During the 1970s, a new type of question was suggested that seemed to eliminate many of the conceptual problems in the media comparison question. Instead of focusing on media, it was recommended (Clark, 1975; Levie & Dickie, 1973; Salomon, 1974b; 1979) that we study "attributes" of media and their influence on the way that information is processed in learning. In this view, many media possess such attributes as the capacity to slow the motion of objects, to "zoom" into details of a stimulus field, or to "unwrap" a three-dimensional object into its two-dimensional form. These attributes were thought to cultivate cognitive skills when modeled by learners so that, for example, a child with low cue-attending ability might learn the cognitive skill of "zooming" into stimulus details (Salomon, 1974a), or novice chess players might increase their skills in recognizing potential moves and configurations of chess pieces through animated modeling of moves and patterns (Blake, 1977). Because this type of question dealt with the way that information is selected and transformed in the acquisition of generalizable cognitive skills, many believed that the possibility of a coherent theory dealing with media attributes was forthcoming (Olson, 1972; Schramm, 1977). In addition, it was exciting to imagine that, because they promised to teach mental transformations that had not yet been experienced, these media attributes might result in unique cognitive skills.

The promise of the media attributes approach is based on at least three expectations: a) that the attributes were an integral part of media and would provide a connection between instructional uses of media and learning; b) that attributes would provide for the cultivation of cognitive skills for learners who needed them; and c) that identified attributes would provide unique independent variables for instructional theories that specified causal relationships between attribute modeling and learning—finally the evidence for a connection between media and learning. Although the final point is most important, it now appears that the media attribute question suffers many of the problems that plagued the media comparison issue. Generally, the evidence suggests that only the second expectation has been fulfilled, which implies that media attribute research may contribute to instructional design but not to theory development.

## Media Attributes and Media

The first expectation was that these media attributes would somehow represent the psychologically relevant aspects of media. Few of the originators of the media attribute construct (Olson & Bruner, 1974; Salomon 1974b) claimed that they were more than "correlated" with different media. Because they were not exclusive to any specific media and were only associated with them by habit or convenience, they were not "media" variables any more than the specific subject matter content of a book is part of the definition of "book." In fact, the early discussions of the construct most often referred to "symbol systems," or symbolic "elements" of instruction. All instructional messages were coded in some symbolic representational system, the argument went, and symbols vary in the cognitive transformation they allow us to perform on the information we select from our environment. Some symbolic elements (animated arrows, zooming) permit us to cultivate cognitive skills. However, because many different media could present a given attribute, there was no necessary correspondence between attributes and media. Media are mere vehicles for attributes; it is misleading to call them *media* attributes.

## Attributes and the Cultivation of Cognitive Skills

The second expectation of the attribute approach was more realistic. Although Mielke (1980) is correct in saying that very few of the skill cultivating attributes have been found and validated, there is positive evidence for Salomons's (1979) claim that "the coding elements of a . . . symbol system can be made to cultivate the mastery of specific mental skills by either activating or overtly supplanting the skills" (p. 216). (Much of the research buttressing this claim is presented in Salomon, 1979, and will not be reviewed in detail here.) The problem lies not in symbol systems being made to cultivate skills but in whether these symbolic elements or attributes are exclusive or necessary to learning. If the attributes identified to date are useful in instruction, they are valuable. However, theory development depends on the discovery of basic or necessary processes of instruction and learning. It is to this point, the third expectation of media attribute theories, that the discussion turns next.

## Attributes as Causal Factors in Learning

Recent evidence shows that attributes of symbol systems are occasionally sufficient but not necessary contributors to learning. In science, sufficient conditions are those events that were adequate to produce some outcome in a past instance. There is no guarantee, however, that sufficient conditions will ever produce the outcome again because the variable that caused the outcome was merely correlated with the condition. For example, a lecture might be sufficient to produce the desired level of achievement in one instance but fail in another. Severing the optic nerve will cause blindness but will not explain the cause of all cases of blindness. This issue is related to the problem of external validity. Although it is often useful instructionally to know about conditions sufficient for producing desirable levels of achievement, our theories seek necessary conditions. Without necessary conditions we run the risk of failing to replicate achievement gains when we change the context, times, or student clients for instruction. Instructional theory (Shuell, 1980) seeks generalizations concerning the necessary instructional methods required to foster cognitive processes. To illustrate this point, the discussion turns next to research evidence for the skill-cultivating function of symbol system attributes.

## The Research Evidence

In the zooming study mentioned earlier, students who had difficulty attending to cues in a visual field learned the skill by seeing it modeled in a film where they saw a camera "zoom" from a wide field to close-up shots of various details (Salomon, 1974a). Here, an analysis of the task suggested that effective cue attending required an attention-directing strategy that began with a view of the entire stimulus and then narrowed the stimulus field until a single, identifiable cue remained. For those students with low cue-attending skill (the requisite cognitive skill to perform the task) Salomon (1974b) reasoned that the required instructional method would be modeling. In this case, the construction of the model followed an analysis of the symbol systems, which allowed this particular method to be coded for delivery to the students. Although the zooming treatment he used was available in many media (e.g., film, television, video disc), the students seemed to model the zooming and used it as a cognitive skill that allowed them to attend to cues.

In a partial replication of this study, however, Bovy (1983) found that a treatment using an "irising" attribute to provide practice in cue-attending was as effective as Salomon's zooming in cultivating the skill during practice. Irising consisted of slowly enclosing cues in a circular, gradually enlarging, darkened border similar to the effect created by an iris that regulates the amount of light permitted through a camera lens. More important, however, was her finding that a treatment merely isolating cues with a static close-up of successive details singled out by the zooming and irising was *even more effective at cultivating cue-attending skill than either zooming or irising*. It may be that only the efficient isolation of relevant cues is necessary for this task.

In a similar study, Blake (1977) taught chess moves to high or low visual ability undergraduates through a standard narration and a) still pictures, b) animated arrows with the pictures, or c) a motion film from which the still pictures were taken. The recommendation is to exercise caution in future research on symbolic elements of media. Although all three conditions worked for the higher-ability students, low visualizers learned the chess moves equally well from the arrow and the motion treatments, which were significantly better for them than the static pictures. Here, as in the Salomon (1974a) study, we presume that the modeled chess moves compensated for the low ability students' lack of spatial visualization. Unlike Salomon, Blake's subjects profited from two operational definitions of the necessary model: animated arrows and moving chess pieces. Different stimulus arrangements resulted in similar performances but, we might expect, led to nominally different cognitive processes being modeled. The necessary process for learning chess moves as well as the visualizing of the entire move allowed each piece could therefore be operationalized in any of various adequate conditions for successful performance.

## Summary

It seems reasonable to assume, therefore, that media are delivery vehicles for instruction and do not directly influence learning. However, certain elements of different media, such as animated motion or zooming, might serve as adequate conditions to ease the learning of students who lack the skill being modeled. Symbolic elements such as zooming are not media (we can have a film or television program that does not contain zooming) but allow us to create conditions adequate to teach required cognitive skills. The determination of necessary conditions is a fruitful approach when analysing all instructional problems, and it is the foundation of all instructional theories. Once described, the necessary cognitive operation is a specification or recipe for an instructional method.

This point of view takes us a great distance from traditional conceptions of the role of media in instruction and learning. It suggests that systems of symbols that are correlated only with familiar media may sometimes serve as adequate (but never necessary) conditions for learning from instruction. They accomplish this by providing operational vehicles for methods that reflect the cognitive processes necessary to successfully perform a given learning task. Generally, treatments such as zooming or animated arrows are but two of the many nominally different treatments that would result in the same performance. Just as some form of medium is required to deliver instruction, some form of a symbol system must be employed to construct a treatment. Similarly, as the medium does not influence learning, neither is the symbolic element chosen to construct the treatment the most direct influence on learning. We can employ a great variety of media and, possibly, a similar variety of symbol systems to achieve the same performance; however, we cannot vary the requirement that the method somehow model the crucial cognitive process required for the successful performance of the task. The critical features of the necessary cognitive process underlie the construction of successful instructional methods and the development of instructional theory (Clark, 1982). These cognitive process features must be translated into a symbol system understandable to the learner and then delivered through a convenient medium. The cognitive feature in the chess study was the simulation of the beginning and ending points of the moves of the various chess pieces. In the cue-attending studies by Salomon and Bovy, the cognitive features were probably the isolation of relevant cues. The external modeling of these features in a compatible symbol system is necessary for learning; neither the medium nor the symbol system yields the required performance. When a chosen symbol system is shaped to represent the critical features of the task and other things are equal, learning occurs. When a medium delivers a symbol system containing this necessary arrangement of features, learning occurs also, but not as a result of either the medium or the symbol system.

There are instructional problems other than learning that may be influenced by media (e.g., costs, distribution, the adequacy of different vehicles to carry different symbol systems, equity of access to instruction). Although space prevents a complete discussion of these more promising areas, there follows a brief overview of studies that deal with research on our beliefs and attributions concerning media. These new questions differ from traditional media research in that there are no media variables in the studies—only variables having to do with our attributions or beliefs about media; this is a subtle but important difference, as we shall see.

# Promising Research:
# Beliefs and Attributions About Media

That we learn (through education and experience) to prefer some media or to attribute varying levels of difficulty, entertainment value, or enjoyment to media might influence instructionally relevant outcomes. Several studies have fruitfully explored the attribution question.

# Perceived Learning Demands of Media and Learning Strategies

Presumably, differences in the qualities attributed to different media may influence learning-related behaviors of students. Ksobiech (1976) and Salomon (1981) have reported studies where students' beliefs about the different demands placed on them by various media influenced their approaches to learning tasks. Ksobiech (1976) told sixty undergraduates that televised and textual lessons were to be a) evaluated, b) entertainment, or c) the subject of a test. The test group performed best on a subsequent test with the evaluation group scoring next best and the entertainment group demonstrating the poorest performance. Also in this study some subjects were allowed to push a button and receive more video or more narrative content (verbal information) about the lessons. The test subjects consistently chose more verbal information presumably because they believed that it was a surer route to the factual information they needed to succeed at the test. Also, the subjects who believed that a test awaited them persisted longer than the other groups.

Salomon (1981) has recently suggested a model for conceptualizing the differences in persistence that result from different media attributions. His model suggests precise relationships between the perceived "difficulty" of different media, the self-efficacy of students, and the resulting effort they invest in learning from a given medium. Again, it is not the medium but the students' perceptions or attributions of the medium and their own abilities that are thought to be casually connected to the effort they invest. It is typical, Salomon reports, for students to attribute great difficulty to learning from computers but to think of television as "shallow" and "easy."

# Enjoyment, Achievement, and Choice of Media

In related studies, Saracho (1982), Machula (1978–1979), and Clark (1982) reported studies where preferences and achievement from media were antagonistic. In a year-long study involving over 250 third- to sixth-grade students, Saracho (1982) found that those assigned to computer-assisted instruction in basic skills liked the computer less but learned more in the computer condition than from other media. Similarly, Machula (1978–1979) instructed 114 undergraduates via television, voice recording, and printed text. Students liked the television less but learned significantly more from it than from the voice recording, which they liked more.

Clark (1982) has reviewed similar studies and has suggested that students choose by mistake those media carrying methods that inadvertently result in less learning for them. Students incorrectly assess the extent to which the instructional method carried by the medium will allow them the most efficient use of their effort. Strong interactions with general abilities are often found in this research. Higher-ability students seem to like methods and media that they perceive as more structured and directive because they think they will have to invest less effort to achieve success. However, these more structured methods prevent higher-ability students from employing their own considerable skills and yield less effort than the less directive methods and media. Lower-ability students typically seem to like less-structured and more discovery-oriented methods and media; they seem to avoid investing the effort required by the more structured approaches to achieve the same disappointing results. These more unstructured approaches offer relative anonymity and the chance to invest less effort for less-able students who actually need the greater structure of the methods they like less. Although medium and method are not the same experience, the methods conveyed by the media in studies such as these probably account for different levels of achievement, and subject attributions about media influence their preferences.

## Attitudes Toward Computers

Hess and Tenezakis (1973) explored the affective responses of predominantly Mexican-American, low SES seventh, eighth and ninth graders to remedial mathematics presented by computer or teacher. Among a number of interesting findings was an unanticipated attribution of more fairness to the computer than to the teacher. It seems that these subjects felt that the computer treated them more equitably (kept promises, did not make decisions based on their heritage) than some of the teachers. They consistently trusted the computer more but also found the computer to be less "flexible" and unresponsive to students' desires to change the course or content of their instruction. Stimmel, Connor, McCaskill and Durrett (1981) found strong negative affect toward computers and computer instruction among a large group of preservice teachers. These same teacher trainees had similar reactions to mathematics and science teaching, and they may have associated computers with these disciplines.

# Conclusions

One might reasonably wonder why media are still advocated for their ability to increase learning when research clearly indicates that such benefits are not forthcoming; of course, these conclusions are disseminated slowly and must compete with the advertising budgets of a multimillion dollar industry that has a vested interest in selling these machines for instruction. In many ways the problem is analogous to one that occurs in the pharmaceutical industry. There we find arguments concerning the relative effectiveness of various media (tablets, capsules, liquid suspensions) and different brand names carrying the same generic drug to users.

An equal contributor to this disparity between research and practice is the high expectation we have for technology of all kinds. Other machine-based technologies similar to the newer electronic media have revolutionized industry, and we have had understandable hopes that they would also benefit instruction. In addition, many educators and researchers are reserved about the effectiveness of our system of formal education. As environments for learning, media seem to offer alternative and more effective features than those available from the conventional teacher in the conventional classroom. Tobias (1982), for example, has provided evidence that we can help overcome student anxiety by allowing anxious students the chance to replay a recording of a lesson. This quality of "reviewability" is commonly thought to distinguish some of the newer media from the conventional teacher's lecture; however, teachers are entirely capable of reviewing material for anxious students (and probably do so often). It is what the teacher does—the teaching—that influences learning. Most of the methods carried by newer media can also be carried or performed by teachers. Dixon and Judd (1977), for example, compared teacher and computer use of "branching" rules in instruction and found no differences in student achievement attributable to these two "media."

The point is made, therefore, that all current reviews of media comparison studies suggest that we will not find learning differences that can be unambiguously attributed to any medium of instruction. It seems that existing research is vulnerable to rival hypotheses concerning the uncontrolled effects of instructional method and novelty.

More recent evidence questions the evidence for the media-based attempts to determine the components of effective instructional methods. These symbol system or media attribute theories seem to be useful for instructional design but of limited utility in explicating the necessary conditions that must be met by effective methods. Future research should therefore focus on necessary characteristics of instructional methods and other variables (task, learner aptitude, and attributions), which are more fruitful sources for understanding achievement increases. Recent studies dealing with learner attributions and beliefs about the instructional and entertainment qualities of various media seem particularly attractive as research directions. There are no media variables in attribution research, however. Independent variables are concerned with learner beliefs, and outcome measures are typically some measure of learner persistence at a task. It seems reasonable to recommend, therefore, that researchers refrain from producing additional studies exploring the relationship between media and learning unless a novel theory is suggested.

## Author's Note

*The author wishes to acknowledge the substantive advice of Gavriel Salomon, William Winn, and anonymous reviewers without making them responsible for errors.*

## References

Blake, T. 1977. Motion in instructional media: Some subject-display mode interactions. *Perceptual and Motor Skills* 44:975–985.

Bovy, R. A. April 1983. *Defining the psychologically active features of instructional treatments designed to facilitate cue attendance.* Paper presented at the annual meeting of the American Educational Research Association, Montreal.

Clark, R. E. 1975. Constructing a taxonomy of media attributes for research purposes. *AV Communication Review* 23, no. 2:197–215.

———. 1982. Antagonism between achievement and enjoyment in ATI studies. *The Educational Psychologist* 17, no. 2:92–101.

Clark, R. E., and R. E. Snow. 1975. Alternative designs for instructional technology research. *AV Communications Review* 23, no. 4:373–394.

Cohen, J. 1977. *Statistical power analysis for the behavioral sciences.* Rev. ed. New York: Academic Press.

Cohen, P., B. Ebling, and J. Kulik. 1981. A meta-analysis of outcome studies of visual based instruction. *Educational Communication and Technology Journal* 29, no. 1:26–36.

Dixon, P., and W. A. Judd. 1977. A comparison of computer instruction and lecture mode for teaching basic statistics. *Journal of Computer Based Instruction* 4, no. 1:22–25.

Glaser, R. 1976. Components of a psychology of instruction: Towards a science of design. *Review of Educational Research* 46, no. 1:1–24.

Glaser, R., and W. W. Cooley. 1973. Instrumentation for teaching and instructional management. In R. Travers, ed., *Second handbook of research on teaching*. Chicago: Rand McNally College.

Glass, G. V. 1976. Primary, secondary and meta-analysis of research. *Educational Researcher* 5, no. 1:3–8.

Hess, R., and M. Tenezakis. 1973. The computer as a socializing agent: Some socioaffective outcomes of CAI. *AV Communication Review* 21, no. 3:311–325.

Hovland, C., A. A. Lumsdaine, and F. Sheffield. 1949. *Experiments on mass communication*. Princeton, N.J.: Princeton University Press.

Jamison, D., P. Suppes, and S. Welles. 1974. The effectiveness of alternative instructional media: A survey. *Review of Educational Research* 44:1–68.

Keller, F. 1968. Good-bye teacher. *Journal of Applied Behavior Analysis* 1:79–89.

Ksobiech, K. 1976. The importance of perceived task and type of presentation in student response to instructional television. *AV Communication Review* 24, no. 4:401–411.

Kulik, C., J. Kulik, and P. Cohen. 1980. Instructional technology and college teaching. *Teaching of Psychology* 7, no. 4:199–205.

Kulik, J., R. Bangert, and G. Williams. 1983. Effects of computer-based teaching on secondary school students. *Journal of Educational Psychology* 75:19–26.

Kulik, J., C. Kulik, and Cohen, P. 1979. Research on audio-tutorial instruction: A meta-analysis of comparative studies. *Research in Higher Education* 11, no. 4:321–341.

Levie, W. H., and K. Dickie. 1973. The analysis and application of media. In R. Travers, ed., *The second handbook of research on teaching*. Chicago: Rand McNally.

Lumsdaine, A. 1963. Instruments and media of instruction. In N. Gage, ed., *Handbook of research on teaching*. Chicago: Rand McNally.

Machula, R. 1978–1979. Media and affect: A comparison of videotape, audiotape and print. *Journal of Educational Technology Systems* 7, no. 2:167–185.

Mielke, K. 1968. Questioning the questions of ETV research. *Educational Broadcasting Review* 2:6–15.

———. Commentary. *Educational Communications and Technology Journal* 28, (1980) no. 1:66–69.

Olson, D. 1972. On a theory of instruction: Why different forms of instruction result in similar knowledge. *Interchange* 3, no. 1:9–24.

Olson, D., and J. Bruner. 1974. Learning through experience and learning through media. In D. Olson, ed., *Media and symbols: The forms of expression, communication, and education* (73rd Yearbook of the NSSE). Chicago: University of Chicago Press.

Reiser, R., and R. Gagné. 1982. Characteristics of media selection models. *Review of Educational Research* 52, no. 4:499–512.

Rosenshine, B. 1971. *Teacher behaviors and student achievement.* London: National Foundation for Educational Research in England and Wales.

Salomon, G. 1974a. Internalization of filmic schematic operations in interaction with learners' aptitudes. *Journal of Educational Psychology* 66:499–511.

——. 1974b. What is learned and how it is taught: The interaction between media, message, task and learner. In D. Olson, ed., *Media and symbols: The forms of expression, communication, and education* (73rd Yearbook of the NSSE). Chicago: University of Chicago Press.

——. 1979. *Interaction of media, cognition and learning.* San Francisco: Jossey Bass.

——. 1981. *Communication and education.* Beverly Hills, Calif.: Sage.

Salomon, G., and R. E. Clark. 1977. Reexamining the methodology of research on media and technology in education. *Review of Educational Research* 47:99–120.

Saracho, O. N. 1982. The effect of a computer assisted instruction program on basic skills achievement and attitude toward instruction of Spanish speaking migrant children. *American Educational Research Journal* 19, no. 2:201–219.

Schramm, W. 1977. *Big media little media.* Beverly Hills, Calif.: Sage.

Shuell, T. J. 1980. Learning theory, instructional theory and adaption. In R. E. Snow, P. Federico, and W. Montigue, eds., *Aptitude, learning and instruction,* vol. 2. Hillsdale, N.J.: Lawrence Erlbaum.

Stimmel, T., J. Connor, E. McCaskill, and H. J. Durrett. 1981. Teacher resistance to computer assisted instruction. *Behavior Research Methods and Instrumentation* 13, no. 2:128–130.

Thorndike, E. L. 1912. *Education.* New York: Macmillan.

Tobias, S. 1982. When do instructional methods make a difference? *Educational Researcher* 11, no. 4:4–9.

# Author

*RICHARD E. CLARK, Professor of Educational Psychology and Technology, University of Southern California, WPH 801 P. 0. Box 77963, Los Angeles, CA 90007. Specialization: Instructional theory.*

# 10

# *Learning with Media**

## Robert B. Kozma

*This article describes learning with media as a complementary process within which representations are constructed and procedures performed, sometimes by the learner and sometimes by the medium. It reviews research on learning with books, television, computers, and multimedia environments. These media are distinguished by cognitively relevant characteristics of their technologies, symbol systems, and processing capabilities. Studies are examined that illustrate how these characteristics, and the instructional designs that employ them, interact with learner and task characteristics to influence the structure of mental representations and cognitive processes. Of specific interest is the effect of media characteristics on the structure, formation, and modification of mental models. Implications for research and practice are discussed.*

Do media influence learning? The research reviewed in this article suggests that capabilities of a particular medium, in conjunction with methods that take advantage of these capabilities, interact with and influence the ways learners represent and process information and may result in more or different learning when one medium is compared to another for certain learners and tasks.

From: Kozma, R. B. 1991. Learning with media. *Review of Educational Research* 61(2):179–211. Copyright 1991 by the American Educational Research Association. Reprinted by permission of the publisher.
*This project was performed pursuant to grant number OERI-GO086-90010 from the Office of Educational Research and Improvement/Department of Education (OERI/ED). The opinions expressed herein do not necessarily reflect the position or policy of the OERI/ED or the Regents of The University of Michigan, and no official endorsement by either group should be inferred. The author acknowledges the comments of many colleagues on earlier drafts, particularly those of Patricia Baggett, Jerome Johnston, Wilbert McKeachie, Paul Pintrich, Nancy Nelson Spivey, and an anonymous reviewer. Also acknowledged is support from the Dana Foundation Fellowship for Computer-Assisted Instruction in the Humanities at Carnegie Mellon University.

This article responds to a challenge by Clark (1983) for "researchers [to] refrain from producing additional studies exploring the relationship between media and learning unless a novel theory is suggested" (p. 457). He extended this challenge after reviewing the existing comparative research on media and concluding that "media do not influence learning under any conditions" (p. 445). Rather, "media are mere vehicles that deliver instruction but do not influence student achievement any more than the truck that delivers our groceries causes changes in our nutrition" (p. 445). The theoretical framework supported by the review herein presents an image of the learner actively collaborating with the medium to construct knowledge. It stands in vivid contrast to an image in which learning occurs as the result of instruction being "delivered" by some (or any) medium. The framework is meant to provide the novel approach required by Clark before research on media and learning can progress.

In this theoretical framework, learning is viewed as an active, constructive process whereby the learner strategically manages the available cognitive resources to create new knowledge by extracting information from the environment and integrating it with information already stored in memory. This process is constrained by such cognitive factors as the duration and amount of information in short-term memory, the task-relevant information that is available in long-term memory, the structure of this information, the procedures that are activated to operate on it, and so on. Consequently, the process is sensitive to characteristics of the external environment, such as the availability of specific information at a given moment, the duration of that availability, the way the information is structured, and the ease with which it can be searched.

The relationship between the internal and external cognitive environments is explicitly addressed by the emerging discussion of *distributed cognition.* There are two perspectives one can take in this discussion: a system view or a personal view (Norman, 1989). Pea (1990) and Perkins (1990) take a system perspective and examine how cognition within the system is augmented by its distribution among individuals and between individuals and artifacts (e.g., computers, calculators, etc.). The theoretical framework developed in this review approaches distributed cognition from the perspective of the individual. This review examines the effects that the sharing of cognition between an individual and a medium has on the cognitive representations and processes of that individual, particularly those effects that endure beyond the immediate interaction (Salomon, 1990).

The subdomain of the external environment examined in this article is *mediated information,* not only information that is intentionally educational (e.g., a computer-based lesson) but also other information that may not have an explicit educational goal (e.g., in popular books, television programs, etc.). This review does not directly address information embedded in what are sometimes called *authentic situations* (Brown, Collins & Duguid, 1989), but it complements learning in such situations. Nor does this article examine the larger social environment within which mediated interactions occur (Perkins, 1985). Although it may be the above contexts, and the ways media are integrated into them, that have the greatest impact on how people think and learn, these broader contexts will be only referenced here. The primary focus of this article is finer-grained. It will examine the specific episodes within which a learner interacts with mediated information to influence learning.

This article will provide a definition of media and use it to examine the theoretical and research literature on learning from books, television, computers, and multimedia environments. Each section will examine how the complementary construction of representations, and operations performed on them, is influenced by characteristics of the medium, designs that take advantage of these characteristics, and the characteristics of learners and tasks. The intent is to demonstrate the relative cognitive effects of learning with various media, particularly effects related to the structure, formation, and modification of mental models.

# Media Defined

Media can be defined by its technology, symbol systems, and processing capabilities. The most obvious characteristic of a medium is its technology: the mechanical and electronic aspects that determine its function and, to some extent, its shape and other physical features. These are the characteristics that are commonly used to classify a medium such as a television, a radio, and so on. The cognitive effects of these characteristics, if any, are usually indirect. Characteristics such as size, shape, and weight make it more likely that a student will learn with a book, but not a computer, while on a bus, although of course this predilection is changing as computers get smaller, lighter, and cheaper. A few cognitive effects of technology, however, are more direct. For example, the size and resolution of many computer screens are such that reading their texts may be more difficult than reading the text of some books (Haas, 1989).

The primary effect of a medium's technology, however, is to enable and constrain its other two capabilities: the symbol systems it can employ and the processes that can be performed with it. For example, a computer with a graphics board or a speech synthesis board can use different symbols in its presentations from those without these features. Computers with enough memory to run expert systems can process information in different ways than those without such a memory. These additional symbol systems and processes are likely to account for the cognitive effects of these systems, rather than the technology.

Symbol systems and processing capabilities have a number of important implications for learning. Salomon (1974, 1979) describes the relationship between a medium's symbol systems and mental representations. Symbol systems are *modes of appearance* (Goodman, 1976), or sets of elements (words, picture components, etc.) that are interrelated within each system by syntax and are used in specifiable ways in relation to fields of reference. (Words and sentences in a text may represent people, objects, and activities and be structured in a way that forms a story.) A medium can be described and perhaps distinguished from other media by its capabilities to employ certain symbol systems. Thus, television can be thought of as a medium that is capable of employing representational (i.e., pictorial) and audiolinguistic symbol systems (among others). Such characterizations can also be used to specify a certain overlap or equivalence of media. Thus video and motion film can be thought of as equivalent in this regard, although they can be distinguished from radio, which can employ only a subset of these symbol systems.

Salomon (1974, 1979) suggests that these characteristics should be used to define, distinguish, and analyze media because they are relevant to the way learners represent and process information from a medium. He contends that certain symbol systems may be better at representing certain tasks and that information presented in different symbol systems may be represented differently in memory and may require different mental skills to process. The research reviewed here supports and elaborates on this contention. For example, studies will be examined that illustrate how symbol systems characteristic of certain media can connect mental representations to the real world in a way that learners with little prior knowledge have trouble doing on their own without the representation of information in these symbol systems.

But, as will be demonstrated, symbol systems alone are not adequate to describe a medium and its cognitive effects. Information is represented not only in memory; it is processed. Media can also be described and distinguished by characteristic capabilities that can be used to process or operate on the available symbol systems. Thus, information can be searched or its pace of progression changed with videodisc in a way that is not possible with broadcast video. Including processing attributes in the definition of media can create useful distinctions between videodisc and broadcast video, even though both have access to the same symbol systems. Computers are, of course, especially distinguished by their extensive processing capabilities rather than their access to a particularly unique set of symbol systems.

The processing capabilities of a medium can complement those of the learner; they may ease operations the learner is capable of performing or perform those that the learner cannot. As Salomon (1988) points out, if such processes are explicit and fall within what Vygotsky (1978) calls the *zone of proximal development,* the learner may come to incorporate them into his or her own repertoire of cognitive processes. This review will examine research that illustrates how the processing capabilities of certain media modify and refine the dynamic properties of learners' mental models.

It is important to remember, however, that whereas a medium can be defined and distinguished by a characteristic cluster, or *profile,* of symbol systems and processing capabilities some of these capabilities may not be used in a particular learning episode (Salomon & Clark, 1977). For example, a particular video presentation may use few or no representational symbols (e.g., a talking head presentation); or a viewer may allow a videodisc presentation to play straight through and not use the available search capabilities. In these cases, a *virtual medium* is created that consists of the profile of symbol systems and processing capabilities that were actually used during the session: In effect, a television becomes a radio; a videodisc player becomes a broadcast television. Only the capabilities of the virtual medium can be expected to have an effect on learning processes and outcomes.

Whether or not a medium's capabilities make a difference in learning depends on how they correspond to the particular learning situation—the tasks and learners involved—and the way the medium's capabilities are used by the instructional design. Tasks vary in their situational characteristics and in the demands they place on the learner to create mental representations of certain information and to operate on that information in certain ways. Learners vary in their processing capabilities, the information and procedures that they have stored in long-term memory, their motivations and purposes for learning, and their metacognitive knowledge of when and how to use these procedures and information.

Many learners, perhaps most, can and frequently do supply useful representations and operations for themselves from the information externally available, regardless of the medium used. But learners will benefit most from the use of a particular medium with certain capabilities (as compared to the use of a medium without these) if the capabilities are employed by the instructional method to provide certain representations or perform or model certain cognitive operations that are salient to the task and situation and that the learners cannot or do not perform or provide for themselves. These representations and operations, in turn, influence problem solving and the ability to generate and use representations in subsequently encountered situations. This view of learning with media as a continuous, reciprocal interaction between person and situation—between learner and mediated information—is compatible with Snow's (1989) evolving aptitude-treatment interaction theory.

# Learning with Books

The most common medium encountered in school learning is the book. As a medium, books can be characterized by the symbol systems they can employ: text and pictures. The following sections of the review will examine the cognitive processes used in processing text and in processing text with pictures. They will discuss how a distinctive characteristic of this technology—its stability—influences the processing of these symbol systems to construct knowledge representations and how these, in turn, are influenced by the individual differences of learners, primarily differences in their prior domain knowledge. The summary will describe how these processes and structures can be supported by the author when designing a book.

## The Reading Processes and the Stability of the Printed Page

The primary symbol system used in books consists of orthographic symbols that, in Western culture, are words composed of phonemic graphemes, horizontally arrayed from left to right. That this arrangement is stable distinguishes text in books from other technologies that use the same symbol system—for example, the marquee on Times Square. This stability also has important implications for how learners process information from books. Specifically, the stability of text aids in constructing a meaning of the text.

Learning with text involves the construction of two interconnected mental representations: a *textbase* and a *situation model* (Kintsch, 1988, 1989). The *textbase* is a mental representation derived directly from the text, at the level of both micro- and macro-structure; it is a *prepositional* representation of the meaning of the text. While progressing through the text, the reader assembles propositions and integrates them with those previously constructed. As memory limits are reached, the most recent and frequently encountered propositions are retained in short-term memory and held together by repetition or the embedding of arguments (Kintsch & van Dijk, 1978). The reader generalizes from these local propositions to form *macropropositions,* or summary-like statements that represent the gist of the text. Integrating the information from the text in this way increases the likelihood that it will survive in short-term memory and be fixed in long-term memory.

*The situation model* is a mental representation of the situation described by the text (Kintsch, 1988, 1989). Whereas the textbase is prepositional, the situation model can be constructed from propositions or spatial information. The situation model is connected to and constructed from information in the text base and from knowledge structures evoked from long-term memory by information appearing early in the text or information activated by the reader's purpose. These structures—called, variously, *schemata* (Anderson, Spiro & Anderson, 1978), *frames* (Minsky, 1975), and *scripts* (Schank & Abelson, 1977—can be characterized as a framework with a set of labeled slots in which values are inserted for particular situations. These structures serve two related purposes: They provide a scaffold upon which the situation model is constructed from the textbase, and they provide default values so that the reader can make inferences about the local situation that were not explicitly mentioned in the text. Learning from text involves the integration of these representations into the comprehender's knowledge system by updating the schemata currently in long-term memory or by constructing a new schema for an unfamiliar situation.

But what does any of this have to do with media? How does this symbol system influence mental representations and cognitive processes in distinctive ways? And why would learning processes and outcomes be any different for books—which store orthographic symbols in a fixed, stable way—than they would be for another medium, say audiotape or lecture, which may convey the same linguistic information but in a different symbol system and in a transient way (i.e., speech)?

In many situations for fluent readers, reading progresses along the text in a forward direction at a regular rate, and the information could just as well be presented in another, more transient medium. But, on occasion, reading processes interact with prior knowledge and skill in a way that relies heavily on the stability of text to aid comprehension and learning.

In the obvious case, the effort required of poor readers to decode the text draws on cognitive resources that would otherwise be used for comprehension, thus increasing the risk of comprehension, or learning, failure (LaBerge & Samuels, 1974). But even fluent readers may have difficulty with longer or novel words, such as technical terms in an unfamiliar domain. In both of these cases, readers will use the stability of text to recover from comprehension failure. When encountering difficulty, readers will slow their rate, making more or longer eye fixations (Just & Carpenter, 1987), or they may regress their eyes, going back to review a word as an aid to retrieving a meaning for it from memory (Bayle, 1942). Alternatively, readers may retrieve several meanings for a word and may make longer or additional fixations or may regress over a phrase, a clause, or even a sentence to determine which is appropriate for a given context (Just & Carpenter, 1987; Bayle, 1942). Such difficulties might arise from unusual syntactic structures (e.g., The thief stood before the black-robed judge entered the courtroom.) or difficulties in interpreting combinations of words to construct local propositions. Readers will slow their rate for a passage on a difficult or novel topic (Buswell, 1937) when they encounter information within a passage that is particularly important to the meaning of the text (Shebilske & Fisher, 1983) or when they must integrate less well-organized sentences into macropropositions (Shebilske & Reid, 1979).

All these are examples of how readers use the stability of the symbol system in books to slow their rate of progression or even to regress over text in a way that would seem difficult or impossible to do with audiotape's ever-advancing presentation of information; however, this distinction is likely to be crucial only in certain situations. For example, readers in the Shebilske and Reid study (1979) reduced their rate from 302 words per minute to 286. This difference is statistically significant, but it may not have practical significance with regard to media use because the typical audiotape presentation rate of 110–120 words per minute would seem to be slow enough to accommodate these comprehension difficulties. Even the apparent inability to regress over speech might be accommodated by the two-second duration of information in acoustic memory (Baddeley, 1981) that would allow a listener to recover the three or four most recently spoken words and achieve the same effect as regression over text. The clearest advantage to the use of the stability of text to aid comprehension is when the reader must regress over segments of information larger than a phrase.

Perhaps more important than the use of the stability of text to recover from local comprehension failure in novel or difficult situations is this use in conjunction with highly developed reading skills (such as those described by Brown, 1980) and elaborate memory structures to strategically process large amounts of text within very familiar domains. This is most dramatically illustrated in a study by Bazerman (1985), who interviewed seven professional physicists and observed them reading professional material in their field. These readers read selectively, making decisions based on highly developed schemata that extended beyond extensive knowledge of accepted facts and theories in the field to include knowledge about the current state of the discipline and projections of its future development as well as personal knowledge and judgments about the work of colleagues. Readers used this specialized, or *domain,* knowledge to serve their reading purposes. Most often their interests were to find information that might contribute to their immediate research goals or to expand their background knowledge of the field, and they made their selections based on these purposes.

Bringing schemata and purposes to bear, these subjects typically read by scanning rapidly over tables of contents and by using certain words to trigger their attention to question a particular title more actively. When a particular term attracted their attention, they looked at other words in the title, with the result that about two-thirds of the titles more closely examined were subsequently rejected based on this additional information. When even more information was needed to make further selections, they turned to the abstract.

Having identified an article of interest, they read parts of it selectively and non-sequentially, jumping back and forth, perhaps reading conclusions then introductions, perhaps scanning figures, and finally reading those sections more carefully that fit their purpose. When an article did not readily fit with their comprehension schemata, the readers weighed the cost of working through the difficulty against the potential gain relative to their purposes. When they chose to read through a difficult article or section, they occasionally paused at length to work through the implications of what had been read or to read it through several times. They sometimes looked up background material in reference works and textbooks.

The studies above show the range of ways that readers take advantage of the stable structure of text to aid comprehension. In the Bazerman (1985) study, strategic readers with considerable domain knowledge sometimes progressed through the text at a rapid rate, using a single word to skip a vast amount of information. Other times, they slowed considerably, moving back and forth within a text and across texts, to add to their understanding of the field. In other studies (Bayle, 1942; Shebilske & Reid, 1979), readers encountering difficulties with unfamiliar words, syntactic structures, or ideas used the stability of the printed page to slow their rate and regress over passages. None of these processing strategies are available with the transient, linguistic information presented in audiotape or lecture.

## Multiple Symbol Systems: Learning with Text and Pictures

Orthographic symbols are, of course, not the only ones available to books. Pictures and diagrams are used in books from primers to college textbooks to technical manuals. But how do readers use pictures? What is the cognitive effect of pictures in combination with text? And how does the stability of these symbols, as presented in books, influence this process compared to another medium—say, television—that presents linguistic and pictorial symbols in a transient way? The following section examines the cognitive effects of pictures and text. The subsequent section directly addresses learning with television.

There is a large body of comparative research on learning from text with and without pictures. Almost all of the studies examine only the impact on cued recall and use traditional experimental designs of the type criticized by Clark (1983); however, there is a consensus, among the reviews of this research, that pictures have positive effects under certain conditions. Pressley (1977), Schallert (1980), and Levie and Lentz (1982) generally concur that the use of pictures with text increases recall, particularly for poor readers, if the pictures illustrate information central to the text, when they represent new content that is important to the overall message, or when they depict structural relationships mentioned in the text. The problem with this type of research is that it does not reveal the mechanism by which pictures and text influence the learning process.

The four studies below examine processes of comprehension and learning with text and pictures. In brief, it appears that the use of both symbol systems aids the construction of the textbase and the mapping of it onto the mental model of the situation; this is particularly helpful for learners having little prior knowledge of the domain.

A study by Rusted and Coltheart (1979) examined the way good and poor fourth-grade readers used pictured text to learn about physical features, behavior, and habitat of unfamiliar animals. Including pictures of animals in their environments along with the text resulted in better retention by both good and poor readers over the use of text alone. It aided retention of all information by good readers but only pictured information (i.e., recall of physical features) by poor readers. Observations of good readers showed that they spent time initially looking at the pictures but rarely looked at them once they started reading; poor readers, on the other hand, frequently moved back and forth between text and pictures. The process data was not detailed enough to be definitive, but it suggested that good readers used the pictures to evoke an animal schema that guided their reading and aided their comprehension. Poor readers moved back and forth, perhaps, to ease the decoding of particular words and to aid in building a mental model of these unfamiliar animals and their habitats.

Stone and Glock (1981) obtained similar findings, using more precise measures, when they examined the reading of second- and third-year college students. Subjects used either text without pictures or text with pictures to learn how to assemble a toy pushcart. The text-only group made significantly more assembly errors, particularly errors of orientation. The pictured-text group was most accurate in its constructions, making only 18 percent of the errors of the text-only group. Eye-tracking data indicated two patterns of picture use. Readers typically spent the first few seconds examining the picture. Then they looked from text to picture as they progressed through the passage, spending an average of more than 80 percent of their time looking at text rather than at pictures. As in the Rusted and Coltheart study (1979), the data suggest that readers initially use the pictures to evoke a schema that serves as a preliminary mental model of the situation. Subsequently, it seems that the text carries the primary semantic message and the pictures are used to map this information onto the preliminary mental model, elaborating on the components of the pushcart and their relative arrangement.

The usefulness of pictures seems to interact with domain knowledge. In a study by Hegarty and Just (1989), college students were tested on mechanical ability and assigned to either a short text or a long text describing a pulley system. The short text merely named the components of the system and described how it operated. The long text also elaborated on the arrangement and structure of the components in the system. All texts were accompanied by a schematic diagram of the pulley system. Precise eye-fixations measured the number and duration of movements back and forth between particular words in the text and specific locations in the diagram. There was a nonsignificant interaction such that low-ability students spent more time than high-ability students looking at the diagram when it accompanied the longer text describing the relationship among the components of the system; the high-ability students spent more time examining the diagram with the shorter text. The results suggest that people low in mechanical ability have difficulty forming mental models of mechanical systems from text and use diagrams to help them construct this representation. People with high mechanical ability seem to construct this model from prior knowledge and information from the text without need to refer to the picture. Interestingly, these high-ability students are better able to encode new information from a diagram when the text does not describe all the information relevant to understanding a mechanical system.

In a study by Kuntz, Drewniak & Schott (1989), university students majoring in either geography or social science read passages that contained concepts and rules on meteorology. They received text either with or without two types of supplements: a) representational pictures depicting spatial arrangement, appearance, and configuration of clouds, and b) a tree diagram that provided an overview of the main concepts, constituting the macrostructure of the text. Students were divided on prior domain knowledge. For students with a higher prior knowledge, the examination of representational pictures did not correlate with post-task comprehension, and the use of the tree diagram correlated negatively with performance. In contrast, subjects with low prior knowledge did better if they often inspected the representational picture and spent some time examining the tree diagram. These data suggest that students with little prior knowledge benefited most from the pictures and the tree diagram. Students with adequate prior domain knowledge relied instead on their own well-developed mental models to aid comprehension. Indeed, the tree diagram may have conflicted with the idiosyncratic structure of these students' domain knowledge and actually interfered with their comprehension.

These studies may also explain Pressley's conclusion (1977) in his review of studies of text and imaging. He found that learners who do not receive pictures but are instructed to generate images during the processing of story prose recall as much as those who receive pictures and more than those who do not receive pictures and are not instructed to generate images. There were developmental differences, however. Children of eight years and older could gainfully generate and use images during text processing, whereas those under the age of six appeared unable to generate useful images in response to text, even when directed to do so. In these studies, age may be a surrogate measure for accumulated world knowledge that allows older children to generate mental models that supplement the text and aid comprehension and recall. Younger children may not have enough world knowledge to generate such mental models; thus, they benefit most from pictures to aid this process.

Greeno (1989) elaborates on the situation model in a way that can be useful in analyzing the relationship between text, pictures, cognitive structures, and processes. Greeno proposes a theoretical framework that defines knowledge as a relationship between an individual and a social or physical situation rather than as a property of an individual only. This framework extends the information processing paradigm, which focuses primarily on internal structures and process, to include structures and processes external to the learner. This relativistic notion of knowledge depends heavily on a model of the situation and has considerable implications for learning with media.

In the framework, objects and events organized in relation to human activities (e.g., hitting a ball, buying and selling merchandise), as well as related abstractions (e.g., force, profit margin), are expressed within our culture in various symbolic notations and structures (verbal descriptions, diagrams, graphs, etc.). Mental representations, or mental models, are derived from these symbolic notations and structures and correspond to real-world objects and events and their abstractions.[1] These mental models consist of symbolic objects, or mental entities, that may have properties associated with the symbol systems from which they were derived (e.g., arrows representing force vectors) as well as properties of objects in situations that the symbolic structures represent (e.g., balls moving through space and time along certain trajectories). Greeno contends that people can reason in this mental space to solve problems by operating on these symbolic objects in ways that correspond to operations in real situations.

Too often in school learning, however, these mental objects and operations have little correspondence to real world objects, events, and their abstractions, and map only onto the symbolic domains from which they were derived. The research above suggests that, for some learners, the use of pictures, in addition to text, may provide information needed to map mental representations derived from the text onto mental representations of the real world. This may be because pictorial symbol systems share more properties with the corresponding objects and events in the real world than do linguistic symbol systems.

## Summary and Implications

We now have a picture of learning with books that illustrates the relationship between human information processes and the characteristic stability and symbol systems of the medium. Readers move along a line of text constructing a representation of the textbase. They build a mental model of the situation described with information from the textbase and schemata activated in long-term memory. They slow down to comprehend difficult or important points, and stop or regress to retrieve the meaning of an unfamiliar word or a confusing clause or sentence. They may also use their knowledge of the domain and highly developed strategies to read very selectively in service of a particular purpose they bring to the task. They use titles and abstracts to skip sections or entire articles or to focus on sections of interest. They read summaries, then overviews, reread portions, and move back and forth between texts.

If a picture is available, they may refer to it to supplement the text. An initial look at the picture will evoke domain knowledge for those that have it. In a less familiar domain, readers will move back and forth frequently between text and picture to clarify the meaning of a word or to construct or to elaborate on a model of the situation. All of these strategies and their resulting mental representations are influenced by the knowledge and purpose the reader brings to the task, by the symbol systems, and by the stability of code that characterizes the book.

An author can use these capabilities in a way that complements the learner's skills and deficiencies. Authors can use the stability of text and pictures in books and knowledge of comprehension processes to design structures within their books that support and aid learning. Such structures may include titles (Brandsford & Johnson, 1972), postquestions (Wixson, 1984), explicitly stated behavioral objectives (Mayer, 1984), cohesive text elements (Halliday & Hasan, 1976), signals (Meyer, 1975, 1985; Mayer 1984), and so on. For example, in the Brandsford and Johnson (1972) study, one group of students had considerable difficulty comprehending a paragraph even though it was linguistically simple and contained no difficult words, constructions, or complex concepts. A second group was presented the same paragraph, but this time the paragraph was preceded by a title. In this second condition, the subjects not only rated the paragraph as more comprehensible but recalled it better. Presumably, the title evoked an appropriate schema that allowed the readers to supply information not explicit in the paragraph but important for its comprehension. Other text strategies might evoke different reading processes, such as conducting backward reviews to aid retention (Wixson, 1984), focusing attention on certain types of information, or building internal connections among concepts in the text (Mayer, 1984). Such devices designed into the text can support the purpose and schema-driven strategies evident in the Bazerman study (1985), at least for students having enough prior knowledge.

An understanding of the cognitive function of pictures can also inform instructional practice. This understanding can provide text authors with information that can be applied heuristically to identify situations where pictures would be useful and to design pictures that would accommodate particular learners and tasks (Winn, 1989). Such guidelines may suggest the positioning of pictures in the text, the degree of realism, and the use of arrows and other highlighting mechanisms. For example, the research above suggests that for knowledgeable readers, pictures should be placed early in the text if they are used at all. On the other hand, a less knowledgeable readership would benefit from interspersed pictures, juxtaposed with the corresponding text. Winn (1989) reviews research that suggests the use of arrows in pictures to highlight critical attributes of objects can aid subsequent identification, but that the inclusion of details in an illustration can actually interfere with the learning of an object's structure or function.

# Learning with Television

Television differs in several ways from books that may affect cognitive structures and processes. As with books, television can employ pictures, diagrams, and other representational symbol systems, but, in television, these symbols are transient and able to depict motion. Linguistic information in television can be orthographic, but more often it is oral and, as with audiotape and radio, transient. Because linguistic and pictorial symbol systems are transient in television and because they are presented simultaneously, viewers may process this information in a way different from the back-and-forth serial processing of linguistic and representational information in books. It is also possible that the symbol systems used and their transient nature affect the mental representations created with television.

## Television's Window of Cognitive Engagement

Popular notions of television viewing portray children as staring zombie-like at the screen, but reality is much different. When alternative activities are available, children generally look at and away from the television between 100 and 200 times an hour (Anderson & Field, 1983). Visual attention increases from very low levels during infancy to a maximum during the late elementary school years, declining somewhat during adulthood (Anderson, Lorch, Field, Collins & Nathan, 1986). Although the median look duration is usually only several seconds, extended episodes as long as a minute are not rare. Looks as long as ten minutes are exceptional. This discontinuous, periodic attention to a medium whose information streams by ceaselessly has important implications for comprehension and learning.

Research indicates that visual attention is influenced by several factors. One set of factors, termed *formal features* by Huston and Wright (1983), includes the use of different types of voices (e.g., children, adult male, adult female), laughing, sound effects, music of different types, animation, cuts, zooms, pans, and so forth. Children's moment-to-moment visual attention may wander from the set, but evidence suggests that they continuously monitor the presentation at a superficial level such that their visual attention is recaptured by certain audio cues. Features that are associated with the onset of visual attention are women's and children's voices, laughter, peculiar voices, sound effects, auditory changes, and visual movement (Anderson, Alwitt, Lorch & Levin, 1979). Features associated with continued viewing are special visual effects, pans, and high physical activity. The offset of visual attention among children frequently corresponds to the use of men's voices, long zooms, and inactivity.

This image of visual attention seems bottom-up and data-driven, but other evidence suggests that these formal features come to be seen by children as corresponding to the presentation of more or less meaningful content, and this second factor, the meaningfulness or comprehensibility of the presentation, guides visual attention. For example, Anderson, Lorch, Field and Sanders (1981) found that visual attention to segments of *Sesame Street* was greater for normal segments than for the same visual presentation for which comprehensibility was experimentally reduced by using backward speech or a foreign language. Anderson and Lorch (1983) hypothesize that, through extensive viewing experience, children come to acquire knowledge about the associations between the typical use of various formal features and the likelihood that the corresponding content will be meaningful and interesting. For example, men's voices may be perceived as generally corresponding to adult-oriented content that is less comprehensible and less interesting to children, and thus male voices do not recruit their visual attention.

Huston and Wright contend that this comprehensibility influences attention in an inverted-U relationship. Content that is very simple or very difficult to comprehend maintains attention less well than content in an intermediate range of difficulty. This creates a window of cognitive engagement, one that is perhaps different for each viewer. Yet, within this window, Huston and Wright (1983) conclude that visual attention is necessary though not sufficient for comprehension; even with visual attention, the depth of comprehension varies.

Salomon (1983) introduces the construct of *amount of invested mental effort,* or AIME, to account for the difference between what is viewed and the depth of comprehension. AIME distinguishes the deep, effortful, nonautomatic elaboration of encountered material from the mindless or shallow processing of information that results in less learning. AIME is in turn influenced by several factors: One is the attitudes people have about the amount of effort required to process a medium's messages; the other is the purpose that people bring to the task.

Salomon (1984) found that a sample of sixth graders rated television as an easier medium from which to learn than books. When assigned to view comparable stories from television or print, the effort spent on learning reported by the reading group was significantly greater than that reported by the group who viewed the television program. Both groups scored the same on a test of factual recognition, but the print group scored higher on a test of inferences based on the story.

Krendl and Watkins (1983) exposed fifth-grade children to a fifteen-minute educational television program. They manipulated the purpose of viewing by telling half of the students to watch it for entertainment purposes; the other half were told that it was an educational program and that they should watch it so that they could answer questions. Whereas recall of the storyline was the same for both groups (i.e., number of recalled actions, facts, scenes, etc.), the group instructed to view the program for educational purposes responded to the content with a deeper level of understanding; that is, they reported more story and character elements and included more inferential statements about the meaning of the show.

These studies suggest that the perceptions students have about a medium and the purposes they have for viewing influence the amount of effort that they put into the processing of the message and, consequently, the depth of their understanding of the story. The following sections elaborate on the cognitive mechanisms involved in effortful learning with television and examine the interaction of these processes with the characteristics of the medium. Three issues related to the processing of televised information are examined: the relationship between simultaneously presented auditory and visual information, the processing pace of transient information, and the use of such transient presentations to inform the transformation functions of mental models. For the first of these issues, there is now a considerable amount of cognitive research available; however, there remains little research on the other two issues.

## The Simultaneous Processing of Two-Symbol Systems

An important attribute of video is the ability to use both auditory and visual symbol systems. Within the window of cognitive engagement, how do these symbol systems work, independently and together, to influence comprehension and learning with television? Can either symbol system convey the meaning of a presentation? Does the presentation of both at the same time inhibit or facilitate learning?

Baggett (1979) found that either pictorial or linguistic symbol systems alone can carry semantic information, such as a storyline. In this study, college students were presented with either a dialogueless movie, *The Red Balloon,* or an experimentally derived, structurally equivalent audio version. They wrote summaries of episodes within the story either immediately after the presentation or after a week's delay. An analysis of the summaries by trained raters found that those written immediately after viewing the dialogue-less movie were structurally equivalent to those written immediately after listening to the story. Subjects could construct a semantic macrostructure (i.e., summary) from either medium, but information obtained visually was more memorable. Summaries written a week after viewing the movie were judged to be more complete than those written a week after listening to the audio version.

Meaning can be conveyed by either symbol system; however, Baggett (1989) concludes that information presented visually and linguistically is represented differently in memory. She contends that visual representations contain more information and are *bushier*. Whereas the phrase *red leaf* contains only the name of an object and a modifier, a mental representation of a red leaf obtained from a picture carries with it information about size, color, and shape. Also, the visual representation has more *pegs* that can be used to associate it with information already in long-term memory. These additional associations also make it more memorable.

But it is a significant attribute of video that the auditory and visual symbol systems are presented simultaneously. How does a viewer process information from both of these sources? Two basic hypotheses exist: One possibility is that the simultaneous presentation of audio and visual information competes for limited cognitive resources and that this competition actually reduces comprehension. Another possibility is that information presented with these two-symbol systems may work together in some way to increase comprehension.

A number of studies have compared a video program with its decomposed audio and visual presentations to determine the role of these two sources of information, individually and together (Baggett & Ehrenfeucht, 1982, 1983; Beagles-Roos & Gat, 1983; Gibbons, Anderson, Smith, Field & Rischer, 1986; Hayes & Kelly, 1984; Hayes, Kelly & Mandel, 1986; Meringoff, 1982; Nugent, 1982; Pezdek & Hartman, 1983; Pezdek, Lehrer & Simon, 1984; Pezdek & Stevens, 1984). In none of these studies did the combination of audio and visual information result in lower recall than recall from either source alone. In most of these studies, the combined use of visual and auditory symbol systems resulted in more recall than visual-only and audio-only presentations. This compels the rejection of the hypothesis that simultaneous presentation of audio and visual information necessarily competes for cognitive resources at the expense of comprehension.

Several of these studies used multiple measures of recall to trace the symbol system source of different kinds of knowledge. In a 1982 study, Meringoff asked nine- and ten-year-old children to draw and talk about their imagery and to make and substantiate inferences about a story, *The Fisherman and His Wife*. Compared to those who heard the story, the children who saw the video drew more details and their pictures were more accurate. Children in the audio groups based their inferences about details on previous learning and personal experiences (more like those of children in the control group unexposed to the story), and they were frequently in error relative to the verbal descriptions. Beagles-Roos and Gat (1983) compared animated and audiotape presentations of two stories to groups of first- and fourth-grade children. These researchers found that the explicit story content was learned equally well by both treatment groups. The visual groups recalled more details from the story, did better at a picture sequencing task, and based their inferences on depicted actions. The audio groups more frequently retold the stories using expressive language and based their inferences on verbal sources and prior knowledge.

People can construct a mental representation of the semantic meaning of a story from either audio or visual information alone, but it appears that when presented together, each source provides additional, complementary information that retains some of the characteristics of the symbol system of origin. Children recall sounds and expressive language from the audio track and visual details from the visual track. It also appears that the bushier nature of representations derived from the visual symbol systems are better for building mental models of the situation than are representations based on audio-linguistic information. Students listening to an audiotape are more likely to get information for this model from memory. Audio may be adequate for those knowledgeable of a domain, but visual symbol systems supply important situational information for those less knowledgeable.

These results parallel those for text and pictures; however, the processing of text appears to be driven by the construction of a representation of the linguistic information. Comprehension of video appears to be driven by the processing of visual information. This is apparent from a study by Baggett (1984), who varied the temporal order of audio and visual information within a video presentation on the names and functions of pieces of an assembly kit. In this study, the narration was presented in synchrony or seven, fourteen, and twenty-one seconds ahead of or behind the visual presentation. College students performed best on immediate and seven-day delayed tests of recall of the synchronous and seven-second, visual-then-audio presentations. The worst performance was by groups with the audio presented first. This suggests that, in a video presentation, the visual symbol system serves as the primary source of information and that the audio symbol system is used to elaborate it.

## The Processing of Transient Information

Another important characteristic of television is that the information it presents can be, and usually is, transient. Comprehension is affected by the pace of this presentation and by its continuity. Wright et al. (1984) used sixteen, fifteen-minute-long children's television programs that varied in pace and continuity. Pace was defined by these researchers as the rate of scene and character change. Low-continuity programs were those with scenes that were independent and unconnected (i.e., magazine formats). High-continuity programs were those with connected scenes (i.e., stories). These programs were shown to groups of elementary school children whose recall was measured using seriation tasks of still pictures from the shows. The children who viewed slow-paced, high-continuity programs performed better on these tasks. The effect was additive for younger children.

Surprisingly little research has been done on the effect of pace on comprehension, but this is a potentially crucial variable that may distinguish the process of learning with television and other transient media from learning with stable media, such as text. Wright et al. (1984) defined *pace* as a characteristic of the presentation—the amount of information presented per unit of time (i.e., scene and character changes). But from a cognitive perspective, the critical consideration is *cognitive pace*—the amount of information processed per unit of time. From this perspective, the hypothetical unit of information is the chunk—a semi-elastic unit whose size depends on the familiarity and meaningfulness of the information (Miller, 1956; Simon, 1974). A single word may be a chunk in the following list of words: Lincoln, calculus, criminal, address, differential, lawyer, Gettysburg. Rearranged into Lincoln, Gettysburg, address, criminal, lawyer, differential, calculus, the chunk might be larger than one word (e.g., Lincoln's Gettysburg address) but only if the phrase had some meaning in long-term memory. Simon (1974) examines the results of several experiments to conclude that the capacity of short-term memory is five to seven chunks. He also concludes that it takes between five to ten seconds to fixate each chunk in long-term memory. Thus, whereas the amount of time it takes to process information is relatively constant (i.e., one chunk per five to ten seconds), the number of words processed per unit of time depends on the size of the chunk. This, in turn, depends on relevant prior knowledge in long-term memory.

With books, the reader creates chunks of variable word size to affect a reading pace (i.e., words per unit of time) that accommodates the cognitive requirements of comprehension. With television, the pace of presentation (i.e., words or visual elements per unit of time) is not sensitive to the cognitive constraints of the learner; it progresses whether or not comprehension is achieved. The television viewer may be familiar enough with the information to process it at the pace presented, even if it is fast. That is, the viewer's chunks may be large enough so that the cognitive pace of processing words and ideas keeps abreast with the pace at which they are presented. Even if attention waivers and information is missed, knowledge of a familiar domain can be used to fill in the gaps by supplying information from long-term memory. If the viewer has little domain knowledge, the chunk size will be smaller, and the cognitive pace will drop, perhaps below the pace at which ideas are presented. Also, there is less information from long-term memory to compensate for the information that might be missed. Because the information is transient, the viewer cannot regress over it to refresh short-term memory. This situation may result in the cascading comprehension failure mentioned by Anderson and Collins (1988). For lack of research, however, such contentions remain speculative and empirical work in this area is needed.

The discussion above concentrates on the potential problems created by the transient nature of video information. But this transience may have some advantages in the development of dynamic mental models. As mentioned, Greeno (1989) contends that people use mental models to reason through the solution of problems. This is possible because a mental model is considered to be composed of a connected, *runnable* set of objects, or mental entities (Williams, Hollan & Stevens, 1983). Each of these has an associated representation of its state, a set of parameters, a set of procedures that modify its parameters, and a set of relationships that connect it with other objects. The model is *run* by means of propagating a change of state in one object over time to the states of connected objects, using the associated procedures and relationships to modify their parameters; thus the representation is transformed from the current state to some future state. This information is used to make inferences and solve problems (Holland, Holyoak, Nisbett & Thagard, 1986).

For example, mental models in physics typically include entities that correspond to physical objects that are encountered in the situation, such as blocks, springs, and pulleys (Larkin, 1983). People operate on the mental entities as they would in real time and make inferences about "what would happen to them next" to solve physics problems.

Holland et al. (1986) contend that learning a representation of the transition function is the critical goal in the construction of a mental model. The prospect exists that the transient, time-based character of video information could be used to inform the dynamic properties of mental models, such as those in physics. The observation of objects moving along paths, for example, could provide learners with information needed to make estimates of changes in state. This information would not be available with static information, such as that in text. Whereas learners familiar with the domain might be able to supply such dynamic information from memory or use their prior knowledge to infer dynamic properties from static pictures, those novice to a domain may not be able to supply such constructions and might benefit from the dynamic character of televised information. However, as will be discussed in the subsequent section on learning with computers, this information may not be comprehensive enough to overcome misconceptions that novices frequently bring to tasks such as those involving the motion of objects (Clement, 1983; diSessa, 1982; McCloskey, 1983). Again, lack of research in the area holds these contentions speculative.

## Summary and Implications

This research paints a picture of television viewers who monitor a presentation at a low level of engagement, their moment-to-moment visual attention periodically attracted by salient audio cues and maintained by the meaningfulness of the material; this creates a window of cognitive engagement. Within this window, their processing is sometimes effortless, resulting in the construction of shallow, unelaborate representations of the information presented. However, when viewing with a purpose, people will attend more thoughtfully, constructing more detailed, elaborate representations and drawing more inferences from them.

The visual component of the presentation is particularly memorable, and the representations constructed with it are especially good for carrying information about situations. The auditory symbol systems carry information about sounds and expressive language and help in interpreting the visual information. Auditory symbol systems alone draw primarily on prior knowledge for a construction of the situation model, and this may be problematic for those with little prior knowledge.

Viewers use their prior domain knowledge to process information at the pace presented and supplement information that they may have missed. The transient information in the presentation may be useful in building the dynamic properties of mental models so that inferences can be made about the phenomena they represent; however, if the topic is unfamiliar, little information exists in long-term memory to supplement viewing. The pace of the presentation may exceed the capacity to process it, and comprehension failure may result.

This knowledge can be used by instructional designers to make media-related decisions; for example, people who are very knowledgeable about a particular domain can process information at a much faster rate and more strategically with text than they can with audiotape or video, suggesting that text would suffice for these learners. However, people who are novices to a domain are likely to benefit from the ability to slow the rate of information processing, regress over text, and move back and forth between text and pictures as they are presented in books. These same people are more likely to fail at comprehending some portion of a video presentation because their pace of processing information may fall below the pace at which it is presented. Thus, for novices, a more stable medium should be used, or the pace of a video production should be slowed (Kozma, 1986). For learners moderately familiar with a topic, television's symbol systems can supply complementary information, particularly useful in constructing a situation model, and its normal pace will accommodate comprehension. In video productions, the linguistic information should be presented simultaneously with or just following the visual information.

# Learning with Computers

So far, media have been described and distinguished from each other by their characteristic symbol systems. Some media are more usefully distinguished by what they can do with information—that is, their capability to process symbols. This is particularly the case for computers, the prototypic information processors. For example, computers can juxtapose, or transform, information in one symbol system to that in another (Dickson, 1985). A learner can type in printed text, and a computer with a voice synthesizer can transform it into speech. The computer can take equations, numerical values, or analog signals and transform them into graphs. Research is reviewed below that shows how the computer can be used to aid students in constructing links between symbolic domains, such as graphs, and the real world phenomena they represent. The research shows that it is the transformation capabilities of the computer, rather than its symbol systems, that are crucial in this regard.

The computer is also capable of *proceduralizing* information; that is, it can operate on symbols according to specified rules, such that a graphic object on the screen can move according to the laws of physics, for example. Research is reviewed below that illustrates the role that this capability can play in aiding learners to elaborate their mental models and correct their misconceptions with the use of microworlds.

## Connecting the Real World to Symbols with MBL

An important part of school learning is acquiring an understanding of the relationship between various symbol systems and the real world they represent. Yet students are frequently unable to connect their symbolic learning in school to real-world situations (Resnick, 1987). The transformational capabilities of the computer can be used to make this connection.

Graphs provide an example of this. Mokros and Tinker (1987) found frequent errors among seventh- and eighth-grade students in the interpretation of graphs. Two patterns were identified. First, there was a strong graph-as-picture confusion. Half the students drawing a graph of a bicyclist's speed uphill, downhill, and on level stretches drew graphs representing the hills and valleys rather than speed. In a less striking pattern, 75 percent of the students responded incorrectly when asked to specify maximum warming or cooling on a graph. About half of the 75 percent selected the highest (or lowest) point on the graph as that showing the most rapid change.

Mokros and Tinker (1987) went on to use a microcomputer-based lab (MBL) with 125 seventh and eighth graders for three months. MBL involves the use of various sensors (temperature probes, microphone, motion sensors, etc.) connected to the computer to collect analog data. The computer transforms these data and displays them in real time on the screen as a graph. In a typical unit, the user can turn a heater on for a fixed period, thereby delivering a fixed quantity of thermal energy to a liquid. Using temperature probes interfaced to the computer, the increase and decrease of temperature is instantaneously graphed over time. Mokros and Tinker found a significant increase from pre- to post-tests on the interpretation of graphs (from m = 8.3 to m = 10.8 on a 16-item test). That students made the greatest gains on items sensitive to the graph-as-picture error was of particular importance.

In a similar study, Brasell (1987) used MBL with high school physics students. One group of students spent a class session collecting and observing MBL data in real time (the standard MBL group). A second group used the MBL equipment to collect data, but it was displayed after a twenty-second delay. One control group plotted data with pencil and paper, and another control group engaged in testing only. Brasell found that the post-test scores from the standard MBL treatment were significantly higher than scores from all other treatments. The analysis indicated that real-time transformation of data (i.e., the difference between standard MBL and delayed MBL) accounted for nearly 90 percent of the improvement relative to the control. Brasell suggests that unsuccessful students lack appropriate techniques for referring to previous events or experience, and they fail to make explicit links between physical events and the graphed data, even when they are displayed after only a twenty-second delay. The transformation capabilities of the computer made the connection between symbols and the real world immediate and direct.

## Building Mental Models with Microworlds

Experts in a domain are distinguished from novices in part by the nature of their mental models and how they use them to solve problems. The processing capabilities of the computer can help novices build and refine mental models so that they are more like those of experts.

In physics, a series of studies (Chi, Feltovich & Glaser, 1981; Hegarty, Just & Morrison, 1988; Larkin, 1983; Larkin, McDermott, Simon & Simon, 1980) has established that experts have extensive domain knowledge organized into large, meaningful chunks, or schemata, that are structured around the laws of physics. These schemata contain not only information about the laws of physics but also information on how and under which conditions they apply. In other words, they contain both declarative and procedural knowledge.

When encountering a textbook physics problem, experts use the objects (e.g., *springs, blocks, pulleys)* and features mentioned in the problem statement to cue the retrieval of one or more relevant schemata (e.g., *force-mass, work-energy).* They construct a mental model that contains both information that has been explicitly provided by the situation as well as information supplied from memory. These mental models include mental entities that correspond to the physical objects mentioned in the problem *(blocks, pulleys;* Larkin, 1983; Larkin et al., 1980), as well as entities that correspond to the formal constructs of physics that have no direct, concrete referent in the real world *(force, vectors, friction, velocity).* The relationships between these entities correspond to the laws of physics; experts reason with this model to test the appropriateness of potential quantitative solutions. Only after this qualitative analysis is complete will the expert use an equation to derive a quantitative solution to the problem.

Novices represent and use information in this domain in a very different way; not only do they possess less knowledge about physics than do experts but they organize it differently. For some novices, their physics-related knowledge is composed of a set of fragments, or *phenomenological primitives,* that are not connected by formal relationships but are based on real-world objects and actions. Some novices evoke these fragments to construct a representation of a particular problem (diSessa, 1988); other novices may have coherent and consistent, though erroneous "theories," or misconceptions, of the phenomenon (Clement, 1983; McCloskey, 1983). These misconceptions may represent procedural relationships that are contrary to established laws of physics; for example: An object remains in motion only as long as it is in contact with a mover, or an object should always move in the direction that it is kicked.

Confronted by a textbook problem, novices will use the same surface cues as experts to evoke this information from memory; however, unlike those of experts, the mental models that novices construct with this information are composed primarily of entities that correspond to the familiar, visible objects mentioned in the problem statement (Larkin, 1983). These representations do not contain entities that represent formal physical constructs, such as *force* or *friction;* nor do they contain information on physical laws and principles, or if they do, this information is inaccurate or incomplete. Thus, either the models are inadequate in determining a solution or the solution that is specified is incorrect.

How do people modify such incomplete and inaccurate mental models to form more accurate, expert-like models? This process is not automatic. Indeed, such misconceptions can be held into adulthood as well as after taking courses in the domain (McCloskey, 1983). Rather, modification of a mental model is triggered by certain conditions, such as the failure of a model to adequately predict or account for phenomena when it is used to achieve some desired goal (Holland et al., 1986). In such cases, a person can drop the current mental model in favor of another, maintain the model but lower confidence in its ability to reliably predict, or modify the model. The last is most often the goal in school learning. One way a model is modified is by elaborating its situational components; these are the criteria used to evoke and select the appropriate model in response to a particular problem. Another way to modify a model is by changing the transformation rules associated with the situation. Which of these various changes ultimately occurs depends on the accumulated previous success with the model (a model that has been used successfully many times is more likely to be modified than replaced), the perceptual elements of the situation that might allow for differentiation (the existence of salient perceptual elements will be used to refine the selection criteria so that it is used in a somewhat different set of situations), and the future success of alternate models and rules when they compete to explain subsequent situations (modifications in the model that successfully predict subsequent situations are more likely to be retained). Expertise is developed through a series of such differentiations and elaborations as a result of extensive experience within a domain—both successful and unsuccessful.

Now, how might the processing capabilities of computers be used by novices to aid them in building more expert-like models? First, an important attribute of the computer is its ability to symbolically represent entities in ways that might inform mental models. First, they can graphically represent not only concrete objects but also formal, abstract entities, entities that novices do not normally include in their models. Second, the computer has the important capability of being able to proceduralize the relationships among these symbols. Abstract concepts can be represented in other media, such as text, by symbolic expressions (e.g., $f = ma$) or denoted in diagrams by arrows; but Greeno (1989) points out that such symbols do not behave like forces and accelerations. With computer models, arrows and other symbols can behave in ways that are like the behavior of forces, velocities, and other abstract concepts. For example, a velocity arrow can become longer or shorter, depending on the direction of acceleration. Furthermore, learners can manipulate these symbols and observe the consequences, successful or otherwise, of their decisions. By using their mental models and manipulating these entities governed by the laws of physics, novices may become aware of the inadequacies and inaccuracies of their models. Through a series of such experiences, they can progressively move from initial fragmented, inconsistent, and inaccurate understanding to more elaborate, integrated, and accurate mental models of the phenomena.

This is illustrated in several studies by White (1984, in press), who examined students as they learned principles of Newtonian dynamics within computer-based microworlds. She extended the work of diSessa (1982), who created a computer-based LOGO environment (called *Dynaturtle*) in which the task was to hit a target through a series of directional "kicks" imparted to the turtle. di Sessa observed that physics-naive elementary school students in his study commonly operated with an Aristotelian model of force and motion expressed thus: If you impart a force on a moving object, it will go in the direction last pushed. This Aristotelian notion of force can be contrasted with the Newtonian principle that the motion of an object is the vectorial sum of the forces that have acted on it. An Aristotelian strategy universally used by these students was to wait until the moving turtle was at the same height as the target and give it a ninety-degree kick directly toward the target. The result in this Newtonian environment would be a compromised motion of forty-five degrees that would miss the target.[2]

White (1984) analyzed the correct Newtonian strategy, decomposing it into component principles (i.e., the scalar sum of forces, the vectorial sum of forces, etc.), and created a series of games that progressively incorporated these component strategies. Each game instantiated both an observable object (e.g., a space ship) and a formal physical object (e.g., a force, represented by a key press). These objects were governed by one of the component Newtonian principles (e.g., combining two forces to increase speed in one direction). The series led up to the target game used by diSessa. White found that the group of high school physics students who used these games for less than an hour not only used the Newtonian strategies in the target game but showed significant improvement on transfer verbal force and motion problems. They also performed significantly better on these problems than did a control group of students who attended a physics class but were not exposed to the games.

White and Frederiksen (1990) present a paradigm for the development of a progression of computer models that support conceptual change. The progression leads the learner from simple models to advanced models, increasing in the number of rules, qualifiers, constraints taken into account, and range of problems accommodated. The models allow students to make predictions, explain system function and purpose, solve problems, and receive feedback and explanations. Each is designed to build upon and aid transformation from the previous model.

White (in press) applied this progressive paradigm to develop a two-month curriculum in Newtonian mechanics. This version contained significant improvements in the design. Additional formal constructs from physics were represented by dynamic symbols; for example, a history of the object's speed was represented by a "wake," and the vectorial components of forces acting on the object were represented by a "datacross." As the learner applied more force to the object, he or she saw not only the resulting effect on the object as it moved but a dynamic decomposition of the force into its orthogonal vectors (i.e., the datacross) and a dynamic representation of the change in velocity (i.e., its wake). The students were also provided with additional structure, such as a set of possible "laws" to test within the microworld and a set of real-world transfer problems; additional forces, such as friction and gravity, could be introduced into the system. Two classes of sixth graders were assigned to this curriculum for forty-five minutes a day instead of their regular science course. At the end of the period, the groups using the microworld scored significantly better on a range of real-world transfer problems than did two classes of sixth graders attending the regular science class. They also scored significantly better on these items than did four classes of high school physics students, including two classes that had just spent two and a half months studying Newtonian mechanics.

## Summary

The studies above examined the processing capabilities of the computer and showed how they can influence the mental representations and cognitive processes of learners. The transformation capabilities of the computer connected the symbolic expressions of graphs to the real-world phenomena they represent. Computers also have the capability of creating dynamic symbolic representations of nonconcrete, formal constructs that are frequently missing in the mental models of novices. More important, they are able to proceduralize the relationships between these objects. Learners can manipulate these representations within computer microworlds to work out differences between their incomplete, inaccurate mental models and the formal principles represented in the system.

White's research (1984, in press) shows that novice learners within these environments benefit from structured experiences of progressive complexity that help them build and elaborate their mental models. Research by Brasell (1987) and others suggests that such symbolic-operational environments would be particularly powerful if directly connected to real-time phenomena. These could help learners connect their more elaborate models to the real-world experiences that they can explain.

# Learning with Multimedia

This final section is the most speculative. Little research (particularly process research) has been done on learning with multimedia environments, in part because most efforts in the field are focused on development and in part because the field is still evolving. However, multimedia present the prospect that the various advantages of the individual media described above can be brought together in a single instructional environment and strategically used to facilitate learning.

The term *multimedia* has been around for several decades (Brown, Lewis & Harcleroad, 1973). Until recently, the term has meant the use of several media devices, sometimes in a coordinated fashion (e.g., synchronized slides with audiotape, perhaps supplemented by video). However, advances in technology have combined these media so that information previously delivered by several devices is now integrated into one device. The computer plays a central role in this environment. It coordinates the use of various symbol systems—presenting text and, in another window, presenting visuals. It also processes information it receives, collaborating with the learner to make subsequent selections and decisions.

The following sections review work on two somewhat different but soon to be integrated approaches to multimedia environments: *interactive videodisc environments* and *hypermedia environments*. The literature reviewed reports on developments within these fields, speculates on the cognitive impact of these environments, and raises issues that must be addressed in future research.

## Connecting Mental Models to the Real World with Interactive Video

*Interactive video* integrates computer and video technologies in a way that allows both video and computer-generated information to be displayed together. In some implementations, this information is displayed on the same screen and can be overlayed. For example, the video could present a view of a boulder rolling down a hill in one window on the screen; the computer could then generate force vectors and overlay them on the moving object. In another window, a graph that plotted velocity or acceleration over time could be generated. Alternatively, the students may be given workspaces within which they could compute acceleration or velocity.

The Cognition and Technology Group at Vanderbilt University (1990; Sherwood, Kinzer, Bransford & Franks, 1987; Sherwood, Kinzer, Hasselbring & Bransford, 1987) has developed a series of interactive video-based, complex problem spaces (or *macrocontexts*) that are anchored in realistic goals, activities, and situations. These macrocontexts provide semantically rich environments in which students and teachers can collaboratively explore concepts and principles in science, history, mathematics, and literature, and use these multiple perspectives to solve realistic problems. The Group contends that the videodisc presentation provides a more veridical representation of events than text and that its dynamic, visual, and spatial characteristics allow students to form more easily rich mental models of the problem situation.

Nationally, a number of interactive videodisc environments are now in the stages of development and formative evaluation. One such environment is *Palenque* (Wilson & Tally, 1990). *Palenque* is intended to be an entertainment and educational exploratory environment for children aged from eight to fourteen. With *Palenque,* the viewer becomes a member of an archaeological team of scientists and children exploring ancient Maya ruins in search of the tomb of Pacal, the twelve-year-old ruler of Palenque during its heyday.

In an "explore mode," the viewer can use a joystick to engage in "virtual travel;" that is, the video uses a subjective camera perspective to allow viewers to "see" what they would be seeing if they were actually there, walking and climbing among the ruins. This is accompanied by a dynamic you-are-here map. The child can use simulated research tools such as a camera, compass, and tape recorder. In the "museum mode," the viewer can browse through a database of relevant information including text, still photographs, motion video, graphics, and so on. These are organized into theme "rooms," such as "Maya glyphs" and the "tropical rain forest." In the "game mode," the viewer engages in such activities as putting back together fragmented glyphs and constructing a jungle symphony. Formative evaluation consists of examining the system's user friendliness, the appeal of the various components, and its comprehensibility.

These systems may be particularly powerful in representing such social situations and tasks as interpersonal problem solving, foreign language learning, or moral decision making. Situational information needed to understand and solve these semantically rich problems is sometimes difficult to represent by computer alone and can be better represented with video. But, as mentioned earlier (Salomon, 1983), video information alone can easily be processed in a mindless, shallow way, thus reducing the inferences that viewers draw from it. With interactive video, the computer can be used to help the learner analyze the rich information present in a video scene and carefully think through all the factors that impinge on the problem.

In one example, Covey (1990) has created a particularly compelling moral case study titled *A Right to Die? The Case of Dax Cowart.* In this environment, students are faced with the real-life dilemma of a young man who, having just returned from the war in Vietnam, is involved in a flaming accident in which he is burned over 60 percent of his body and loses his sight. In addition, as part of his burn therapy he must be subjected to daily painful antiseptic washings. He demands to have the treatments discontinued and to be allowed to die. If the treatments are continued, he can be rehabilitated to a functional but disabled life. Students are confronted with an important moral decision: Should the treatments be discontinued?

The goal of the program is not to teach or argue the students toward a specific position but to provide them with a moral sensorium within which to explore these issues. Covey (1990) contends that to understand the moral position of another person one must do more than walk in his shoes: One must live in his skin. With this program, which is based on a true case and filmed with the actual people involved, the students can see the patient's treatments and, in effect, "talk" to the patient, the patient's mother, the doctors, a nurse, and a lawyer. The students are guided through a consideration of the issues of pain and suffering, competence and autonomy, quality of life, and the role of health professionals. No matter which decision students make, they are presented with contrary information intended to push them toward a deeper understanding of the issues.

Cross-media research on the Dax case study is currently underway to examine the impact of video alone, text alone, and interactive video on the representation and processing of this information and on the moral reasoning of the learners. Also being examined is the interaction between these media and students' prior knowledge, experience, and opinions. Of particular interest will be the social and interpersonal cues embedded in the video information and how these are moderated by computer-generated text and guidance to affect the learners' construction of a model of the situation.

Stevens (1989) shows how these cues can be built into a system and used in problem solving. In this system, a subjective camera view is used to put the learner at the head of a conference table in the role of team leader. The task before the team of programmers is to review and critique program code generated by various members of the team. Critiques can, of course, be done in ways that generate defensiveness and otherwise reduce team productivity, and such incidents are built into the episode as it is played out. The task of the learner/team leader is to manage the meeting and interject comments at appropriate times to aid group process; the precise timing and nature of these interjections is left open and up to the learner. Successful behavior within the system must be responsive to social information embedded in the presentation. The learner can interrupt the session at a particular point and use various menus to construct a verbal statement and give it an affective, emotional loading. The feedback is also contextual; an expert system knowledge-base is used to present the reactions of the team members as they might happen in a real meeting.

Holland et al. (1986) indicate that mental models of social worlds are also filled with misconceptions and stereotypes. Typically, people believe social behavior is more predictable at the level of the individual than it is actually. People tend to explain social behavior according to the actors' dispositions rather than the character of the situation confronting the actor. Interactive video environments, such as the ones above, may help learners to build models of social situations and to use them in understanding social behavior and in solving social problems.

## Navigating Through Symbolic Expressions with Hypermedia

To this point, this article has spent a considerable amount of time discussing the relationship between media and the construction of situation models. Kintsch (1989), however, points out that some texts, such as literary texts, are studied in their own right. In these cases, a major component of the task is to understand a text in the context of other texts and cultural artifacts to which it refers and within which it was constructed. This section describes an example of multimedia called *hypermedia* and speculates on its cognitive effects.

Although *hypertext* and *hypermedia* have become common terms only recently, they are ideas that have been around for several decades. The terms were coined by Nelson (1987/1974) in the 1960s, but his thinking was strongly influenced by the earlier work of Bush (1945). As defined by Nelson, *hypertext* is nonlinear text. In its many emerging uses, it has come to mean a set of windows on the computer screen that are linked to information in a database (Conklin, 1987). *Hypermedia* is an extension that includes a variety of symbolic expressions beyond texts.

These terse definitions can benefit from an illustration. Picture a text document displayed in a window on the computer screen. This document can be searched by various means, including a Boolean key word search using logical functions such as AND and OR. Imagine that the document is an English translation of Plato's *Republic* and that, if desired, the user could display the document in Greek as well as in another window on the screen. In the English version, one could select a word, and the computer could identify its corresponding word in the Greek text; this operation would be reciprocal. There may be other information connected to a word or passage in the text. For example, a passage could be connected to a contemporary scholarly article that comments on it; this article could be retrieved from the database and displayed on the screen. A reference to Homer would allow the user to retrieve and display *The Iliad*. A word could be associated with a dictionary definition, a diagram, a sound, or a bit-mapped, high-resolution photograph of an ancient artifact, sculpture, or building. The name of a city or country could be linked to a map of it. The title of a play could be linked to a video enactment of its dramatization that could be displayed in yet another window.

Much of the educational development of hypermedia is occurring in a few universities, for instance, Project Perseus at Harvard (Crane, 1990), Intermedia at Brown University (Landow, 1989), and Hyperties at the University of Maryland (Marchionini & Schneiderman, 1988). The domains include the Greek classics, works of English literature, and technical material.

Spiro and Jehng (1990) contend that hypertexts ease the application and transfer of complex knowledge to new situations. Such cognitive flexibility requires the representation of knowledge along multiple rather than single conceptual dimensions. The ill-structured nature of complex situations also requires the assembly of representations, rather than the retrieval of an intact schema. According to Spiro and Jehng (1990), hypertext aids this cognitive flexibility because it allows students to use various concepts or themes to explore a topic in multiple ways; this results in the development of integrated, flexible knowledge structures interconnected by criss-crossing conceptual themes that promote the use of this knowledge to solve a wide range of problems. Each concept can be subsequently used in many ways, and the same concept can apply to a variety of situations.

The potential cognitive effects of such systems become apparent when one compares their capabilities to the reading behavior of experts as described in the previously mentioned Bazerman (1985) study. These experts read selectively, making strategic decisions based on a particular purpose and on highly developed schemata of their field. They scanned tables of contents and read parts of articles selectively and in a personally constructed order. At times, they progressed through the text rapidly; at other times, they slowed, moving back and forth within and across texts. This nonlinear reading would certainly appear to be aided by the richness of information and the nonlinear structure of hypertext.

The process may also be speeded by a hypertext that is not yet widely used. Most current implementations of hypertext systems are search-and-browse systems. The learner is presented with an established database, structured by the author, and is free to navigate through it in whatever way he or she may desire. Other systems (e.g., Kozma, in press; Kozma & Van Roekel, 1986; Scardamalia, Bereiter, McLean, Swallow & Woodruff, 1989) allow learners to add their own information and to construct their own relationships, perhaps symbolically representing them by graphic, node-and-link structures. Such systems can be made to correspond to the processes learners use when constructing interrelationships among concepts in real memory. As Salomon (1988) points out, this may prompt learners not only to think about ideas but to think about how they are interrelated and structured. More important, they provide an explicit model of information representation that, under certain conditions, learners may come to use as mental models of their thinking.

Beyond the considerable literature that lauds the potential for such systems and describes individual projects, there is little research on hypertext to date. Those studies that have been done (e.g., Gay, Trumbull & Mazur, in press; Marchionini, 1989; Egan, Rernde, Landauer, Lochbaum & Gomez, 1989) focus on the more rudimentary functions of hypertext (such as search functions) and relatively simple tasks (e.g., identifying specific information in text) rather than on learning or on problem solving. There are some encouraging preliminary findings in these studies to indicate that hypertext both calls on and develops cognitive skills in addition to those used with standard text, but much more research is needed. The Bazerman (1985) study suggests that much of the reading behavior exhibited by expert physicists is a result of their considerable domain knowledge and skill with the medium. Similar research is needed on the impact of domain knowledge and skills in hypertext.

Indeed, in a note of caution, Charney (1987) suggests that some of the very features that make hypertext so appealing may make it more difficult to use for certain students. For example, the nonlinear nature of hypertext requires readers to decide which information to read and the order in which to read it; building such sequences is likely to be particularly difficult for readers new to a domain. By comparison, the author-determined sequence of information in text and the use of certain cues to signal structural relationships may particularly improve comprehension for novices. Getting lost in hypertext is another potential problem, particularly for novices who lack the extensive schemata that would allow them to easily locate new information within that previously encountered. Finally, lacking domain-based selection criteria, novices may end up reading a great deal of irrelevant material. Thus, hypertext seems to hold some promise, but it also poses some challenges that warrant research in this area.

## *Summary and Implications*

Integrated multimedia environments bring together the symbolic and processing capabilities of the various media described above to help learners connect their knowledge to other domains. Interactive videodisc environments hold the potential for helping learners build and analyze mental models of problem situations, particularly social situations. Hypermedia environments are designed to help the reader build links among texts and other symbolic expressions and construct meaning based on these relationships. Plausible rationales have been given for the expected effectiveness of such environments, but these must be tested, and in some cases serious questions have been raised. Nonetheless, instructional designers will find these to be powerful development environments having important implications for practice.

For example, these environments may dramatically change the nature of the media decisions made by instructional designers. Until now, the selection of media has been a macrolevel decision. That is, the decision—should video be used or is audiotape sufficient?—has been based on various instructional considerations in balance, and it applies to the entire instructional presentation and to all learners. The desirability of presenting visual information for one component of the task would have to be balanced against the increased cost for the entire presentation.

The structure of these traditional, macrolevel decisions has affected the conduct of media research. The important question for media researchers has been this: What is the overall impact of one medium versus another across learners, and is this impact going to be sufficient enough to justify the additional production and delivery costs that might be involved? This is the meta-question that has driven research on media for the past thirty years and has resulted in little understanding of learning with media.

Still, media decisions for integrated multimedia environments will be microlevel decisions. With these environments, it is possible to reconfigure a presentation in response to the needs of a particular learner. The moment-to-moment selection of appropriate media can respond to specific learner needs and task demands. Audiolinguistic or even text information may be adequate for most of the presentation or for most learners, but visual information can easily be presented to a particular learner, for a particular segment, at a particular moment, and for a particular purpose.

The macrolevel decision still exists; the cost of such multimedia delivery environments is high relative to other devices. Equipment costs, however, are likely to continue to come down, and they are, for the most part, one-time costs; production costs can even be lower for such systems. Only selected segments need be videotaped; a single segment can be produced based on pedagogical grounds without having to incur the costs of videotaping the entire presentation. Design costs need not go up if the system is used to make these decisions as the interaction progresses; this will avoid the need for programming all possible branches in advance (Stevens, 1989).

A shift from macro- to microlevel design decisions requires an understanding of the moment-by-moment collaboration between a particular learner and the medium. This collaboration raises a different set of questions for the media researcher: What is the prior knowledge of a particular learner? How is this knowledge represented and structured, and how does the learner operate on it to solve problems? What is the range among learners of such representations and operations? What symbol systems can best represent various components of the task domain? How do these correspond to the way learners represent the task? What skills do the learners have in processing various symbol systems? How do they process various symbol systems together? How can the medium process these in a way that supports the learner?

Many of these questions were addressed in the research reviewed above, and this research can inform microlevel media decisions. However, the fact that these questions are now asked from within an integrated, multimedia environment will raise other, more novel questions—ones not yet addressed in research.

# Conclusions

Do media influence learning? Clark (1983) contends that media do not influence learning under any condition, but the research reviewed in this article suggests that this position must be modified. Some students will learn a particular task regardless of the delivery device. Others will be able to take advantage of a particular medium's characteristics to help construct knowledge.

Various aspects of the learning process are influenced by the cognitively relevant characteristics of media: their technologies, symbol systems, and processing capabilities. For example, the serial processing of linguistic and pictorial information in books is very much influenced by the stability of this technology. Some learners rely on pictures to help construct a textbase and map it onto a model of the situation; others can provide this model from information in memory and do not need pictures or find audio presentations sufficient. The processing of linguistic and visual information in television is very much influenced by the simultaneous presentation of these symbol systems and the information in their codes. Some learners use these to build rich representations of situations, particularly of their dynamic aspects; others can supply this information from memory, and text or audio presentations suffice. The process of learning with computers is influenced by the ability of the medium to dynamically represent formal constructs and instantiate procedural relationships under the learner's control. These are used by some learners to construct, structure, and modify mental models; other students can rely on prior knowledge and processes, and the use of computers is unnecessary.

However, Clark (1983) contends that, even if there are differences in learning outcomes, they are due to the method used, not the medium. With this distinction, Clark creates an unnecessary schism between medium and method. Medium and method have a more integral relationship; both are part of the design. Within a particular design, the medium enables and constrains the method; the method draws on and instantiates the capabilities of the medium. Some attributions of effect can be made to medium or method, but there is much shared variance between them, and a good design will integrate them. In the various studies cited above, learning was influenced by the methods used, but it was in part because they took advantage of the medium's cognitively relevant capabilities to complement the learner's prior knowledge and cognitive skills. Many of these methods would have been difficult or impossible to use in other media.

Finally, Clark (1983) calls for a moratorium on media research, but this article provides a rationale for additional research on media. There is a growing understanding of the mechanisms of learning with media, but a number of questions remain, and the cognitive effects of the more recently developed environments are speculative. Research is needed to extend this understanding.

This research can itself be promoted by the use of media. Computers provide a unique opportunity to examine learning processes and how these interact with the capabilities of a medium. Particularly useful is the computer's ability to collect moment-by-moment, time-stamped log files of key presses, typed responses, menu selections, and so forth. These data, supplemented by videotapes of students working individually and thinking aloud, can be used to examine the effects of media on learners' mental representations and cognitive processes (Ericsson & Simon, 1984). Videotapes of several students working together and talking can provide insights into how cognition is shared among students and between students and media (Roschelle & Pea, 1990). The integration of computer and video records will allow for powerful analyses of qualitative data, and the sharing of these analyses among researchers. The examination of the same raw qualitative data by psychologists, anthropologists, and sociologists can bring multiple disciplinary perspectives to bear on media research as well as help link these knowledge domains; indeed, too often they go unconnected.

Ultimately, our ability to take advantage of the power of emerging technologies will depend on the creativity of designers, their ability to exploit the capabilities of the media, and our understanding of the relationship between these capabilities and learning. A moratorium on media research would only hurt these prospects.

# Notes

1. Greeno also points out that at least in some cases information in the situation may be used directly without the need to construct and operate on mental representations. Pictures can be considered either as symbolic expressions or as concrete objects in the environment. Pictures as situated objects may be a more efficient source for processing certain kinds of information, quite apart from how that information is represented in memory. See, for example, Larkin and Simon (1987) and Larkin (1989).

2. It is important to keep in mind that graphic objects, such as those used by di Sessa (1982), may not be symbolic. That is, the objects may not be viewed as having a referent in another domain (e.g., physics), and students may learn to operate on them directly in their own right without taking them to represent concrete objects or physical concepts. The extent to which objects refer to other domains, and thus serve as symbols, should be explicitly addressed in research with symbolic environments.

# References

Anderson, D. R., and D. Field. 1983. Children's attention to television: Implications for production. In M. Meyer, ed., *Children and the formal features of television* (pp. 56–96). Munich, Germany: Saur.

Anderson, D. R., and E. P. Lorch. 1983. Looking at television: Action or reaction? In J. Bryant and D. R. Anderson, eds., *Children's understanding of television* (pp. 1–33). New York: Academic Press.

Anderson, D. R., and P. A. Collins. 1988. *The impact on children's education: Television's influence on cognitive development* (Working Paper No. 2). Washington, D.C.: Office of Educational Research and Improvement.

Anderson, D. R., E. P. Lorch, D. E. Field, and J. Sanders. 1981. The effects of TV program comprehensibility on preschool children's visual attention. *Child Development* 52:151–157.

Anderson, D. R., L. F. Alwitt, E. P. Lorch, and S. R. Levin. 1979. Watching children watch television. In G. A. Hale and M. Lewis, eds., *Attention and cognitive development* (pp. 331–361). New York: Plenum.

Anderson, D. R., E. P. Lorch, D. E. Field, P. Collins, and J. Nathan. 1986. Television viewing at home: Age trends in visual attention and time with television. *Child Development* 57:1024–1033.

Anderson, R. C., R. J. Spiro, and M. C. Anderson. 1978. Schemata as scaffolding for the representation of information in discourse. *American Educational Research Journal* 15:433–440.

Baddeley, A. 1981. The concept of working memory: A view of its current state and probable future development. *Cognition* 10:17–23.

Baggett, P. 1979. Structurally equivalent stories in movie and text and the effect of the medium on recall. *Journal of Verbal Learning and Verbal Behavior* 18:333–356.

———. 1984. Role of temporal overlap of visual and auditory material in forming dual media associations. *Journal of Educational Psychology* 76:408–417.

———. 1989. Understanding visual and verbal messages. In H. Mandi and J. Levin, eds., *Knowledge acquisition from text and pictures* (pp. 101–124). Amsterdam, The Netherlands: Elsevier.

Baggett, P., and A. Ehrenfeucht. 1982. Information in content equivalent movie and text stories. *Discourse Processes* 5:73–99.

———. 1983. Encoding and retaining information in the visuals and verbals of an educational movie. *Educational Communication and Technology Journal* 31, no. 1:23–32.

Bayle, E. 1942. The nature and causes of regressive movements in reading. *Journal of Experimental Education* 11:16–36.

Bazerman, C. 1985. Physicists reading physics. *Written Communication* 2, no. 1:3–23.

Beagles-Roos, J., and I. Gat. 1983. Specific impact of radio and television on children's story comprehension. *Journal of Educational Psychology* 75, no. 1:128–137.

Brandsford, J. D., and M. K. Johnson. 1972. Contextual prerequisites for understanding: Some investigations of comprehension and recall. *Journal of Verbal Learning and Verbal Behavior* 11:717–726.

Brasell, H. 1987. The effect of real-time laboratory graphing on learning graphic representations of distance and velocity. *Journal of Research in Science Teaching* 24, no. 4:385–395.

Brown, A. L. 1980. Metacognitive development and reading. In R. Spiro, B. Bruce, and W. Brewer, eds., *Theoretical issues in reading comprehension* (pp. 453–481). Hillsdale, N.J.: Lawrence Erlbaum.

Brown, J. S., A. Collins, and P. Duguid. 1989. Situated cognition and the culture of learning. *Educational Researcher* 18, no. 1:32–42.

Brown, J., R. Lewis, and F. Harcleroad. 1973. *AV instruction: Technology, media, and method.* 4th ed. New York: McGraw-Hill.

Bush, V. 1945. As we may think. *Atlantic Monthly* (July):101–108.

Buswell, G. 1937. *How adults read.* Chicago: University of Chicago Press.

Charney, D. 1987. Comprehending non-linear text: The role of discourse cues and reading strategies. In J. Smith and F. Halasz, eds., *Hypertext '87 proceedings* (pp. 109–120). New York: Association for Computing Machinery.

Chi, M. T., P. J. Feitovich, and R. Glaser. 1981. Categorization and representation of physics problems by experts and novices. *Cognitive Science* 5:121–152.

Clark, R. 1983. Reconsidering research on learning from media. *Review of Educational Research* 53:445–459.

Clement, J. 1983. A conceptual model discussed by Galileo and used intuitively by physics students. In D. Genter and A. Stevens, eds., *Mental models* (pp. 325–340). Hillsdale, N.J.: Lawrence Erlbaum.

Cognition and Technology Group at Vanderbilt University, The. 1990. Anchored instruction and its relationship to situated cognition. *Educational Researcher* 19, no. 6:2–10.

Conklin, J. 1987. Hypertext: An introduction and survey. *IEEE Computer* 20, no. 9:17–41.

Covey, P. April 1990. *A right to die?: The case of Dax Cowart.* Paper presented at the annual meeting of the American Educational Research Association, Boston.

Crane, G. 1990. Challenging the individual: The tradition of hypermedia databases. *Academic Computing* 6, no. 11:36–41.

Dickson, W. P. 1985. Thought-provoking software: Juxtaposing symbol systems. *Educational Researcher* 14, no. 5:30–38.

diSessa, A. 1982. Unlearning Aristotelian physics: A study of knowledge-based learning. *Cognitive Science* 6:37–75.

———. 1988. Knowledge in pieces. In G. Forman and P. Pufall, eds., *Constructivism in the computer age* (pp. 49–70). Hillsdale, N.J.: Lawrence Erlbaum.

Egan, D. E., J. R. Remde, T. K. Landauer, C. C. Lochbaum, and L. M. Gomez. April, 1989. *Acquiring information in books and SuperBooks.* Paper presented at the annual meeting of the American Educational Research Association, San Francisco.

Ericsson, K., and H. Simon. 1984. *Protocol analysis: Verbal reports as data.* Cambridge, Mass.: MIT Press.

Gibbons, J., D. R. Anderson, R. Smith, D. E. Field, and C. Rischer. 1986. Young children's recall and reconstruction of audio and audiovisual narratives. *Child Development* 57: 1014–1023.

Goodman, N. 1976. *Languages of art.* Indianapolis, Ind.: Bobbs-Merrill.

Greeno, J. 1989. Situations, mental models, and generative knowledge. In D. Khahr and K. Kotovsky, eds., *Complex information processing* (pp. 285–318). Hillsdale, N.J.: Lawrence Erlbaum.

Haas, C. 1989. "Seeing it on the screen isn't really seeing it": Computer writers' reading problems. In G. Hawisher and C. Selfe, eds., *Critical perspectives on computers and composition instruction* (pp. 16–29). New York: Teachers College Press.

Halliday, M. A., and R. Hasan. 1976. *Cohesion in English.* London, England: Longman.

Hayes, D. S., and S. B. Kelly. 1984. Young children's processing of television: Modality differences in the retention of temporal relations. *Journal of Experimental Child Psychology* 38:505–514.

Hayes, D. S., S. B. Kelly, and M. Mandel. 1986. Media differences in children's story synopses: Radio and television contrasted. *Journal of Educational Psychology* 78, no. 5:341–346.

Hegarty, M., and M. A. Just. 1989. Understanding machines from text and diagrams. In H. Mandl and J. Levin, eds., *Knowledge acquisition from text and pictures* (pp. 171–194). Amsterdam, The Netherlands: Elsevier.

Hegarty, M., M. A. Just, and I. R. Morrison. 1988. Mental models of mechanical systems: Individual differences in qualitative and quantitative reasoning. *Cognitive Psychology* 20:191–236.

Holland, J., K. Holyoak, R. Nisbett, and P. Thagard. 1986. *Induction: Processes of inference, learning, and discovery.* Cambridge, Mass.: MIT Press.

Huston, A., and J. Wright. 1983. Children's processing of television: The informative functions of formal features. In J. Bryant and D. R. Anderson, eds., *Children's understanding of television* (pp. 35–68). New York: Academic Press.

Just, M. A., and P. A. Carpenter. 1987. *The psychology of reading and language comprehension*. Newton, Mass.: Allyn Bacon.

Kintsch, W. 1988. The role of knowledge in discourse comprehension: A construction-integration model. *Psychological Review* 95, no. 2:163–182.

———. 1989. Learning from text. In L. Resnick, ed., *Knowing and learning: Essays in honor of Robert Glaser* (pp. 25–46). Hillsdale, N.J.: Lawrence Erlbaum.

Kintsch, W., and T. van Dijk. 1978. Toward a model of text comprehension and production. *Psychological Review* 85, no. 5:363–394.

Kozma, R. 1986. Implications of instructional psychology for the design of educational television. *Educational Communications and Technology Journal* 34:11–19.

———. In press. Constructing knowledge with learning tool. In P. Kommers, D. Jonassen, and T. Mayes, eds., *Mindtools: Cognitive technologies for modeling knowledge*. Berlin, Germany: Springer-Verlag.

Kozma, R. B., and J. Van Rockel. 1986. *Learning tool*. Ann Arbor, Mich.: Arborworks.

Krendi, K. A., and B. Watkins. 1983. Understanding television: An exploratory inquiry into the reconstruction of narrative content. *Educational Communications and Technology Journal* 31, no. 4:201–212.

Kuntz, G. C., U. Drewniak, and F. Schott. April 1989. *On-line and off-line assessment of selfregulation in learning from instructional text and picture*. Paper presented at the annual meeting of the American Educational Research Association, San Francisco.

LaBerge, D., and S. J. Samuels. 1974. Toward a theory of automatic information processing in reading. *Cognitive Psychology* 6:293–323.

Landow, G. P. 1989. Course assignments using hypertext: The example of Intermedia. *Journal of Research on Computing in Education* 21, no. 3:349–365.

Larkin, J. H. 1983. The role of problem representation in physics. In D. Genter and A. Stevens, eds., *Mental models* (pp. 75–98). Hillsdale, N.J.: Lawrence Erlbaum.

———. 1989. Display-based problem solving. In D. Khahr and K. Kotovsky, eds., *Complex information processing* (pp. 319–342). Hillsdale, N.J.: Lawrence Erlbaum.

Larkin, J. H., and H. Simon. 1987. Why a diagram is (sometimes) worth ten thousand words. *Cognitive Science* 11:65–100.

Larkin, J. H., J. McDermott, D. Simon, and H. Simon. 1980. Expert and novice performance in solving physics problems. *Science* 80, no. 4,450: 1335–1342.

Levie, W., and R. Lentz. 1982. Effects of text illustrations: A review of research. *Educational Communication and Technology Journal* 30, no. 4:195–232.

Marchionini, G. April 1989. *Information seeking in electronic encyclopedias*. Paper presented at the annual meeting of the American Educational Research Association, San Francisco.

Marchionini, G., and B. Schneiderman. 1988. Finding facts vs. browsing knowledge in hypertext systems. *IEEE Computer* 21, no. 1:70–80.

Mayer, R. 1984. Aids to prose comprehension. *Educational Psychologist* 19:30–42.

McCloskey, M. 1983. Naive theories of motion. In D. Genter and A. Stevens, eds., *Mental models* (pp. 299–324). Hillsdale, N.J.: Lawrence Erlbaum.

Meringoff, L. April 1982. *What pictures can and can't do for children's story understanding.* Paper presented at the annual meeting of the American Educational Research Association, New York.

Meyer, B. J. F. 1975. *The organization of prose and its effects on memory.* Amsterdam, The Netherlands: Elsevier.

———. 1985. Signaling the structure of text. In D. Jonassen, ed., *The technology of text* (pp. 64–89). Englewood Cliffs, N.J.: Educational Technology Publications.

Miller, G. A. 1956. The magical number seven plus or minus two: Some limits of our capacity for processing information. *Psychological Review* 63:81–97.

Minsky, M. A. 1975. A framework for representing knowledge. In P. H. Winston, ed., *The psychology of computer vision* (pp. 211–277). New York: McGraw-Hill.

Mokros, J., and R. Tinker. 1987. The impact of microcomputer-based labs on children's ability to interpret graphs. *Journal of Research in Science Teaching* 24, no. 4:369–383.

Nelson, T. 1987. *Computer lib.* Redmond, Wash.: Tempus Books.

Norman, D. June 1989. *Cognitive artifacts.* Paper presented at the Workshop on Cognitive Theory and Design in Human-Computer Interaction, Chappaqua, New York.

Nugent, G. C. 1982. Pictures, audio, and print: Symbolic representation and effect on learning. *Educational Communication and Technology Journal* 30, no. 3:163–174.

Pea, R. April 1990. *Distributed intelligence and education.* Paper presented at the annual meeting of the American Educational Research Association, Boston.

Perkins, D. April 1990. *Person plus: A distributed view of thinking and learning.* Paper presented at the annual meeting of the American Educational Research Association, Boston.

Perkins, D. N. 1985. The fingertip effect: How information-processing technology shapes thinking. *Educational Researcher* 14, no. 7:11–17.

Pezdek, K., and E. F. Hartman. 1983. Children's television viewing: Attention and comprehension of auditory versus visual information. *Child Development* 54:1015–1023.

Pezdek, K., and E. Stevens. 1984. Children's memory for auditory and visual information on television. *Developmental Psychology* 20:212–218.

Pezdek, K., A. Lehrer, and S. Simon. 1984. The relationship between reading and cognitive processing of television and radio. *Child Development* 55:2072–2082.

Pressley, M. 1977. Imagery and children's learning: Putting the pictures in developmental perspective. *Review of Educational Research* 47:585–622.

Resnick, L. 1987. Learning in school and out. *Educational Researcher* 16, no. 9:13–20.

Roschelle, J., and R. Pea. April 1990. *Situated learning: Computer-based multimedia analysts of learning activities.* Paper presented at the annual meeting of the American Educational Research Association, Boston.

Rusted, R., and V. Coltheart. 1979. The effect of pictures on the retention of novel words and prose passages. *Journal of Experimental Child Psychology* 28:516–524.

Salomon, G. 1974. What is learned and how it is taught: The interaction between media, message, task, and learner. In D. Olson, ed., *Media and symbols: The forms of expression, communication, and education* (pp. 383–408). Chicago: University of Chicago.

Salomon, G. 1979. *Interaction of media, cognition, and learning.* San Francisco: Jossey-Bass.

———. 1983. The differential investment of mental effort in learning from different sources. *Educational Psychologist* 18, no. 1:42–50.

———. 1984. Television is "easy" and print is "tough"; The differential investment of mental effort in learning as a function of perceptions and attributions. *Journal of Educational Psychology* 76, no. 4:647–658.

———. 1988. AI in reverse: Computer tools that turn cognitive. *Journal of Educational Computing Research* 4, no. 2:123–134.

———. April 1990. *If intelligence is distributed, what about the cultivation of individuals' abilities?* Paper presented at the annual meeting of the American Educational Research Association, Boston.

Salomon, G., and R. Clark. 1977. Reexamining the methodology of research on media and technology in education. *Review of Educational Research* 47:99–120.

Scardamalia, M., C. Bereiter, R. McLean, J. Swallow, and E. Woodruff. 1989. Computer-supported intentional learning environments. *Journal of Educational Computing Research* 5:51–68.

Schallert, D. L. 1980. The role of illustrations in reading. In R. Spiro, B. Bruce, and W. Brewer, eds., *Theoretical issues in reading comprehension* (pp. 503–524). Hillsdale, N.J.: Lawrence Erlbaum.

Schank, R. C., and R. P. Abelson. 1977. *Scripts, plans, goals, and understanding.* Hillsdale, N.J.: Lawrence Erlbaum.

Shebilske, W. L., and D. F. Fisher. 1983. Eye movements and context effects during reading of extended discourse. In K. Rayner, ed., *Eye movements in reading* (pp. 153–179). New York: Academic Press.

Shebilske, W. L., and L. S. Reid. 1979. Reading eye movements, macro-structure and comprehension. In P. A. Kolers, M. E. Wroistad, and H. Bouma, eds., *Processing of visible language,* vol. 1 (pp. 97–110). New York: Plenum.

Sherwood, R., C. Kinzer, J. Bransford, and J. Franks. 1987. Some benefits of creating macrocontexts for science instruction: Initial findings. *Journal of Research in Science Teaching* 24, no. 5:417–435.

Sherwood, R., C. Kinzer, T. Hasselbring, and J. Bransford. 1987. Macro-contexts for learning: Initial findings and issues. *Applied Cognitive Psychology* 1:93–108.

Simon, H. A. 1974. How big is a chunk? *Science* 183: 482–488.

Snow, R. 1989. Aptitude-treatment interaction as a framework for research on individual differences in learning. In P. Ackerman, R. Stemberg, and R. Glaser, eds., *Learning and individual differences* (pp. 13–60). New York: Freeman.

Spiro, R., and J. Jehng. 1990. Cognitive flexibility and hypertext: Theory and technology for the nonlinear and multidimensional traversal of complex subject matter. In D. Nix and R. Spiro, eds., *Cognition, education, and media* (pp. 163–206). Hillsdale, N.J.: Lawrence Erlbaum.

Stevens, S. 1989. Intelligent interactive video simulation of a code inspection. *Communications of the ACM* 32, no. 7, 832–843.

Stone, D., and M. Glock. 1981. How do young adults read directions with and without pictures? *Journal of Educational Psychology* 73, no. 3:419–426.

Trumbull, D., G. Gay, and J. Mazur. 1992. Students actual and perceived use of navigational guidance tools in a hypermedia program. *Journal of Research on Computing in Education* 24(3):315–328.

Vygotsky, L. S. 1978. *Mind in society.* Cambridge, Mass.: Harvard University Press.

White, B. 1984. Designing computer games to help physics students understand Newton's laws of motion. *Cognition and Instruction* 1(1):69–108.

White, B. In press. A microworld-based approach to science education. In E. Scanlon and P. O'Shea, eds., *New directions in educational technology.* New York: Springer-Verlag.

White, B., and J. Frederiksen. 1990. Causal model progressions as a foundation for intelligent learning environments. In W. Clancey and E. Soloway, eds., *Artificial intelligence and learning environments* (pp. 99–158). Cambridge, Mass.: MIT Press.

Williams, M. D., J. D. Hollan, and A. L. Stevens. 1983. Human reasoning about a simple physical system. In D. Genter and A. Stevens, eds., *Mental models* (pp. 131–154). Hillsdale, N.J.: Lawrence Erlbaum.

Wilson, K., and W. Tally. 1990. The "Palenque" Project: Formative evaluation in the design and development of an optical disc prototype. In B. Flagg, ed., *Formative evaluation for educational technologies* (pp. 83–98). Hillsdale, N.J.: Lawrence Erlbaum.

Winn, W. 1989. The design and use of instructional graphics. In H. Mandl and J. Levin, eds., *Knowledge acquisition from text and pictures* (pp. 125–144). Amsterdam, The Netherlands: Elsevier.

Wixson, K. 1984. Level of importance of postquestions and children's learning from text. *American Educational Research Journal* 21, no. 2:419–433.

Wright, J.C., A. C. Huston, R. P. Ross, S. L. Calvert, D. Tolandelli, L. A. Weeks, P. Raeissi, and R. Potts. 1984. Pace and continuity of television programs: Effects on children's attention and comprehension. *Developmental Psychology* 20, no. 4:653–666.

# 11

# Who Needs Computers in Schools, and Why?

## David Hawkridge

*What are the popular rationales for using computers in schools? Are there others that are being neglected? How do they stand up to criticism? Are they the same in developing countries as they are in industrial countries? Is there any evidence that priorities are changing? This paper addresses these questions and draws particularly on recent research, funded by the Harold Macmillan Trust, in developing countries of Africa, Asia, and the Arabic-speaking world.*

## Who Needs Computers in Schools, and Why?

Imagine for a moment that you are minister of education in some country, not this one (England). Do you like the idea? Perhaps the thought of all the perks crosses your mind, or even the notion of entertaining Sir Kenneth Baker (Minister of Education when this article was written), as he may well be before long. Or perhaps you instantly recoil from having as many problems on your hands as he has. At any rate, you may be sure that, as minister, sooner or later, probably sooner, you will have to consider seriously this question of who needs computers in schools, and why. You will receive plenty of advice, and not simply from your officials. And you will want a sound rationale.

Reprinted from *Computers & Education* 15:1, D. Hawkridge, "Who needs computers in school and why?", pp. 1–6 (1990) with permission from Elsevier Science.

I will spell out four popular rationales for using computers in schools and subject them to some criticism; then I will draw comparisons between such rationales in industrial countries and developing ones. What I have to say is based on recent work I have been doing with two British colleagues in Africa, Asia and the Arab-speaking world.[1] I am glad that the Harold Macmillan Trust funded our project, paying our coworkers in seven of those countries. Finally, I will consider whether priorities are changing. Are governments shifting their ground as they try to justify putting computers into schools?

# Uses of Computers in Schools

First, let us remind ourselves what children use computers for. In industrial countries, children use them in schools for four main purposes:

- to become generally aware of the uses and limitations of computers;

- to learn computer programming (usually in BASIC but sometimes other languages such as Pascal or LOGO);

- to learn to use programs for word-processing, spreadsheet analysis, graphics process control and information retrieval from databases;

- to learn selected topics from school subjects right across the curriculum, with the computer and educational software either complementing or temporarily replacing the teacher.

Teachers also use computers for record keeping; some teachers even keep track of the progress of individual children. Administrators use them to support such managerial and administrative functions as scheduling and financial accounting. All this is well known. Now let us consider the popular rationales behind these uses.

# Four Popular Rationales

To justify using computers in schools, the strongest reason offered by policy makers is that all children of secondary school age (and perhaps even those of primary school age) should be *aware and unafraid of how computers work,* because computers are pervading industrial societies and are likely to be important in all countries. Because schools prepare children for life, teachers should demystify computers and prepare children to deal with them. Many politicians also believe that modernisation of schooling involves bringing computers into schools. If children need to become literate and numerate, today they need also to know something about computers. All children should take courses in "computer awareness." This is what I call the Social Rationale, and I shall return to it later.

A second reason offered is that many children should learn to *operate* computers. Teaching children programming gives them some confidence in their ability to control computers, and it may be a foundation for a career in computer science. Teaching children how to use applications programs does not require them to learn programming, but it does give them skills that may be useful to them as children and possibly when they move into jobs. Specific vocational training will come later, from employers or postsecondary institutions. At school, runs the reasoning, many children, boys and girls, should take courses in "computer literacy" or even "computer science." This is the Vocational Rationale.

A third reason advanced is that children should be able to use computers in learning physics, art, or any other subject where CAL offers advantages over other methods. Schools in industrial countries such as the United States and the United Kingdom now have access, given the funds, to a considerable stock of CAL software; this is the Pedagogic Rationale, based on a strong belief that *computers can teach.*

A fourth reason is that *schools can be changed* for the better by the introduction of computers. Teaching, administrative and managerial efficiency may be improved. Some educators assert that when computers arrive in a school, its staff, parents, and children are more open to change than they usually are. Computers help children to become less dependent on the teacher as expert. Computers require children to do less memorising of facts and more information handling and problem solving. Computers encourage children to learn by collaborating rather than by competing with other children. Computers help administrators bring about change. Computers are seen as catalysts, enabling desired change in education to occur; this is the Catalytic Rationale.

## Scrutinising These Rationales

Each of these four rationales probably sounds to you reasonable enough, and quite familiar, but each is rather too simplistic. Each deserves to be scrutinised, lest its proponents be guilty of merely jumping on a bandwagon.

What does the Social Rationale lead to? Ministries of education think they must provide "computer awareness" in classes or clubs that teach an awareness of the principles on which computers work, including some elementary BASIC programming. Most children commonly get only a little hands-on experience, and usually there is no examination or test of their achievement. In industrial countries, large numbers of children are now receiving such computer education.

Where are the roots of the Social Rationale? Are they in liberal thinking, which urges free and equal access for all children to computers, the wonder machines of our age, and which wants the citizenry to be more fully developed as individuals? If so, what are governments doing to provide free and equal access? Is there strength in the idea that children can realise their individual potential because of computers in schools?

Is this Social Rationale based on the socialist utilitarian desire to bring the greatest benefit to the greatest number, in the service of all? That would mean at least avoiding the emergence of elites, or domination of the machines by one racial group or gender; yet this is not what is happening in socialist countries, let alone capitalist ones. It is not even the declared policy in any of them.

Is the Social Rationale fear-driven, in the sense that we fear lest our children should be unable to cope with these new monsters, which must be demystified? Yet it is well known that children cope with them better than we adults do!

Or is this Rationale being subtly put about by politicians in league with international capitalist financiers and manufacturers who see great profits to be made out of widespread acceptance of computers? It claims the high-ground morally, this Rationale, being for the people. But is it true that schools have been stampeded into teaching computer awareness? They have certainly been assailed by technological hype, generated by multinational companies selling information technology and information itself.

Or is the Social Rationale merely a piece of after-the-fact justification for the rather low level of what has happened in many schools? Some people argue that using computers in this way, to generate computer "awareness" is a waste of resources, because computers are potentially very powerful educational tools.

I have raised a lot of questions about the Social Rationale. But let me turn now to the Vocational Rationale. Adoption of this rationale leads to "computer studies" courses, quite often aimed at preparing secondary school children for a public examination. Such courses include substantial knowledge of how computers are designed and used, plus plenty of hands-on experience of applications such as word processing and spreadsheet analysis, and some training in programming, usually in BASIC but sometimes in Pascal.

The Vocational Rationale has a Thatcherite, market-oriented ring to it: Computers help children to prepare for jobs in the marketplace. Computers will take them to successful moneymaking, wealth-creating careers. But other major British political parties have also declared that computers are vital to our economy and students should learn how to use them. Remember James Callaghan (Prime Minister just before the article was written)? Political arguments arise instead over whether school is the right place for vocational training. Because the Vocational Rationale calls for far more time to be spent on computer education than does the Social Rationale, the question of curriculum priorities comes up. What should computers displace? Because computer-related technology and jobs are changing fast, governments adopting this rationale may be uncertain about the course content. Obsolescence is a huge problem. Worse, the lack of well-trained teachers often means that programming is poorly taught, and children must later unlearn what they learned at school once they are in jobs or postsecondary education. Wouldn't they be better off doing physics? The Vocational Rationale is not without its difficulties.

Next, the Pedagogic Rationale. This focuses on improving teaching and learning, and may well be the one that commands greatest support, perhaps overwhelmingly so, at CAL 89! It has an idealistic tone. Let me quote: We want "to enrich the existing curriculum and improve the way in which it is delivered, by using computers as sophisticated educational tools which can extend traditional ways of presenting information to children and offer new opportunities through techniques (such as simulation), possible only with computers."[2] "Enrich," "improve," "extend," and "offer" are all good positive verbs to use.

The rationale is not faulty, even if enthusiasts exaggerate a little. But the technical and financial means of following it through may be lacking as we struggle to develop satisfactory educational software. Many papers being read at CAL 89 reflect research going on to realize the potential of computers in helping children to learn. We already see examples of what computers can teach that teachers alone cannot. Some of our best hopes may lie in using computers for monitoring and sensing within science, for data logging, for robotics and computer aided design, and for information retrieval in the humanities. Clearly, we do not want children using computers in schools to learn that which teachers can teach better. The Pedagogic Rationale is essentially hopeful, if only the resources can be found.

Of these four Rationales, I think the Catalytic Rationale contains the most hidden power, but it also promises a Utopian future that will never arrive. First, it speaks of schools as they might become if computers could be present in large enough numbers and use the kind of software that would enable children and teachers to change. Supporters of this Rationale say that computers will help children to move away from rigid curricula, rote learning, and teacher-centered lessons by giving more control to children of their own learning. "Let the child program the computer, not the computer program the child," shout the likes of Seymour Papert, and it is indeed a powerful idea. Somehow, we are told, not only will teachers will adopt "more relevant" curricula by using computers but they will bring educational opportunities to a larger number of students.

I think these people are pinning their hopes on computers because their ideals for schools have not been achieved by other means. I have some sympathy for them. Optimists among us hope that LOGO, microworlds, word processing, and computer conferencing will soon favourably affect the curriculum and schools. Certainly the British Government's desire, expressed through the National Curriculum Council, is to see computers embedded in the new centralized curricula introduced in the 1990s.

Second, the Catalytic Rationale speaks of organisational change. Pessimists—and I am sure there are none here—insist that NO desirable organizational change will ever come about through introducing computers. Such people are gloomy about present attempts to computerize management information systems in schools. But administrators are already changing the way they manage schools, and they are turning to computers to help them.

Despite these qualifications, I believe that only a blind optimist or a Conservative Party politician would use the Catalytic Rationale to justify future expenditure on the basis of what has changed so far. Schools, whether they opt out or not, now have to raise funds and control expenditure. Computers help, even if one disagrees, as I do, with the underlying ideology. But computers follow the law, the law does not follow computers. They are seldom catalytic in the broad sense, although they change working practice.

# Other Rationales

These four, Social, Vocational, Pedagogic and Catalytic, are the most popular rationales being used to justify putting computers into schools, but I want to mention the three others, which I shall call the Information Technology Industry Rationale, the Cost-Effectiveness Rationale and the Special Needs Rationale.

The Information Technology Industry Rationale runs like this: In our country (it could be the United Kingdom or Zimbabwe) we want to build up a strong information technology industry. On the hardware side, we want to manufacture, or at least assemble, computers and their components. On the software side, we want to build up a highly skilled workforce of programmers capable of undertaking contract programming for customers from this and other countries.

Proponents of this rationale tend to be from within the industry, and they favor placing large numbers of locally made or assembled computers in the schools, at government expense; they comment that this will bring down the average cost of hardware and may indeed be the only way in which the national enterprise can work to the benefit of industry and commerce. The manufacturers and/or importers bring pressure to bear on ministries of education to prescribe the models they sell. Once the machines are in the schools, they expect the Vocational Rationale to prevail and have little interest in the others. They have made their market once, and may be able to make it again if the country does indeed build up a workforce of programmers. This rationale is market-driven, without doubt, under the guise of serving national interest. It often hides behind one of the four rationales I have already discussed.

The Cost-Effectiveness Rationale commands little support, even in the World Bank, but its proponents (such as Carnoy *et al.*)[3] argue that computer hardware and software can substantially replace teachers and be more cost-effective. Perhaps they draw their evidence from industrial and commercial training, where computers have in fact proved to be cost-effective in certain settings.[4] As yet, you would have to go a long way to find a private primary or secondary school based mainly on teaching through computers, and it would be operating at a loss. The rationale is faulty because it does not take into account the socialising and other humanistic roles of schools, which parents will not sacrifice; rightly, I feel.

The Special Needs Rationale asserts that children with special needs, including those with moderate or severe learning difficulties, and those who are sensorily or physically disabled, benefit greatly from using computers, which can motivate slow learners and compensate for disabilities.[5] Here the rationale is sound, but there is no general panacea: Instead, extremely patient assessment of each child's needs is essential before computer-based solutions are offered. The cost of assessment and of the technology is high.

# Rationales in Developing and Industrial Countries

Which rationale or rationales does each country choose? Do developing countries choose different ones from industrial countries? It is clear that national strategy on putting computers into schools depends to a large extent on the dominant rationale. The Social Rationale does not lead to the same strategy as the Vocational Rationale; for example, if a government wants to teach computer awareness in secondary schools, it may try to introduce low-cost microcomputers into a large number of schools. The government will expect every school to employ several teachers who, between them, can teach all children for two to three hours a week in, say, the second year. But if a government strongly influenced by the Vocational Rationale wants to introduce computer studies, possibly as an examination subject near the end of secondary schooling, medium-priced microcomputers will be needed, teachers will have to be much better trained, and probably only selected classes of children will be able to take the course. In fact, the government will probably decide to limit hardware and software provision to a minority of secondary schools in the country on the grounds of shortage of resources as well as a small national requirement for school graduates with computer studies.

Governments influenced by the Pedagogic and Catalytic Rationales must face a far larger bill for hardware and software. Consider the CAL software side for a moment. The cost of developing and marketing suitable CAL software is very high, as we know to our cost in the United Kingdom. Indeed, it is so high that few countries have tried on a large scale. The rest are importing software or doing without it. Those importing it are usually unhappy with what they get, for pedagogical as well as cultural reasons. Those doing without it are escaping from these two rationales: They are giving up hope and they may indeed be very sceptical of trials elsewhere; doubtless they have not sent representative to CAL 89.

I will not dwell here on the question of whether developing countries need computers in their schools. That is for them to decide, and many are saying yes, they do, and are stating their rationales. Though these countries advance similar rationales to those given by industrial ones, most of them place greatest emphasis on the Vocational Rationale and much less on the Social, Pedagogic and Catalytic Rationales. For example, China, which committed about £50 million in 1984 to support its policy on computers in schools, not only selects children to study computers but expects them to proceed to computer science or to be useful to their employers; China perceives computers an essential part of its drive towards modernization. India at first showed its determination to give selected children a chance to enter this field of computer technology, but educationalists there called for a less elitist project based on the Social Rationale and, to some extent, on the Pedagogic Rationale. There were even some who sought to bring the Catalytic Rationale to bear, to change Indian schools. Lately, however, the Vocational Rationale appears dominant, with the Ministry of Electronics playing a major role.

Pakistan, working on a much smaller scale than India, has a pilot project aided by an international bank. The rationale adopted so far is clearly Vocational. Six countries in Southeast Asia have planned a computer literacy course for all secondary children, with elective computer studies courses for senior classes; but hardly any CAL to serve the Pedagogic Rationale and no mention at all of the Catalytic Rationale. Of the six, some possess resources to adopt the plan in full, others not. Singapore decided some years ago that software development, in particular, would be an important part of its economic future. The Singapore Ministry of Education requires every secondary school student to take a twenty-hour computer familiarisation course, and it subsidises computer clubs in many of the schools. Mauritius and Sri Lanka are taking similar Social and Vocational lines, with undertones of the Information Technology Industry Rationale. Could these islands, with their well-educated peoples, become data-entry and software sweatshops for Asia and Africa?

Two other island nations, Fiji and Trinidad, found that their desire to follow the Pedagogic Rationale was frustrated because the British origins of their curricula clashed with the U.S. origins of the software, bought to run on U.S. machines. In Kenya, not run by the ministry, there has been a well-founded, but not entirely successful, attempt to follow the Pedagogic and Catalytic Rationales as well as the Social and Vocational. There, the market for computer-related skills is still small and can be met by children from only a few secondary schools.

# Is There Evidence of Changing Priorities?

There is no time to talk about Bahrain and Botswana, Jamaica and Jordan, Egypt, Lesotho, Nigeria, or Tunisia; and I do not know what is happening in the Latin American countries. But is there evidence of changing priorities in any country, industrial or developing? Are governments shifting their ground as they try to justify putting computers into schools?

Our recent study certainly indicates that ministries of education without a policy on computers in schools are realizing that they need one and that it must be based on a clear rationale. The trouble is, the computers arrive anyway, whether through donations or by purchase with nongovernment funds. Manufacturers and their agents are indeed asserting great pressure, which can be damaging in developing countries. Without a policy, computers, some of them obsolete, arrive in uncoordinated fashion. Teachers are not trained. Software is scarce. Hardware is incompatible. Spares, repairs, and maintenance hardly exist. Expensive private schools with a network of foreign contacts probably survive best; these schools quickly widen the gap between their children and the rest. Ministries without a policy will probably formulate one soon, but does that mean priorities are changing? Not necessarily, because for them computers may have to remain a low priority for lack of resources.

Ministries of education with a policy, backed by a rationale or rationales, may still lack the money to do all they want to, of course, and they may be unable to give computers high priority. But at least they are able to make important decisions within the policy. For example, should they allow their schools to accept donations of hardware, particularly of obsolete hardware? Should they require schools to have at least one properly trained teacher before obtaining a computer? Should they set up a center for support services and possibly to develop educational software? What degree of dependence on other countries can they tolerate? Ministries with a policy can also determine, at the right time, whether computers should receive higher priority.

Ministries of education with a policy that has been tested for some years are changing their priorities. Even in the United States, where legislatures in states such as California have been persuaded to put very large sums into computers for schools, there is pause for reflection. Here in the United Kingdom, we have a three-year study of the effects of computers on schools, accompanied yet again by short-term programs for hardware, software, and support. At the same time, subject working parties for the National Curriculum Council are being pushed to embed CAL in all the core subjects. Nobody knows what the final outcome will be for British schools. Probably the dark realities of costs will slowly be recognized, and with the dawning recognition priorities may shift again.

The Social and Vocational Rationales are gathering strength in developing countries, and the Pedagogic Rationale in richer industrial ones. The Catalytic Rationale, noble as it is, is there in the background to give us hope. The rationale finally chosen and adopted by each country will be the affordable one.

# Summary

Let me summarize. I have advanced what I consider to be the four popular rationales for using computers in schools, and I have touched on three others that are possibly being neglected. I have offered you some criticisms of each. I have shown that these rationales are not influencing developing and industrial countries in the same way. Indeed, there are interesting differences and some evidence that priorities are changing as the true costs are calculated. No matter what our personal rationales may be for using computers in schools, I believe we can look forward to an absorbing and intellectually exciting period as countries shake out the wrinkles and decide exactly what they want to do, why, and whether they can afford it.

*Acknowledgement*—My thanks to Harry McMahon for very helpful comments on a draft of this paper.

# Notes

1. D. Hawkridge, J. Jaworski, and H. McMahon, *Computers in Third World Schools,* in press (London: Macmillan, 1990).

2. Commonwealth Secretariat, "Microcomputers in Schools" (report and papers of a meeting of Commonwealth specialists, Edmonton, Alberta, 1986).

3. M. Carnoy, H. Daley, and L. Loop, *Education and Computers: Vision and Reality* (Division of Educational Sciences, Contents and Methods of Education, Paris: UNESCO, 1987).

4. D. Hawkridge, W. Newton, and C. Hall, *Computers in Company Training* (London: Croom Helm and Methuen, 1988).

5. D. Hawkridge, T. Vincent, and G. Hales, *New Information Technology in the Education of Disabled Children and Adults* (London: Croom Helm and College Hill Press, 1985).

# 12

# Displays and Communication

## Malcolm L. Fleming

The design of displays that communicate is not a stand-alone part of the instructional development process, but grows out of prior analyses of learner characteristics, tasks, and learning situations. Consequently, what follows assumes that such preparatory analyses have been done.

This chapter deals with the problem of translating the products of earlier stages of the instructional development process into a specific and detailed design for instruction. This design is typically in the form of a script or story board which includes the words and the pictures that the instructor or the medium will present, though these will be in provisional form—sketches instead of final art or photography. Translating this instructional design into final media forms is a process specific to each medium and is not directly dealt with here.

Paraphrased, the above title might read, "What kinds of displays communicate?" That is the question addressed in this chapter. A more research-oriented statement would be, "What kinds of stimuli tend to lead to what kinds of responses, for example, attention, perception, learning, concept formation?"

The principles presented as guidelines to instructional design are stated in a language and a form that translates readily to practice. These principles are expected to inform the creative processes of the designer, increasing the probability of wise decisions without guaranteeing them. Thus, although the principles are based on large bodies of research, testing of prototype designs is essential, followed by redesign and retesting as needed.

From: Fleming, M. L. "Displays and communication" in *Instructional Technology: Foundations*, R. Gagné, ed., Ch. 9, pp. 233–60. Reprinted with permission from Lawrence Erlbaum.

# Some Definitions

*Medium.* Several concepts used in the following sections require clarification at this time. To begin with, conceptions of medium range from "the medium is the message" to the medium is only a delivery system. I believe neither view to be satisfactory. Even if we reduce our conception of media to simply that of delivery systems we still must make intelligent choices among them. True, seldom is one medium the only appropriate choice (given access to several), but neither is it likely that all media will adequately meet a particular instructional requirement.

To avoid some of the conceptual pitfalls associated with use of the word *medium,* I prefer a word that broadens the concept to a position of centrality in the instructional process. The substitute word is *mediator,* which is defined as "an intervening cause or instrument, something that intervenes between parties at variance to reconcile them." There are two advantages. First, mediator defines a role or function, that of arranging effective relations between two key parties to the instructional process: the learner and the subject matter. Learning is a lifelong process between humans and their environment, while instruction (by any mediating person or agency) is a deliberate intervention between learner and subject matter. Hence, effective instruction is seen as mediating optimally between learner and subject matter, taking into account the characteristics of both.

A second advantage of the term *mediator* is that it is eclectic. Anything in an instructional system that performs the mediational role is a mediator, from live teacher to latest device. Thus, because it denotes a function essential to instruction and because it avoids some undesirable associations with the word media, the concept of mediator serves well within the systems approach, and will be used here to refer to the vehicle which delivers the instructional message. In contrast, *display* will be used to refer to the actual instructional stimulus: the page of a book mediator, the speech of a teacher mediator, the projected image of a film mediator, the images displayed by a computer mediator.

*Learner.* I use the term *learner* not simply because one hopes the receiver in the instructional situation does learn, but also because I conceive of that person as a learner wherever he or she is, and at whatever stage in life. Such a person is actively interacting with the environment much of the time, mentally and physically.

The idea of *learner strategy* is pervasive in contemporary research literature. It is presumed that for every kind of subject matter or task there is a corresponding cognitive strategy, which, if applied by the learner, will lead to acquisition of the subject matter or performance of the task accurately and efficiently. According to this conception, the designer of instruction can arrange for a match between a learner's cognitive strategy and a particular task in any of several ways: assume the learner knows and will apply the appropriate strategy, remind the learner to use a known strategy, build the strategy into the instructional method (called embedded strategy, after Rigney, 1978), or teach the strategy as a separate part of the instruction. Full application of the learner-strategy concept to instructional design awaits further study of how to induce or teach the strategies. Some task-specific work has been done, for example, on geometry problems (Greeno, 1978), reading (Cook & Mayer, 1983), language learning (Paivio, 1983). Application of a few general memory strategies is now possible and will be discussed in a following section on learning.

Other chapters in this book focus on learner differences (particularly, Chapter 8). The design principles here are addressed to general learner characteristics. Adapting these principles to different learners is assumed to involve more changes in degree than in kind.

*Task.* I will use the term *task* here in place of subject matter or content, although knowledge or information are occasionally used to avoid the behavioral aspect of "task."

Further, particular kinds of tasks will be referred to by name, for example: skill, concept, problem.

The term *schema* is used here to refer to the way knowledge is represented in memory. A schema is presumed to be an organized cluster of related information in memory. Although the designer may expect the existence of a close relation between the organization of information in a display and the presumed organization of schemata in memory, this relation does not necessarily follow.

Here are a few caveats concerning the communication principles to be described:

1. Principles will be numbered and underlined.

2. Principles have been selected primarily from four areas *(attention, perception, learning, and concept formation)* which are judged to be most pertinent to design decisions.

3. The sources cited in parentheses following each principle are mostly reviews of research. The bibliography in each review may, of course, be consulted for more specific credit to individual studies and investigators.

4. Instructional effects have multiple causes, hence the effects of any one principle may be modified by other factors.

5. The principles are broad, superordinate statements. Qualifications are omitted, hence the limits of appropriate application are not specified.

6. The applications suggested for the principles are intended as illustrative rather than prescriptive.

7. The application of research often involves over-generalization. The risk of misapplication is acceptable, however, if the designer tests and revises each instructional design as necessary.

# Attention

Attention, perception, and learning are not discrete processes. They are richly intertwined—both practically and theoretically. Even so, it is frequently advantageous to discuss them separately.

Quite simply, without attention there can be no learning. Designers typically seek both to obtain the learner's attention and to keep it. Influence on attention comes both from the display and from the learner, and the designer has some control of both.

1. *Attention is highly selective* (Treisman, 1974). We can give attention to only a small part of the environment at one time, and of that we see most sharply only the tiny, central portion of the visual field. We cope with the complexities of the environment by continually repositioning the eyes so that bit by bit we construct a functional, perceptual representation. Designers must learn to accommodate to and use this selective process called attention.

2. *Attention is drawn to what is novel or different* (Berlyne, 1970). By manipulating instructional displays the designer can readily introduce novelty. This need not be something that is entirely new to learners; it need only be different from what they have just recently experienced. For example, in speech, change the volume or inflection; in print, change

the typeface or color; in film or television, change the pace or introduce a novel element such as a sound effect. In instructional displays, novelty should be used to draw attention to the information to be learned, not to the novel element per se.

Novelty can further be understood as the introduction of change. From that perspective come the following subprinciples:

2a. Changes in brightness and particularly in motion are strong attention getting factors. Sensitivity to these factors is present even in infants, hence the designer can use them with all ages.

2b. Once attention is gained, continuing changes in the ongoing stream of instruction can help maintain it.

3. *Attention is drawn to moderate complexity* (Forgus, 1966). Obviously, this can be overdone, leading to learner avoidance. On the other hand, a too simplistic display may get very little attention.

4. *Lean displays focus attention.* This has been called attribute isolation (Bovy, 1981). The procedure here is simply to include only the most relevant information. For example, in motion pictures and TV, use close-ups; in text, delete nonessentials and use footnotes for less central information; in pictures delete irrelevant background information and superfluous interior detail in figures.

The above principles do not depend on prior learning, and hence can be used by the designer for all ages.

5. *Learned cues can direct attention* (Bovy, 1981). Examples are arrows, underlinings, circles, or rectangles around items. Such attention-directing cues are effective only with "literate" learners. Another very effective cue is simply to direct the learner verbally to look for or listen to certain features. See Figure 12.1.

Captions can have a strong effect on the amount and kind of attention given pictures. Pictures without attention-directing prompts may be scanned superficially and processed at a very shallow level (Levie & Lentz, 1982). See Figure 12.1.

6. *Learner expectations can strongly influence attention* (Eysenck, 1984). The learner's expectations (sometimes called mental set) are a powerful determinant of attention. Designers can have a strong effect on learner set or expectation by means of task instructions. Challenging questions, for example, can strongly influence what a learner attends to in a paragraph or picture, and thus determine what can be remembered.

Expectations can also influence the amount of mental effort that learners are willing to invest in attention to a display. For example, Salomon (1984) has shown that learners may have a set or expectation that television provides entertainment, and hence may not give it the careful attention necessary for systematic learning.

7. *Moderate uncertainty may induce careful attention* (Mouly, 1973). This implies that displays that are too easy or obvious may fail to gain or hold attention. The amount of uncertainty may vary with the task, less for concepts and more for problem solving.

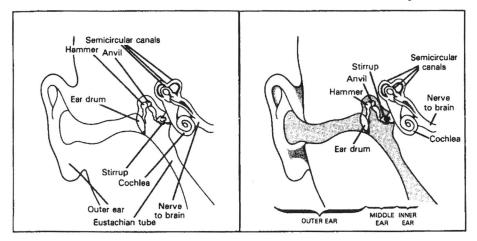

***Fig. 12.1.*** **Effects of display organization. In the improved version (right) important figures stand more clearly from the background. Labels and arrows are grouped by three major areas, simplifying attention and memory.**

# Perception

Learning is limited by what the learner perceives, and that can be influenced directly by the designer. Subsequent learning is controlled by other less direct factors which will be considered later. Perception is conceived here as an active, ongoing, constructive process. A learner presented with a display may select some part of it, compare it with some schema (organized information) in memory and immediately recognize the displayed object. Or, lacking a match between display and schema, the learner may scan further information in the display or seek another schema for comparison. This interactive, goal-oriented process may continue until an adequate match is found, an existing schema is modified, or a new schema is constructed. While principles of perception operate in all sensory modalities, the following discussion emphasizes the two modalities by which most instruction is received: visual and auditory modalities.

8. *Perception is organized* (Eysenck, 1984). Learners try to construct meaningful wholes from their environment: objects, events, ideas. Unorganized stimulation is difficult to understand and remember. The designer who produces displays that are readily organized reduces the possibility that the learner will organize the material differently and perhaps erroneously. See Figure 12.1.

8a. Perhaps the most basic organizational step in the perceptual process is the separation of the visual field into figure and ground. For example, key figures (objects, persons) in a picture are selected and given more attention than the background scene. The designer should make the essential information figural and therefore dominant. See Figure 12.1.

8b.  Orderly displays invite systematic perceptual processing (Winn, 1982). Since perception takes time, logically organized displays save instructional time and also increase the probability of correct interpretation. For example, hierarchical orderings can influence comprehension of graphic displays. Other orderings, for example, cause-effect, before-after, can simplify perception.

9.  *Perception is relative* (Helson, 1974). Perception is not registered in absolute values; rather, it functions by comparison. The implications are many.

9a.  Judgments of brightness and loudness are relative. A medium gray may be perceived to be dark gray relative to white and light gray relative to black. The apparent loudness of a musical passage will be influenced by the level of the just preceding passage.

9b.  Judgments of size or quantity are relative. The size of an unknown pictured object cannot be determined without reference to some standard, for example, a hand or ruler.

9c.  Judgments of depth or distance are relative. For instance, size and depth are inversely related; the smaller a familiar object appears to be the farther away it will be judged to be. Perceived size in a picture or screen is influenced by the frame—large if it's filled and smaller if it's not.

9d.  Judgments of time are relative. For example, judgments of time duration are relative to the concurrent activity—short if it's interesting and long if it's not. Moral to designers: keep instruction moving.

9e.  Judgments of motion are relative. Perceived motion is relative to some reference point, for example, the frame or background in a picture.

10.  *Perception is most influenced by the informative areas of a display.* The informative areas are those which are most effective in reducing uncertainty and providing a match between display structure and learner schema. Examples follow.

10a.  Contours are given more attention than uniform areas, probably because there is more information there; contours define figures (Graham, 1965). This may help explain the perceptual effectiveness of outline drawings.

10b.  Learners attend to and remember figures better than the details inside the figures (Mandler & Johnson, 1976).

11.  *Vision is most sensitive to colors in the middle of the spectrum, yellow and yellow-green, and least sensitive to those at the ends of the spectrum, violet/blue and red. Similarly, audition is most sensitive to pitches in the middle, two to three octaves above middle C, falling off toward both lower and higher pitches* (Murch, 1973; Van Bergeijk, Pierce, & David, 1960). The falling off of sensitivity toward the ends of the range can be partly compensated. For vision, add white pigment or white light (more energy) to the blue or red. For audition, special audio equipment can compensate for losses by boosting the levels of low or high frequencies.

12.  *Displays and display elements that appear similar tend to be grouped in perception and associated in memory* (Haber & Hershenson, 1973). Similarity is a pervasive factor whose influence extends to concept formation

(grouping and labeling similar things). Similarity can be made apparent in many ways: perceptually (form, size, color) as well as procedurally and conceptually. It follows that the designer has many ways of manipulating similarities; for instance, by accentuating some cues, and by eliminating or rearranging others. When objects, events, ideas are to be related, associated, organized, or conceptualized together, employing similarity factors can be facilitative.

Similarity also influences the amount of transfer of learning from one situation to another. Where extensive transfer is desired, the designer should provide for similar practice in varied contexts.

13.     *Displays or elements that appear close together in space or time tend to be grouped in perception and memory* (Murch, 1973). This principle has been called the law of proximity in perception and the law of contiguity in memory. These relationships are critical for the designer to arrange since many instructional processes depend on them.

13a.    Proximity is often a determinant of perceived causality, for example, when one event or condition, the apparent cause, is closely followed by another, the apparent effect. Film editors have often used this device to suggest cause-effect or before-after relationships.

13b.    Two proximate (side-by-side) displays invite perceptual comparison of similarities and differences. This relationship can be manipulated to emphasize similarities despite differences, and vice versa. See Figure 12.2 for an example.

13c.    Contiguity, either spatial or temporal, is a basic factor in forming associations in memory (Bugelski, 1971). Putting two symbols together in space, for example, a picture of an object together with its label, facilitates associative memory. So, too, does putting two symbols one after the other in time, for instance, words in a spoken sentence.

13d.    Classical forms of learning, such as conditioning and reinforcement, depend on contiguity factors.

14.     *Displays that are different tend to separate ideas in perception and memory* (Fleming & Levie, 1978). Display differences can be in time of presentation, in spatial location within the display, or in style or format. Such differences are common across mediators: separate paragraphs or chapters in books, fades to black between film or TV sequences, pauses in lectures, verbal cues for change, for example, "before that," "next," "in contrast." Such devices have the effect of signaling the boundaries between ideas.

When two things are quite difficult to distinguish, other methods are required, as follows.

14a.    For difficult discriminations a side-by-side (instead of separate) arrangement may be necessary to facilitate perception of the differences.

14b.    For discrimination, maximize differences. This can be done by exaggerating critical differences or eliminating similarities.

14c.    Begin with examples that are most different (easy to discriminate) and continue with those having finer differences (difficult to discriminate) (Gibson, 1969).

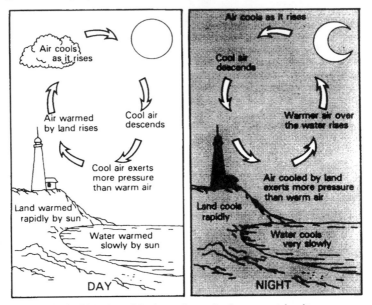

*Fig. 12.2.* **Side-by-side (proximate) placement invites comparison. Critical information is contrasted between the two, increasing its saliency. Less important information is held constant.**

# Learning

## *Representing the Information*

One might expect this section to begin with the several classical laws of learning (frequency, effect, conditioning). Instead, a generally sequential order of principles is used, depending roughly on when a designer might consider them. Thus, principles dealing with an initial presentation will precede those dealing with repeating it (frequency) and those involving learner responses following it (effect).

Probably the most important objects perceived by learners are the various kinds of symbols used in instruction, for instance, words, numbers, pictures, which refer to important phenomena in the environment. One of the more common and puzzling choices that designers make is among symbol types.

Distinctions important to the designer can be made here.

15.  *The kinds of mental operations evoked by a display are related to but not limited by the symbol systems used* (Winn, 1982). For example, a displayed picture often arouses mental words as well as mental images. A displayed word may arouse mental images (picture-like) as well as mental words. Displayed numbers can also lead to verbal or imaginal processing. Such dual-processing effects do not necessarily occur, but when they do they may facilitate learning.

16. *The kinds of information that can be presented in a display are dependent on the nature of the symbol systems used.* This is partly a function of the characteristics of the sensory modalities involved. Vision is especially sensitive to changes across space, while audition is especially sensitive to changes across time. Words are perceivable through either modality: through vision as print and through audition as speech. In contrast, pictures are generally perceivable only through vision. These sensory differences affect instruction.

16a. Words are instructionally more flexible than pictures in that they can be perceived through either the visual or the auditory modality (Fleming & Levie, 1978). This provides the designer with more mediator choices and the learner with more choices in recording and manipulating the symbols.

16b. Print and pictures are more durable than speech, that is, they are available—to processing longer (Fleming & Levie, 1978). This is due to the temporal nature of the auditory channel. Typically, the learner has one moment to perceive a spoken word but can perceive a printed word over more time. (Obviously the mediator involved can limit perception time as well; fixed-pace mediators, such as TV and motion pictures, limit both picture and print duration.)

   Thus, print and pictures are more suitable than speech (live or recorded) for presentation of complex tasks which require prolonged attention. Where auditory symbols are desired, very good sound quality and listening conditions are required.

17. *Concreteness in displays facilitates learning* (Gagné & Rohwer, 1969). This principle requires explanation; for, despite its positive effect on memory, concreteness by itself may be undesirable; although it is effective when used to exemplify abstractions. Following are more examples and explanations.

17a. The demonstration or modeling of skills can lead to their acquisition by observers (Berliner & Gage, 1976). Many motor, social, and cognitive skills are learned from models: parents, teachers, peers. The designer can make effective use of live or recorded models; for example, one can use experts in the task being taught.

17b. Pictures are better remembered than words (Gagné & Rohwer, 1969). This has been supported by many controlled studies, but the implications for instruction are not self-evident. For example, a picture may give too much information, and the most essential part for instruction may not be evident. Hence pictures generally need the constraining context of words (Mills, 1980), or selective simplification, as in line drawings (Dwyer, 1972). A common use of pictures is to repeat the information verbally stated in a display. This has been shown repeatedly to increase significantly learning of that over is learned from the verbal display alone (Levie & Lentz, 1982).

17c. Concrete words are better remembered than abstract words (Paivio, 1971). One explanation of this well-established finding is that concrete nouns more readily elicit mental images than do abstract nouns. Though designers often cannot avoid use of abstract words, they can define them with concrete words or provide examples or analogies that are concrete.

17d.   Concreteness is more effective on the stimulus side of an association than on the response side (Gagné & Rohwer, 1969). This fits well the use of pictures as stimuli and words as responses or descriptions.

17e.   Pictures and words can be reciprocally beneficial; words can delimit and interpret pictures and pictures help define, exemplify, and make memorable words (Mills, 1980). Captions and labels can have a determinative effect on how or whether pictures are studied.

17f.   Realism per se is not necessarily a virtue in instruction (Winn, 1982). This is probably apparent from the foregoing outline, but needs emphasis because picture-mediator enthusiasts have sometimes overlooked the fact that abstraction is often the intent of instruction.

18.    *Meaningful displays facilitate learning* (Eysenck, 1984). An earlier S-R psychology avoided the concept of "meaning," but yielded ample evidence that learners of nonsense syllables resorted to many techniques to make enough sense out of nonsense-syllable stimuli to permit memorization, for example, similarity to words, alphabetical order, phonics, rhymes. Current cognitive psychologists are more accepting of the concept of meaning but not much more successful in defining it. However, two factors emphasized as strongly influencing it are display organization, for example, advance organizers (Ausubel, 1968), and learners' prior knowledge of display characteristics (Reigeluth, 1983).

       To be stressed here is the power of meaningfulness over memory; the more meaningful the display the less drill or repetition necessary to memorize it. Numerous principles in this chapter contribute to meaningfulness: for example, relating instruction to learner's prior knowledge (24), making criterial cues dominant (20), make organization apparent (25), giving corrective feedback (29), and others.

19.    *The amount of displayed information that can be processed at one time is quite limited* (Moray, 1967). It follows that the information provided by the designer should be rationed. Following are some important considerations.

19a.   Information in a display is divided by the learner into chunks of a size suitable for perception and memory (Miller, 1968). Prechunking by the designer may be facilitative, in effect increasing processing capacity. Displays can be prechunked by spatial grouping, by temporal pacing and pauses, or by semantic grouping of related concepts. For example, a process of 20 steps can be divided into 4 groups of 5 steps. Though more information will be involved, that is, the names of the 4 groups, all of it is likely to be learned more efficiently.

19b.   A general limit of seven plus or minus two familiar items can be perceived and reported at one time (Miller, 1968). Perhaps five is a more dependable limit for instruction. Item size, and hence capacity, will depend on prior learning; for instance, a familiar superordinate word can be made to stand for a quantity of subordinate information.

19c.   Processing capacity is influenced both by the quantity of information involved and the type or depth of processing required (Eysenck, 1984). For example, explaining the various relationships between objects in a picture would require deeper processing than simply naming the separate objects. Thus, both the size of the display and the complexity of the task need to be controlled to keep within processing capacity limits. (However, deeper or more extensive processing generally leads to more learning.)

19d.  Familiar displays or elements require less processing capacity than unfamiliar (Haber & Hershenson, 1973). Thus, including familiar terms or examples, or using analogies to something familiar can increase capacity.

19e.  Capacity is partly determined by sensory modality; there can be more when two modalities are used concurrently than when either is used separately (Craik, 1979). For example, using both the visual modality (pictures) and the auditory modality (speech) increases capacity over either one separately. However, this effect occurs when information in the two modalities is related rather than redundant or discrepant. Also, adding more information to both modalities can overload the system so much that the learner must choose to attend to one or the other.

Directly related to the capacity problem, much research has been devoted to finding the optimum size of step in programmed instruction, but without much success. There are apparently too many factors involved to permit simple generalizations. However, Margolius and Sheffield (1961) referred to a useful measure, the *demonstration-assimilation span,* or the amount of information that can be presented before the learner must respond by rehearsing, answering questions, or applying the information. They defined this measure as the amount of information on which 75% of learners tested immediately can score 100%. Similarly, Brophy (1980) reports that effective teachers use small steps but a rapid pace to keep learners involved. The indicator for the teacher is that learners can answer correctly about 70-80% of questions. It thus appears that problems of pace and size-of-step must ultimately be answered through formative evaluation of initial designs.

20.  *Displays which make criterial information salient make learning more efficient* (Fleming & Levie, 1978). Two aspects should be noted here. First, criterial information in a complex display is often highly selective (based on a careful task analysis), and hence may not be apparent to a naive learner. Second, salience is required because of the important distinction between the nominal stimulus (what's available in the display and perfectly clear to the designer) and the effective stimulus (what the learner selectively attends to). To minimize the discrepancy between the two, the designer must make the essential part salient, dominant, noticeable. What information is criterial in Figure 12.2?

The manipulations available to the designer for the above purpose are many: eliminating the nonessential (picture background), adding the essential (definitive examples), selectively emphasizing the essential (making it larger, colored, moving, underlined, repeated). Several emphatic devices have been noted in a previous section.

Special mention should be made here of color. Despite widespread opinion, color has not been shown to have any unique effect on instruction (Lamberski, 1980). True, learners typically prefer it, but they generally learn as well without it. Color seems to be an important characteristic of displays where it is criterial, that is, essential to the subject matter (color which identifies a particular bird), where it is selectively used to direct attention to what is essential (a word printed in red), or where it is used to differentiate or group objects or ideas (color coding of a map).

21. *Contextual information may be necessary to perception, learning, and understanding* (Horton & Mills, 1984). Whereas the previous principle favors a bare-bones display, this one favors adding or retaining some contextual information. The difference is one of degree. Information that is too isolated can be misinterpreted or forgotten. This is because of the basic relational nature of cognition: figures are perceived relative to a ground, memory functions by connecting a and b (assimilating to an existing schema). For example, much recent research on reading demonstrates the dependence of word meanings on a sentence context and sentence meaning on a paragraph context (Horton & Mills, 1984).

22. *Learning can be aided where displays in initial learning stages are highly manipulated to influence attention and memory, and where, in subsequent displays, these manipulations are gradually eliminated* (Anderson & Faust, 1973).

    Maximum assistance is given the learner initially to minimize error. Then the assistance is gradually faded until the learner can respond correctly and without aid to the real situation. This method doesn't avoid maximum manipulation but attempts to remedy its undesirable effects.

23. *Alternately, learning can be facilitated where initial displays are only minimally manipulated. Criterial questions are asked; and additional manipulation, called brightening, is provided only as and if the learner requires it to give correct answers* (Ellson et al., 1965). This method avoids overmanipulation, but requires a knowledgeable tutor to keep evaluating the learner and providing remedial assistance (more manipulation, more prompts) as needed. However, this procedure can be systematized with a graduated series of questions and prompts so that nonprofessional tutors can be trained to manage it quite effectively.

    Also, the degree and kind of manipulations that are desired in instructional displays and processes depend on the characteristics of the learner, a factor dealt with in other chapters of this book. In general, the more skilled and knowledgeable the learner the less the manipulation required.

24. *Learning is highly dependent on the prior knowledge of the learner* (Reigeluth, 1983). The prior knowledge presumably provides a schema which subsumes or modifies the new information. Thus, what is already familiar to the learner can be used to acquire new learning. Many kinds of prior knowledge can be facilitative: knowledge of symbol systems, of related concepts or skills (superordinate, coordinate, subordinate), of preceding steps in a process, of known relationships (alphabetical, hierarchical), of cognitive strategies.

    While some newness or unfamiliarity in a display is necessary in order for learning to occur, limiting the new to what is necessarily new—that is, making as much use of the familiar as possible—reduces the processing and memory load, saving capacity for the essential new elements. There is a limit to this principle, for too familiar displays may be given only superficial processing that overlooks essential information. In such cases, some added difficulty in task or unfamiliarity in display may be necessary (Wickelgren, 1981).

Notice that the familiarity principle seems to contradict the novelty principle (2) discussed earlier. The difference is in the designer's intent: to attract attention, use novelty; to facilitate memory, use familiarity. It may be difficult to maintain a proper balance between the two.

## Organizing and Sequencing Instruction

Once some of the decisions on the representation of information have been made, the designer faces important alternatives in organization and sequence.

25. *Organized displays facilitate learning* (Winn, 1981). This principle extends an earlier one (8) noting the positive effect of organization on efficient perceptual processing. However, there are several ways to conceptualize and achieve organization. Three representations of organization are: the structure of the knowledge to be taught, the structure of the display, and the structure of the learner's cognitive schemata. The designer's task might be conceptualized as bringing these three representations into congruence. Relating the first two can be fairly straightforward, providing that task analysis yields a representation of the substantive relationships. For example, a spatial diagram may be employed, probably hierarchical for concepts and sequential for skills. However, dealing with the last factor, cognitive schemata, in any direct and reliable way, is beyond our present capability in most areas of knowledge. However, enough can be inferred from a learner's knowledge about a task and skills for dealing with it to permit the designer to proceed—that is, to train prerequisite skills, or embed them in the design, or assume the learner has the skills (based on pretests or prior instruction successfully completed). The next two principles are intended to influence the learner's selection and development of cognitive processes appropriate to the task at hand.

26. *What occurs in the first display or last display of an instructional unit can have a critical effect on learning* (Gagné, 1978). As a concept in the learning literature the idea of an introduction, whatever it may be called, is widely reported and valued. A sample of the various conceptions follows.

26a. Primacy and recency effects are very common in memory research; what the learner encounters first and last in a stimulus is better remembered than that in between (Berelson & Steiner, 1964).

26b. An introduction that is relatively abstract and provides an organization that subsumes the following information can aid learning. This kind of introduction, called an advance organizer, is said to provide an assimilative context for what follows. Advance organizers have been widely studied with mixed results, although when the organizers are properly designed and effects are measured by a transfer test, the results are generally positive. This seems especially true when the information is otherwise poorly organized or the learners are poorly informed (Mayer, 1979).

26c. Introductory questions have a determinative effect on learning (Anderson & Biddle, 1975). Information related to the prequestions tends to be better learned than information not related to them. Further, the type of question influences the kind of cognitive processing induced, from recall to analysis, synthesis, and evaluation (Hall, 1983).

26d. Various other kinds of introductory information affect subsequent cognitive processing and facilitate learning: instructions, statements of objectives, and topic sentences (Gagné, 1978); headings and titles (Resnick, 1981). There is evidence that what appears at the top of a display is judged to be superordinate to what follows and thus more inclusive or general, more important, or superior, relative to what follows (DeSoto, London, & Handel, 1968).

26e. Concluding material such as postquestions, summaries, and reviews can also affect what is learned. Postquestions appear to have a broader effect on learning than prequestions in that they facilitate learning of both related and unrelated information (Anderson & Biddle, 1975).

It is apparent from the foregoing that the start and finish positions in an instructional sequence provide the designer with a variety of opportunities to influence the course of cognitive processing.

27. *Repetition increases learning* (Wickelgren, 1981). This is the classical Law of Frequency, and is commonly employed by teachers and learners alike, that is, in drill and practice. It should, however, be used selectively by designers.

27a. Use repetition where meaningfulness is minimal. Use it more for rote memory tasks than for concepts (DeCecco & Crawford, 1974).

27b. Use repetition for skills that need to be maximized in precision (golf swing or basketball free-throw) and in speed (addition, multiplication, reading, writing). Also, repetition may be required to produce automatization of skill (Neves & Anderson, 1981).

27c. The newer the information the more practice and more time per repetition may be necessary (Kumar, 1971).

27d. Spaced or distributed practice generally leads to more learning than massed practice (Wickelgren, 1981). Cramming before a test (massed practice) may appear to be an exception, but does not favor long-term retention.

28. *Repetition with variety is superior to verbatim repetition* (Tulving & Thomson, 1973). This not only makes the repetition less boring but also increases the generality of the learning. Repetition in varied contexts increases transfer of learning.

The designer should keep in mind that repetition and meaningfulness are reciprocal, that is, the more meaningful the display the less need for repetition, and vice versa. Thus, a considerable investment in meaningfulness can be cost effective. See Principle 18.

## Feedback to the Learner

At this point, if not earlier, it is important for the designer to consider what learner responses might be to the tentative design resulting from the preceding, and what effect these might have on learning and on next design decisions.

29. *Feedback to learners after they have responded facilitates learning* (Kulhavy, 1977). This is the classical Law of Effect, the basic tenet of reinforcement theorists. What happens after a response is made to a display affects whether that response will be repeated, that is, learned. The association is presumably strengthened where the effect is positive and weakened where negative.

This principle has been very widely studied and applied, and should be known by designers as a central concept behind programmed instruction. However, studies have not found it to be uniformly effective, particularly in studies of programmed instruction in which learners were permitted to peek at the answers before making a response (Anderson et al., 1971). Some limitations and qualifications for its use follow. A common distinction in the literature is between feedback that is intended to reward the learner ("Well done!" "Excellent!") and that is intended to inform the learner ("Correct answer was _____"). When the learner's response is correct, rewarding feedback may be more reinforcing; while when the response is incorrect, feedback is more informative. With learners of some maturity, Estes (1972) found informative feedback to be more effective than a reward.

29a. Give praise for correct responses and more help for incorrect ones (Levin & Long, 1981). However, feedback after errors is generally more important than confirmation of correct responses (Kulhavy, 1977).

29b. Feedback for incorrect responses should include corrective procedures and further testing and feedback as necessary. This approach was found to be essential in recent research on mastery learning (Bloom, 1984). Corrective procedures can extend to probing learner errors to find why they were made (Levin & Long, 1981). This probing of errors is particularly useful in formative evaluation of an initial design in order to inform the designer of problems to remedy in a redesign.

29c. Immediate feedback is not always essential or even desirable. Delays of 24 hours can sometimes facilitate learning (Kulhavy, 1977). However, immediacy is probably important where the task is difficult or where each step is dependent on correct responding to the previous one.

29d. Feedback should be frequent in initial instruction, then reduced, and finally eliminated (Anderson & Faust, 1973).

All of the above feedback principles assume that a responsive mediator (teacher, computer, or other) is available.

## *Activity and Strategy of the Learner*

The designer can assume the learner is active, overtly or covertly. The problem is that of guiding and sustaining the learner's on-task activity and reducing or eliminating the off-task activity.

30. *Learning is facilitated where the learner reacts to or interacts with the criterial information, and the more activity the more learning, within limits* (Levin & Long, 1981). Although, as noted earlier, repetition can increase learning, the emphasis here is on more varied activity.

30a. Both overt and covert activity can aid learning. Thus, mental activity of various kinds is included in the above principle, the designer's problem being how to induce it. This is related to the concept of level of processing, that is, from a rote superficial level to a higher conceptual or problem-solving level. Results from study of processing levels have shown greater learning associated with deeper levels of processing, generally induced through higher cognitive tasks. Though some investigators (e.g., Horton & Mills, 1984) have explained this kind of result as mental elaboration or mental effort, the levels-of-processing concept provides the designer a useful heuristic for finding ways to maximize learner cognitive involvement.

30b. Learner involvement varies with type of task, over which the designer has considerable control. For example, as discussed earlier, the insertion of questions in displays can markedly influence the learner's level of activity, both quantitatively and qualitatively. See Figure 12.3 for an example of the use of questions with an illustration.

As noted in the introduction to this chapter, learners acquire strategies (systematic ways of dealing with information) partly from trial-and-error learning, partly from strategies embedded in instruction, and partly from direct instruction. Two of the best-established and most widely useful memory strategies will be discussed here.

31. *A learner strategy that consists of the generation of relational mental images can markedly increase learning* (Eysenck, 1984). A mental image is a representation in the learner's mind that corresponds to some degree to concrete objects and events. Extensive research has established that where two words (concepts) are to be associated, forming a mental image of the object, event, or idea which each word refers to can lead to twice as much learning as subvocal repetition of the word pair, provided the two images interact in some way (Bower, 1972). Several qualities of mental images have been compared. The results suggest that while image vividness and bizarreness may sometimes be helpful, it is essential that there be some interaction between the images to be associated such that a single, composite image be formed.

    There is evidence that, for a particular task, provision of a picture of interacting objects may lead to more learning than provision of instructions for the learner to form interacting mental images of the objects (Levin, 1979). However, there is also long-range merit in training learners to use mental imagery as a memory strategy that is easy to learn, inexpensive to apply, and widely applicable (Higbee, 1979).

32. *A learner strategy that consists of the generation of a sentence or paragraph context for embedding words to be memorized can increase learning* (Bower, 1973). This is a form of mental elaboration upon the given information, such that meaningful relations are formed between the words to be remembered and the sentence context. This has the effect of raising the level of processing from rote to conceptual. Even the use of simple rhymes can facilitate memory; for example, use "i" before "e," except after "c."

The above two principles raise again the issue as to how far instruction should go in supplanting learner strategies (with pictures or verbal structures) instead of inducing them (mental imagery or mental elaboration). While the designer's decision in any particular case can be argued, there seems to be a consensus that learners can and should be taught a wide range of cognitive strategies, such as imagery and elaboration. There is also evidence that repeated performance of a cognitive task can lead to automatization of the strategies involved (Gagné & Dick, 1983). This greatly increases efficiency on that task and may result in strategies that can be transferred to other tasks. There is further evidence that repeated exposure to a certain mediator can induce learning of cognitive strategies characteristic of that mediator. For example, repeated zooming into details of a painting seems to induce a more analytical strategy toward study of subsequent paintings (Salomon, 1979). But such effects may not always be positive. Extensive exposure to broadcast TV may lead to preferences for shallow processing and low investment of mental effort.

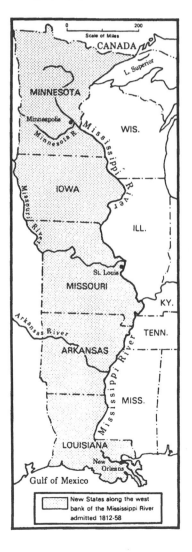

**Fig. 12.3.** Use of questions to influence learner involvement. 1) Name the new states created along the west bank of the Mississippi River. 2) Which has an international boundary? 3) What effect might the Mississippi and its tributaries have on settlement to the west?

# Concept Formation

Concepts are commonly thought of as names or labels (common nouns) for groups of things. More precisely, concepts are what common nouns refer to, that is, a set of referents (objects, events, or ideas) which have some characteristics or defining attributes in common. Concepts enable us to group a very large number of things into a finite number of categories. Without them, learning to cope with our environment would be very difficult. Concepts are built on the important regularities observed in the environment, and thus are the core of classroom learning.

As implied above, a concept is more than its label. It is also more than its definition. Both label and definition can be memorized, but concept formation ultimately requires a higher cognitive process, a generalization across a varied set of examples. Thus, another group of principles is required to assist the designer in moving learners from memorization processes to conceptualization processes.

Because of recent research, some older concepts about concepts have been modified. The classical view that all examples have *common* defining attributes is now seen as largely limited to mathematics and science concepts. For other concepts, the attributes may be only probable and be based on the relative similarity of examples to a prototypical example. Such concepts are common in the social sciences and humanities (Medin, 1984). Thus, despite an effort toward achieving clear-cut classical-type concepts, many remain with fuzzy borders and with examples having a gradient of representativeness.

Just what may be the instructional implications of the above range of concept types is not yet clear. Consequently, the principles which follow will in general assume classical-type concepts, for they have been most extensively studied in learning contexts.

As discussed in the preceding section on learning, what occurs first in concept instruction may have a determinative effect on what follows. For example, prior learning of relevant words (names of attributes, examples, related concepts) and prior familiarization of relevant objects would be facilitative (Brien, 1983).

33. *Concrete concepts are generally easier to learn than abstract concepts* (Clark, 1971). This mainly serves to extend a memory principle encountered earlier (17). It assumes that concrete (more memorable) examples will be used in instruction.

34. *Abstract concepts can be learned from various verbal structures: definitions, descriptions of attributes, descriptions of examples, synonyms* (Klausmeier et al., 1974). While pictures may be more memorable than words, as noted in 17b, abstract concepts are unlikely to have readily picturable examples. Even abstract pictures may include too much without very careful control of noncriterial attributes. Hence, the use of relatively concrete words (more memorable) to describe abstract concepts (less memorable) seems appropriate. Analogies may be very useful as well.

## *Selection of Examples and Nonexamples*

Five kinds of information are useful for concept instruction: name, definition, attributes, and examples and nonexamples; and this is the sequence in which they are often selected and presented by designers. The opposite view is taken here, that is, choose examples first because only from them can the common attributes be reliably determined;

and only from those attributes can an accurate definition be derived. However, when the choice has been made to begin with a definition, the designer must be sure to verify it with reference to examples. The definition must reliably and efficiently distinguish between examples and nonexamples.

35. *Use both examples and nonexamples in instruction* (DeCecco & Crawford, 1974). Often instruction includes only examples. However, it is the non-examples that clarify for the learner just what is distinctive about the concept, that is, what distinguishes examples from nonexamples.

36. *Use a wide variety of examples to represent their full range of divergence* (Tennyson, 1980). These examples would be expected to be alike in criterial attributes but as varied as possible in noncriterial attributes. The effect is to clarify for the learner what defines the concept (doesn't change) and what is irrelevant to it (does change). Figure 12.4 provides an example.

37. *Use nonexamples that are close in to (similar to) examples* (Tennyson, 1980). These close-in nonexamples are very important instructionally, for they are the very ones that learners will find confusing and thus require special help with. These nonexamples will be similar to examples in one or more criterial attributes, or noncriterial attributes, or both.

38. *Use sufficient examples to suggest the applicable range of the concept. Use close-in nonexamples to cover the most common and confusing ones and to delimit the concept* (DeCecco & Crawford, 1974). This provides a basis for controlling the number and kinds of examples and nonexamples needed for instruction.

## *Presentation of Examples and Definitions*

Presentation order has been much debated. The definition (rule) can be presented first and then the examples. This deductive approach has been dubbed "ruleg." Or, the examples can be presented first, followed by the definition (rule). This inductive approach has been called "egrule." A combined approach has much to recommend it. First, present a simple and clear example or two, derive from them a rule (definition or set of criterial attributes), then apply it to a wide range of examples and nonexamples (Engelmann, 1969). The initial example(s) could be eliminated when it is considered that the learner would understand the concept in abstract verbal form, that is, by its definition.

39. *Display of the criterial attributes increases concept learning as opposed to a presentation requiring the learner to discover them* (Anderson & Faust, 1973). This can be done in several ways: present a definition, present a list of attributes, direct attention to the attributes in examples. Where a discovery method is preferred, more examples may be required, and criterial attributes should be as few and as apparent to the learner as possible (Anderson & Faust, 1973).

40. *Initial examples should be representative of the concept, relatively familiar, and with unambiguous criterial attributes* (Anderson & Faust, 1973). *Subsequent presentations should include both examples and nonexamples and be arranged in order of increasing difficulty* (Tennyson, 1980). This is essentially a reiteration of the simple-to-complex order recommended earlier for instruction.

41.  *Display examples and nonexamples simultaneously or in close succession while keeping earlier ones in view* (DeCecco & Crawford, 1974). This reduces memory load and permits direct comparisons of similarities among examples (see Figure 12.4) and differences between examples and nonexamples. This is another application of the proximity-contiguity principle (13).

Some writers (Ali, 1981; Tennyson, 1980) also recommend presentation of matched pairs: an example and then a close-in nonexample, the pair being similar in non-criterial attributes. This would certainly draw learner attention to criterial attributes.

42.  *Displaying the concept name in contiguity with examples facilitates associating the two* (DeCecco & Crawford, 1974). Contiguity can mean either close together in space (computer terminal) or in time (voice over picture).

43.  *Displaying a definition as an organized list of attributes can increase concept learning over the usual sentence format* (Markle, 1975). This technique selectively emphasizes each attribute that might otherwise be lost in a long definition.

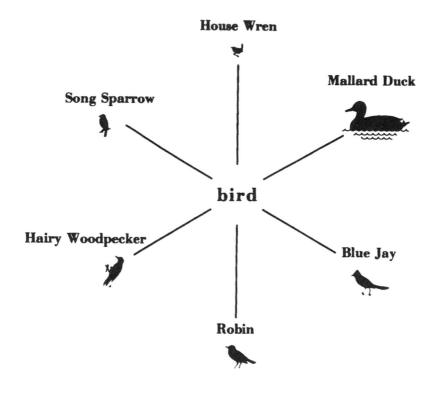

**Fig. 12.4.** Concept (bird) related to a range of divergent examples. Common attribute (configuration) is accentuated by similar poses across examples. Irrelevant attribute (size) is eliminated by variation across examples.

44.  *When dealing with a concept that is probable (not classical), present the central meaning, then a series of carefully chosen examples, for example, model example, contrary example, related example, borderline example, together with the context of use* (Hall, 1983). As noted in the beginning paragraph of this section, there have not been many studies contrasting instructional methods for this type of concept with those for classical concepts.

  Practice with newly learned concepts is important, as would be expected from learning principles such as 27.

45.  *Consolidation of new conceptual learning depends on further learner activity, including opportunities to practice identifying additional examples and nonexamples, to describe criterial attributes, and to apply the concept to various situations* (Klausmeier et al., 1974).

# Other Cognitive Processes

Considerable recent research has examined problem solving, primarily with reference to the cognitive processes or strategies employed. Most results appear to be task specific, for example, solving geometry problems, (Greeno, 1978), playing poker (Langley & Simon, 1981), solving spatial-aptitude problems (Cooper, 1980), learning maps (Stasz & Thorndyke, 1980), inductive reasoning (Pellegrino & Glaser, 1980). However, it is generally found that good problem solvers engage in certain kinds of activities, for instance, systematic study of the situation, planning moves, trying alternatives, monitoring the effects, evaluating.

Thus it seems apparent that certain task-specific strategies have been analyzed and can now be taught (Greeno & Simon, in press). Also, general problem solving strategies, if such there be, need further study.

# Summary

One way of summarizing this chapter would be through a four-part model of the learner. As here conceived, the learner actively seeks *stimulation* (information) in the environment, is particularly attentive to *order* (regularities) there, requires some *strategy* for dealing with that stimulation and order, and as a general consequence of this ongoing process derives *meaning* from the environment (Fleming, 1980). In general, *any instructional situation should provide for these four learner needs.*

These learner needs can serve as an organizing aid to memory for many of the foregoing principles by forming them into four clusters. Under *stimulation* could be grouped these attention principles: selectivity, and novelty; plus these learning principles: concreteness, prior knowledge, and salient criterial attributes; as well as these concept formation principles: varied examples, and close-in nonexamples. Under *order* could be grouped these perception principles: organization, similarity, and proximity-contiguity; plus these learning principles: limited capacity, similarity, and primacy-recency; as well as this concept-formation principle: simultaneous display of examples. Under *strategy* could be grouped the perception principle: expectancy; and the learning principles: activity, strategy, mental imagery, and elaboration. Under *meaning* could be grouped the attention principle, uncertainty; and the learning principles, meaningfulness and feedback.

# Author's Notes

*MALCOLM L. FLEMING is Professor Emeritus, Indiana University Audio-Visual Center and Department of Instructional Systems Technology, School of Education, Indiana University.*

*Special thanks are expressed to Dr. W. Howard Levie for a thorough critique of the manuscript and numerous thoughtful suggestions for improving it. Appreciated as well are the illustrations by Suzanne Hull, Michael Neff, and Irene Lee. Indiana University Audio Visual Center.*

# References

Ali, A. M. (1981). The use of positive and negative examples during instruction. *Journal of Instructional Development,* 5(1), 2–7.

Anderson, R. C. & Biddle, W. B. (1975). On asking People question, about what they are reading. In G. H. Bower (Ed.), *The psychology of learning and motivation* (Vol. 9). New York: Academic Press.

Anderson, R. C. & Faust, G. W. (1973). *Educational psychology, The science of instruction and learning.* New York: Dodd, Mead.

Anderson, R. C., Kulhavy, R. W. & Andre, T. (1971). Feedback procedures in programmed instruction. *Journal of Educational Psychology,* 62, 148–156.

Ausubel, D. P. (1968). *Educational psychology: A cognitive view.* New York: Holt, Rinehart, and Winston.

Berelsen, B. & Steiner, G. A. (1964). *Human behavior: An inventory of scientific findings.* New York: Harcourt, Brace & World.

Berliner, D. C. & Gage, N. L. (1976). The psychology of teaching methods. In N. L. Gage (Ed.), *The psychology of teaching methods.* NSSE Yearbook (Vol. 75, Pt. 1). Chicago: University of Chicago Press.

Berlyne, D. E. (1970). Attention as a problem in behavior theory. In D. I. Mostofsky (Ed.), *Attention: Contemporary theory and analysis.* New York: Appleton-Century-Crofts.

Bloom, B. S. (1984). The 2 Sigma problem: The search for methods of group instruction as effective as one-to-one tutoring. *Educational Researcher,* 13(6), 4–16.

Bovy, R. C. (1981). Successful instructional methods: A cognitive information processing approach. *Educational Communication and Technology Journal,* 29, 203–217.

Bower, G. H. (1973). How to . . . ah . . . remember. *Psychology Today,* 7(5), 62–70.

Bower, G. H. (1972). Mental imagery and associative memory. In L.W. Gregg (Ed.), *Cognition in learning & memory.* New York: Wiley.

Brien, R. (1983). Sequencing instruction. A cognitive science perspective. *Programmed Learning and Educational Technology,* 20(2), 102–114.

Brophy, J. (1980). *Recent Research on Teaching.* Paper presented at annual meeting of Northeast Educational Research Association. (ERIC No. ED 204280)

Bugelski, B. R. (1971). *The psychology of learning applied to teaching.* Indianapolis: Bobbs-Merrill.

Clark, D. C. (1971). Teaching concepts in the classroom: A set of teaching prescriptions derived from experimental research. *Journal of Educational Psychology*, 62. 253–264.

Cook, L. K. & Mayer, R. E. (1983). Reading strategies training for meaningful learning from prose. In M. Pressley & J. R. Levin (Ed.), *Cognitive strategy research, educational applications.* New York: Springer-Verlag.

Cooper, L. (1980). Spatial information processing: Strategies for research. In R. E. Snow, P. A. Federico & W. E. Montague (Eds.), *Aptitude, learning, and instruction* (Vol. 1). Hillsdale, N.J.: Lawrence Erlbaum.

Craik, F. I. M. (1979). Human memory. *Annual Review of Psychology*, 30, 63–102.

DeCecco, J. P. & Crawford, W. R. (1974). *Psychology of learning and instruction: Educational psychology.* Englewood Cliffs, N.J.: Prentice-Hall.

DeSoto, C. B., London, M. & Handel, S. (1968). Reasoning and spatial representations. *Journal of Verbal Learning & Verbal Behavior*, 7, 351–357.

Dwyer, F. M. (1972). *A Guide for improving visualized instruction.* State College, Pa.: Learning Services.

Ellson, D. G., Barber, L., Engle, T. L. & Kampwerib, L. (1965). Programmed tutoring: A teaching aid and a research tool. *Reading Research Quarterly,* 1, 77–127.

Engelmann, S. (1969). *Conceptual learning.* San Rafael, Calif.: Dimensions.

Estes, W. K. (1972). Reinforcement in human behavior, *American Scientist*, 1972, 60, 723–729.

Eysenck, M. W. (1984). *A handbook of cognitive psychology.* Hillsdale, N.J.: Lawrence Erlbaum.

Fleming, M. (1980). From seeing and hearing to remembering: A conception of the instructional process. *Instructional Science*, 9, 311–326.

Fleming, M. & Levie, W. H. (1978). *Instructional message design: Principles from the behavioral sciences.* Englewood Cliffs, N.J.: Educational Technology.

Forgus, R. H. (1966). *Perception: The basic process in cognitive development.* New York: McGraw-Hill.

Gagné, E. D. (1978). Long-term retention of information following learning from prose. *Review of Educational Research,* 48, 629–665.

Gagné, R. M., & Dick, W. (1983). Instructional psychology, *Annual Review of Psychology,* 34, 261–295.

Gagné, R. M. & Rohwer, W. D. (1969). Instructional psychology. *Annual Review of Psychology,* 20, 381–418.

Gibson, E. J. (1969). *Principles of perceptual learning and development.* New York: Meredith.

Graham, C. H. (1965). *Vision and visual perception.* New York: Wiley.

Greeno, J. G. (1978). A study of problem solving. In R. Glaser (Ed.), *Advances in instructional psychology,* (Vol. 1). Hillsdale, N.J.: Lawrence Erlbaum.

Greeno, J. G. & Simon, H.A. (in press). Problem solving and reasoning. In R. C. Atkinson, R. Herrnstein, G. Lindzey & R. D. Luce (Eds.), *Stevens' handbook of experimental psychology.* (Revised ed.). New York: Wiley.

Haber, R. N. & Hershenson, M. (1973). *The psychology of visual perception.* New York: Holt, Rinehart and Winston.

Hall, K. A. 1983. Content structuring and question asking for computer-based education. *Journal of Computer-Based Instruction,* 10(1–2), 1–7.

Helson, H. (1974). Current trends and issues in adaptation- level theory. In P. A. Fried (Ed.), *Readings in perception: Principle and practice.* Lexington, Mass.: Heath.

Higbee, K. L. (1979). Recent research on visual mnemonics: Historical roots and educational fruits. *Review of Educational Research,* 49, 611–629.

Horton, D. L. & Mills, C. B. (1984). Human learning and memory. *Annual Review of Psychology,* 35, 361–394.

Klausmeier, H. J., Ghatala, E. S. & Frayer, D. A. (1974). *Conceptual learning and development: A cognitive view.* New York: Academic Press.

Kulhavy, R. W. (1977). Feedback in written instruction. *Review of Educational Research,* 47, 211–232.

Kumar, V. K. (1971). The structure of human memory and some educational implications. *Review of Educational Research,* 41, 379–417.

Lamberski, R. J. (1980). *A comprehensive and critical review of the methodology and findings in color investigations.* Paper presented at the annual convention of the Association for Educational Communications and Technology, Denver, Colo.

Langley, P. & Simon, H. A. (1981). The central role of learning in cognition. In J. R. Anderson (Ed.), *Cognitive skills and their acquisition.* Hillsdale, N.J.: Lawrence Erlbaum.

Levie, W. H. & Lentz, R. (1982). Effects of text illustrations: A review of research. *Educational Communication and Technology Journal,* 30, 195–232.

Levin, J. R. (1979). *On functions of pictures in prose.* Wisconsin University, Madison: Research and Development Center for Individualized Schooling. (ERIC No. ED 186847)

Levin, T. & Long, R. (1981). *Effective instruction.* Alexandria, Va.: Association for Supervision and Curriculum Development. (ERIC No. 200572)

Mandler, J. M. & Johnson, N. S. (1976). Some of the thousand words a picture is worth. *Journal of Experimental Psychology: Human Learning & Memory,* 2, 529–540.

Margolius, G. J. & Sheffield, F. D. (1961). Optimum methods of combining practice with filmed demonstrations in teaching complex response sequences: Serial learning of a mechanical assembly task. In A. A. Lumsdaine (Ed.), *Student response in programmed instruction.* Washington, D.C.: National Academy of Sciences, National Research Council.

Markle, S. M. (1975). They teach concepts, don't they? *Educational Researcher,* 4(6), 3–9.

Mayer, R. E. (1979). Twenty years of research on advance organizers: Assimilation theory is still the best predictor of results. *Instructional Science,* 8, 133–167.

Medin, D. L. & Smith, E. E. (1984). Concepts and concept formation. *Annual Review of Psychology,* 35, 113–138.

Miller, G. A. (1968). The magical number seven, plus or minus two: Some limits on our capacity for processing information. In R. N. Haber (Ed.), *Contemporary theory and research in visual perception.* New York: Holt, Rinehart and Winston.

Mills, M. I. (1980). A study of human response to pictorial representations on *Telidon. Telidon Behavioral Research 3.* Quebec: Montreal University.

Moray, N. (1967). Where is capacity limited? A survey and a model. In A. F. Sanders (Ed.), *Attention and performance*. Amsterdam: North-Holland.

Mouly, G. J. (1973). *Psychology for effective teaching*. New York: Holt, Rinehart, and Winston.

Murch, G. M. (1973). *Visual and auditory perception*. Indianapolis: Bobbs-Merrill.

Neves, D. M. & Anderson, J. R. (1981). Knowledge compilation: Mechanisms for the automatization of cognitive skills. In J. R. Anderson (Ed.), *Cognitive skills and their acquisition*. Hillsdale, N.J.: Lawrence Erlbaum.

Paivio, A., (1971). *Imagery and verbal processes*. New York: Holt, Rinehart and Winston.

———. (1983). Strategies in language learning. In M. Pressley & J. R. Levin (Eds.). *Cognitive strategy research: educational applications*. New York: Springer-Verlag.

Pellegrino, J. & Glaser, R. (1980). Components of inductive reasoning. In R. E. Snow, P. A. Federico & W. A. Montague (Eds.), *Aptitude, learning, and instruction* (Vol. 1). Hillsdale, N.J.: Lawrence Erlbaum.

Reigeluth, C. M. (1983). Meaningfulness and instruction: Relating what is being learned to what a student knows. *Instructional Science,* 12, 197–218.

Resnick, L. B. (1981). Instructional psychology. *Annual Review of Psychology,* 32, 659–704.

Rigney, J. W. (1978). Learning strategies: A theoretical perspective. In H. F. O'Neil (Ed.), *Learning strategies*. New York: Academic Press.

Salomon, G. (1979). Media and symbol systems as related to cognition and learning. *Journal of Educational Psychology,* 71, 131–148.

———. (1984). Television is "easy" and print is "tough": The differential investment of mental effort in learning as a function of perceptions and attributions. *Journal of Educational Psychology.* 76, 647–658.

Stasz, C. & Thorndyke, P. (1980). *The influence of visual-spatial ability and study procedures on map learning skill*. (N-1501-ONR). Santa Monica, Calif.: Rand.

Tennyson, R. D. (1980). The teaching of concepts: A review of instructional design research literature. *Review of Educational Research,* 50, 55–70.

Treisman, A. M. (1974). Selective attention in man. In P. A. Fried (Ed.), *Readings in perception: Principle and practice*. Lexington, Mass.: Heath.

Tuiving, E., and D. M. Thomson. (1973). Encoding specificity and retrieval processes in episodic memory. *Psychological Review,* 80, 352–373.

Van Bergeijk, W. A., Pierce, J. R. & David, E. E. (1960). *Waves and the ear*. Garden City, N.Y.: Anchor Books.

Wickelgren, W. A. (1981). Human learning and memory. *Annual Review of Psychology.* 32, 21–52.

Winn, W. (1982). *Status and trends in visual information processing*. Paper presented at the annual meeting of the Association for Educational Communication and Technology, Dallas, Tex.

———. (1981). The meaningful organization of content: Research and design strategies. *Educational Technology,* 21(8), 7–11.

# 13

# Development and Use
# of the ARCS Model of
# Motivational* Design

### John M. Keller

The ARCS Model of motivation was developed in response to a desire
to find more effective ways of understanding the major influences on the
motivation to learn, and for systematic ways of identifying and solving problems
with learning motivation. The resulting model contains a four category synthesis of variables that encompasses most of the areas of research on human
motivation, and a motivational design process that is compatible with typical
instructional design models. Following its development, the ARCS Model
was field-tested in two inservice teacher education programs. Based on the
results of these field tests, the ARCS Model appears to provide useful assistance to designers and teachers, and warrants more controlled studies of its
critical attributes and areas of effectiveness.

Keller, J. M. 1987. Development and use of the ARCS model of motivation design. *Journal of
Instructional Development* 10(3)2–10. Reprinted with permission of Association for Educational
Communications and Technology.
*Original title: Development and Use of the ARCS Model of Instructional Design.

# Can Motivation Be Systematically Influenced?

Seldom do the arguments about the boundaries of a teacher's responsibilities or whether teaching is an art or science become more animated than when discussing the motivation of students. Instructional designers have similar concerns. Typically, motivation is viewed as highly unpredictable and changeable, subject to many influences over which the teacher or designer has no control. Consequently, both teachers and designers often view their responsibility as providing good quality instruction, and assume it is the student's responsibility to decide whether or not to take advantage of the opportunity to learn.

This is, however, a rationalization in that we know that no matter how motivated learners are when they begin a course, it is not too difficult to bore them, if not kill their interest completely. Conversely, it is possible to stimulate or even inspire the students' desire to achieve. Perhaps the rationalization results from the assumption that because motivation is a largely uncontrollable state, it is easier to think of it as the student's responsibility.

With respect to students' social behavior, most teachers do assume that motivation can be controlled by the appropriate application of rules and reinforcements; but when it comes to inspiring interest in a school subject, the popular view is that it requires intuition and native talent. How many times have you heard a teacher or designer say, "I know my subject, but I'm not really an entertainer?"

A concern for these issues led to the exploration of two questions. First, is it possible to synthesize the many concepts and theories of human motivation into a simple, meaningful model, or schema, that would be useful to a practitioner? Second, is it possible to develop a systematic, as opposed to intuitive, approach to designing motivating instruction? Exploration of these questions led to a review of the literature, the development of an approach called the ARCS Model, and field tests of the model with two different groups of teachers.

## What Is the ARCS Model?

The ARCS Model (Keller, 1984) is a method for improving the motivational appeal of instructional materials. It has three distinctive features. First, it contains four conceptual categories that subsume many of the specific concepts and variables that characterize human motivation. Second, it includes sets of strategies to use to enhance the motivational appeal of instruction. And third, it incorporates a systematic design process, called motivational design (Keller, 1987), that can be used effectively with traditional instructional design models. Each of these is described in further detail below.

## Why the ARCS Model?

When work began (Keller, 1979) on the development of the ARCS Model, there were no macro theories or models that directly addressed the question of how to create instruction that would stimulate the motivation to learn. Most of the application-oriented theory and research on motivation dealt either with psychological approaches to changing individual motivational characteristics (e.g. McClelland, 1965), or with job satisfaction and work performance (e.g. Steers & Porter, 1987).

In education, motivation was most generally studied in terms of classroom control (e.g. Doyle, 1985), reinforcement of learning (e.g. Skinner, 1961), or the affective outcomes of instruction (e.g. Krathwohl, Bloom, & Masia, 1964). There were some good applications-oriented materials (e.g. Mager, 1968; Wlodkowski, 1978), but they tended to be somewhat restricted in their approach and theoretical foundation. They did not help the designer or teacher know how many or what types of strategies to use with a given audience, and they did not incorporate important principles from several areas of motivational research that have been studied in recent years (e.g. curiosity, sensation seeking, and intrinsic motivation). Subsequently, work has been done to help students learn how to be self-motivated (e.g. McCombs, 1984), and Wlodkowski (1985) has expanded the scope of content and application of his work. But none of these models takes a design or problem-solving approach.

# Where Did the ARCS Model Originate?

The ARCS Model is based upon the macro theory of motivation and instructional design developed by Keller (1979, 1983). It is grounded in expectancy-value theory which derives from the work of Tolman (1932) and Lewin (1938). Expectancy-value theory assumes that people are motivated to engage in an activity if it is perceived to be linked to the satisfaction of personal needs (the value aspect), and if there is a positive expectancy for success (the expectancy aspect).

In the original model (Keller, 1979, 1983), these two categories were expanded to four. The category called *value* was subdivided into two categories, *interest* and *relevance*. The third category, *expectancy,* remained the same, and a fourth category called *outcomes* was added. *Interest and relevance* were separated to make a distinction between a set of variables, or constructs, that are concerned primarily with curiosity and arousal versus other motives such as "need for achievement" and "perceived utility." All of these variables have an influence on what people think is important, but *interest* refers more to attentional factors in the environment, and *relevance* refers more to goal directed activity.

The third category, *expectancy,* refers to one's expectation for being successful. It includes several areas of research that are concerned with people's self-confidence and their feelings of control over their lives and environment. There is no doubt that a person's perception of the likelihood of being successful influences the actual degree of success (Jones, 1977).

The fourth category, *outcomes,* refers to the reinforcing value of instruction. The outcomes of goal-directed behavior have an influence on subsequent levels of perceived value and expectancy for success and, therefore, form the final category of motivational variables in the ARCS model. The *outcomes* category includes the appropriate application of reinforcement as explained in operant conditioning theory, and the environmental outcomes that help maintain intrinsic motivation (e.g., Deci, 1975). More detailed explanations of this syntheses and its rationale are provided by Keller (1983). Building on this conceptual foundation, the ARCS Model was created by generating a large list of motivational strategy statements and then sorting them to see whether the four categories of the model provided a conceptually valid typology. All the strategies used in the development of the model were derived from research findings and from practices that have resulted in motivated learners. Strategy statements were obtained from research studies in the primary areas of research on human motivation from practical handbooks and from interviews with practitioners. The strategy statements were then sorted into the four categories, and were further divided into useful subcategories (see Tables 13.1, 13.2, 13.3, and 13.4). Four people worked on the classification process, and the correspondence of judgments for the placement of strategies into categories was acceptable. The reliability estimate based upon the intraclass correlational method (Winer, 1971) was .78.

During the transition from the original model to the ARCS Model, the four categories were renamed as indicated below to strengthen the central feature of each and to generate a useful acronym. The resulting catalog of strategies is used in the process of identifying and solving motivational problems in instructional materials and methods (Keller & Kopp, 1987), and in computer assisted instruction (Keller & Suzuki, 1987).

## *Table 13.1.* Attention Strategies

| | |
|---|---|
| **A1:** *Incongruity, Conflict* | |
| A1.1 | Introduce a fact that seems to contradict the learner's past experience. |
| A1.2 | Present an example that does not seem to exemplify a given concept. |
| A1.3 | Introduce two equally plausible facts or principles, only one of which can be true. |
| A1.4 | Play devil's advocate. |
| **A2:** *Concreteness* | |
| A2.1 | Show visual representations of any important object or set of ideas or relationships. |
| A2.2 | Give examples of every instructionally important concept or principle. |
| A2.3 | Use content-related anecdotes, case studies, biographies, etc. |
| **A3:** *Variability* | |
| A3.1 | In stand-up delivery, vary the tone of your voice, and use body movement, pauses, and props. |
| A3.2 | Vary the format of instruction (information presentation, practice, testing, etc.) according to the attention span of the audience. |
| A3.3 | Vary the medium of instruction (platform delivery, film, video, print, etc.). |
| A3.4 | Break up print materials by use of white space, visuals, tables, different typefaces, etc. |
| A3.5 | Change the style of presentation (humorous-serious, fast-slow, loud-soft, active-passive, etc.). |
| A3.6 | Shift between student-instructor interaction and student-student interaction. |
| **A4:** *Humor* | |
| A4.1 | Where appropriate, use plays on words during redundant information presentation. |
| A4.2 | Use humorous introductions. |
| A4.3 | Use humorous analogies to explain and summarize. |
| **A5:** *Inquiry* | |
| A5.1 | Use creativity techniques to have learners create unusual analogies and associations to the content. |
| A5.2 | Build in problem-solving activities at regular intervals. |
| A5.3 | Give learners the opportunity to select topics, projects and assignments that appeal to their curiosity and need to explore. |
| **A6:** *Participation* | |
| A6.1 | Use games, role plays, or simulations that require learner participation. |

**Table 13.2.** Relevance Strategies

| | |
|---|---|
| *R1: Experience* | |
| R1.1 | State explicitly how the instruction builds on the learner's existing skills. |
| R1.2 | Use analogies familiar to the learner from past experience. |
| R1.3 | Find out what the learners' interests are and relate them to the instruction. |
| *R2: Present Worth* | |
| R2.1 | State explicitly the present intrinsic value of learning the content, as distinct from its value as a link to future goals. |
| *R3: Future Usefulness* | |
| R3.1 | State explicitly how the instruction relates to future activities of the learner, |
| R3.2 | Ask learners to relate the instruction to their own future goals (future wheel). |
| *SR4: Need Matching* | |
| R4.1 | To enhance achievement striving behavior, provide opportunities to achieve standards of excellence under conditions of moderate risk. |
| R4.2 | To make instruction responsive to the power motive, provide opportunities for responsibility, authority, and interpersonal influence. |
| R4.3 | To satisfy the need for affiliation, establish trust and provide opportunities for no-risk, cooperative interaction. |
| *R5: Modeling* | |
| R5.1 | Bring in alumni of the course as enthusiastic guest lecturers. |
| R5.2 | In a self-paced course, use those who finish first as deputy tutors. |
| R5.3 | Model enthusiasm for the subject taught. |
| *R6: Choice* | |
| R6.1 | Provide meaningful alternative methods for accomplishing a goal. |
| R6.2 | Provide personal choices for organizing one's work. |

***Table 13.3.* Confidence Strategies**

| | |
|---|---|
| *C1:*    *Learning Requirements* | |
| C1.1 | Incorporate clearly stated, appealing learning goals into instructional materials. |
| C1.2 | Provide self-evaluation tools that are based on clearly stated goals. |
| C1.3 | Explain the criteria for evaluation of performance. |
| *C2:*    *Difficulty* | |
| C2.1 | Organize materials on an increasing level of difficulty; that is, structure the learning material to provide a "conquerable" challenge. |
| *C3:*    *Expectations* | |
| C3.1 | Include statements about the likelihood of success with given amounts of effort and ability. |
| C3.2 | Teach students how to develop a plan of work that will result in goal accomplishment. |
| C3.3 | Help students set realistic goals. |
| *C4:*    *Attributions* | |
| C4.1 | Attribute student success to effort rather than luck or ease of task when appropriate (i.e. when you know it's true!). |
| C4.2 | Encourage student efforts to verbalize appropriate attributions for both successes and failures. |
| *C5:*    *Self-Confidence* | |
| C5.1 | Allow students opportunity to become increasingly independent in learning and practicing a skill. |
| C5.2 | Have students learn new skills under low-risk conditions, but practice performance of well-learned tasks under realistic conditions. |
| C5.3 | Help students understand that the pursuit of excellence does not mean that anything short of perfection is failure; learn to feel good about genuine accomplishment. |

***Table 13.4.*** **Satisfaction Strategies**

| | |
|---|---|
| **S1:** *Natural Consequences* | |
| S1.1 | Allow a student to use a newly acquired skill in a realistic setting as soon as possible. |
| SI.2 | Verbally reinforce a student's intrinsic pride in accomplishing a difficult task. |
| S1.3 | Allow a student who masters a task to help others who have not yet done so. |
| **S2:** *Unexpected Rewards* | |
| S2.1 | Reward intrinsically interesting task performance with unexpected, non-contingent rewards. |
| S2.2 | Reward boring tasks with extrinsic, anticipated rewards. |
| **S3:** *Positive Outcomes* | |
| S3.1 | Give verbal praise for successful progress or accomplishment. |
| S3.2 | Give personal attention to students. |
| S3.3 | Provide informative, helpful feedback when it is immediately useful. |
| S3.4 | Provide motivating feedback (praise) immediately following task performance. |
| **S4:** *Negative Influences* | |
| S4.1 | Avoid the use of threats as a means of obtaining task performance. |
| S4.2 | Avoid surveillance (as opposed to positive attention). |
| S4.3 | Avoid external performance evaluations whenever it is possible to help the student evaluate his or her own work. |
| **S5:** *Scheduling* | |
| S5.1 | Provide frequent reinforcements when a student is learning a new task. |
| S5.2 | Provide intermittent reinforcement as a student becomes more competent at a task. |
| S5.3 | Vary the schedule of reinforcements in terms of both interval and quantity. |

# Components of the ARCS Model

The ARCS Model defines four major conditions (Attention, Relevance, Confidence, and Satisfaction) that have to be met for people to become and remain motivated. As previously indicated, each of these conditions subsumes several areas of psychological research (Keller, 1979, 1983), and has been divided into specific subcategories with sample motivational strategy prescriptions (Keller, 1983; Keller & Kopp, 1987, Keller & Suzuki, 1987). Following is a brief description of each of the four major conditions.

## Attention

The first condition, attention, is an element of motivation and is also a prerequisite for learning. The motivational concern is for getting and sustaining attention. As an element of learning, the concern is for directing attention to the appropriate stimuli. As a tone level, it is fairly easy to gain attention. A dramatic statement, a sharp noise, a quiet pause—all of these and many other devices are used.

Getting attention is not enough, however. A real challenge is to sustain it, to produce a satisfactory level of attention throughout a period of instruction. To do this, it is necessary to respond to the sensation-seeking needs of students (Zuckerman, 1971) and arouse their knowledge-seeking curiosity (Berlyne, 1965), but without overstimulating them. The goal is to find a balance between boredom and indifference versus hyperactivity and anxiety. The strategies listed under categories A5 and A6 (Table 13.1) are particularly useful in sustaining attention.

## Relevance

How many times have we heard students ask, "Why do I have to study this?" When a convincing answer is not forthcoming, there is a relevance problem. To answer this question, many course designers and instructors try to make the instruction seem relevant to present and future career opportunities for the students (categories R2 and R3, Table 13.2). Others, in a more classical tradition, believe that learning should be an end in itself, something that students come to enjoy and treasure. Both of these can be important, but there is a third way: It focuses on process rather than ends.

Relevance can come from the way something is taught; it does not have to come from the content itself (categories R4 and R5, Table 13.2). For example, people high in "need for affiliation" tend to enjoy classes in which they can work cooperatively in groups. Similarly, people high in "need for achievement" enjoy the opportunity to set moderately challenging goals, and to take personal responsibility for achieving them. To the extent that a course of instruction offers opportunities for an individual to satisfy these and other needs, the person will have a feeling of perceived relevance.

## Confidence

Some people never quite achieve success even when the odds are in their favor; others always seem to excell no matter what the odds.

Differences in confidence, the third major component of the model, can influence a student's persistence and accomplishment.

Several factors contribute to one's level of confidence, or expectancy for success. For example, confident people tend to attribute the causes of success to things such as ability and effort instead of luck or the difficulty of the task (Weiner, 1974; Dweck, 1986). They also tend to be oriented toward involvement in the task activity and enjoy learning even if it means making mistakes. Confident people tend to believe that they can effectively accomplish their goals by means of their actions (Bandura, 1977; Bandura & Schunk, 1981). In contrast, unconfident people often have more of an ego involvement; they want to impress others and they worry about failing (Dweck, 1986).

Fear of failure is often stronger in students than teachers realize. A challenge for teachers in generating or maintaining motivation is to foster the development of confidence despite the competitiveness and external control that often exist in schools.

The preceding research results are reflected in the confidence-building strategies (Table 13.3) that can be used by an instructional designer or teacher. The purpose of most of these strategies is to help the learner form the impression that some level of success is possible if effort is exerted. It is, of course, important to avoid creating this impression if it is false. If success is not possible with a reasonable amount of effort, the instruction should be redesigned or the student should be given appropriate counsel.

## Satisfaction

This category incorporates research and practices that help make people feel good about their accomplishments. According to reinforcement theory, people should be more motivated if the task and the reward are defined, and an appropriate reinforcement schedule is used (categories S3 and S5, Table 13.4). Generally this is true, but people sometimes become resentful and even angry when they are told what they have to do, and what they will be given as a reward. Why would this be so? An important part of the answer seems to be "control."

When a student is required to do something to get a reward that a teacher controls, resentment may occur because the teacher has taken over part of the student's sphere of control over his or her own life. This is especially likely to happen when the behavior you control is one that the student enjoys for intrinsically satisfying reasons. The establishment of external control over an intrinsically satisfying behavior can decrease the person's enjoyment of the activity (Lepper & Greene, 1979).

There are appropriate ways to use extrinsic rewards in learning situations, and to stimulate intrinsic reward. A challenge is to provide appropriate contingencies without overcontrolling, and to encourage the development of intrinsic satisfaction (categories S1, S2, and S4, Table 4).

In summary, these four categories form the basis of the ARCS Model. Within each are subcategories that include prescriptive motivational strategies (see Keller & Kopp, 1987; Keller & Suzuki, 1987). However, given the purpose of this model for helping to identify specific ways to make instruction more appealing, there is still the question of procedure: How is the ARCS Model used in instructional development or lesson planning? The following two sections provide a brief description of this process, and the results of using the model with two groups of teachers.

# Using the ARCS Model

The ARCS Model includes a systematic design process that can be used with typical instructional design and development models. It can be conveniently separated into the steps of define, design, develop, and evaluate (see Table 13.5).

## Define

Prior to the field tests reported in the next section, the define phase had two purposes; audience analysis and preparation of objectives. During the field tests a third purpose called "problem classification" was added as the first step in the process. It became clear that an unstated but important constraint of the ARCS Model is that, in its present form, it is designed to help make a course of instruction more motivating for a reasonably typical class of students, one in which some people will be cooperative and interested, others will be indifferent and bored, and some may even be slightly antagonistic.

*Table 13.5.* The Motivational Design Model

| DEFINE | DEVELOP |
|---|---|
| Classify problem<br>Analyze audience motivation<br>Prepare motivational objectives | Prepare motivational elements<br>Integrate with instruction |
| DESIGN | EVALUATE |
| Generate potential strategies<br>Select strategies | Conduct developmental try-out<br>Assess motivational outcomes |

There can be motivational challenges that differ from situation to situation. For example, lack of perceived relevance might be the primary problem in a world history class, and low expectancy for success (i.e., low confidence) in a required algebra class for non-college-bound students; however, the assumption is that the group as a whole will be responsive if an effective set of motivational strategies is employed.

The ARCS Model, as presently constituted, is not designed as a behavioral change model; that is, it is not intended for use in solving individual personality problems or in teaching students how to be self-motivated. It could be adapted easily and used as a frame of reference for organizing strategies for teaching meta-cognitive strategies for self-motivation, but that was not its function in the field tests. For work in the area of self-motivation, see McCombs (1984), and Schmitt & Newby (1986).

Consequently, the first step in applying the ARCS Model is to classify the motivational problem to be solved. If the problem is one of improving the motivation appeal of instruction for a given audience, it is appropriate to use the model.

The second step is to do an audience analysis to identify motivational gaps. In some situations, a group of students will be highly motivated for a particular course as a result of their intrinsic interest in the topic, or because of external factors that make the course important to them. In other cases, the students' motivation will have to be stimulated after they arrive at the class. In the first case, the designer, or instructor, will have to maintain the motivation, but in the second case, strategies to establish motivation will be required. An even more specific level of analysis can be performed to discover whether there are particular problems in one or more of the four motivational categories (Keller & Suzuki, 1987).

The third step in the define phase is to prepare motivational objectives (Table 13.5). The audience analysis should reveal the specific areas that are most likely to require special attention in the development of motivational strategies. Of course, it is always possible that a balanced focus will be most appropriate in a given setting; that is, a designer or teacher might not discover an acute problem area, but simply might have to give balanced treatment to all four areas.

Motivational objectives, like instructional objectives, should identify the behavior, conditions, and criteria that apply. For example, a motivational objective might be, "By the end of the first module of work, all the students in the class will express confidence that they can finish the unit successfully if they try hard." By creating specific motivational objectives, the designer or instructor is better able to choose appropriate strategies.

# *Design*

The first step in design is to create a list of potential motivational strategies for each of the objectives. At this point, it is generally best to use a brainstorming approach to create a broad range of strategy ideas. The goal is to move away from the analytical thinking that characterizes the define phase and to begin thinking in an uncritical, more creative mode. By creating a variety of possible strategies, the likelihood of finding optimal strategies is increased.

The next step is to critically review the potential strategies and select the ones to be used. Five guidelines that help accomplish this are that the motivational strategies should: a) not take up too much instructional time, b) not detract from the instructional objectives, c) fall within the time and money constraints of the development and implementation aspects of the instruction, d) be acceptable to the audience, and e) be compatible with the delivery system, including the instructor's personal style and preferences.

All these criteria exemplify the central concern for motivation as a means to an end, not an end in itself. For example, if students come to class already motivated, do not inject a large number of motivational strategies; this could slow the instruction and cause the students to focus on the entertaining motivational strategies to the detriment of the instructional objectives. This is illustrated by a foreign language teacher who spent so much time with the students planning a culturally enriching banquet that she covered only half of the required content. At first the students enjoyed it, but they became annoyed when they realized that they would not be properly prepared for the next level of study. Motivational strategies should stimulate the motivation to learn (Brophy, 1983), and not detract from the learning process.

The strategies included in the model are proven in that they are based on research and successful practices; but their effectiveness and the way in which they are adopted depends in part on the personality of the instructor and the type of atmosphere that he or she prefers (e.g. formal versus informal). Consequently, the final selection of strategies for a given instructional event is based, in large part, upon the judgments of the designer and teacher rather than upon objective criteria. In this sense, even though the ARCS Model contains prescriptive strategies, the overall model is more heuristic than prescriptive or algorithmic. It helps ensure a solution to motivational problems, but it does not guarantee one as does a correctly applied algorithm. It requires experience and judgment, and perhaps even some trial and error from the designer.

# *Develop*

During the development phase, it is time to create any special materials that are required and integrate them into the instruction. This usually requires revision of the instructional materials to ensure continuity and internal consistency.

# *Evaluate*

It is important to base the evaluation of the materials on motivational as well as learning outcomes. Too often, decisions about the effectiveness of motivational strategies are based on gain scores or other achievement measures. This is not a good practice because achievement is affected by many factors, not just motivation (see Keller, 1979, for a more complete discussion of this point). To judge motivational consequences, it is best to use direct measures of persistence, intensity of effort, emotion, and attitude.

# Developmental Test of the ARCS Model: Two Case Studies

The ARCS Model was field-tested in two teacher training workshops. The first was with eighteen teachers of middle school children between the ages of twelve and fourteen. All the teachers were from the same school district in central New York, and most were from the same school. The primary purpose of the overall inservice program was to improve instruction in problem solving, and the ARCS Model was included as one part of each workshop session. It was included as a problem solving approach to improving motivation, and to assist the teachers in designing the motivational aspects of the instructional materials they were designing.

The workshop took place over four months, with four-hour afternoon meetings twice a month. It was conducted by a trainer who was familiar with the motivational material encompassed by the ARCS Model, and included one session in which the author presented the specific strategies and procedures of the model.

During the four months of the project, the teachers went through the complete process of defining a motivational problem, formulating objectives, selecting strategies, preparing a plan, enacting the plan, and reporting results. Most of the teachers worked on developing or revising modules of instruction to make them more interesting, but some worked on the motivational problems of specific students.

There were two criteria for success in this developmental test, both of which were attitudinal. First was that the participants would, after being taught the basic characteristics of the model, regard it as being comprehensible and useful. This criterion was important because the ARCS Model draws upon a broad base of psychological concepts and research that has not been studied by most teachers. For the ARCS Model to be acceptable to practitioners, it has to be presented in familiar, practical language.

The second criterion was that after using the ARCS Model, participants would believe that the model helped them do a better job of improving the motivational appeal of instruction than they would have done otherwise.

In response to a questionnaire with five-point response scales ranging from strongly disagree to strongly agree, all the participants responded positively (agree or strongly agree) to the first criterion, and sixteen (89 percent) responded positively to the second. The other two were neutral. In a "Comments" section, they said that they gained some insights from learning and using the model, but they used more or less the same motivational strategies that they would have used anyway. Both of these teachers, according to comments from the principal and other teachers, had excellent reputations as motivators. Given the overall positive responses, this test of the ARCS Model was judged to be supportive of its acceptability and utility.

An interesting consequence of using the ARCS Model in this setting occurred: In their conclusions, some of the teachers suggested that the key factor in the process was that they had simply paid more attention either to the student or to the class. At first, this seemed to be a disappointing result for the ARCS Model. Why have a reasonably complex, formalized model if "paying more attention" is all that is required?

Upon reflection, it became clear that the teachers were not giving themselves enough credit for what they had actually accomplished. After analyzing their action plans and logbooks, it was obvious that they had used specific strategies to bring about the change. For them, "attention" was simply a convenient word to summarize a great many specific acts.

A second test was conducted with another group consisting of sixteen teachers from primary, middle, and secondary schools within a single school district in northeastern New York. This was a six-day workshop on motivational design conducted by the author and two assistants for two days each in three successive months. One day each month was spent in a working session with the teachers, and the other day each month was used for classroom visitations and individual consultation.

At the end of the first session, the teachers had defined their motivational problems. During the next four weeks, they were to work on collecting data to verify the problem and to develop a preliminary strategy list. They were enthusiastic at the end of the first session, but by the beginning of second session one month later, several had encountered difficulties and become discouraged.

After analyzing their problem statements and progress reports, it appeared that the differences were caused primarily by the type of problem chosen by the participant. The workshop leaders had encouraged the participants to work on instructional improvement problems that were fairly small in scope; that is, to chose a unit or lesson that they could analyze and improve with respect to its motivational characteristics. Instead, several of the teachers had chosen to work on the personal motivational problems of individual students; some of these students had personal problems and family situations that would be a challenge even for an experienced psychotherapist.

In general, the teachers who chose instructional improvement projects had made better progress and felt more positive. However, some of these teachers enlarged the scope of the project after the first session, or failed to reduce the scope as recommended by the workshop leaders. Consequently, the first part of the second session was spent reviewing the chosen problems and scope of work. After the concerned teachers redefined their problems into something more manageable, their progress improved quickly.

The difficulties experienced with the second group were reflected in the ratings obtained from the questionnaires on the two criteria as described above in the first study. After the second session, ten of the twelve teachers (83 percent) agreed that the model seemed comprehensible and useful. At the end of the workshop, nine of the twelve teachers (75 percent) believed that use of the model had helped them improve the motivational appeal of their instruction.

Why, we wondered, did the ARCS Model work better with the first group, which included several teachers who chose behavior modification problems? In that group, the workshop leader had worked with the school district and with the same group of teachers on several other projects during the preceding three years. The earlier projects were concerned with helping the teachers learn to use systematic development and research procedures for creating and validating instructional improvement projects in curiosity and cognitive problem-solving skills.

In the second group, most of the teachers had not had an inservice training program in many years, and some had never had one. Consequently, these teachers were starting from "scratch" in orienting themselves toward a productive experience in the workshop and toward the specific processes of systematic development. They had to learn the generic problem solving and design processes as represented in the specific context of the ARCS Model, and in the content of the model itself. Furthermore, these teachers had to work independently during the four weeks between sessions. They could not get immediate personal advice from the workshop leaders because of the distance to their work location, and they did not mail materials to the workshop leaders for review as they had been invited to do. In summary, this group chose too many problems that, although interesting and important to them, fell outside the scope of the ARCS strategies or the time constraints of the workshop, and they had no previous experience in working independently on instructional improvement projects.

## Conclusion

The results of these two field tests provide support for the comprehensibility and utility of the ARCS Model as a means of assisting in the motivational design of instruction, and they illustrate some of the requirements for its successful use. ARCS is a problem-solving model, and it does require some time to acquire an understanding of the basic strategies and concepts included in it. If a potential user has never learned to work with a systematic instructional design model, the concepts of problem identification, solution design, and implementation must be learned in conjunction with the content and processes of the ARCS Model.

Furthermore, care must be exercised in the first step of the application to ensure that participants select problems that are appropriate for the model. These would be problems concerned with the improvement of instruction, and not with changes in the personalities of the students.

A limitation of this study is that, even though positive support was found in two settings and there is research support for the various elements of the model, there were many uncontrolled aspects to the field tests. For example, the author of the model was involved in both studies; however, a more objective test of the model would result from having trainers other than the author involved. More objective measures of the effectiveness of the model could also be used; for example, a checklist of motivational characteristics applied to preworkshop samples of materials developed and taught by the participants could be compared to postworkshop samples. It is essential that several replications of the study be conducted to test for consistent results; this type of action research can never be highly controlled, and the dynamics that can develop in any given group can have a strong influence on the outcomes. Given the initially positive responses to the model, more controlled studies of its critical attributes and areas of effectiveness appear to be warranted.

## Author's Note

*The author gratefully acknowledges the contributions of Bernard Dodge, Bonnie Keller, and Fulya Sari to the development of the strategies included in the ARCS Model, and to Roger Kaufman for his careful review of a draft of this paper.*

## References

Bandura, A. 1977. Self efficacy: Toward a unifying theory of behavioral change. *Psychological Review* 84:191–215.

Bandura, A., and D. H. Schunk. 1981. Cultivating competence, self-efficacy, and intrinsic interest through proximal self-motivation. *Journal of Personality and Social Psychology* 41:586–598.

Berlyne, D. E. 1965. Motivational problems raised by exploratory and epistemic behavior. In S. Koch, ed., *Psychology: A study of a science,* vol. 5. New York: McCraw-Hill.

Brophy, J. 1983. Conceptualizing student motivation. *Educational Psychologist* 18:200–215.

Deci, E. L. 1975. *Intrinsic motivation.* New York: Plenum Press.

Doyle, W. 1985. Classroom organization and management. In M. Wittrock, ed., *Handbook of research on teaching,* 3d ed. New York: Macmillan.

Dweck, C. S. 1986. Motivational processes affecting learning. *American Psychologist* 41:1040–1048.

Jones, R. A. 1977. *Self-fulfilling prophecies: Social psychological and physiological effects of expectancies.* New York: Halsted Press.

Keller, J. M. 1979. Motivation and instructional design: A theoretical perspective. *Journal of Instructional Development* 2, no. 4:26–34.

———. 1983. Motivational design of instruction. In C. M. Reigeluth, ed., *Instructional design theories and models: An overview of their current status.* Hillsdale, N.J.: Lawrence Erlbaum.

———. 1984. The use of the ARCS model of motivation in teacher training. In K. E. Shaw, ed, *Aspects of educational technology volume XVII: Staff development and career updating.* London: Kogan Page.

———. 1987. Motivational design. In *Encyclopedia of Educational Media, Communications, and Technology,* 2d ed. Westport, Conn.: Greenwood Press.

Keller, J. M., and T. Kopp. 1987. Application of the ARCS model of motivational design. In C. M. Reigeluth, ed., *Instructional theories in action: Lessons illustrating elected theories and models.* Hillsdale, N.J.: Lawrence Erlbaum.

Keller, J. M., and K. Suzuki. 1987. Use of the ARCS motivation model in courseware design. In D. H. Jonassen, ed., *Instructional designs for microcomputer courseware.* Hillsdale, N.J.: Lawrence Erlbaum.

Krathwohl, D. R., B. S. Bloom, and B. B. Masia. 1964. *Taxonomy of educational objectives, the classification of educational goals. Handbook II: Affective domain.* New York: David McKay.

Lepper, M. R., and D. Greene. 1979. *The hidden costs of reward.* Morristown, N.J.: Lawrence Erlbaum.

Lewin, K. 1938. *The conceptual representation and measurement of psychological forces.* Durham, N.C.: Duke University Press.

Mager, R. F. 1968. *Developing attitude toward learning.* Belmont, Calif.: Fearon.

McClelland, D. C. 1965. Toward a theory of motive acquisition. *American Psychologist* 20:321–333.

McCombs, B. L. 1984. Processes and skills on underlying continuing intrinsic motivation to learn: Toward a definition of motivational skills training. *Educational Psychologist* 4:190–218.

Schmitt, M. C., and T. J. Newby. 1986. Metacognition: Relevance to instructional design. *Journal of Instructional Development* 9, no. 4:29–33.

Skinner, B. F. 1961. Teaching machines. *Scientific American* 205:90–102.

Steers, R. M., and L. W. Porter. 1987. *Motivation and work behavior.* 3d ed. New York: McGraw-Hill.

Tolman, E. C. 1932. *Purposive behavior in animals and men.* New York: Century.

Weiner, B., ed. 1974. *Achievement motivation attribution theory.* Morristown: N.J.: General Learning Press.

Winer, B. J. 1971. *Statistical principles in experimental design.* 2d ed. New York: McGraw-Hill.

Wlodkowski, R. J. 1978. *Motivation and teaching. A practical guide.* Washington, D.C.: National Education Association.

———. 1985. *Enhancing adult motivation to learn.* San Francisco: Jossey-Bass.

Zuckerman, M. 1971. Dimensions of sensation seeking. *Journal of Consulting and Clinical Psychology* 36:45–52.

# 14

# Distance Teaching and Industrial Production:*
## A Comparative Interpretation in Outline

### Otto Peters

      The more one attempts to grasp and explain the phenomenon of distance teaching, and especially the more one tries to identify the particular educational opportunities distinguishing this form of teaching from other forms of imparting academic knowledge, the clearer it becomes that the conventional range of educational terminology is not sufficiently comprehensive. Distance study represents facts new to education in several aspects. Compared with other forms of study it was novel in the form in which it made its first breakthrough over 90 years ago. With even greater justification it can be called novel in its present form in which it is currently spreading throughout the world, contributing towards the discovery of the educational opportunities provided by the modern media, such as radio and television. It is, above all, novel and pointing towards the future when it makes use of electronic data processing equipment and wideband cable transmission techniques. It is no coincidence that university study at a distance, in its early form of correspondence teaching, began its development only about 130 years ago, as it requires conditions that only existed from then on. One necessity, for example, is a relatively fast and regular postal and transport service. The first railway lines and the first correspondence schools were established around the same time. When one further realises how much technical support distance teaching establishments need nowadays in order to cater effectively for large groups of students, it becomes clear that distance study is a form of study complementary to our industrial and technological age. Lectures, seminars and practice sessions, on the other hand, have developed from forms of teaching derived from ancient rhetoric and practised at medieval universities; the colloquium originates from the dialogic teaching methods of the humanistic era.1 These forms of teaching have changed little in their basic structure since the beginning of the 19th century. They proved almost completely resistant to combination with technical support facilities. In this context they can therefore be described as pre-industrial forms of study.

On account of these differences, distance study can only be described and analysed to a limited extent using traditional educational terms. They are not wholly adequate for this new form of study. This is understandable insofar as these terms developed from pre-industrial forms of teaching. If one applies them to distance study one will think in conventional concepts. To emphasise the point, one looks at a new form of study from an old perspective and has one's view of the essential structural characteristics distorted.

Industrialisation is the symbol of a new epoch in the development of man fundamentally different from all previous epochs. It is without example in history, above all, on account of the basic changes in most spheres of human existence. Academic teaching alone seems to have remained largely unscathed by industrialisation—with the exception of distance study, for this form of study is remarkably consistent with the principles and tendencies of industrialisation. For this reason, experimentally, structural elements, concepts and principles derived from the theories of industrial production are used here to interpret the distance study phenomenon. This does not mean that the teaching and learning processes occurring in distance study are equated with processes in industrial production. The comparison is purely heuristic.

A comparison of this kind between a form of teaching and processes from another sphere of life is legitimate and not without example in the history of educational theory. Amos Comenius, the "founder and virtuoso of the method of parallel comparison"[2] in his *Didactica Magna,* for example, compared the 'art of teaching' in unusual detail with the art of printing, also a technical process. Theodor Litt identified the nature of pedagogic thinking by comparing it with artistic creativity, technology and the processes of growth.[3] In the sixties, experiments were carried out which tried to explain the teaching and learning processes using the technical model of the feedback control system, in order to find approaches to a 'cybernetic pedagogy.'[4] Most impressive, however, was the achievement by Gottfried Hausmann who, in 1959, condensed the analogy between the dramatic arts and education into a 'dramaturgy of teaching'. In it he interprets the educational structure of teaching and learning processes in detail using the terms and principles of the dramatic art in the theatre. Paul Heimann saw the merit of this comprehensive and detailed comparison in the possibility that "it might give rise to a complete revision of our teaching and learning models."[5]

Furthermore, it may not be without significance for this planned interpretation that for another important aspect of university or college work, namely research, comparisons with the production process already exist. In 1919, Max Weber defined structural similarities between research institutes and capitalistic organisations,[6] and, in 1924, Helmut Plessner pointed out that the "mechanisation, methodisation and depersonalisation of the manufacturing process equally dominate the production of economic as well as cultural goods."[7] The following comparison between distance study and the industrial production process will prove similar consistencies.

From the start, distance study has a special relationship with the industrial production process insofar as the production of study materials in itself is an industrial process built into the whole teaching process as a constituent part, quite unlike the production of text books, for example. In the case of commercial distance teaching establishments the further question of selling the printed or otherwise duplicated study units adds calculations of applied economics to the teaching process. Even the distance teaching departments of government-financed universities are not entirely free from these considerations. it would be interesting to examine how far these facts have influenced the structure of distance teaching already.

In order to facilitate the discovery of further relationships between distance teaching and the production process, the following structural changes—essentially brought on by industrialisation—in the development of the production of goods should be noted:

1. According to the principle of rationalisation, individual work as it was traditional in the craftmen's trades, changes at an early stage to a production based on the division of labour (e.g. in factories), and this later leads to the development of assembly lines and mass production.

2. Work processes initially characterised by the use of tools are increasingly re-structured by mechanisation and, later, automation.

3. In detail, these changes lead to the following results:

   • The preparatory phase becomes increasingly important.

   • Success depends, among other things, on systematic planning and organisation. Scientific measures of control are needed.

   • Work processes must be formalised and products standardised.

   • The production process is objectified. Each developmental step towards increased mechanisation leads to changes in the function of those involved in the production process.

   • Small concerns are no longer able to raise the investment needed for developmental work and technical equipment. A strong tendency towards concentration and centralisation becomes noticeable.

The terms used in business studies to describe these facts will be outlined briefly and—where possible—applied to distance teaching.

# Rationalisation

By rationalisation we mean all 'methodical, i.e., rationally guided measures' with the purpose of achieving output with a comparatively (compared to earlier situations) lower input of power, time and money.[8] Scientific discoveries should "be evaluated for practical use in such a way as to achieve the best possible results in view of the continually necessary development and redevelopment of economic and technical processes."[9]

Applied to the practical example of the production process this means that "the entire production line, from raw material to end product, is carefully analysed to allow each single work process to be planned so as to make the most effective contribution possible towards achieving clearly formulated business tasks."[10]

Georges Friedmann emphasises that this is a dynamic process aiming at continuous improvement in quality through "continuous progress in the study of materials, accuracy and precision."[11] Rationalisation of this type has only started to develop with increasing industrialisation at the end of the 19th century.[12]

Management Science believes the reason for the considerable obstacles to rationalisation lie in human nature itself, because "human inadequacy inhibits the motivation to gain unprejudiced views and the willingness to act according to rational convictions."[13] Further obstacles are considered to be tradition, convention, habits and fashion.

In education, a rationalising way of thinking is nothing new. In a general form, it influences the reasoning for numerous educational decisions. For example, the introduction of lectures to larger groups of students, the use of printed books and the specialisation of university lecturers were considerable steps towards the rationalisation of the academic teaching process. Every university teacher will, when planning a lecture, choose those subjects that will help him most to fulfil the purpose of that particular lecture. In distance teaching, however, ways of thinking, attitudes and procedures can be found which only established themselves in the wake of an increased rationalisation in the industrialisation of production processes. The characteristic details are, among others, as follows:

1.  In distance study the teaching process is based on the division of labour and detached from the person of the University lecturer. It is therefore independent from a subjectively determined teaching situation, thus eliminating part of the earlier mentioned obstacles to rationalisation. The division of labour and the objectification of the teaching process allow each work process to be planned in such a way that clearly formulated teaching objectives are achieved in the most effective manner. Specialists may be responsible for a limited area in each phase.

2.  The use of technical equipment (duplicating machines, organisation systems, transporting devices) makes it possible to convey the knowledge, ability and teaching skills of a university lecturer, by means of the detached objectivity of a distance study course of constant quality, to a theoretically unlimited number of students. The rationalisation effect of mass production becomes apparent here.

3.  The rigorous application of organisational principles and means saves teachers as well as students unnecessary effort.

4.  At some of the newer distance teaching establishments, modern means of technical support, such as film, television and electronic data processing installations, have replaced teaching staff in certain areas of their work, in particular, in the fields of giving information and assessing performance.

5.  Students work through a course which has been tested prior to going to print; this prevents misunderstandings and stops students from going in the wrong direction.

6.  The quality of a distance study course can be improved, because its effectiveness can be monitored at any time by scientific methods.

If the number of students required in a society outgrows the number of university teachers available, rational thinking should be able to find ways and means of changing teaching methods in such a way that the teaching resources of the university teachers available are used to the best effect, quantitatively as well as qualitatively. Distance study can be regarded as a result of such endeavours.

# The Division of Labour

The division of labour has played an important role in the sociological theories of the last 100 years.[14] Applied to the production process it means that the work is split in the sense of "dividing one complete work process into a number of elementary procedures,"[15] as described by Adam Smith at an early stage.[16] With an extensive division of labour "training periods become shorter, more people are able to carry out the work and wages can be lowered."[17]

A result of the advanced division of labour is increased specialisation. The following statement, by Adam Smith in 1776, applies to everyone involved in a production process where a division of labour exists:

---

"Men are much more likely to discover easier and readier methods of attaining any object, when the whole attention of their minds is directed towards that single object than when it is dissipated among a great variety of things. It is naturally to be expected therefore that some one or other of those who are employed in each particular branch of labour should soon find out easier and readier methods of performing their own particular work, whenever the nature of it admits of such improvement."[18]

---

Just as the division of labour is a precondition for the mechanisation of work processes and for industrialisation as a whole, it has made university study at a distance possible. The division of labour is the main prerequisite for the advantages of this new form of teaching to become effective. The principle of the division of labour is thus a constituent element of distance teaching.

The 'complete work process', which is split in distance teaching, consists of the teaching activity of the university lecturer, i.e. the entirety of the measures he takes in order to initiate and guide learning processes in students. Initially, the two basic functions of the university teacher, that of conveying information and of counselling, were allocated as separate responsibilities in distance teaching departments of universities or colleges. Both functions, above all however that of transmitting information, are now even further divided. If, for example, the number of students enrolled on a distance study course is high, regular assessment of performance is not carried out by those academics who developed the course. The recording of results is the responsibility of yet another unit; and the development of the course itself is divided into numerous phases, in each of which experts in particular fields are active.

This specialisation may bring the following advantages:

- Materials required for the development of the distance study course can be assembled by leading experts in the specialist fields concerned.

- Having completed the manuscript the author can then be freed from the time-consuming processes of exact source references and of lecturing.

- Educationalists and experienced practitioners of distance teaching are able to revise the manuscripts of study units to make the planned teaching process more effective.

- Even colleagues from the 'academic middle tier' may be involved in the correction of exercises carried out by students. There are cases where even senior students have taken over such tasks, especially where they are concentrating on marking the exercises from a limited number of correspondence units. As in the industrial manufacturing process, the level of previous training may be lower on account of the division of labour and, as there, 'more people are able to carry out the work'. Since with extensive specialisation of this type the number of scripts one university teacher is able to mark may be much higher, this process is also cheaper.

# Mechanisation

Mechanisation means the use of machines in a work process.[19] These machines replace the work done by the muscles of men or animals. In part they even take over elements of brain work. There are varying degrees of mechanisation. The preindustrial stage is characterised mainly by craftwork making use of tools. The first. level of industrialisation was reached with the use of 'dependent machines'. The second level of industrialisation led to mass production as a result of the use of 'semi-independent machines' and assembly lines. Finally, the third level of industrialisation is characterised by the spread of automation (with automatic control or feedback). The changes occurring at each level are so great that, in this context, one author has spoken about a first, second and third technical or industrial revolution.[20]

In order to remain with this analogy, distance study could be ascribed to the industrial levels, as it cannot take place without the use of machines. Duplicating machines and transport systems are prerequisites, and later forms of distance teaching have the additional facilities of modern means of communication and electronic data processing installations.

In contrast, when considering the framework of conventional study one cannot help thinking that its forms of teaching belong to the pre-industrial level. There the university teacher is comparable to a craftsman as he uses 'tools' (pictures, objects, books), without these changing the structure of the teaching process to any considerable degree.

# Assembly Line

Buckingham referred to the importance of the assembly line principle in connection with the use of machines. Both these factors, among others, had made mass production possible.[21] Assembly line work is characterised by the fact that the worker remains at his place of work, whilst the workpieces travel past him.

The formal similarity between distance teaching and the production process becomes particularly noticeable here. In the development of the distance study course the manuscript is passed from one area of responsibility to another and specific changes are made at each stage. The study units are printed on a large scale, stored, sent to the distance learner, completed by him, sent to the script marker who checks the work, and finally submitted to the administration, where the performance of the distance learner and the effort of the script marker (to calculate fees) are recorded. The rationalisation effect achieved by the fact that many university teachers and thousands of students do not have to meet in one place in order to participate in teaching events—is at least the same as that a car manufacturer tries to achieve when, instead of sending the worker to the vehicle to be built, he transports the necessary parts to the worker. In both cases the production process as well as distance teaching—time, energy and money are saved.

# Mass Production

In modern sociology the term *'mass trend'* has rid itself of its negative cultural connotation, making it a largely neutral expression.[22] Mass trend nowadays merely denotes a structural characteristic of an advanced industrial society and indicates "that in a pure consumer society such as ours, the rise in the standard of living is due purely to the fact that industry produces certain consumer goods and commodities in large quantities, thus making them generally accessible."[23]

Mass production is by its nature only possible where there is a sufficiently large 'mass of consumers'. This, in turn, requires an efficient transport system providing a connection between producer and consumer who, as is typical in today's system, are geographically distant. In order to work profitably, the producer needs to research consumer requirements and find standards acceptable to all consumers for his product. He must continually improve his goods (aim at perfection), as each shortcoming is multiplied by the number of items produced.

If one equally rids the term *'consumer'* of its negative cultural connotation, one can speak of the student as a 'consumer of academic education'. Quite obviously, 'demand' outstrips 'supply' at universities and colleges, and this had led to the large scale operation at our universities and colleges. As traditional forms of academic teaching originally envisaged small groups of students, and today's practice of applying methods designed for small groups to large groups must be seen as a perversion of an educational concept, (e.g., several lecture rooms with loudspeaker connection), one can understand it if various governments see distance teaching, on account of its similarity with the mass production process, as a means of providing very large groups of students more adequately with academic teaching than conventional methods would allow it.

Indeed, the multiplication effect achieved by technology and the postal delivery system mean that the university teacher and the distance learner—like producer and consumer—no longer need to live in the same geographical location.

From an economic point of view, the production of distance study courses represents mass production. Apart from reasons of profitability, the large number of courses produced forces distance teaching organisations to analyse the requirements of potential distance learners far more carefully than in conventional teaching and to improve the quality of the courses. For example, in the USSR the Public Accounts Authority complained at one time that too many students dropped out of distance study and it is suspected that this might have been the reason that led to an examination of the study materials. Most American distance study courses are revised and re-issued at regular intervals (every one to four years). As American universities charge fees to cover the greatest part of the budget allocated to distance teaching departments, the quality of distance study courses must not be allowed to deteriorate. When, on account of mass production, the University of California has more distance study courses to offer than there is demand for them, it occasionally places advertisements for students in newspapers.

Statistics prove that the number of graduates in areas without a university is lower than in areas near universities. It is possible that, according to the principle of mass production, distance teaching will one day equalise the opportunities to study, just as industrial mass production has assimilated consumer patterns in town and country. Analogous to the increase in the standard of living, this would make a general increase in the level of education possible—which might not otherwise have been achieved.

# Preparatory Work

In a production situation where a division of labour prevails, economy, quality and speed of the work processes depend on the right type of preparation. This is necessary in industries producing a variety of articles and needs to be carried out by senior specialist staff in special departments (thinking departments), as workers, foremen and masters involved in the production process lack the necessary knowledge and experience. During the preparatory stages one determines how workers, machines and materials can usefully relate to each other during each phase of the production process. In addition, there are developmental and constructional tasks. The more thorough the preparation, the less is a successful production process dependent on the particular abilities of the workers involved. Consequently, workers can easily be exchanged. Normally, considerably larger sums of investment are required for preparatory work than was the case previously in the manufacture of goods.

As distance teaching institutions have to develop a great variety of distance teaching courses, the comparison with a firm producing a variety of goods comes to mind. In distance teaching too success depends decisively on a 'preparatory phase'. It concerns the development of the distance study course involving experts in the various specialist fields with qualifications also often higher than those of other teachers involved in distance study. Here too, each section of the course can be carefully planned. The use of technical support and a suitable combination of this with individual contributions from distance tutors and advisers play an important role in this. Compared to university teachers in conventional study, who are responsible for the entire teaching process, distance tutors and advisers are more easily exchangeable on account of the thorough preparatory work. Finally, the development of distance study courses also requires investment to an extent that has never before been considered at establishments of higher education.

The separation of preparatory work and individual instruction and the distribution of these functions among several persons is a particularly clear example of analogy with the production process.

# Planning

An essential element of preparation is planning which needs to be far more comprehensive and detailed in the industrial manufacturing process than in manual production, as it requires the coordination of many interacting factors. By planning we mean that "system of decisions which determines an operation prior to it being carried out."[24] In more detail this means that "all measures necessary for the economical execution of an order—from placement to delivery—must be introduced according to plan."[25]

Management Science distinguishes two methods of planning. Effective planning consists of choosing the most advantageous of several alternatives and forecasting the future development of data. Contingency planning is applied where market situations suddenly change.[26]

In the developmental phase of a distance study course planning plays an important role, as the contents of correspondence units, from the first to the last, must be determined in detail, adjusted in relation to each other and represented in a predetermined number of correspondence units. Where distance study is supplemented by residential weeks on campus or weekend seminars, planning becomes even more important; these supplementary teaching events are not intended to repeat academic contents already offered, nor have an 'enrichment' function, but should be structurally integrated in the distance study course. When combining distance teaching with other media, one has to consider carefully which type of contents suits what medium. Finally, where computers are used in distance study, preparatory planning is most advanced and demands by far the greatest expenditure as the teaching activity of the computers needs to be programmed.

In all these efforts to predetermine and arrange the course of teaching processes as far as possible, we are dealing with effective planning. Intervention by advisers and tutors during the course of distance study, however, is regarded as contingency planning, which supplements effective planning.

# Organisation

Planning largely concerns itself with the organisation of the production cycle. In organisational management terms, organisation means "creating general or permanent arrangements for purpose-orientated activity."[27] As a consequence of the division of labour, the production process has to be rationally ordered according to organisational principles and with specially developed organisational means, since "the continuous interacting of numerous people towards a specific purpose requires organisation,"[28] and furthermore, productivity depends on the type and degree of organisation. Distinguished from organisation are improvisation (preliminary and provisional regulations) and disposition (special regulations).[29]

In distance study, likewise, there is an immediate connection between the effectiveness of the teaching method and rational organisation. Organisation, for example, makes it possible for students to receive exactly predetermined documents at appointed times, for an appropriate university teacher to be immediately available for each assignment sent in, for consultations to take place at fixed locations at fixed times, or for examinations to be held, or for a counsellor to inform himself at any time of the progress of a student or a group of students. Organisation becomes easier in large distance teaching establishments, as trained personnel and modern means of organisation are available. These enable them to supplement the organisation of distance teaching with improvisation and disposition.

The importance of organisation in distance teaching can be assessed by the fact that it is often difficult to distinguish between the operational (technical) organisation of distance study and the methodical organisation of the actual academic contents.

# Scientific Control Methods

In recent decades the principles of scientific management have made a gradual breakthrough. According to them work processes are analysed systematically, particularly by time studies, and in accordance with the results obtained from measurements and empirical data the work processes are tested and controlled in their elementary details in a planned way, in order to increase productivity, all the time making the best possible use of working time and the staff available. Frederick Winslow Taylor describes this process as the application of scientific engineering techniques to management.[31]

In distance teaching, similar tendencies can be shown. For example, some distance teaching institutions commission experts to analyse scientifically the success of their courses. Michael Young outlines the educational function of the research techniques applied by remarking that they replace the eyes and ears of academics in face-to-face teaching: they register students' reaction to the distance study course and aim at improving its effectiveness accordingly.[32] These research techniques are not only used to determine the effectiveness of the course for individual students, but—and this is even more important—its effectiveness for the whole group of students involved. With its efforts to measure the success of a teaching method, distance teaching has doubtless introduced a hitherto neglected aspect into university teaching.

# Formalisation

On account of the division of labour and mechanisation in the manufacturing process there is a much greater need to predetermine the various phases formally than in manual production. It is only the emphasis on formality which makes the cooperation of all those involved in the production process possible, as each of them has to rely on previous work having been carried out according to plan. Most activities and interactions in an industrial set-up must therefore be determined according to agreed rules.[33]

In distance study, likewise, all the points in the cycle, from student to distance teaching establishment to the academics allocated, must be determined exactly. Communication is standardised by the use of forms. Authors of correspondence units are recommended to consider the incorporation of standard formalised aspects that have proved to be of advantage. Lecturers marking assignments also work to standard guidelines. Assessment is, in parts, largely formalised through the frequent use of multiple choice questions, where the student only has to place a cross against the right answer. In the most modern forms of distance teaching, formalisation goes as far as students marking the results of their learning on a punchcard in coded form and this is then input to a computer.

# Standardisation

It is characteristic of a production situation involving the division of labour and high technology that manufacture is limited to a number of types of one product, in order to make these more suitable—for their purpose, cheaper to produce and easier to replace.[34] Georges Friedmann pointed out that this does not at all represent a threat of dullness and uniformity. On the contrary, the elementary parts produced could be combined in extremely diverse ways.[35]

The application of the principle of the division of labour and the use of machines, as well as the duplication of correspondence units in often large numbers, force distance teaching institutions likewise to adopt a greater degree of standardisation than is required in conventional teaching. Not only is the format of the correspondence units standardised, the stationery for written communication between student and lecturer, and the organisational support, as well as each phase of the teaching process, but also the academic contents.

Whereas the academic giving a conventional lecture may indulge in—an interesting deviation, because he sees educational advantages in this with a certain group of students, the distance study lecturer has to be aware that when writing a correspondence unit, addressing such a large group of students that situation-dependent improvisation becomes impossible, find a standard adequate, as far as possible, for every, student admitted to the distance study course in question. This is achieved by developing a model for the course, perfecting it through the involvement of several experts and then approximating it to the required standard by testing it on a representative group of students before printing large numbers of copies. Just as the production of a branded article can only remain economical if its quality is continuously adapted to the constant needs of a large group of consumers, a distance teaching institution has to standardise the academic contents of its courses in such a way that it can be sure they appeal to all distance learners as equally as possible. The adaptation to any number of students, however large, forces the lecturer more strongly than in conventional study to consider the necessary standard that is, at the same time, realistic for as many students as possible.

Consequently, the choice of contents of a distance study course is less likely to be a reflection of the particular interests of an academic giving conventional lectures, but rather of the objective requirements of the total course profile.

# Change of Function

On account of the division of labour and the use of various types of machines, the function of the worker in the production process has changed considerably. Whereas it was typical for the craftsman to plan the production of a piece of work as well as acquire the necessary materials, carry out the work and finally sell the finished piece of work himself, industrialisation led to a more marked functional differentiation. When preparatory work and selling became separate from production and, within these three phases, many individual functions were allocated to different individuals, a loss of function naturally occurred for each single worker. On the other hand, new roles were created and new achievements became possible. For example, "in jobs where, due to mechanisation, the processing of the material has been taken out of the worker's hand, speed and energy of execution are no longer required; they have been replaced by accuracy and diligence; the work no longer shows quantitative but qualitative critera."[36]

As a result of the division of labour, the function of the lecturer teaching at a distance also changes. The original role of provider of knowledge in the form of the lecturer is split into that of study unit author and that of marker; the role of counsellor is allocated to a particular person or position. Frequently, the original role of lecturer is reduced to that of a consultant whose involvement in distance teaching manifests itself in periodically recurrent contributions. In order to ensure the effectiveness of the four functions mentioned, numerous support functions of an operational-technical type are particularly important, as, without them, distance study could not take place.

As tutors and consultants have largely been relieved from the task of conveying course matter, they are able to devote themselves to a considerable degree to more demanding tasks, such as aiding motivation, providing individual support, structuring course contents for students, identifying problems, establishing connections, etc. Here, too, a loss of function is compensated for by a gain in function whereby, at the same time, an otherwise almost unattainable level of quality can be achieved.

# Objectivication

The more the production process is determined by machines and organisational principles, the more it loses its subjective element which used to determine craftmen's work to a considerable degree. Hermann Schmidt pointed out that this process already started when man began to substitute tools provided by nature, such as—hands, fists, and teeth—with tools taken from his surroundings. Objectification was not possible until the item to be objectified had become the subject of reflection.[37]

Considering that, since Frederick Winslow Taylor, there has been a change over to analysing each single phase of the industrial production process with scientific means and to purposefully organising the contribution of workers and machines accordingly, it becomes clear what a high degree of objectification has been achieved. This development has found a climax in automated production where man's involvement in production process has largely been eliminated.

In this respect too, the relationship between distance study and conventional study is the same as between industrial production and mechanical fabrication. The university lecturer who lectures from his chair or leads a seminar discussion has the freedom and the opportunity to allow his subjectivity to influence his way of teaching: he is free to decide how and how much to prepare, he determines his own academic aims and methods and is able to change them spontaneously during a lecture, whereby not all the changes in his teaching method need to be reflected. In distance teaching, however, most teaching functions are objectified as they are determined by the distance study course as well as technical means. Only in written communications with the distance learner or possibly in a consultation or the brief additional face-to-face events on campus has the teacher some individual scope left for subjectively determined variants in his teaching method. In cases where a computer is used in distance study, even this opportunity is limited further.

The advantages of objectifying the teaching process in the form of a distance study course lie in the fact that the teaching process can then be reproduced, thus making it available at any time and, above all, that it can be manipulated. Without objectification distance study courses could not take place anywhere and at any time and be continuously improved.

The objectification of teaching practice in distance study is of particular importance in societies where, on account of an hierarchic structure of universities and colleges, the function of the provider of knowledge is combined in many academics with that of a holder of very great authority. As a result of this the relationship between student and lecturer is similar to that of subordinate and superior. As distance study has largely been freed from subjectivity, the process of providing knowledge is hardly affected by situations of this kind. In this context, distance study is particularly suitable for the further education of adults.

# Concentration and Centralisation

The investment required for mechanised mass production involving the division of labour has led to large industrial concerns with a concentration of capital, a frequently centralised administration, and a market that is not seldom monopolised.

In this context it is significant that some distance teaching establishments cater for very large groups of students. The largest universities teaching at a distance in the USSR and in South Africa have over 40,000 students, and the Open University in England has more than 70,000. Each of these three establishments—as well as their Spanish equivalent—caters for the national demand. Obviously, a minimum number of students is necessary to make the technical installations and the establishment of an efficient organisation feasible. Economically, it is therefore more worthwhile to create a large central distance study establishment rather than 10 or 20 small regional institutions. Just as the industrial markets for certain products have long expanded beyond narrow regional frontiers, such centralised distance teaching establishments must cross the traditional areas of the responsibility of universities and the educational administration.

If all the said principles of distance teaching are rigorously applied, monopoly-like prestige positions in teaching activity are created for leading experts in various disciplines. Just as no record producer would use a mediocre singer when he can engage a Fischer-Dieskau, a distance teaching institution has to try and gain the best lecturers in their field for the development of its distance study courses. Just as in industry, however, one must ensure that such monopoly-like positions do not hinder free competition.

The possible consequences of a rigorous concentration and centralisation of distance teaching were hinted at, for the first time in 1966, in a memorandum from the British Government concerning the then proposed University of the Air.[38] In future, universities would no longer pursue the same objectives in all subjects, but specialise in some disciplines and cater for the national requirements for distance study in these.

# Summary

From the above comparisons the following conclusions in relation to distance teaching may be drawn:

1.  The structure of distance teaching is determined to a considerable degree by the principles of industrialisation, in particular by those of rationalisation, division of labour and mass production.

2.  The teaching process is gradually re-structured through increasing mechanisation and automation.

3.  These changes are the reason for the following structural characteristics to have emerged:

    *   the development of distance study courses is just as important as the preparatory work taking place prior to the production process.

    *   the effectiveness of the teaching process is particularly dependent on planning and organisation.

    *   courses must be formalised and expectations from students standardised.

    *   the teaching process is largely objectified.

    *   the function of academics teaching at a distance has changed considerably vis à vis university teachers in conventional teaching.

    *   distance study can only be economical with a concentration of the available resources and a centralised administration.

The result of this comparative interpretation permits the addition to recent explanations of distance study based on traditional educational concepts of a definition which is apt to point to the specific characteristics of the new forms of teaching and learning, thus structurally separating them from conventional forms of teaching and learning. This definition is as follows:

*Distance study is a rationalised method—involving the definition of labour—of providing knowledge which, as a result of applying the principles of industrial organisation as well as the extensive use of technology, thus facilitating the reproduction of objective teaching activity in any numbers, allows a large number of students to participate in university study simultaneously, regardless of their place of residence and occupation.*

This definition shows that, within the complex overall distance teaching activity, one area has been exposed to investigation which had regularly been omitted from traditional didactic analyses. Contrary to other attempts at definitions, new concepts are used here to describe new facts.

It was not a purpose of this comparative interpretation to pass judgements on the industrial structures which have been shown to apply to distance teaching. Presumably, the striking advantages of these structures, from a point of view of educational policy and organisation, are also connected with important educational disadvantages. This question has yet to be discussed. In this context it shall merely be hinted that it must be disadvantageous to a society if the developments outlined here have not been, or have not been fully, recognised, or are even denied. Such deep structural changes in academic teaching merit everyone's attention, no matter what hopes or fears are connected with them. If society's awareness lags behind the speedily developing technological and industrial opportunities, this is bound to lead to painful malfunctions, even in the area of academic teaching. They can be detected and remedied more easily, when the industrial structures characteristic of distance teaching are recognised and taken account of when the appropriate educational decisions are taken.

*This contribution is the revised and re-edited version of the 2nd chapter of the monograph *Das Fernstudium an Universitäten und Hochschulen*, which the author had published by Beltz in 1967.

# Notes

1. Hausmann, G.: *Dramaturgie des Unterrichts*. Heidelberg 1959, p. 153.

2. Ibid, p. 68.

3. Litt, T.: *Führen und Wachsenlassen*, Stuttgart 1958. App. 1: Das Wesen des pädagogischen Denkens, p. 83ff.

4. Frank, H.: *Kybernitetische Grundlagen des Lernens und Lehrens*, Stuttgart, 1965.

5. Didaktik als Theorie und Lehre, in: *Die Deutsche Schule*, Heft 9, 1962, p. 421.

6. Wissenschaft und Beruf, in: *Gesammelte Aufsätze zur Wissenschaftlehre*, 2nd ed., Tübingen 1951, pp. 566–597. Quoted from Schelsky, H.: *Einsamkeit und Freiheit*, Hamburg, 1963, p. 192.

7. Zur Soziologie der modernen Forschung und ihrer Organisations in der deutschen Universität, in: Scheler, M. 9th ed.): *Versuche zu einer Soziologie des Wissens*, München, 1924, pp. 407–425, quoted from Schelsky, H., in: *Einsamkeit und Freiheit*, Hamburg, 1963, p. 192.

8. Seischab, H. and Schwantag, K. (eds.): *Handwörterbuch der Betriebswirtschaft*, c.e. Poeschel Verlag, 3rd ed., Stuttgart, 1960, Vol. III, column 4530.

9. Ibid.

10. Buckingham, W.: *Automation und Gesellschaft*, S. Fisher Verlag, Frankfurt am Main, 1963, p. 24f.

11. Friedman, G.: *Der Mensch in der mechanisierten Produktion*, Köln, 1952, p. 203.

12. Seischab, H. and Schwantag, K.(eds.): as above, Vol. III, column 4531.

13. Ibid, column 4530.

14. Durheim, E.: *De la division du travail social*, and *Die Theorie der Arbeitsteilung*, by Gustav Schmoller.

15. König, R. (ed.): *Soziologie, Das Fischer Lexicon*, p. 27. The author refers here to Adam Smith.

16. Smith, A.: *The Wealth of Nations*, quoted from the chapter "Division of Labor" in Lewis, Arthur D. (ed.) *Of Men and Machines*. A Dutton Paperback Original, New York, 1963, pp. 110–113.

17. König, R. (ed.): *Soziologie, Das Fischer Lexicon*, Frankfurt am Main, 1958, p. 27. The author quotes Charles Babbage (1792–1871).

18. Smith, A.: Division of Labour, In: Lewis, Arthur D. (ed.): *Of Men and Machines*. A Dutton Paperback Original, New York, 10963, pp. 110–111.

19. Buckingham, W.: *Automation und Gesellschaft*. S. Fischer Verlag, Frankfurt am Main, 1963, pp. 17–27.

20. Buckingham, W.: As above, p. 17.

21. Ibid, p. 20.

22. König, R. (ed.): *Soziologie, Das Fischer Lexicon*, Frankfurt/Main, 1958, p. 171.

23. Ibid.

24. Seischab, H. and Schwantag, K.(eds.); as above, Vol. III, column 4341.

25. Seischab, H. and Schwantag, K. (eds.); as above, Vol. I, column 1742.

26. Seischab, H. and Schwantag, K.(eds.); as above, Vol. III, column 4348

27. Mayntz, R.: Soziologie der Organisation, rowohlt's deutsche enzyclopädie, Reinbeck near Hamburg, 1963, p. 86.

28. Mayntz, R.: as above, p. 7.

29. Koziol, E.: *Grundlagen und Methoden der Organisationsforschung*, Berlin, 1959, p. 18ff, quoted from Mayntz, R.: Soziologie der Organisations, rowohlt's deutsche enzyclopädie, Reinbeck near Hamburg, 1963, p. 86.

30. Scheischab, H. and Schwantag, K. (eds.): Vol. I, column 1055.

31. McConnell, J. W.: In Henry Pratt Fairchild, *Dictionary of Sociology and Related Sciences*, Littlefield, Adams, Totowa, N.J., 1966, p. 268.

32. *The Home Study review*, Washington D.C., Spring, 1965, p. 37.

33. Mayntz, R.: as above, p. 86.

34. Friedmann, G.: *Der Mensch in der mechanisierten Produktion*. Köln, 1852, p. 394.

35. Ibid.

36. Ibid, p. 389

37. See *Lexicon der kybernetischen Pädagogik und der Programmierten Indstruktion*. Schnelle, Quickborn, 1966, p. 133.

38. A University of the Air. Presented to the Parliament by the Secretary of State for Education and Science by Command of her Majesty, London: Her Majesty's Stationery Office, February 1966, 7 pages.

# The Profession

**Robert M. Morgan (1978):**
*Educational Technology—Adolescence to Adulthood*

## The Profession

It is important to make a distinction between Part 1, The Field, and Part 4, The Profession. The field incorporates all the elements that compose an area of research and practice. The field includes the theories and rationales that are perceived to be within the boundaries. The field is defined and elaborated in Seels and Richey (1994).

A profession is the *application* of the substantive elements that make up the field: Curriculum content prepares people for service in the field; organizations of practitioners create cohesion within the field; the ethical conduct of personnel guides the decisions made by personnel; and recognition by other related professions all help to create a synergy that eventually identifies a profession. Finn (1953) spells out the characteristics of a profession: an intellectual technique; a practical application of the technique; a long period of training; and an association and communication among members.

The field of instructional technology has been preoccupied with its status for many years. The attempts to define the field since the early days of the twentieth century (Reiser and Ely, 1997) offer evidence regarding this dilemma. Charters (1945) asks, "Is there a field of educational engineering?" and Heinich (1973) asks, "Is there a field of educational communications and technology?" Others have used a documentary approach to spell out the history of the field (Saettler, 1968, 1990), and in a briefer treatment, Reiser (1987) outlines the highpoints of the field's development. The body of this literature has grown and the both the facts and the perceptions have confirmed the legitimacy of the field.

Instructional technology professionals have been critical about their role and status of the field. Hawkridge's early article, "New Year, Jerusalem! The Rise of Educational Technology" (1976) pulls no punches as he describes the tentative growth of the field at that time. Heinich's "The Proper Study of Instructional Technology" (1984) carries on the exploration. Morgan explores the field in the same fashion but with the pronouncement that others have been reluctant to voice: "As a discipline, educational technology is about to pass from its late adolescence to early adulthood." This was published in 1978.

Where are the voices today? What are they saying? How has the field changed? How does it need to change? Professionals should continue to seek answers to such questions if the profession is to grow and prosper.

# References

Charters, W. W. 1945. Is there a field of educational engineering? *Educational Research Bulletin* 24, no. 2:29–37, 53.

Finn, J. D. 1953. Professionalizing the audio-visual field. *Audio-Visual Communication Review* 1, no. 1:6–18. In D. P. Ely and T. Plomp, *Classic writings on instructional technology* (Englewood, Colo.: Libraries Unlimited, 1996.)

Hawkridge, D. G. 1976. Next year, Jerusalem! The rise of educational technology. *British Journal of Educational Technology* 1, no. 7:7–30.

Heinich, R. M. 1973. Is there a field of educational communications and technology? *Audiovisual Instruction* 18, no. 5:44–46. In D. P. Ely and T. Plomp, *Classic writings on instructional technology* (Englewood, Colo.: Libraries Unlimited, 1996.)

———. 1984. The proper study of instructional technology. *Educational Communications and Technology Journal* 32, no. 2:67–87. [In this volume, Part I]

Reiser, R. A. 1987. Instructional technology: A history. In R. M. Gagné, *Instructional technology: Foundations.* Hillsdale, N.J.: Lawrence Erlbaum, 11–48.

Reiser, R. A., and D. P. Ely. 1997. The field of educational technology as reflected through its definitions. *Educational Technology Research and Development* 45, no. 3:63–72.

Seels, B. B., and Richey, R. C. 1994. *Instructional technology: The definition and domains of the Field.* Washington, D.C.: Association for Educational Communications and Technology.

# 15

# *Educational Technology— Adolescence to Adulthood*

### Robert M. Morgan

As a discipline, educational technology is about to pass from its late adolescence into early adulthood. If its birth can roughly, and perhaps arbitrarily, be placed in the late 1950s, then educational technology is nearly two decades old. Some would say that a discipline about whose name there is no certainty is no discipline at all, and educational technology has a variety of other labels—instructional systems development, instructional design, and, occasionally, educational engineering. Putting aside for the moment these variations in name preference, it may be useful, as we anticipate our "coming of age," to take stock of where we are, where we came from, and where we might be going.

It could be argued that educational technology is still trying to become a legitimate academic discipline. We have no professional society exclusively ours, although educational technologists find acceptance in other associations, such as the American Psychological Association and the American Educational Research Association, and in some of the traditional education societies. We have few journals. However, an increasing number of institutions offer graduate degree specialties in educational technology, and there is a sizable and growing body of research literature in the field. The academic programs at such universities as Indiana, Southern California, Brigham Young, Syracuse, Florida State, and Arizona State are sufficient to assure the future viability of educational technology. So although educational technology does not yet have the traditions or history of such disciplines as biology, psychology, or physics, it is likely here to stay.

From: Morgan, R. M. 1978. Educational technology—Adolescense to adulthood. *Educational Communication and Technology Journal* 26(2):142–152. Reprinted with permission of Association for Educational Communications and Technology.

# Contributions from Other Fields

The paternity of educational technology is not altogether clear. It might be argued that it all started with Carleton Washburne of Winnetka fame or with James Finn, whose programs at the University of Southern California contributed significantly to educational technology development, or even with Thomas Edison. The strongest case can be made, I believe, for dating the origin of educational technology from the work of B. F. Skinner and others on programmed instruction (Skinner, 1958). The ideas reflected in that work have been a tremendous catalytic force in education, causing the convergence of three disciplines, which, in turn, gave rise to the new discipline of educational technology. Although educational technology has freely but selectively borrowed from many sources, its foundation is derived from a) communications, b) management science, and c) behavioral science. Joining the tools and knowledge of the relevant portions of these disciplines and focusing them upon the problems of education has been much of the substance of educational technology these past twenty years.

## Communications

The field of communications, with its research on information storage and retrieval, message transmission, and complex communications networks, has contributed much to education. Indeed, for many people, the equipment of communication has come to represent the substance of educational technology. For years such equipment as opaque and overhead projectors, slide/tape devices, motion-picture projectors, and radio and television have been used in classrooms for instructional purposes. More recently, exotic communications systems using the computer and the satellite have been added to this inventory. Although these tools have been useful, their impact on the quality of student learning has been limited. They represent improvements in the means of message transmission, but efficient learning demands more than simple reception of information. A joint effort between the psychologist and the communications specialist is essential if the principles of learning are to affect the shape, sequence, and nature of information transmission. Each of these specialists has expertise not easily available to the other, the amalgam of which can lead to improved conditions for learning.

## Management Science

The second contributor to the new discipline of educational technology has been management science. Modern management technology has evolved from the time/motion studies of the 1920s to such techniques as systems analysis, cost/benefit approaches, program evaluation, and review techniques. These approaches have made possible the planning and management of otherwise nearly incomprehensible tasks. Military, industrial, and scientific leaders have made much use of these management tools, but educators traditionally have not been under the same pressures to "produce" efficiently, even though education is no less complex an endeavor. Program planning and budgeting, systems management, and cost effectiveness are as important to education as they are to any other sector of the socioeconomic system. The management specialist can help predict and evaluate the effects of the introduction of a new educational practice from the unique perspective of that discipline: How will the change affect the logistics of the learning environment? What happens to personnel, space, and time usage? Do the benefits of the change justify its various costs? Indeed, is the change affordable at all?

The management perspective, when fused with communications and psychological approaches, yields an interdisciplinary linkup that should be useful in the educational domain.

## *Behavioral Sciences*

The behavioral sciences, particularly the discipline of psychology, have much to contribute to improving the educational process. Psychologists have been investigating the variables associated with the learning process for over half a century, and several alternative theories of learning have resulted from that work. Psychologists have also been interested in the concept of individual differences, and a wealth of information is now available on the variations in human characteristics. An outgrowth of this area of inquiry has been a sophisticated technology of tests and measurement. Bridging the gap between research and application is always difficult and time-consuming, and much of what has been known to psychologists has, historically, been slow to result in improved instructional practices.

In the case of programmed instruction, a concerted effort was made to design a teaching tool capable of using some of the important principles of learning that are difficult to apply in a traditional classroom. The first linear programs of instruction were in print form; in some instances they were dramatically successful in their teaching effectiveness. It is probably difficult for newcomers to educational technology to imagine the excitement (and sometimes the frustration) of the first developers of programmed instruction in the early 1960s. Although many programs didn't work very well, some did. For perhaps the first time, at least some conditions of human learning were brought under a measure of experimental control. In many ways it was like the discovery of gold in California! Programmed instruction became in only a few months a "movement" complete with zealots if not fanatics. Attracted to the movement were business investors, fast-buck artists, and, fortunately, more than a few rigorous experimental psychologists and educators. By 1963, more than sixty private companies had been formed in this country to develop and market programmed materials. Unhappily, many of the premature promises made for programmed instruction by its advocates did not materialize. Too much was expected too quickly. When it became evident that programmed instruction was not education's Sutter's Creek, the money-seekers moved on to other bonanzas and programmed instruction disappeared from the pages of the *Wall Street Journal.*

Despite the rapid rise and fall of programmed instruction, a large quantity of programmed text materials had been developed by 1965. There was enormous variation in the quality and teaching effectiveness of these materials, and partly because of this programmed instruction never experienced widespread use in schools at any level. Others have done complete postmortems on programmed instruction. What is of interest now is to explore the residual and continuing benefits to education of the programmed instruction effort.

# Enduring Effects of Programmed Instruction

It may be that the single most important effect of programmed instruction was to attract to the educational arena some types of professionals who had not before shown much interest in school events. Robert Gagné, Robert Mager, R. L. Bright, Leslie Briggs, Lloyd Homme, Bob Glaser, and many others brought new perspectives and problem-solving tools to school learning. Of greatest value was their empirical approach to the task. Although many of the newcomers to education during this period eventually returned to their original fields, a large number, fascinated by the challenges of educational improvement, appear to be in education to stay—often under the rubric of educational technology.

Another, more pervasive, effect has been a change in outlook on the basic nature of the educational phenomenon. Their numbers increasing from a few at first, by now a fairly large number of people in education have shifted their orientation from a preoccupation with the processes of education to a much greater emphasis on the outcomes. The Model-T's of programmed instruction were analytically derived and their instructional intentions were certainly more objectively defined than were the purposes of conventional instructional materials. These first programs made obvious the absolute requirement of more precisely and operationally defined learning outcomes. Conventional instruction could tolerate vague objectives, but programmed instruction by its nature demanded more precision. It is easy to forget that programmed instruction was the parent of behavioral objectives and not the reverse (Popham, 1968; Mager, 1962).[1] The concept of behavioral objectives thus born was, and still is, surrounded by considerable controversy. Even so, there is much greater acceptance of the concept by educators than might have been predicted only a few years back. With this (albeit grudging) tolerance of objectification of learning outcomes, the educational stage was set for the idea of criterion-referenced testing of student performance and for the notion that schools could be held accountable for student learning.

A related shift in attitude has taken place with regard to learning potential of students (Bloom, 1968). More educators began to believe that learning conditions could be arranged so that virtually all students could learn. It became somewhat less acceptable to blame the student solely for failure. Lack of background, low motivation, and low intelligence are not so readily accepted as legitimate causes for student failure now as they were in past years. Educators are beginning to look at teaching and other instructional modes as being at least partly to blame for some failures.

It may be giving programmed instruction more credit than it is due to say that it has been responsible for these positive attitudinal shifts. However, it is unlikely that such shifts would have occurred without the ferment of the programmed instruction movement.

Other direct effects of programmed instruction are apparent in the area of instructional design. Professionals working in the early days of programmed instruction encountered a wide range of problems. Their creative responses to these problems have added significantly to the subject matter of educational technology. Because the chaining of these events is not well documented, there is little general knowledge of what happened and why. Different researchers tackled different aspects of the instruction problem. For example, Lloyd Homme in his programmed instruction laboratory in Albuquerque observed that students, Skinner notwithstanding, did not find studying programmed instruction for any sustained time intrinsically motivating. To be sure, students who stayed with the programs learned well, but, short of coercion, it was difficult to keep the students at work. The problem was not unique, and others tried various extrinsic reinforcers—from money to candy—as study payoffs. Recognizing that youngsters satiate quickly on either money or candy, Homme borrowed an idea from Premack and began to use reinforcement contingency management as a tool in the learning process.

Others concentrated on improving and expanding the range of instructional resources. The work of Leslie Briggs (Briggs, Campeau, Gagné, & May, 1967), then at the American Institute of Research, exemplifies this approach. They asked if the application of learning principles to instruction using a printed format yielded good results, could the same be done with a variety of media? Briggs and others then began to program interactive mixes of media following the same iterative development and revision processes that were being used with printed programmed instruction. The returns on this investment of effort were real. Programmed multimedia helped ameliorate the learner-motivation problem, and student achievement levels were high.

At about this same time Pat Suppes (1968) of Stanford, concerned about the stimulus-and-response patterns of programmed instruction, began to experiment with the computer as a means of presentation control. The outcome of this work was computer-assisted instruction (CAI). The computer was used in essentially two ways—in an interactive, tutorial mode and as a means of providing drill and practice for students. In both cases, the student received instruction online, at a computer terminal. This form of instruction was prohibitively expensive for operational use in public schools, and others began to look for more economical uses of the computer for instructional purposes (Morgan, 1969). Don Bitzer of the University of Illinois concentrated on the development of more cost-effective computer and terminal hardware systems. This resulted in the development of the PLATO system. Walter Dick (Dick & Gallagher, 1972) and his associates at Florida State started looking for variations in use of conventional computer systems that would be cost competitive in instruction.

What had been learned about programmed multimedia, coupled with what was known about the information management properties of the computer, led in 1970 to the development of the first operational course taught by computer-managed instruction (CMI). This early effort was used in a graduate course, "Techniques of Programmed Instruction." Skills and technical aspects of programming as well as information about programmed instruction were taught. At first all of the instructional resources were selected from available, off-the-shelf materials. In subsequent revisions, some of the less-effective materials were replaced with new materials especially designed for use in the course. The computer served to mediate among the individual student, the course objectives, and the extensive inventory of instructional resources selected to teach the objectives. Using a CRT terminal, the student accessed the computer, which was programmed to query the student until a fix was made on which of the course objectives the student had and had not mastered. At this point, the computer scanned the available instruction resources to identify those for the first objectives in the course sequence on which the student was deficient. Thus was accomplished, on a periodic and continuing basis, an individual diagnosis of learning needs and an individual prescription of instructional events. The prescribed instructional events were limited only by what was logistically available to the course. Audiovisual lessons such as films, slide-tape presentations, and instructional television were included. Also available were text selections, scheduled teacher demonstrations, small-group work, and periodic large-group presentations. The student could also be routed to the professor or an assistant for tutorial guidance. Later, CAI was selectively added as an additional instructional resource.

In the early phases of this experimentation two findings stood out: a) instruction by means of CMI was a great deal cheaper to deliver than conventional live instruction; and b) even at the beginning the accomplishment of course objectives by students was done as well through CMI as through live instruction. The computer's capacity to support learning activities reliably and to store, analyze, and retrieve large amounts of data on each student has been clearly demonstrated (Suckley & O'Dell, 1976; Alessi, Anderson, & Beddle, 1976). Computer-managed instruction has come into fairly widespread use, with courses now being offered by industry, the military, and some universities.

Once a course has been developed, its use by students is limited only by availability of a terminal connected to the main computer and access to the associated instructional materials. The initial cost of developing such courses is relatively high. Dick and Gallagher (1972) estimate that for a typical college course, where mostly off-the-shelf materials are used, the development cost may range from $8,000 to $12,000. Also, the acquisition and set-up cost of a large time-sharing computer is very high—although the total cost per student for computer time in a single course is low. Cost data from several CMI courses suggest that a total cost of 512 to $20 per student, per course is a reasonable expectation.

# Performance Assessment for Instructional Improvement

A variation of CMI has been developed recently, making it possible to take advantage of the feedback to the learner component of CMI without the development of the special inventory of instructional resources (Oosterhof, 1977). Also, rather than using individual student terminals for testing the learner, a series of tests over the course objectives are developed. Students can request tests for whatever objectives they feel ready to be tested on. The test is then scored on the spot by an optical scanner and the central computer prints out for the student a record of successes and deficiencies in attaining the course objectives. This process differs from CMI in that the computer does not prescribe any instruction for the student. The student's learning follows the conventional pattern of hearing the teacher lecture, receiving reading and work assignments, and engaging in the kinds of behavior associated with usual classroom instruction. The major difference is that all the learning objectives for the course have been specified and sequenced, and criterion-referenced test items have been developed for each objective and stored in the computer. Students are told the objectives at the beginning of the course and advised that they can go to a campus testing center at any time to be examined on any of the objectives.

The process contributes to learning effectiveness in several important ways. Students can keep track of their progress with respect to the course expectations on a continuous basis. Even though the students in a particular course are being tested at various times, the computer periodically aggregates the data for the teacher. Thus the teacher can monitor the progress of the class and each of the students; it can be determined on a weekly, or even daily, basis which objectives or parts of the course are giving the students difficulty and should be allotted more instructional time. Guidance to students who need special instruction is also facilitated. In contrast with CMI, no special instructional materials are being developed at this time; but if such a need becomes evident, the accumulated test data will identify those areas where the needs are most pressing.

Students can submit to retesting one or more times on those objectives they failed the first time. Objectives from the early parts of the course are retested, on a sampling basis, in subsequent tests to determine retention. This process serves both a formative and summative testing function, greatly reducing the amount of in-class testing time needed while increasing the overall performance assessment for each student. Although uniform mastery has not been attained, course failure and near failures have been virtually eliminated.

Most of the activities described up to this point have focused on media forms. They have attempted, sometimes successfully, to engineer the interaction between diagnosis and dynamic choice of instructional event in ways that facilitated learning.

Meanwhile, other researchers were wondering whether the principles of programmed instruction might be applicable to the functioning of the total classroom environment (Flanagan, 1968; Flanagan, Shanner, Brudner, & Marker, 1975). There were several independent starts in the individualization of classroom instruction in the mid-1960s.

The frontrunners were Robert Glaser of the University of Pittsburgh, Thorwald Esbensen of the Duluth, Minnesota public schools, and Robert Boston of the Bloomfield Hills, Michigan school system (Glaser, 1968; Esbensen, 1968). In a short time many other individualized programs got underway around the country, but very few were as well conceived and carried out as the first three. Just as it was difficult to distinguish good, properly developed programmed instruction from junk programmed instruction without hard data on its teaching effectiveness, it was not easy to distinguish good individualized programs from bad ones by superficial inspection. As a result, many schools copied the forms of individualized instruction but gave little or no attention to the substance. The difficult, expensive, and time-consuming development processes were not undertaken by many schools; it should not be surprising that evaluations of individualized programs have not been very encouraging. Similarly, differentiated staffing and performance contracting have much conceptual appeal but have been carried out in such slapdash ways that they rarely come off looking very well.

When researchers started working in real schools they discovered a whole new world of problems that constrained the improvement of the educational process. These problems were political, economic, and procedural. Once more, educational technologists had to widen their focus to include more of the whole of education. Now we hear some of our colleagues talking about needs assessment, change processes, systems studies, alternative models, and more (Kaufman, 1972; Branson, et al., 1975; Flanagan, et al., 1975). Arguments are voiced that "little solutions" in education have not been solutions at all.

## The Future

We need the means of making immense improvements in educational accomplishments. This end must be attained with human and material resources presently available and affordable. The processes and products of educational technology must be included among the inventory of resources that can contribute to quickening the pace of educational improvement. As long as the approaches of educational technology are responsive to the changing problems in education, this new discipline will have its raison d'etre. If in the years ahead it becomes enmeshed in its own traditions and ceases to be fresh and responsive, it will undoubtedly be replaced by some more relevant set of ideas.

## Notes

1. A number of readers will recall that behavioral objectives were around long before programmed instruction. I learned to write behavioral objectives in 1946 in a course taught by James D. Finn at Colorado State College of Education. I also learned to use behavioral objectives as an evaluation technique from R. S. Gilchrist and W. L. Wrinkle (*Secondary Education for American Democracy*. N.Y.: Rinehart, 1942). (And that's not even mentioning Ralph Tyler, who preceded the other three.) However, there were two important differences between these early efforts and programmed instruction: Early efforts used behavioral objectives not to *develop* instruction, but to set the stage for instruction and to evaluate it; and earlier behavioral objectives lacked precision and did not emphasize a level of performance. [Editor's note-R.H.]

# References

Alessi, S. M., T. T. Anderson, and B. W. Beddle. 1976. Hardware and software considerations in computer based course management. *Educational Technology* 16, no. 4:16–21.

Bloom, B. S. 1968. Learning for mastery. *Evaluation Comment* 1, no. 2. Los Angeles: Center for the Study of Evaluation of Instruction Programs, UCLA.

Branson, R., G. T. Rayner, J. L. Cox, J. P. Furman, F. T. King, and W. H. Hannum. 1975. *Inservice procedures for instructional sytstems development* (TRADOC Pam. 350–330 and NAVEDTRA 106A, 5 vols.). Ft. Monroe, Va.: U.S. Army Training and Doctrine Cornmand.

Briggs, L. J., P. L. Campeau, R. M. Gagné, and M. May. 1967. *Instructional media. A procedure for the design of multimedia instruction.* Monograph 2. Pittsburgh: American Institute for Research.

Dick, W., and P. Gallagher. 1972. Systems concepts and computer-managed instruction: An implementation and validation study. *Educational Technology* 12, no. 12:33–39.

Esbensen, T. 1968. *Working with individualized instruction: The Duluth experience.* Palo Alto, Calif.: Fearon Publishers.

Flanagan, J. C. 1968. Project Plan. In Aerospace Education Foundation, *Technology and innovation in education.* New York: Praeger.

Flanagan, J. C., W. M. Shanner, H. J. Brudner, and R. W. Marker. 1975. An individualized instruction system: PLAN. In H. Talmage, ed., *Systems of individualized education.* Berkeley: McCutchan.

Glaser, R. 1968. *The program for individually prescribed instruction.* Paper presented at the annual meeting of the American Educational Research Association, Chicago.

Kaufman, R. A. 1972. *Educational systems planning.* Englewood Cliffs, N.J.: Prentice-Hall.

Mager, R. F. 1962. *Preparing instructional objectives.* Palo Alto, Calif.: Fearon.

Morgan, R. 1969. A central computer utility for educational systems. *Journal of Engineering Education* (American Society for Engineering Education) (February):475–477.

Oosterhof, A. 1977. *Cost effectiveness and interactive assessment of student achievement.* Tallahassee: Florida State University, Center for Educational Development and Evaluation.

Popham, W. J. 1966. *Educational objectives.* Los Angeles: Vimcet Associates.

———. 1967. *Selecting appropriate educational objectives.* Los Angeles: Vimcet Associates.

———. 1968. Probing the validity of arguments against behavioral goals. Paper presented at the annual meeting of the American Educational Research Association, Chicago.

Skinner, B. F. 1958. Teaching machines. *Science* 128:969–977.

Suckley, M. H., and R. T. O'Dell. 1976. The open learning model using computer-managed instruction. *Educational Technology* 16, no. 2:39–42.

Suppes, P. 1968. How far have we come? What's just ahead? *Nation's Schools* 82:52–53. (Interview)

# INDEX